EVOLUTION, DEVELOPMENT, AND CHILDREN'S LEARNING

GOODYEAR DEVELOPMENTAL PSYCHOLOGY SERIES
Alex Siegel, Series Editor

Evolution, Development, and Children's Learning
Harold D. Fishbein

EVOLUTION, DEVELOPMENT, AND CHILDREN'S LEARNING

Harold D. Fishbein
University of Cincinnati

Goodyear Publishing Company, Inc.
Pacific Palisades, California

Library of Congress Cataloging in Publication Data

Fishbein, Harold D.
  Evolution, development, and children's learning.

  (Goodyear developmental psychology series)
  Bibliography: p.
  Includes index.
  1.   Genetic psychology.   2. Learning, Psychology
of.   3. Child psychology.   I. Title.   (DNLM:
1. Child development.   2. Evolution.   3. Learning
—In infancy and childhood.   WS105 F532e)
BF701.F55   155.7   75-13478
ISBN 0-87620-282-2

Library of Congress Catalog Card Number: 75-13478

ISBN: 0-87620-282-2
Y-2822-8

Current printing (last number):
10 9 8 7 6 5 4 3 2 1

Printed in the United States of America

cover design: Jackie Thibodeau

To
Sara, Max,
Diane,
Jeremy, and Aaron

CONTENTS

FOREWORD

This book discusses children's learning in a new way, by linking findings from research with children together with findings from contemporary studies of evolution, the brain, and paleoanthropology. It offers a careful effort to bring together the incisive experimental analyses of psychology and the imaginative naturalism of anthropology and ethology. We need a connected system of thought. We need data on human behavior. We need to interpret those data in the light of a convincing and meaningful outlook on man's adaptation to nature.

Long ago, evolutionary questions gave life to the several psychologies of today: stimulus-response psychology, psychoanalysis, ethology, genetic epistemology, mental testing, etc. Each began with some thought and some assumptions about human evolution, and each then led out to an inquiry in part determined by those assumptions. Why, then, write a book in the 1970s to connect learning with evolution? Such a book seems necessary to reconstruct old intellectual connections that have become inadequate as our knowledge has grown.

Systematic research on human learning has existed for about 50 years, with some of the methods and ideas that gave form to the work going back another 50 years. Ebbinghaus and G. E. Muller were studying human learning in German laboratories in the 1880s, but not too much was made of the problem of learning in those laboratories. Just after the turn of the century, Edward B. Thorndike in the United States and Ivan Pavlov in Russia set forth some basic patterns of inquiry that were to serve as models for a subsequent great flowering of a research movement dedicated to the analysis of learning. Their laboratories were prototypic for the development of the later laboratories. Just as important, their views of the meaning of learning in evolution became embodied as central to the technology and the ideology of the later work.

In scientific work, it is often equally important to find questions as it is to find answers. In effect, Thorndike and Pavlov found the questions about learning to which the learning laboratories of the 1900s sought to find answers. By the 1930s, the learning theory movement was in full flower. There were laboratories studying "instrumental conditioning" (the learning of Thorndike) and "classical conditioning" (the learning of Pavlov). By the late 1930s and early 1940s, a series of scientific prospectuses had been set forth by Tolman, Hull, and Skinner. Programmatic papers and normal science filled the journals. In the 1950s and the 1960s, the cycle began to come to a close. The new findings and the new assumptions that could be harmonized under the traditional learning theories now began to be buried under unassimilable findings and assumptions. Completely different insights and perspectives on learning were developed in the coexisting inquiries of neuropsychology, ethology, information-processing, and genetic epistemology. All this was scientifically healthy and pretty much according to plan. The early learning theorists were intent on being explicit in order to stimulate their own downfall. But the last step in the cycle they initiated has not yet been taken and it is that step, I believe, that this book tries to take. It states some new questions about learning.

We always pose our general questions about learning by imagining a creature in the natural environment, endowing that creature with some built-in behaviors needed to adapt to that environment, and then asking what mechanism or mechanisms might serve to complete the creature's adaptive repertoire. So the study of learning always depends on assumptions about what the organism is endowed with and what it has to go out and get.

What we find at the core of most contemporary discussions of learning is an archaic creature, browsing in the shadows of newer creatures. The archaic creature is the conceptual creature of Thorndike and Pavlov. Thorndike's part of the creature, in particular, was deliberately built very simply, with a great fear of anthropomorphism, and with a great faith that science proceeds best on parsimony, and few assumptions. The archaic creature, therefore, does not know much and cannot do very much. It is a creature of reflexes or, if you like, S-R connections. It is solitary. It adapts by adding behaviors to its store and by selecting from its store pieces of behavior that best fit pieces of the environment. It is fundamentally inert, moving only when its drives are aroused, steering by means of cues, rewards, and habits. Most psychologists, put face to face with this conceptual creature, would instantly deny its validity as a basis for the discussion of learning. But, nonetheless, it still lives concealed at the bottom of the learning chapters of our textbooks. Other chapters of those textbooks, chapters dealing with habituation, attachment, perceptual learning, Piagetian equilibration, reflect the shadows of newer and more valid conceptual creatures. Can we bring forth into the light a whole new conceptual creature, posing the question of the meaning of learning in terms suitable to the breadth of our contemporary knowledge about human adaptation?

Harold Fishbein's book incorporates an impressive range of our current knowledge about human adaptation. A central theme in the book is Waddington's notion of *canalization*. More and more evidence suggests that human behavior has a high degree of preorganization which causes the paths human learning can take to be constrained. The human being is designed to organize in certain ways as he grows. There are some kinds of human development that come naturally.

Questions about heredity versus environment evoke human concerns about fate and predestination, and such questions often stimulate a rigid emotionalism that seems to demand that a theorist vote one way or the other. Since Fishbein feels that the possibility of human learning is conditioned by preorganization, is he arguing for instinctivism (fate)? No. If humans operated through instincts their behavior patterns would be preorganized at birth and they would develop in ways that were impervious to environmental influences. One hardly finds instinctive organizations that strong above the level of Fabre's insects. From McDougall and Watson on, the scholars who have been typecast as heroes or villains of the heredity-environment debate have argued in vain that they do not believe human development to be conditioned exclusively by heredity or environment, but by their *interaction*. The beauty of the canalization notion is that it allows us for the first time to see, dimly, what the interaction might look like.

Some people seem to hold that genetics determines the form and the behavior of the human infant at birth and that what happens after birth is nongenetic. Others, at times, seem to feel that genetic programming is only fully realized not in fixed forms, physical or behavioral, but in dynamic processes—the growing up of the child, the life styles of the child, the adult, and both together. We are made so that, other things being equal, we will fall into certain kinds of organizations as individuals or as groups. The constraints are not absolute. There is openness. But the openness, the capacity for change and adaptation, may be as much a part of genetic programming as the constancies.

With the notion of canalization, with some of the work and the thinking of contemporary anthropology and ethology, we can ask some new questions about learning. We can embed those questions in a new conceptual learning creature, one less parsimonious than Thorndike's but more plausible and interesting, and we can ask what the creature has and what it has to go out and get. Fishbein suggests some of the themes that might govern the preorganizations of human behavior: cooperative hunting, sharing of food, manufacture of tools, husband-wife reciprocity, symbolic communication, rule giving and following. It would be seriously wrong to regard this as anything like a list of instincts. It is a list of systems, of organizations, or resultants. Humans have inbuilt constructive capacities—motor and nervous system organization, short- and long-term memory systems, proclivities to perceive and emote to certain things—that all together tend towards predictable channels of development and organization. The resultants of all these tendencies are functional systems of behavior for humans in groups, not just any old systems but systems designed by Nature's art to serve human adaptation.

This book places emphasis on those preorganizations that serve the life of the hunter-gatherer. The assumption among anthropologists, one gathers, is that almost all of man's evolutionary history has been spent in hunting and gathering. His canalizations are organized that way. Farming began last week and an urban-bureaucratic existence an hour ago. We awkwardly strive to use old canalizations for new ecologies. The theme of civilization and its discontents is always very near us when we address human adaptation in this way. Freud wrote long ago about the problem of old sexual canalizations in new places, Lorenz not so long ago about similar problems in the canalizations of human aggression. Many of our serious contemporary questions about the plasticity of human development boil down to questions about the possibility of using old human canalizations in changing environments.

I believe that future books on children's learning will come to address the data and the issues in the framework set forth here. What we have in this volume is scientific validity of a new order. It is not enough to discuss children's learning only from the vantage point of the learning laboratory. Science has by now sought out the nature and conditions of human adaptation in many laboratories and field sites. All the work is germane. It takes effort and courage to bring it all together, but this kind of approach and only this kind of approach is in the true spirit of Science. Science cannot be a matter of stockpiling research findings and it cannot be done in the spirit of safety, security, and stolidity. The essence of scientific work is the struggle to find order in nature, to find the pattern of the phenomena. No writing on children's learning begins to compare with this volume in that regard.

One final comment, perhaps a comment about the rewards for the venturesome. There is an emergent esthetic quality about this book that is worth noting. There is the breath of life in these pages. Some time ago, John Dewey defined psychology as "the ability to transform the living personality into an objective mechanism for the time being." For many years since Dewey we have conceptually transformed people into telephone switchboards, trait and factor lists, mathematical models, computer programs, deductive networks, game theory and information theory homunculi, etc.—but never for the time being, never so that we have been able to recognize the living personality in our objective mechanism. Now, here and there in this scientific reconstruction, we catch glimpses of a living child, his learning and the goals and meaning of his learning. Art moves a step towards life. Moving through the work, it is exciting to catch these glimpses and to sense in them our own deepened understanding. Science is, I think, ultimately an esthetic affair. There is beauty in the art that comes to imitate life. It is good, at last, to see a scientific book about children's learning with a little beauty.

Sheldon H. White
Harvard University

PREFACE AND
ACKNOWLEDGEMENTS

The starting point for me in conceiving this book was the conviction that in order to understand the development of human behavior, one must understand human evolution. Although this conviction is obvious to biologists (especially ethologists) and anthropologists, it is not commonly held by contemporary, American-trained psychologists. I was "converted" to this view in the winter of 1970, after reading John Bowlby's book *Attachment* (1969). One essential point Bowlby made was that in order to understand human instinctive behavior in general, and attachment behavior in particular, one must examine the behavior in the context of the environment in which man evolved and adapted.

It then occurred to me that there are many "learned" behavior patterns which are universal or nearly universal in the human species. Further, these behaviors appear to develop in a more or less fixed sequence from infancy to adulthood. During this time I was also working with Professor Sheldon White on the influence of Herbert Spencer's writings on developmental psychology. Spencer was a contemporary of Darwin, and the two of them were the most important evolutionary theorists of the latter half of the nineteenth century. White and I became convinced that Spencer either directly or indirectly influenced most of the major developmental theorists of the twentieth century, including Freud, Gesell, Werner, and Piaget. Weren't these developmental theorists writing about, theorizing about, and describing invariant developmental sequences of behavior?

The next step was the big one. It started with the following questions (not consciously stated by me at the time). (1) What is the relationship between evolution and development? (2) From an evolutionary view, why do the *particular* invariancies or universals seen in human behavior occur? These two questions spawned a host of other questions, which on the one hand led me into somewhat unfamiliar areas of study, such as paleoanthropology and embryology, and on the other hand forced me to view familiar areas in new ways, e.g., learning, developmental theory, primate studies. The more I read and thought, the greater became the perceived magnitude of the task I had set for myself—everything I read, heard, or saw seemed to be relevant. For example, it occurred to me that the form jazz improvization takes is a good analogy for both the constraints and the flexibility inherent in developmental processes. At some point I said to myself "enough, write what you know, the task is endless." Here it is, first in an overview form (Chapter 1), then in detail (the rest of the book).

In the preparation and writing of this book I received a great deal of assistance from a large number of people. For the first seven chapters of the book, the following individuals at the University of Cincinnati were especially helpful. Professors Anthony Perzigian and Gustav Carlson of the Department of Anthropology not only suggested many readings and lent their books to me, but also read and commented on an early draft of these chapters. Professor Alex Fraser of the Department of Biological Sciences also suggested readings, lent books, and read and commented on these chapters. Alex performed yeoman services especially on Chapters 1, 2, and 3, and drew Figure 5, the epigenetic landscape. Professors Larry Erway and Carl Huether of the Department of Biological Sciences read all or parts of an early draft of these chapters and made many helpful comments. Professor Kenneth Caster of the Department of Geology read and commented on Chapters 2, 4, and 5, and reread and commented on a second draft of Chapter 4. Professor Marvin Schwartz of the Department of Psychology read and commented on Chapter 5, and made general comments about the organization of these chapters.

The following members of the Department of Psychology at the University of Cincinnati read and commented on one or more of the last five chapters of the book: Professors Donald Schumsky, Leonard Lansky, Wesley Allinsmith, Richard Honeck, and Mr. Alfred Nigl. Mr. Robert Hoffman, of the same department, was especially helpful, and in addition prepared the Index, for which I am very thankful.

Professor Sheldon White of the Department of Social Relations and Psychology at Harvard University and Professor Alexander Siegel of the Department of Psychology at the University of Pittsburgh read and commented on two drafts of the entire manuscript. They have been extremely helpful and encouraging. They, along with Alex Fraser, can share much of the credit for what has merit in this book, but I take full responsibility for errors, illogic, poor writing, etc. I am also delighted that Shep White agreed to write a Foreword. I'm sure that it will provide the reader with a useful framework with which to manage the book.

Last, but certainly not least, three secretaries labored through my barely legible handwriting and various drafts of the book. They are Mss. Phyllis Trosper, Frances Kennedy, and Sherry Traub. I thank them.

Portions of the writing of this book were supported by Grant OEG 0 72 1616 from the Office of Education, U.S. Department of Health, Education and Welfare.

ILLUSTRATION CREDITS

Figure 1

Le Gros Clark, *The Antecedents of Man*, Edinburgh University Press, 1962, Figure 14, "Some of the living members of the order Primates." Reprinted by permission of the publisher.

Figure 2

Biological Science: An Inquiry into Life, Harcourt Brace Jovanovich, Inc., page 733. Reprinted by permission of the Biological Sciences Curriculum Study.

Figure 5

Alex Fraser, The epigenetic landscape, drawn especially for this volume.

Figure 8, Figure 9, Figure 10

Keith Moore, *The Developing Human*, W. B. Saunders Company, 1973, Figures 1-1, 5-5, and 8-12. Reprinted by permission of the publisher and the author.

Figure 11

Lauri Saxén and Juhani Rapola, *Congenital Defects*, Copyright © 1969 by Holt, Rinehart and Winston, Publishers, Figure 8.11, page 202. Reprinted by permission of Holt, Rinehart and Winston, Publishers.

Figure 13

Alexander Alland, *Evolution and Human Behaviour*, Tavistock Publications Ltd., 1967, Figure 7, page 24. Reprinted by permission of the publisher.

Figure 15

Sherwood L. Washburn, *Tools and Human Evolution*, Copyright © 1960 by Scientific American, Inc. All rights reserved.

Figure 16

From Campbell, 1966; Harrison and Montagna, 1969; Jay, 1968; Jolly, 1972; Tobias, 1970. The relationship between brain size and age of puberty in selected Catarrhini.

Figure 17, Figure 18, and Figure 19

Paul D. MacLean, "The Brain, Empathy and Medical Education," *Journal of Nervous and Mental Disorders* 1967, 144, Figures 2, 3, and 4, pages 377-378. Copyright © 1967 The Williams & Wilkins Co., Baltimore. Reprinted by permission of the publisher.

Figure 20 and Figure 21

J. Z. Young, *An Introduction to the Study of Man*, The Clarendon Press, Oxford, 1971, Figure 34.1, page 471, and Figure 35.1, page 488.

Figure 22

J. M. Tanner, *Growth at Adolescence*, 2nd edn., Blackwell Scientific Publications Ltd., Oxford, 1962. Reprinted by permission of the publisher.

Figure 23 and Figure 24

Hans Kummer, *Primate Societies*, Aldine Publishing Company, 1971, Figures 3.12 and 4.4. Copyright © 1971 by Hans Kummer. Reprinted by permission of the author and Aldine Publishing Company.

Figure 25 and Figure 26

R. V. S. Wright, "Imitative Learning of a Flaked Stone Technology. The Case of an Orangutan," *Mankind* 1972, 8, Plates II and III, pages 296–306. Reprinted by permission of the Editor of *Mankind*.

Figure 27

K. J. Connolly, *Mechanisms of Motor Skill Development*, Academic Press Inc. Ltd., 1970, Figure 1, page 167. Reprinted by permission of the publisher and the author.

Figure 28

R. Held and A. Hein, "Movement Produced Stimulation in the Development of Visually Guided Behavior," *Comparative Physiological Psychology* 1963, 56, Figure 1, page 873. Copyright 1963 by the American Psychological Association. Reprinted by permission.

Figure 29

A. Hein and R. Held, "Dissociation of the Visual Placing Response into Elicited and Guided Components," Science 20 October 1967, 158, Figure 2, pages 390-392. Copyright 1967 by the American Association for the Advancement of Science.

Figure 30

R. Held and J. A. Bauer, "Visually Guided Reaching in Infant Monkeys after Restricted Rearing," Science 10 February 1967, 155, Figure 1, pages 718-720. Copyright 1967 by the American Association for the Advancement of Science.

Figure 31

B. L. White, P. Castle, and R. Held, "Observations on the Development of Visually-Directed Reaching," Child Development 1964, 35, Table 1, page 357. Copyright © 1964 by The Society for Research in Child Development, Inc., and reprinted by permission.

Figure 32

M. Lewis, S. Goldberg, and H. Campbell, "A Developmental Study of Information Processing Within the First Three Years of Life: Response Decrement to a Redundant Signal," Monographs of the SRCD 1969, 34, no. 9 (Ser. #133), Figure 1, page 10. Copyright © 1969 by The Society for Research in Child Development, Inc., and reprinted by permission.

Figure 33

M. Lewis, "Infants' Responses to Facial Stimuli During the First Year of Life," Developmental Psychology 1969, 2, pages 75-86. Copyright 1969 by the American Psychological Association. Reprinted by permission.

Figure 34

Jerome Kagan, "The Determinants of Attention in the Infant," American Scientist 1970, 58, no. 3, Figure 7, page 303. Reprinted by permission of the editors of American Scientist.

Figure 35

V. P. Zinchenko, Van Chzhi-tzin, and V. V. Tarakanov, "The Formation and Development of Perceptual Activity," Soviet Psychology and Psychiatry 1962, 2, pages 3-12. Reprinted by permission of International Arts and Sciences Press.

Figure 36

E. Vurpillot, "The Development of Scanning Strategies and Their Relation to Visual Differentiation," Journal of Experimental Child Psychology 1968, 6, Figure 1, page 634. Reprinted by permission of Academic Press Inc.

Figure 37

L. Ghent, "Perception of Overlapping and Embedded Figures by Children of Different Ages," *American Journal of Psychology* 1956, 69, Figure 3, page 580. Reprinted by permission of the University of Illinois Press.

Figure 38

G. A. Hale and R. A. Piper, "Developmental Trends in Children's Incidental Learning: Some Critical Stimulus Differences," *Developmental Psychology* 1973, 8, pages 327-335. Copyright 1973 by the American Psychological Association. Reprinted by permission.

Figure 39

L. Bagrow and R. A. Skelton, *History of Cartography*, C. A. Watts & Co., London, 1964, map on page 251. Reprinted by permission of the publisher.

Figure 40 and Figure 42

J. Piaget and B. Inhelder, *The Child's Conception of Space*, New York: Humanities Press; London: Routledge and Kegan Paul, 1956, Figures 1 and 18, pages 256 and 263. Reprinted by permission.

Figure 41

E. J. Gibson, J. J. Gibson, A. D. Pick, and H. Osser, "A Developmental Study of the Discrimination of Letter-Like Forms," *Journal of Comparative and Physiological Psychology* 1962, 55, page 256. Copyright 1962 by The American Psychological Association. Reprinted by permission.

Figure 43

M. Laurendeau and A. Pinard, "The Development of the Concept of Space in the Child," International Universities Press, 1970, Figure 15, page 182. Reprinted by permission of Delachaux and Niestle, Switzerland, and International Universities Press, Inc.

Figure 44

H. D. Fishbein, S. Lewis, and K. Kieffer, "Children's Understanding of Spatial Relations," *Developmental Psychology* 1972, 7, page 276. Copyright 1972 by the American Psychological Association. Reprinted by permission.

Part One

OVERVIEW AND THEORY

Chapter 1

OVERVIEW AND SUMMARY

The peculiar title of this chapter means that it should be read first as an overview of what the book is about, and second as a summary of the remaining eleven chapters. When reading it as an overview, do it quickly and don't puzzle long on some idea or description that does not seem clear. When reading it as a summary (or as the nonexistent Chapter 13), take your time. Hopefully on this reading all the ideas and descriptions will be clear.

EVOLUTION, LEARNING, AND ADAPTATION

Genetic evolution and learning are the two major processes by which the members of a population or a species become progressively adapted to a particular environment. *Adaptation* is both a condition of a local population, i.e., we say the population is adapted, and it is a set of processes by which the members of a population reach the condition of being adapted. Adaptation as a condition, or state of being, is defined as the ability of a population to survive and reproduce in a given environment. It should be emphasized that from an evolutionary point of view, *populations* and not *individuals* are in the adapted condition in a particular environment. Adaptation is not a static state of being; rather the members of a population are constantly acting on the environment, and the environment is constantly acting on the population. Perhaps the most dramatic example of the dynamic quality of this interaction involves predatory activity. The members of a human population act on the environment by preying on certain animals, and the environment acts on the population through the predatory activity of certain animals on people. During relatively stable periods, when the climate is unchanged and no new plants or animals enter the area, the environment-population interaction is balanced or in equilibrium.

1

This is manifested in a stable population level for each of the species inhabiting the particular environment.

The qualities which make a population adapted to a particular environment are the *phenotypic characteristics* of the members of the population. Phenotypic characteristics refer to all the individual and collective attributes of the members of the population, which include anatomical, physiological, and behavioral attributes as well as social organization. The two major processes underlying the acquisition of phenotypic characteristics are evolution and learning. Although evolutionary processes act directly on the phenotypes of a population, they act indirectly on phenotype acquisition. This is because evolutionary processes have their effect by determining which members of a population will pass their genes on to the next generation. Thus, it is genetic material and not phenotypic characteristics which are acquired, and it is the next generation which acquires the genetic material. Learning processes, on the other hand, directly affect phenotype acquisition, and do so in one generation. Unless the population has acquired some method for storing the acquisitions brought about by learning, they will have to be learned anew in each succeeding generation.

Evolutionary and learning processes are not independent of each other. Within limits, the greater the learning ability of members of a population and the better the products of learning can be transmitted across generations (cultural learning), the greater is the ability of the population to adapt to varied environments. Hence, there is less pressure on the population to evolve when its native environment undergoes change. For example, temperatures began to fluctuate widely about one million years ago. Man, with his great learning ability, learned to stay warm during the cold periods by using the furry skins of other animals and building fires, rather than by evolving a thick, furry skin himself. Consistent with this view, Stebbins (1971) and Mayr (1963) have argued that for approximately the last 40,000 years the great changes in man's adaptation have stemmed primarily from cultural learning rather than evolution. This is not to say that man has stopped evolving, but rather that the recent changes brought about by learning have been much more rapid and dramatic than those brought about by evolution.

The learning ability of members of a population is an important factor in determining the *flexibility* of the adaptation of a population. The more flexible the adaptation, the greater is the diversity of environments to which the population can adapt, i.e., survive and reproduce. Flexibility is a particularly important characteristic when the environment undergoes a substantial change, or when a population moves into a new environment. Both of these changes in environment-population interactions have been characteristic of human evolution, and obviously man has adapted to these changes thus far.

How is learning defined? In the American learning theory tradition, there are three consenses concerning the definition of learning. First, that it is extremely difficult to give a good definition; second, that learning is a process (or processes), which is inferred from noting changes in behavior; and third, that learning has a more or less permanent, as opposed to transitory, quality. The following definition, offered somewhat tenuously by Hilgard and Bower (1966), is of this genre:

def. →

Learning is the process by which an activity originates or is changed through reacting to an encountered situation, provided that the characteristics of the change in activity cannot be explained on the basis of native response tendencies, maturation, or temporary states of the organism (e.g., fatigue, drugs, etc.).*

The definition of learning used in this book bears some resemblance to the preceding definition. It is very similar to the definition recently employed by White and Fishbein (1971). Learning is defined as a set of functions or processes which progressively organize the individual's future sensory experiences or motor activities or both. These functions are set into motion when the individual interacts with his environment, and their long-range effect is to enable the individual to better coordinate his behavior with the environment. Learning is not just reactive to experience, but rather the individual imposes an organization on his experience, the nature of this imposition being a function of his previous learning history and level of maturation. Baldwin (1895) and Piaget (1950) refer to this imposition on experience as "assimilation" and the consequent sensory or motor reorganization produced by the learning functions as "accommodation." Consider a child who has "learned" that dogs are friendly. Upon seeing a strange dog, he approaches it, owing to his assimilation of the new sensory experience—the strange dog—to his old organization of the dog category. The dog bites him, producing a reorganization or accommodation of his dog category. For him, dogs are now perceived as being generally friendly, but potentially dangerous. This reorganization has the effect of modifying his behavior with respect to other dogs in the environment.

Unlike Hilgard and Bower's definition, the preceding definition of learning does not rule out native response tendencies and maturational factors. The view taken in this book is that human evolution has produced a species with great plasticity but also a species in which certain kinds of learning will almost inevitably occur, e.g., language and motor skills. This channeling or native response tendencies have been crucial to our success as a species. Learning and maturation are intimately connected and cannot be separated, at least in the child. A child does not mature in the absence of encounters with the environment, and successive encounters with the environment occur at different maturational levels. What must be understood is how learning and maturation are keyed to and interact with each other.

EVOLUTIONARY THEORY

Our discussion of evolutionary theory must begin with the relationship between the genotype, the phenotype, and the environment. The genotype of an individual is the collection of all the genes inherited from his parents. Each human being has about 500,000 genes distributed across forty-six chromosomes. The genotype is set when the male's sperm unites with the female's ovum, forming a single cell called the zygote. The genotype can be thought of as a set of instructions for the ways in which the developing individual (the phenotype) will interact with its environment (Waddington 1962). It does not contain, as was previously thought, a preformed program directing the

---

*Ernest R. Hilgard and Gordon H. Bower, *Theories of Learning*, 3rd ed., p. 2, © 1966. Reprinted by permission of Prentice-Hall, Inc., Englewood Cliffs, N.J.

phenotype to "unfold" in completely determined ways. These ideas will be discussed in further detail in the next section of the chapter.

The changing milieu in which the zygote divides, and continues to divide during prenatal growth and development, is the prenatal environment. The changing milieu in which the newborn grows and develops throughout his lifetime is the postnatal environment. This includes the actions of other individuals, which have been a crucial aspect of primate evolution. The important points to emphasize about environments are that they are never absolutely constant from one moment to the next, and that selective aspects of the environment are always impinging on the developing organism. Hence, each individual moves through a sequence of environments from conception to death.

The phenotype of an individual consists of *all* of his characteristics, e.g., his anatomy, physiology, behavior, from the moment the zygote is formed until the individual dies. Hence, the phenotype is constantly changing. The rate of change is most rapid in the early stages of life, and gradually slows down as the individual matures. There are exceptions to this "rule," e.g., the adolescent growth spurt (Tanner 1970), but it is accurate enough for our purposes. It is important to note that not all of an individual's characteristics are changing at all times. This fact is crucial in understanding environmentally induced congenital defects, a topic which will be briefly discussed in another chapter.

Waddington (1960a, 1968) refers to the relationship between the genotype, phenotype, and environment as an *epigenetic system*. The genotype determines the potential for phenotypic development, and the particular way the phenotype develops, including how and what the individual learns, is a function of an individual's genotype and the particular sequence of environments in which the development occurs. Thus, any genotype would lead to different phenotypes in different environments. In some environments, the individual might not reach the stage of being born; in others, he might survive childhood but no more; in still others he might reach a ripe old age and produce many children. Hence, the epigenetic system should be viewed as an adaptive system which "attempts" to maintain a balance or equilibrium between genetic instructions, phenotypic development, and environmental stresses.

Evolutionary processes operate on the epigenetic systems of members of a population. The modern synthetic theory of evolution (e.g., Mayr 1963, Stebbins 1971) identifies five major processes: genetic mutation, chromosomal mutation, genetic recombination, reproductive isolation, and natural selection. The present discussion will be restricted to genetic recombination and natural selection. Genetic recombination refers to the random process in which one half of the chromosomes from the male parent and one half from the female parent come together to form the genotype of the zygote. There are 2^{46} possible ways in which the chromosomes from two parents can be combined into a new single genotype.

Genetic recombination is important from an evolutionary point of view because different genotypes lead to different *Darwinian fitness* in given environments. Darwinian fitness is how much an individual reproduces relative to other individuals (this will be expanded later). Individuals who have many surviving offspring have higher Darwinian fitness than those who have few or

no surviving offspring. Obviously those individuals who do not survive to a reproductive age, e.g. those who die in childhood, have low Darwinian fitness.
Natural selection is a weeding out process operating at all stages of development which is measured by Darwinian fitness. It operates directly on the
phenotypes of individuals in given environments, and only indirectly does it
affect the genotypes of the next generation. Hence, a genotype may lead to high
Darwinian fitness in one sequence of environments, and low fitness in all other
sequences of environments.

Rensch (1959) has referred to evolution as an "experiment" in design, and
Lorenz (1969) has referred to it as a "trial-and-success" experiment. What they
mean is that each individual epigenetic system is a trial run or test run of a
particular design. The design is coded in the genotype, and as the phenotype
carries out the genetic code (the instructions for development) in a given sequence of environments, an experiment is run. If the experiment is successful,
then the epigenetic system is viable, and the individual not only survives but
has high Darwinian fitness, thus transmitting his genes (his design) to the next
generation. If the experiment is unsuccessful, the individual has low Darwinian fitness. If the offspring of the parents with successful designs develop in a
sequence of environments similar to that which their parents experienced, then
it is highly probable that their designs will also be successful. What happens if
the offspring find themselves in a sequence of environments different from that
for which they were designed? In all likelihood their Darwinian fitness will be
low. If the sequence of environments for all offspring is very different from that
experienced by their parents, then the species as a whole may become extinct.
The evolutionary record, in fact, indicates that there are far more extinct
species than living ones (Newell 1963).

The final point to be made in this section is that life processes in general, and
evolutionary processes in particular can be viewed as fundamentally involved
with the acquisition of information or knowledge about the environment (Lorenz 1969, Piaget 1971, Waddington 1960a). In general, the greater the *knowledge* an individual member of any species has of the environment, the greater
are the chances that the individual will survive and reproduce in that environment. In order for an epigenetic system to be viable, the genetic code must contain information (knowledge) of the environments in which the individual is
to develop. That is, the set of instructions contained in the genotype is designed
for interactions in a particular sequence of environments—the environments
to which the parents were adapted. This is why Darwinian fitness decreases
when the environments of the offspring are different from those of the parents
—the knowledge contained in the genotype becomes incorrect or, at least,
inadequate.

In the higher animals—the vertebrates—evolutionary processes have produced two basic sets of mechanisms for the acquisition and transmission of
knowledge. The first are the hereditary mechanisms contained in the
genotype. The second set of mechanisms is ultimately dependent on the first,
but to some extent they develop a life of their own. These are the learning
mechanisms. It is the genotype which determines the development of the particular structures and functions which enable learning to occur, and species

vary considerably in the extent to which they are equipped with these mechanisms. Species also vary in the extent to which the learning of one individual can be transmitted to others in the following generation. As we indicated earlier, this phenomenon—transgenerational or cultural learning—has been one of the key features in human evolution, and is no doubt linked with the tremendous memory capacities of the species.

From a reading of the works of Waddington, Lorenz, and Piaget, it becomes clear that the primary short-range function of the acquisition of knowledge, whether in the genotype or through phenotypic acquisition, is to enable the organism to act effectively in the environment. For Piaget, all phenotypically acquired knowledge starts with action, and is always translatable into action. The long-range function of the acquisition of knowledge is the survival of the species, which also involves effective action in the environment.

The preceding discussion on evolution as a knowledge process has been relatively abstract. One concrete example given by Lorenz (1969) dealing with the phobic response of protozoa to noxious stimulation may bring the subject into sharper focus. When these animals are moving in either a neutral or a continuously improving environment, they keep moving in the same direction. However, when they enter a deteriorating environment or encounter a noxious stimulus, the animals stop, move backwards a certain distance, and then move forward again after they have performed a turning response. The usual outcome of the turn is to alter the subsequent direction of movement away from the noxious stimulus. However, sometimes the animals turn 360° and proceed to move again into the noxious stimulus, setting the whole pattern in motion again. This knowledge process is completely encoded in the genotype—which stimuli are noxious, which are neutral or positive, and the phobic response to a noxious stimulus.

EVOLUTION, DEVELOPMENT, AND BEHAVIORAL ADAPTATION

As already mentioned, evolutionary processes act on the epigenetic system, which is essentially a system of development. Thus, any changes produced in the average genotype of a species will of necessity change the ways in which members of the species develop. The epigenetic system is constructed in such a way that only certain types of changes are possible, i.e., only certain types of genetic changes have the potential for being adaptive in any environment. You can't change a fish directly into an elephant; but elephants do, in fact, come from fish, with an extremely large number of intervening evolutionary steps. At each step the epigenetic system has to be adaptive in order for the step to be taken. Hence, developmental processes and evolutionary processes are conservative, both operating on the principle: "If it works, keep it if you can, modify it if you have to." If the epigenetic system is modified too much, it will not be adaptive. This principle makes it easier to understand the presence of such human embryonic structures as the *branchial arches* which closely resemble, and through evolutionary processes are derived from gill slits in fish. In fact, when development goes awry, the branchial arches do develop into gill-like structures.

The primary reason for the conservatism in evolution and development must be found, then, in the nature of the epigenetic system itself. The genotype of this system has been described as containing a set of instructions for the potential interactions of the phenotype with the environment. This implies that the genotype in some sense contains an image, template, or target of what the phenotype should be like at each point in development. There is some plasticity in the way the phenotype will attain the target, but the extent of this plasticity is severely limited. If the target is missed by too much, the individual will either not survive, or not reproduce. In other words, as in jazz improvisation, some variations work, and other don't. The ones that work in jazz must operate within the constraints set by the rhythm, melody, harmonic structure, and tempo of the tune. The variations in epigenesis which "work" must operate within the constraints of the genotype as a whole, the particular state of development of the individual, and the particular state of the environment when a given set of genetic instructions is set in motion.

There is another aspect of plasticity in the epigenetic system which Waddington (1960a, 1962) has called *canalization*. Canalization involves a set of genetic processes which ensure that development will proceed in normal ways, that the phenotypic targets will be attained despite the presence of minor abnormal genetic or environmental conditions. Canalization processes operate at each point in development to correct minor deflections from the sought-for phenotypic targets. Presumably canalization processes ensure that important phenotypic constancies will occur in all members of a species, e.g., in humans the presence of two eyes, one nose, two hands, language, bipedal locomotion. Canalization is a *collusion* of genes to keep the developing organism in balance. Not all characteristics of an individual are canalized, nor are those which are, equally canalized. Concerning this last point, Fraser has shown, for example (Waddington 1962), that when a major gene controlling hair follicle growth in mice is replaced by a mutant gene, the primary facial whiskers are heavily canalized, i.e., are strongly resistant to change, the secondary facial whiskers are moderately canalized and the hair coat is either weakly canalized or not canalized at all.

One of the major assumptions of this book is that canalization processes operate to bring about behavioral constancies throughout the entire lifetime of individuals, and not just the anatomical constancies found during the prenatal stages of development. (No canalization research has ever been carried out with humans or with behavior.) In other words, it is assumed that not only reflex behavior, but also how we learn and what we learn are canalized. This assumption has also been made by Lorenz (1969, 1972), Piaget (1971), and Waddington (1960a). Lorenz (1972) states this assumption as follows:

> Ethology has . . . demonstrat(ed) irrefutably that all behavior, exactly like all bodily structure, can develop in the ontogeny of the individual only along the lines and within the possibilities of species—specific programs which have been mapped out in the course of phylogeny and laid down in the code of the genome.*

---

*Konrad Z. Lorenz, "The Enmity Between Generations and its Probable Ethological Causes," in *Play and Development*, ed. M. W. Piers (New York: W. W. Norton, 1972), p. 65.

Lorenz (1969) asserts that one underlying mechanism by which these constancies are brought about is *induction*. Induction is a term used in embryology (Moore 1973, Waddington 1962) to describe the influence certain embryonic tissues (the inductors) have on the development of adjacent tissues —an important component of canalization processes. The inductors organize the particular ways in which the adjacent tissue will develop, and the particular way is a function of the developmental stage of the embryo and the part of the genetic code which is active at that time. As an example, there are three primary germ layers in the embryo—the ectoderm, mesoderm, and endoderm. The ectoderm has the potential for developing into the lens of an eye, the neural tube which eventually develops into the brain, or simple skin. The particular structure which develops depends on which inductor is active at the particular developmental stage.

Lorenz (1969) points out that the developmental constancies in embryology occur because evolutionary processes have assured that the prenatal environment will change in certain regular ways in conjunction with preceding changes of the phenotype. He argues that it is immaterial, from an adaptive point of view, whether the induction ". . . comes from another subsystem pertaining to the same organism, or from an environmental circumstance to whose regular occurrence the species is phylogenetically adapted. In other words, all adaptive modification is essentially identical with induction."* A behavioral example of induction cited by ethologists is imprinting in birds. In the natural environment chicks are normally induced to follow their mothers because they are inevitably exposed to their mothers at a certain point in development. In the laboratory, however, the chicks may be induced to become imprinted on men.

Given the existence of anatomical and behavioral invariancies or constancies during development, it makes sense to assume that these phenotypic characteristics have survival value at that time to the individual or to the species. However, this is not necessarily the case. There are four possible reasons for the existence of constancies:

1. The characteristic has survival value at that point in development, e.g., the presence of a placenta.
2. The characteristic does not have survival value at that point in development, but is necessary in order to build another characteristic which eventually will have high survival value, e.g., the presence of an optic cup on which an eye is built.
3. The characteristic does not have survival value at that point in development, but will eventually be combined with other characteristics, the combination eventually having high survival value, e.g., the individual bones of the head.
4. The characteristic itself does not have survival value, but is the outcome of a characteristic which falls in one of the first three categories, e.g., the appearance of reflexes in infants which occur owing to the immaturity of the brain.

---

* Konrad Z. Lorenz, "Innate Bases of Learning," in *On the Biology of Learning*, ed. K. Pribram (New York: Harcourt Brace Jovanovich, 1969), p. 35.

How does one determine whether a behavioral characteristic is adaptive and has survival value? Tinbergen (1965) has strongly argued that nothing short of looking at the characteristic in the environment can provide an answer. He states ". . . how useless and even unscientific it is to pronounce an opinion on the question whether or not 'a certain feature is adaptive' until one has tried to find out."* In his paper, Tinbergen gives examples of the two main methods he and his colleagues have used to try "to find out." In the first method, a particular environmental pressure is singled out, e.g., defense against predators, and the way members of a given species meet the challenge of this pressure is investigated. They have discovered, for example, that the nearly invariant behavior of eggshell removal from the nest by the black-headed gull decreases the probability that the offspring will be killed by predators. In the second method, an invariancy or constancy of behavior or anatomy is observed and the question is asked, how does the characteristic contribute to individual or species survival? For example, in his own work with the three-spined stickleback, Tinbergen noted that the males almost always "fanned" the water over the nest where developing eggs were laid. When fanning was prevented by removing the males, or when the nest was covered by glass, the eggs died. However, if the male and glass were removed but freshly aerated water was run through the nest, the eggs survived. Thus, fanning was found to be adaptive because it ventilated the eggs.

To what extent has the adaptive value of various aspects of human behavior been determined by these or comparable methods? Almost none at all for children or adults. In a recent book entitled *Ethological Studies of Child Behavior* (Jones 1972), a start has been made. However, these studies consist largely of descriptions of behavior-function relationships from which *inferences* are made as to the probable survival value of the behavior. For example, in Konner's chapter about the Bushmen, a hunter-gatherer people in Africa, he notes that family size is kept down by abstention from sexual intercourse for up to fifteen months after childbirth. He also notes that Bushmen women do most of the food gathering and carry their zero to two year-old infants during this time. The inference is then made that spacing births too closely would interfere with food gathering, and hence would be maladaptive. As another example, Konner points out that such reflexes as headraising and "crawling" movements made by newborns have limited adaptive value for babies placed in cribs. But for babies who are almost constantly being carried upright in slings by their mothers, these movements not only allow them to readjust to their mothers' changes in posture, but also probably prevent them from being smothered.

Given the present status of canalization studies and ethological studies of human behavior, some of the discussions in this book will be speculative. Where constancies or invariancies in human development are observed, it will be assumed that canalization and induction processes were operating, and that as a consequence the characteristics must have had adaptive value at some

---

*N. Tinbergen, "Behavior and Natural Selection" in *Ideas in Evolution and Behavior,* ed. J. A. Moore (Garden City, N.Y.: Natural History Press, 1965), p. 35.

point in human evolution. What was it? Answers to this question will be attempted, based primarily on inferences drawn from anthropological, paleontological, and neurological studies.

THE PRIMATE EVOLUTIONARY LINES

Several points have been emphasized in the preceding sections. Evolution was described as both an experiment in design and as a knowledge process. Evolution leads to the acquisition of knowledge through the development of two sets of acquisition mechanisms—the hereditary mechanisms of the genotype, and the learning mechanisms which are programmed in the genotype. These mechanisms not only determine how members of a species will learn, but to a certain extent, what they will learn.

We also emphasized that evolution, development, and learning are interdependent, conservative processes. This conservatism is due to the nature of the epigenetic system itself, a system compared to jazz improvisation in the sense that in order for a variation (evolutionary, developmental, or learning) to work, it must fit in with the overall plan of the system (in jazz, the tune itself). What is the nature of man's epigenetic system? Since man is a primate—a variation of the primate plan—we must know something about the nature of the primate plan to answer this question. First we will examine the course of primate evolution—the evolutionary record—and then we will compare the living primate variations.

The primate order started to evolve approximately sixty-five million years ago, about forty million years after placental mammals started to emerge, from a ground-living order of mammals called *insectivores*. The first primates were very small, probably rat-like in appearance, closely resembling contemporary tree shrews. Their initial adaptation (design) was for life in the trees in tropical or sub-tropical climates. Most contemporary primates still maintain this adaptation (Jolly 1972).

The paleoanthropological record—primarily bones and teeth of varying ages—suggests the following evolutionary course of the primates. The first primate suborder to evolve from our tree shrew-like ancestors were the Lemuroidea, which include the contemporary tree shrews and lemurs of the Old World tropics. Fifty to sixty million years ago the next suborder emerged, the Tarsiodea, whose contemporaries, the tarsiers, live in the Asian tropics. Forty to fifty million years ago the remaining two primate suborders emerged, the Platyrrhini, which include all the contemporary New World monkeys, and the Catarrhini, which include all the contemporary Old World monkeys, apes, and man. All the surviving Platyrrhini maintain an arboreal adaptation, whereas some of the surviving Catarrhini returned to the ground. About forty million years ago the Catarrhini diverged into two superfamilies, the Cercopithecoidea (Old World monkeys), and the Hominoidea (apes and man). About thirty million years ago the Hominoidea started to diverge, with the first line leading to the contemporary gibbons and the second line leading to the contemporary orangutans, both of which live in Asia. Finally, about twenty million years ago the hominoid lines leading to the chimpanzees, gorillas, and man started to diverge in Africa (Campbell 1966, Hulse 1963, Pilbeam 1972). (See Figure 1.)

It is risky to categorize any living primate as representative of a given stage in hominoid evolution because each living species is a result of millions of years of independent, divergent evolution. With this in mind, Le Gros Clark (1959), the most emminent paleoanatomist of our times, believes that it is useful to

Figure 1

Some living members of the order Primates, representing a series that, broadly speaking, links man anatomically with some of the most primitive of placental mammals: 1, tree shrew; 2, lemur; 3, tarsier; 4, Old World monkey; 5, chimpanzee; 6, Australian aboriginal (From Le Gros Clark 1959).

compare living primates to show the anatomical links between the first primates and man. This linkage is shown in Figure 1.

Arboreal adaptation produced in the primates, as distinct from other mammals, major anatomical-functional changes involving the brain, vision, touch and grasping, and posture and locomotion (Le Gros Clark 1959, Campbell 1966). The changes in the brain primarily involved a reduction of the structures underlying smell, and substantial expansion of the cerebral cortex, especially the areas underlying vision. The former change reflects the fact that a highly developed sense of smell is of limited survival value in trees, and the latter change reflects the need for coordination and integration of sensory information from the distance receptors of audition and vision. The changes underlying vision involved enlargement of the eyes to increase sensitivity to light, movement of the eyes to the center of the face to produce varying degrees of stereoscopic vision, and in the Catarrhini, the development of excellent visual acuity and color vision. The changes in the hand were profound. With the evolution of freely mobile digits (fingers) with sensitive pads (fingertips), the hand became prehensile—it could grasp objects by wrapping the fingers around them. The thumb also evolved with varying degrees of opposability —the ability to touch one or more fingers with it. In short, the hand became an instrument for exploring the environment as well as for manipulating objects. Regarding posture and locomotion, primates move primarily on all fours (quadrupedal locomotion) when on the ground, with the exception of man and the gibbons. In the trees, however, almost all non-human primates do a certain amount of swinging through the branches, arm to arm, known as *brachiation*. From the point of view of posture and locomotion, the importance of brachiation is twofold: it leads to a certain degree of independence between the arms and the legs along with a fair amount of mobility in both, and it encourages an upright posture. As a consequence, most primates sometimes walk bipedally (on two limbs).

We will now turn to the social adaptations of the primates, restricting our discussion to the Catarrhini (Old World monkeys, apes, and man). Hallowell (1961, 1963) has pointed out that an understanding of primate evolution requires an understanding of their social structure. This is especially true of the catarrhines, who are all diurnal animals. (Many of the New World primates are nocturnal.) Hallowell (1961) has described this social structure as follows:

> . . . what we find as the common social core of all but the lowest primate groups, despite their variation, is the continuous association of adults of both sexes with their offspring during the portion of the latter's life cycle that covers the period from birth to the threshold of maturity. This core pattern of associated individuals, when considered with reference to their interrelated roles, is linked with the fact that basic functions are involved, that is, the procreation, protection, and nurture of offspring—born singly, relatively helpless at birth, and dependent for a period thereafter. Variations in mateship and size of group may occur without affecting these functions.*

*Irving A. Hallowell, "The Protocultural Foundations of Human Adaptation," in *Social Life of Early Man*, ed. S. L. Washburn (Chicago: Aldine Publishing, 1961), p. 239. Reprinted by permission of Aldine Publishing.

There are several variations among the catarrhines (including human hunter-gatherers) on this basic pattern, each species having its own characteristic social structure. The major types are:

1. For the chimpanzee, a mother and one or two young offspring comprise a family, with the social group as a whole consisting of many of these families, along with free-ranging juveniles and young and older adults, most in hearing distance of one another.
2. For the gorillas and most monkeys who live on the ground of forests and savannas, the social group consists of many adult males and females and their offspring, all in close visual proximity to one another.
3. For monkeys living on the ground in very dry areas, the basic social group is a "harem" consisting of one adult male, several adult females, and their offspring. The Hamadryas and gelada baboon harems collect together in the evening and sleep in large groups.
4. For human hunter-gatherers, the family consists of a monogamous couple and their children, with several families forming a social group.

Other primates, like the gibbons, are monogamous, but the families in these species do not form larger social groups. In these variations all members of the group are known to each other, and the newborns and young infants are almost always in constant contact with their mothers. As the infants mature, become more mobile, and are able to feed themselves, they nevertheless remain in sight of their mothers (Campbell 1966, Jolly 1972).

Several other features of the catarrhine social group should be pointed out. First, all the groups are seminomadic in that they maintain a home range which they exploit for food and protection from predators but build no permanent sleeping sites within it. Apparently none of the catarrhines are territorial in the sense of defending the boundaries of their home range against intruders of the same species, with the possible exception of the gibbons. Typically, when members of different groups meet at the boundaries of their home range, they either ignore each other or move away from each other. Fighting between different groups is rare (Kummer 1971).

A second common feature of the catarrhines, including the human hunter-gatherers who live in tropical and semitropical areas, is that they subsist primarily on fruits or other vegetation. Most of the catarrhines will periodically eat insects, and a few of them—some baboon species and chimpanzees—will eat meat on occasion. But in all cases meat and insect consumption comprise only a small portion of the diet. In the case of human hunter-gatherers, however, this portion is significant (Lee and DeVore 1968).

Finally, the primary way the young become socialized into the group is through play and observation of older members. Play is most characteristic of the later infancy and juvenile periods of development, after which its frequency drops off markedly. The young usually play with their peers, occasionally with their mother, and rarely with adults. This is true for human hunter-gatherers as well, although unlike the other primates some intentional teaching or instruction by adults does take place in these groups. It is important to emphasize here that if the young are not appropriately socialized into the group

—if they don't become socially competent—they will either not survive to a reproductive age, or they will reproduce less than the more socially competent of
the group. This, of course, is natural selection operating to maintain the design
of the species.

THE HUNTER-GATHERER EVOLUTIONARY LINE

We are now prepared to examine the primate variation of greatest interest to
us—modern man. The paleoanthropological record from more than one million
years ago to approximately ten thousand years ago strongly indicates that the
evolutionary design of man was that of a warm-zone, seminomadic hunter-
gatherer. Thus man has lived in ways similar to other advanced primates for
ninety-nine percent of his existence—in small groups made up of families, as a
hunter of animals and a gatherer of vegetation. The tremendous deviancies
from this adaptation which now characterize man started to occur only about
ten thousand years ago with the establishment of pockets of small, permanently
settled village-farming communities. The widespread existence of villages and
cities did not come about for another five thousand years (Braidwood 1967).

An important assumption of this book is that our present design is still that of
a hunter-gatherer—that the evolutionary changes which have occurred over the
past five thousand years have had little effect on the epigenetic system which
evolved over the preceding one million years. How does one determine the nature of this system? There are three interdependent ways: examination of the
paleoanthropological record, examination of contemporary hunter-gatherer
societies, and examination of certain aspects of human development from birth
to maturity. In this section we will look at the first two ways.

Modern man, *Homo sapiens*, is the only surviving member of the family of
primates called the Hominidae. There are three known genera of the
Hominidae—*Ramapithecus*, *Australopithecus*, and *Homo*. The fossil record
suggests the following evolutionary course of the hominids (Campbell 1966,
Howells 1973, Pilbeam 1972). The first hominids, the ramapithecines, emerged
at least fourteen million years ago in Africa, and by ten million years ago they
were widespread in Africa and Asia. They were forest-living apes, and based
upon the shape and size of their teeth, they appear to have been seed and root
eaters. This suggests that they were primarily ground-living as opposed to
tree-living animals (Howells 1973). By five million years ago the ramapithecines had become extinct, and the next hominids, the australopithecines,
had emerged in Africa.

The fossil evidence from three million years ago suggests that at least two
species of *Australopithecus* existed, *A. robustus* and *A. africanus*. These two
species were similar in the following ways: their brain size was about the same
as that of contemporary chimpanzees, both walked bipedally, both were primarily vegetarians, and both probably lived in savanna areas and on the fringes of
forests. The major differences between the two species were: *A. robustus* was
much larger than *A. africanus* (about 150 pounds versus 70 pounds); *A. africanus* was a meat-eater, whereas *A. robustus* was not; and *A. africanus*
manufactured crude stone tools, whereas *A. robustus* did not. The *A. robustus*
line became extinct about one million years ago, but about two million years
ago the *A. africanus* line evolved into another species, *A. habilis*. These latter

"man-apes" had larger brains and more mobile hands than their ancestors, walked upright more efficiently, and more closely resembled man than did *A. africanus*. They clearly lived in the open savannas and hunted small animals such as toads and rabbits.

It is believed that about one million years ago the first men, *Homo erectus*, evolved from *A. habilis*. These men physically resembled modern man in all ways except for the shape of the face and head and the size of the brain. They made a variety of tools, used fire, and cooperatively hunted large game. The early members of *H. erectus* had an average brain size about two-thirds that of modern man, and the later members—those living about half a million years ago—had an average brain size about three-fourths that of modern man. *Homo sapiens* evolved from *H. erectus* about 250,000 years ago, and the contemporary form, Cro-Magnon man, made his full appearance about 40,000 years ago.

There are four major sets of anatomical-functional changes which characterize man's evolution (Campbell 1966, Howells 1973, Pilbeam 1972, Washburn and Moore 1974, Went 1968). The first set is a very complex one involving brain function and anatomical connections between the brain and the hand and the brain and the neck. As indicated in the preceding section, the primate hand, and especially that of the Catarrhini, is a very flexible "tool" for grasping, manipulating, and exploring the environment. Man's hand differs from that of other primates primarily in the extent to which the thumb is opposable. The reason for the way we use our hands, however, lies in the brain. In comparison with other primates, human brain anatomy underlying the hand differs in two important ways: the hand, especially the thumb, is more extensively represented in both the primary sensory areas and primary motor areas; and the related areas of the cortex involved with executing hand movements are more extensive in man than in nonhuman primates.

At some point in human evolution, and it is debatable just when, man acquired spoken language. In the brain this acquisition is indicated by the presence of a set of interrelated structures not found in other primates. But these changes had to be accompanied by changes in the neck and throat for spoken language to be possible. If other primates had our brain, they would not be able to speak because of the anatomy of their necks and throats. Regarding brain function, changes underlying memory occurred primarily in the expansion of old structures in the brain—the hippocampus, which is phylogenetically very old, and the temporal neocortex, which is phylogenetically more recent. Similarly, changes in the brain underlying spatial understanding occurred primarily in the expansion of existing structures in the parietal lobes of the brain which are characteristic of the advanced primates. The result of all these separate expansions is reflected in the evolutionary record by a tremendous growth of the brain—a tripling of brain size from *A. africanus* to *H. sapiens*.

The second set of anatomical-functional changes involved posture and locomotion. As indicated in the preceding section, all the advanced primates have a tendency to walk bipedally. The evolutionary record (shape of the bones of the feet and shape of the pelvis) clearly indicates that the australopithecines almost always walked bipedally. However, they were not as efficient walkers as *H. erectus*, whose gait was indistinguishable from *H. sapiens*. The primary advantage of bipedal locomotion is that it frees the hands for carrying and manipulating objects. Washburn (1960) believes that bipedal locomotion was the essential condition for determining the future of *Australopithecus-Homo* evolution.

The third set of anatomical-functional changes involved body size, a factor on which Went (1968) places great emphasis. There are not enough fossils to allow a statement to be made about the size of the ramapithecines, but it is clear that the australopithecines were far smaller than *H. erectus.* A fair assumption is that *A. africanus* was between three and four feet tall, and *H. erectus* about five-and-a-half feet tall. Went (1968) points out that if a club proportional to a man five foot eight inches tall were used by him, and another club proportional to a man five foot tall were used by the latter, the taller, heavier man would have twice the striking force as the shorter, lighter one. A comparably fitted individual three foot tall could only produce one-twenty-fifth of the impact. To use clubs or stones for hunting large game and for protection against predators required the strength and size of *H. erectus* which *A. africanus* lacked.

The fourth set of anatomical-functional changes involved rate of maturity. A comparison of living primates indicates that the rate of maturity is slowest for man, followed by the chimpanzees and gorillas, and then the Old World monkeys. It is argued that natural selection operated to produce longer periods of childhood in man because "there is so much to learn" (Hallowell 1963, Washburn and Moore 1974). A lengthened period of immaturity of offspring placed additional stresses on our ancestors—the dependent young had to be fed and protected for increasingly longer periods of time. An alternate view is that slower maturation was not selected for as such, but rather that it was a concommitant or covariation of a characteristic that was selected for—increased brain complexity. This argument will be developed in greater detail in a later section.

We will now turn briefly to the social adaptations of the hominids. As with the anatomical-functional changes, it is assumed that social adaptations are canalized or induced behavioral characteristics. Man learns them because he was designed to learn them. There are six of these broad characteristics: tool manufacture and tool use; symbolic behavior, e.g., language and art; cooperative hunting and sharing; cooperative gathering and sharing; monogamous families; and rule giving and rule following. The fact that all these characteristics are manifested in almost all contemporary hunter-gatherer groups, and that some of them are manifested in the paleoanthropological record, is indirect support for the assumption that they are canalized.

The evolutionary record indicates that tool manufacture and use is a hominid characteristic at least 2.6 million years old. Although the onset of language cannot be dated, the construction of art objects is at least 40,000 years old, and the ritual burying of dead at least 70,000 years old (Pfeiffer 1972). Evidence for cooperative hunting and sharing is more indirect, but "butchering" sites have been dated at half a million years, and the killing of large game at a million years. Of the other characteristics, the evolutionary record is mute.

Following the analyses of Hallowell (1963), G. H. Mead (1934), Simpson (1949) and Waddington (1960b), one key to understanding the form human evolution took is the idea of *reciprocal obligations.* In the hunter-gatherer group, like other primate groups, group identification, i.e., knowing who is and who is not a member of one's group, is a fundamental characteristic of survival. However, in the nonhuman primate groups individual members by and large are not reciprocally obligated to one another. For example, in human groups cooperative hunting and food sharing requires a mutual interdependency among the hunters along with the prohibition of keeping the food for oneself. They follow the assumption: "If I am successful in the hunt and share the kill with you and your family, then you are obligated to do the same for me." Similarly, if a man finds a wife, they not only reciprocally obligate one another regarding the sharing of food and care of children, but they become obligated to remain sexually monogamous. The reciprocal obligations between husband and wife consequently have the effect of permitting others in the group to find mates. It is safe to say that hunter-gatherer groups involve a large number of these obligations.

Hallowell and Mead believe that the necessary condition for the establishment of reciprocal obligations is self-awareness—the ability to objectively view one's self or to reflect upon one's self. At a minimum, this requires that a person be aware of his actions in a given situation and of the subsequent reactions of others. Another important characteristic of self-awareness emphasized by Mead is the ability to be empathic—to take the other's point of view. Thus, in order to be reciprocally obligated it is necessary to be aware of the *potential* effects your actions will have on others, and consequently to act in ways which would be satisfying to yourself if you were in the other's place. This is the "Do unto others," etc., of the Bible. When did self-awareness, empathy, and reciprocal obligations emerge in human evolution? One suggestion is that these characteristics date back to *H. erectus*, and perhaps earlier, based on the early existence of a division of labor between males and females as evidenced by the hunting of large game, and the assumed sharing of meat and vegetation by members of the group. It is hard to conceive of such a complex food distribution system without reciprocity.

ASPECTS OF HUMAN DEVELOPMENT

From an evolutionary point of view, the major developmental task of any primate is to fit into his group and be (or become) a contributor to the *genetic* survival of the group. The word "genetic" is included because reproduction and survival of the young are the most fundamental characteristics of life. Although the primates and mammals as a whole share a large number of developmental requirements, e.g., protection of the young and nursing of infants, each species has its own particular requirements. If the young do not physically mature appropriately and become socialized in such a way as to fit into the group, they will not become contributors to the genetic survival of the group. In fact, their existence may become detrimental to group survival.

The aspects of human development dealt with in this book are those concerning *social competency*. From an evolutionary point of view, the most pertinent aspects of social competency are those related to the major hunter-gatherer social characteristics described in the preceding section. In order for a hunter-gatherer to contribute to his group, he must learn the language, learn how to make and use tools, learn how to identify suitable animals or vegetation for food and how to pursue their "capture," learn to cooperate and share in these and other endeavors, learn to give and follow rules, and learn the appropriate roles for being a husband or wife and parent.

These are enormous tasks for any individual, but they are natural tasks because of the way our epigenetic systems evolved. Just as it would be unnatural for us, and perhaps impossible, to learn to lead the life of baboons or gorillas, it would conversely be impossible for them to learn to be hunter-gatherers. We were designed for the hunter-gatherer adaptation, and the other primates were designed for their typical adaptations. This does not imply that we cannot learn some of the characteristics of chimpanzee social competency, for example, or vice versa, but rather that our evolutionary heritage ensures that we will almost inevitably learn ours. (Recall that Lorenz spoke of this as "induction" and Waddington as "canalization".)

Which aspects of human social competency should we examine, and how can we determine whether they are canalized or induced? The answer to the first part of the question rests on our analysis of hunter-gatherer characteristics and the related available psychological literature. As we indicated in a previous section, no one has determined the adaptive value, in Tinbergen's sense, of behavior patterns seen in childhood. Further, there has been little psychological research done on tracking the acquisition of hunter-gatherer social competency. Nevertheless, there is an enormous literature on the psychology of human development, and some of it is relevant to the approach of this book. Concerning the second part of the question, the only possible direct answer lies in genetic research, probably modeled on the work of experimental embryologists or Waddington and his students. The indirect answer chosen here is to identify constancies or invariancies in psychological development and assume that the behaviors were canalized or induced. This, of course, is Piaget's approach, and before him, that of Gesell. This is also the approach of many who are concerned with the identification and treatment of abnormal behavior.

There are six psychological characteristics necessary for the development of hunter-gatherer social characteristics. These are: motor skills development, development of attention, development of memory, language development, development of spatial understanding, and moral development. A selective review of research done in these areas indicates that the learning or knowledge acquisition that occurs in each appears to form an invariant sequence. Moreover, despite the fact that the learning which occurs is continuous, three sets of age ranges keep cropping up in which the learning seems either quantitatively or qualitatively different. These are when children are one to two years old, five to seven years old, and nine to eleven years old. The first two age ranges correspond roughly to the end of the sensory-motor and preoperational periods of development respectively. The third age range occupies the middle of the concrete operations period of development (Piaget 1970).

In order for a child to become an effective tool maker and user he must not only become familiar with the materials used to fashion tools, and the particular way they should be fashioned, but he must also develop a set of motor skills which can be employed to make and use a variety of tools. Skilled behavior is an organized sequence of goal-directed, sensory-motor activities which are either guided or corrected by feedback, e.g., riding a bike or writing letters. The exquisite insect-catching abilities of mantisses and frogs lack this feedback component, and hence do not meet the definition.

Bartlett (1958) has pointed out that three time measures can be made in relation to the movements of skilled behavior:

1. reaction time, e.g., the time that elapses between the perception that a baseball will fly over your head and your first movements backwards to correct this discrepancy;
2. the interval between successive movements in a sequence or "timing," e.g., the time between picking up a baseball and moving your arms in order to throw the ball to first base;
3. movement time, e.g., the speed with which you move your arms down to pick up a ground ball.

Laboratory research dealing with these three time measures has been carried out primarily with individuals aged four to twenty-four years. The basic finding is that the most rapid improvements occur in the age range four to nine, after which the improvements are more gradual.

Two other important aspects of motor skill development are considered in detail in the chapter dealing with this topic—the development of the complementary use of two hands, and visually guided tool use. These two topics are of particular interest because they appear to go to the heart of the way we use our hands.

We will turn now to language development, one of the fastest growing research areas in psychology. Observation of deaf children and adults makes it clear that all the major hunter-gatherer characteristics can be acquired without spoken language. Language certainly makes it easier to learn these characteristics, however, and no doubt deaf individuals had a lower survival rate than their hearing friends in preagricultural days. From an evolutionary point of view, language acquisition must have been extremely important in light of how rapidly it is learned. The average child starts to speak his first single words at about one year of age, his first two-word "sentences" using about fifty words one year later, and by age five he seems to know virtually all the grammatical rules of his native tongue. Contrast this with the development of the understanding of complex spatial relationships which doesn't start to emerge until about age five, and moral knowledge, i.e., an understanding of reciprocal obligations, until about age seven.

The chapter dealing with attention and memory attempts to show the linkage or interdependency between the two processes. No learning occurs without memory, and little memory occurs without attention, a point which Penfield (1969) has emphasized. Stated another way, attentional processes determine which information will get into the system and to some extent how it will be processed once there, and memory processes determine which of this information will remain in the system. However, the attentional processes themselves are modified by what is remembered or known, and that obviously changes as children get older. Although research on the development of attention has dealt separately with vision, hearing, and touch, some common themes or findings can be discerned. The existence of these themes suggests that all modes of attending are determined by higher order, or evolutionary advanced structures of the brain. These advanced structures not only interrelate information received from different sensory modalities, but they also determine how the various modalities will be employed for gaining new information. In the area of memory, much of the research indicates that as children mature, the way they organize information undergoes substantial and systematic change, resulting in increased accuracy and quantity of what is remembered.

Turning now to spatial understanding, three evolutionary factors stand out:

1. the home range of humans is much larger than those of the non-human primates;
2. unlike other pack-hunting animals such as wolves, olfactory cues play little part in helping man know where he is and where he should go next;
3. the parietal lobes, which underlie spatial perception and spatial understanding, underwent tremendous expansion in man's evolution.

An analysis of the way man knows the world and represents it indicates that spatial understanding is fundamental. For example, we recapture (or capture) temporal relations by transforming them into spatial relations, e.g., clocks and calendars; we use spatial metaphors for capturing sounds and movements, e.g., musical notes and dance rotation; and we can combine several of these relations at once into a static spatial array, e.g., a route map. Vision, though important to this understanding, is not crucial—blind people obviously have spatial knowledge. From a developmental perspective, Piaget has performed the most profound analysis of this developmental problem. The chapter on spatial analysis will deal primarily with his research and that of others who have been influenced by his thinking. What is so surprising about this research is that it shows that the development of spatial understanding is far from complete at the onset of puberty, unlike the development of language understanding.

The final chapter of this book deals with moral development. It is thought that moral development goes to the core of understanding the mutual regulation of members of subsistence groups. The writings of a variety of scholars have asserted that there are at least five factors which determine moral action: authority-acceptance, or obedience (Waddington 1960b); external rewards and punishments; internal rewards and punishments, or ego-ideal and conscience (Freud 1949); the norms of reciprocity (Gouldner 1960); and cognitive-language factors (Kohlberg 1969, Piaget 1932). The development of empathy probably underlies the development of the norms of reciprocity and the development of the cognitive-language factors. The major part of the chapter deals with providing tentative answers to the following five questions. First, what are the child-rearing antecedents of obedience, and to what extent does obedience change with age? Second, what are the child-rearing antecedents of the acquisition of guilt, identification with one's parents, and imitation? Third, what is the developmental course of the acquisition of empathy? Fourth, what is the developmental course of the acquisition of the norm of reciprocity? And fifth, what is the developmental course of the cognitive-language factor of moral development?

Chapter 2

THEORY
OF
EVOLUTION

HISTORY

Precursors of Darwin and Spencer

The three major concerns in evolutionary theory and genetics have been:

1. the nature of the inheritance mechanism
2. the evolution and variation of species
3. individual development (Dunn 1965).

Between the latter part of the nineteenth century and approximately 1935, knowledge of these major concerns increased enormously, and the science of genetics, unknown prior to the twentieth century, came to the foreground in biology. In the 1930s, a new, synthetic view of evolution began to emerge which integrated the various earlier views. This theory will be summarized in the next major section of the chapter.

The theory of evolution, like any theory, was invented (some may prefer to say discovered) as a response to challenges to older theories. The challenges were the newly discovered facts about the environment which were apparently inconsistent with widely held eighteenth-century religious beliefs about the earth and its inhabitants (Eiseley 1958). Three of these major beliefs, summarized as the "Divine Creation," were

1. that God created the earth and all the species on it, which implied that the various species would always continue to exist
2. that the various species were immutable or fixed, which implied that each species was perfectly suited to its environment and would not change
3. that the creation occurred about 5,000 years ago.

Ironically, the man whose work inadvertently led to overturning these beliefs, Carolus Linnaeus (1707–78), believed in them himself.

Linnaeus was the great systematizer of the eighteenth century. In 1758 he published a taxonomy of the animal and plant kingdoms, the *Systema Naturae*, which was based on the external and internal characteristics of the organisms. The taxonomy was arranged in a hierarchical fashion showing the similarity between different species. The most similar organisms were categorized as belonging to the same species, the most similar species to the same genus, the most similar genera to the same order, and so on. Although Linnaeus assumed a separate creation for each species, the relationship between man and the apes, for example, was clearly evident from his tables. Linnaeus' taxonomy was excellent. Although it has been expanded and modified in the past 200 years, it is still the basis for biological taxonomy and a cornerstone in evolutionary theory.

Linnaeus was a widely honored and acclaimed man in his lifetime. His work was largely instrumental in creating an atmosphere in which many sought to discover new species and to learn more about the similarities between known species. Relative to pre-Linnaeun times, this activity was almost explosive. For example, many trading and exploration ships included "naturalists" as part of their crew. This burst of activity brought to light new facts and put old facts under a different light. Some of the new facts were the existence of bones of extinct species, the existence of geological data which indicated that the earth was hundreds of thousands and perhaps millions of years old, and the existence of extinct species in one geographical region which were not extinct in others. One of the old facts seen in a new light was the breeding experiments with plants and animals which showed that species characteristics could be altered. Linnaeus himself engaged in plant experiments and was so impressed with them that in later editions of the *Systema Naturae* he deleted the statement that no new species could emerge.

Even with these facts and Linnaeus' own doubts, the idea of Divine Creation did not quickly crumble. It took approximately eighty years following the death of Linnaeus for the idea of evolution to gain a stronghold and to start replacing Divine Creation. The seminal events were the works of two unique and very different men—Charles Darwin's *On the Origin of Species* (1859) and Herbert Spencer's *Principles of Psychology* (1855, revised 1870). It is to Darwin that we attribute the beginning of modern evolutionary theory, and rightly so, because it was he who first identified the process of *natural selection* as a major factor in evolution. But natural selection was not considered to be so important until the beginning of the twentieth century. Spencer used the concept of evolution in all fields—from cosmology to neurology to sociology. He was the grand speculator and his influence on the acceptance of the theory of evolution was profound.

Darwin and Spencer were not the first evolutionists. Many preceded them, but the most influential of these, both in terms of affecting their thinking and in changing the intellectual climate of the mid-nineteenth century, was Jean Lamarck (1744–1829). He developed the first general theory of evolution. In his *Philosophie Zoologique* (1809) he presented a full account of the transformation and evolution of species. The essential features of his theory were the following:

1. Different environments require different types of adaptations.

2. Adaptation is related to the behavior of animals.
3. Some of these behaviors produce structural changes from the use or disuse of the various bodily organs.
4. These structural changes can be inherited.

Hence, evolution was seen as a progression of acquired characteristics finely tuned to their adaptive value in particular environments. Stated more generally, Lamarck emphasized the relationship between inherited structures, the way these structures functioned, and the given environment in which they evolved—the relationship which a good theory of evolution must account for. Figure 2, p. 24, depicts a Lamarckian explanation of the giraffe's long neck.

Lamarck was bitterly attacked for his theory and had no influential following until the latter half of the nineteenth century, when his theory became very popular, probably because both Darwin and Spencer incorporated the Lamarckian evolutionary mechanism of the inheritance of acquired characteristics into their theories. For Spencer, the primary inheritance mechanism was Lamarckian, and for Darwin it was a secondary, but important mechanism.

Three other writers had a marked influence on the thinking of Darwin and Spencer. They were Thomas Malthus (1766–1834), Karl von Baer (1792–1876), and Charles Lyell (1797–1875). In 1798 Malthus published an essay, *The Principles of Population,* which related man's reproductive potential to available resources. It was clear to Malthus that population growth was far less than reproductive potential, and that "very powerful and obvious checks" were operating in the environment to bring about the observed population growth. Some of the powerful checks noted by Malthus were food supply, disease, and war. Both Spencer and Darwin extrapolated this view and asserted that those individuals and species best adapted to a hostile environment survived and reproduced. Evolution must then involve a "weeding out" process.

Von Baer is referred to as the father of comparative embryology. Although he was not an evolutionist, his work contributed greatly to Spencer's and Darwin's thinking. In his *Development of Animals* (1828), von Baer presented an empirically based description of the embryology of animals emphasizing development as proceeding from a general form to a more special one via the process of differentiation. Von Baer also noted the similarity between embryos of higher and lower species. Both Spencer and Darwin saw these similarities as supporting the notion of continuity in the evolution of species, and both their works viewed evolution as proceeding from the general to the specific.

In 1832 Lyell published his monumental *Principles of Geology.* Two views concerning the creation were then prevalent. The first and older view was that the earth and the various species were created at about the same time. The second was known as the "catastrophe theory," in which several successive creations were followed by catastrophes which eliminated almost all plant and animal life. Lyell argued that the earth itself had undergone a *long, slow,* continuous process of evolution, and maintained that geological phenomena could be explained without resorting to statements about unknown factors. Lyell's views were readily accepted by many in the scientific community, but he had been careful to exclude animal evolution from his conclusions. Spencer and Darwin benefited in two ways from Lyell's work: first, they extrapolated his views into the realm of biological evolution, and second, Lyell's views had changed the intellectual climate regarding evolution. Although Lyell was a

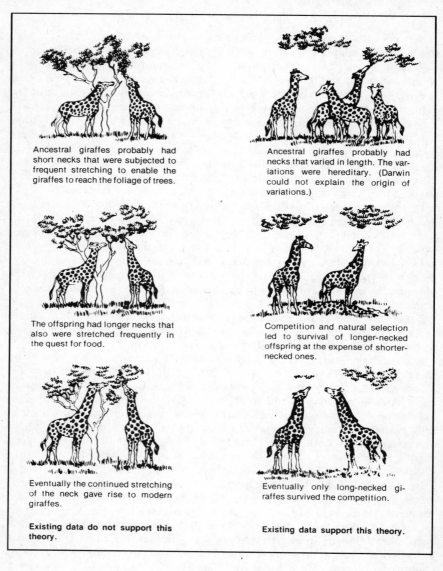

Ancestral giraffes probably had short necks that were subjected to frequent stretching to enable the giraffes to reach the foliage of trees.

Ancestral giraffes probably had necks that varied in length. The variations were hereditary. (Darwin could not explain the origin of variations.)

The offspring had longer necks that also were stretched frequently in the quest for food.

Competition and natural selection led to survival of longer-necked offspring at the expense of shorter-necked ones.

Eventually the continued stretching of the neck gave rise to modern giraffes.

Eventually only long-necked giraffes survived the competition.

Existing data do not support this theory.

Existing data support this theory.

Figure 2

Illustration showing how the origin of the giraffe's long neck is explained according to the now discredited Lamarckian theory of the inheritance of acquired modifications and according to the generally accepted Darwinian theory of natural selection.

friend of Darwin's, it was not until about ten years after *On the Origin of Species* was published that Lyell accepted the theory of biological evolution and became an ardent supporter of it.

Darwin and Wallace

Darwin was born in 1809 into a family of some wealth. Shortly after completing his studies for the ministry at Cambridge University, where he was an undistinguished student, he joined the crew of the H.M.S. *Beagle* as a "naturalist." This was in 1831 and the voyage lasted until 1836. It was during this voyage that Darwin became convinced that evolution had and was taking place. In the three years following the voyage, the idea of natural selection as the primary evolutionary mechanism took shape in Darwin's mind. A key event was his reading of Malthus in 1838. By the age of thirty he had discovered a major facet of evolutionary biology—natural selection (Eiseley 1958, Ghiselin 1973).

During the next twenty years Darwin worked on a full-length treatment of his theory, which he never completed. In 1858 Alfred Russel Wallace (1823–1913), an acquaintance and fellow naturalist, sent Darwin a paper he had written seeking his advice and opinion. In this paper Wallace outlined the theory of evolution by natural selection. After consulting with friends, Darwin suggested to Wallace that each present his views on evolution at the 1858 session of the Linnaeun Society of London, which they did. Between 1858 and 1859 Darwin wrote an "abstract" of his treatise—the well-known *On the Origin of Species*.

Campbell (1966) summarizes the Darwin-Wallace theory as the following four propositions (P) and three deductions (D):

P.1. Organisms produce a far greater number of reproductive cells, and, indeed, young individuals, than ever give rise to mature individuals.

P.2. The number of individuals in populations and species remains more or less constant over long periods of time.

D.1. *Therefore there must be a high rate of mortality both among reproductive cells and among immature individuals.*

P.3. The individuals in a population are not all identical but show variation in all characters, and the individuals that survive by reason of their particular sets of characters will become the parents of the next generation.

D.2. *Therefore the characters of those surviving organisms will in some way have made them better adapted to survive in the conditions of their environment.*

P.4. Offspring resemble parents closely but not exactly.

D.3. *Therefore subsequent generations will maintain and improve on the degree of adaptation realized, by gradual changes in every generation.**

In subsequent editions of his book Darwin identified four major factors in evolution (listed here in decreasing order of importance): natural selection, ac-

---

* Bernard G. Campbell, *Human Evolution* (Chicago: Aldine Publishing, 1966), p. 9. Reprinted by permission of Aldine Publishing.

quired characteristics based upon use and disuse, hereditary changes induced by the environment, and spontaneous variations. A natural selection explanation of the giraffe's neck is depicted in Figure 2 on p. 24.

Evolutionary Theory and Genetics to 1935

No one knew much about the mechanics of hereditary transmission in the nineteenth century. Gregor Mendel (1822–84) published his "Experiments in Plant Hybridization" in 1866. This paper received little attention at the time, and was "lost" until its rediscovery in about 1900. Mendel's research is the cornerstone for the science of genetics. He chose discrete, as opposed to continuous, characteristics of purebred strains of peas for study, e.g., color, position of the flowers, texture of the peas. He then either cross-fertilized or self-fertilized the plants for several generations and counted the number (proportion) of these discrete characteristics in each generation.

Mendel's major discovery was that heredity has a *particulate* basis, i.e., each parent transmits a set of non-blending particles to the offspring. From the results of his experiments Mendel derived two basic laws, the Law of Segregation and the Law of Independent Assortment. The former "law" states that the units of inheritance are genes (this word was coined by Johannsen, not Mendel), and that for any inherited character, each parent contributed one gene allele to its offspring. These two alleles, which may be the same or different, separate during the production of reproductive cells so that one half the germ cells contain the allele from the paternal side and one half contain the allele from the maternal side. The latter "law" states that the distributions of the different genes are not mutually dependent, e.g., the genes underlying color and texture are independent. These two laws have played a very important role in the development of genetics. However, as you will see in the next section of this chapter, they need further clarification.

The next major figure in evolutionary theory was August Weismann (1834–1914), a Neo-Darwinian and anti-Lamarckian. He rejected all of Darwin's theory except the idea of natural selection. For Weismann, evolution *was* natural selection. By clarifying the conceptual relationship between germ cells (the cells of reproduction—sperm cells and ova) and the body cells, he laid the groundwork for the acceptance of genetic mechanisms of evolution and strongly undermined Lamarckian explanations of evolution.

We now arrive at the twentieth century and the almost simultaneous rediscovery of Mendel by Hugo de Vries (1848–1935) and Wilhelm Johannsen (1857–1927). De Vries published his mutation theory of evolution in 1901 and received a wide following. He had observed that new varieties of the evening primrose plant occurred spontaneously through what he termed *mutations* of the underlying hereditary material. He extrapolated from this observation to the generalization that mutations are the sole cause of evolution for plants and animals. De Vries assumed that mutations were random, and saw success in evolution as stemming from preadaptation to changing environments rather than as adaptation to stable environments.

Although Johannsen was a supporter of the mutation theory, his major contribution to evolutionary theory was clarification of the relationship between the *genotype* and the *phenotype*, two terms which he originated (Dunn 1965). Johannsen defined the genotype as the genetic make-up of an individual—the totality of the genes he received from his parents, and the phenotype as the expression of the genotype in the environment or environments in which the individual develops. The phenotype is not static, but continuously changes or develops through time. Hence, individuals with the same genotype could have very different characteristics (phenotypes) if they developed in different environments. In the experiments leading to these conclusions, Johannsen showed that he could develop pure lines (populations) of beans whose offspring differed in such phenotypic characteristics as seed weight, length, or breadth, i.e., the genotypes of these populations were different. However, within a population, size of the offspring was unrelated to size of the parent. He concluded that the different phenotypes within a population were caused by environmental effects.

Related to Johannsen's work on the relationship between heredity and environment was the idea of *norm of reaction* (Dunn 1965). This phrase was coined by Richard Woltereck in 1909, based on his research with fresh-water crustaceans. Woltereck (1877–1944) raised different pure lines of crustaceans in different controlled environments and found that each line had a characteristic range of responses to the varied environments, i.e., different norms of reaction. He concluded that although the norm of reaction was a phenotypic characteristic, the determinants of the norm were hereditary or genotypic.

Laboratory studies of genetics have mushroomed since 1910. Perhaps the most influential and productive geneticist during the early part of this century was T. H. Morgan (1866–1945). Dunn (1965) refers to him as "the chief architect of the gene." Morgan and the brilliant group of students he assembled worked primarily with the fruit fly, *Drosophila*. Some of their early studies dealt with sex-linked traits which led to a clarification of Mendel's Law of Independent Assortment, i.e., that it applied to chromosomes and not to genes. Morgan's later work dealt with further elaborations of the relationship between genes and chromosomes. Towards the end of his career he shifted his major research efforts to embryology, the discipline which had led him into genetics.

MODERN SYNTHETIC THEORY OF EVOLUTION

The early evolutionary theorists tried to evaluate the relative importance of acquired characteristics, genetic mutations, and natural selection in species evolution. Many of the theorists tended to see these factors as being mutually exclusive. We have indicated that most contemporary evolutionary biologists do not believe in Lamarckianism, although the issue is not completely dead (e.g., Koestler and Smythies 1968). One of the intuitively appealing aspects of Lamarckianism is the observation that so many species seem to be exquisitely adapted to the environments they inhabit, and the notion of acquired characteristics "explains" this relationship. In a similar vein, the idea that mutations were the driving force in evolution had a wide following in the early part of the century. The effects of mutations *could* be observed, and the idea was also intuitively appealing. Because evolution does produce differences, mutations "explained" the genetic basis of these differences. However, with the entry of sophisticated statistical techniques into genetic theorizing, and with the aid of the computer, contemporary geneticists have concluded that although mutations are the original source of genetic variation, benign mutations do not occur frequently enough to play more than a small role in evolution (e.g. Stebbins 1971, Waddington 1968).

Finally we saw that natural selection *by itself* could not be the cause of evolution. It is a "weeding out" process which operates on phenotypic differences (or variations in the characters) between members of a species, but natural selection is not the source of these variations. We have noted that phenotypic differences are produced by differences in the genotype, differences in the environment, or both. Given that evolution has a hereditary basis, the source of variation which natural selection must ultimately affect is the genetic source. If not mutations, then what is the genetic source of variation?

The modern synthetic theory of evolution attempts to answer this and related questions. It is a theory which began to emerge in the 1930s, with the signal event, according to Stebbins (1971), being Dobzhansky's *Genetics and the Origin of Species*. Other early major contributors were J. Huxley, J.B.S. Haldane, and Waddington. Dobzhansky and other standard-bearers of the theory have synthesized the apparently conflicting views of the Neo-Darwinians who stressed natural selection as the vehicle of evolution, and the Neo-Mendelians, who stressed mutations. There is no single version of the synthetic theory on which all proponents can agree. Rather, there is a common approach and a collection of core ideas, assumptions, and considerations. Hence, the brief and simplified version of the theory presented here will of necessity be selective. It is based primarily on books written by Campbell (1966), Dobzhansky (1962), Mayr (1963), Rensch (1959), and Stebbins (1971), and book chapters by Waddington (1960a, 1968).

Definitions, Evolutionary Strategies, and Inventions

In the synthetic theory, a *species* is defined as the largest population of potentially interbreeding individuals *reproductively isolated* from other populations (Mayr 1963). In its general sense, reproductive isolation refers to the fact that members of a species don't reproduce with members of another species, e.g., the members of two species, though genetically compatible, become sexually mature at different times during the year and hence don't mate; or members of different species mate and the egg is fertilized, but owing to genetic incompatibility the developing offspring dies before sexual maturity (Mayr 1963). A *deme*, or local population, is a breeding group of a species at a given locality. Theoretically, any two adult members of the deme have an equal probability of mating with each other. Evolution operates at the level of the deme (Mayr 1963).

Campbell (1966) discusses the flexibility of adaptation of the deme (his term is "fitness"). In order for a deme to be flexibly adapted, there must be sufficient genetic stability for the distribution of phenotypes of the deme to remain relatively constant in a stable environment, and there must be sufficient genetic variability for the distribution of phenotypes to change in a changing environment. A deme which has little genetic variability might become extinct in certain changing environments. The paleontological record indicates that there are far more extinct species than there are surviving ones.

Evolution is defined as follows: it is essentially an adaptive response to environmental stress which is accompanied by a change over time in the distribution of gene frequencies of the deme. In other words, evolution implies that a transformation has occurred. Although there are other possible causes of shifts in gene frequencies, our discussion will be restricted to those involved with an environmental stress. In Chapter 1, adaptation was defined as a homeostatic relationship between the population of a species and its environment. An environmental stress changes the environment and disturbs the homeostasis. Some examples of environmental stress are the entry of new predators, climate changes, a drop in sea level, a rapid swelling of the population of the same species due to immigration or unusually high reproductive rates, and movement of the population itself into a different environment. If the population *evolves* in response to the stress, it achieves a different, genetically based homeostatic relationship with the environment. If the population adapts to the stress by *learning* new behaviors, and there is no accompanying change in the gene distribution, then evolution has *not* occurred.

Figure 3 presents a highly simplified example of what we mean by the preceding definition. Assume that the deme in question was adapted to the old environment and had four types of genes—A,B,C, and D—with genes A and B each having four possible forms or alleles, gene C having three alleles, and gene D two alleles. Assume, as in Mendel's experiments, that the different alleles are associated with different phenotypic characteristics. Each individual in the deme has two alleles of each gene (one from each parent) which may be the same or different, e.g., A_1A_1, A_1A_2. Owing to the small number of alleles, genetic variability, i.e., the number of genetic combinations, is limited. If the deme were large, many of the individuals would be genetically identical. In the old environment, the most frequent of the A alleles was A_1, which implies that relative to the other A alleles, A_1 led to some adaptive advantage for the deme. A similar conclusion would be drawn for the allele C_1. Among genes B and D, however, the alleles had no differential frequency, which implies that there was no differential advantage associated with these alleles. Following the environmental stress and adaptation to the new environment, allele distribution shifts for genes A and D, but remains unchanged for genes B and C. In the new environment, A_4 and D_2 are the most frequent for the A and D alleles, which implies that there is now a relatively higher adaptive advantage associated with them. Owing to the adaptive response by the deme to the new environment, which is accompanied by a shift in the gene distribution, we say that evolution has occurred.

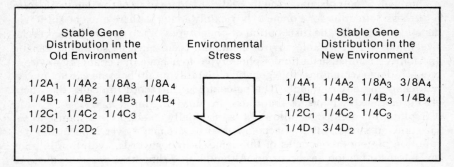

Figure 3

Hypothetical example of evolution. The fractions refer to the proportion of alleles in the deme.

We have defined evolution as essentially an adaptive response of the deme to environmental stress. In general, there are two broad strategies or directions a deme can take to accommodate to the stress. In the first, members of a deme develop specialized structures and functions (behavioral and physiological) to accommodate the deme to the specific environmental stress. For example, in man's evolution, when our ancestors came down from the trees and eventually left the forests for a life in the savannas (grassy plains), they developed a specialized mode of locomotion—bipedal walking. As a consequence, the structural changes underlying bipedal walking made life in the trees nearly impossible. In the second adaptive strategy, the deme develops generalized structures and functions which accommodate to the specific environmental stress as well as to other potential stresses. For example, the evolution of the temperature-regulating system of placental mammals allowed them to accommodate to both large increases and decreases in the external temperature. Relative to reptiles and amphibians, the temperature range to which placentals can adapt is enormous. Another example of a generalized structure is the human brain.

Evolution can be described as an experiment in design, or what Rensch (1959) calls "inventions," or a "trial-and-success" experiment (Lorenz 1969). The experiment is usually a fortuitous one, and one with high stakes —extinction or survival. If the design is a good one, then the deme adapts to the changed environment, but if it is not, the members die out. The following analogy might help clarify this view. A farmer from the plains of central Ohio decides to move to the banks of the Ohio River. He knows that the Ohio floods periodically, which means that he must protect his house from this eventuality. He also knows that the old style house from central Ohio is very vulnerable to this disaster, so he invents or designs a house on stilts which he thinks will be protected against floods. If the design is a good one, he won't be flooded out. If not, he will. In this analogy we've used the concepts "thinks," "knows," and "decides." With the exception of plant and animal breeding experiments, where these concepts apply, the majority of evolutionary inventions should be viewed as unplanned. The evolutionary inventions we are talking about are certain genotypes which lead to certain clusters of phenotypic characteristics. When a given invention—a given genotype—is successful, it leads to greater reproduction relative to other genotypes of that deme. Thus, the successful invention is propogated in the species. When a given invention is not successful, then either the individual having that genotype dies before reproducing, or he or she reproduces less than the norm for the deme. In more technical terms, the successful genotypes are said to have higher *Darwinian fitness* or higher *selective value* than the less successful genotypes. One further clarification is in order. An invention is never successful in and of itself, but is always related to a particular environment and a particular pattern of exploiting it, i.e., the environmental niche of a deme. The farmer's house on stilts might be fine next to flooding rivers, but awful in areas with high winds.

What has been implied above is that in order to understand the inventions or design of a species, the environmental niche to which that species adapted must be described. In the most general terms, the term environmental niche refers to the total surroundings of a deme affecting it, and the reciprocal effects of the deme on the environment. Thus the environmental niche for animals consists of such diverse elements as the climate, the type of available food and shelter, the type and nature of predators, other plants and animals, and the nature of the deme, i.e., the individuals in the deme, their activities, and their social organization. The nature of the deme is particularly complicated because it is simultaneously a product of evolution and a part of the niche. The environment is not static, nor are all the changes which occur in it reversible. This has been the case especially for environments which modern man has entered. For example, although man had been a predator of the American bison for hundreds of years, many bison demes were completely eliminated when the rifle was introduced, and the species almost became extinct. As another example, up until about 400 years ago shellfish were a major food source for the native Americans living along the banks of the Ohio. Whether the Ohio shellfish died out because of heavy human predation or water pollution, or both, is not known. However, their disappearance is apparently irreversible.

For many species, the response or invention to a particular climate or particular food source was the crucial factor in their evolution and adaptation. If a particular food becomes unavailable, the species may die out. For example, the South American three-toed sloth will only eat fresh cecropia leaves, which makes their habitation in North American zoos next to impossible. For some species, the type of social organization invented was the crucial factor in their evolution and a crucial environmental factor. This is clearly seen in the social insects, e.g., ants and bees, but it will be argued in the forthcoming chapters that this is also true of man's evolution.

To summarize, evolution operates at the level of the deme, as contrasted with either the species as a whole or with individuals. It has been defined as essentially an adaptive response to environmental stress which is accompanied by a change over time in the distribution of gene frequencies of the deme. Evolution is considered to be an experiment in design which generally follows one of two strategies—the members of the deme develop specialized structures and functions which adapt them to the particular stress, but make the prestress mode of life nearly impossible; or they develop more generalized structures and functions which allow them to adapt to a variety of environments which may include the prestress environment. A particular design is never successful in and of itself, but is always related to a particular environment and a particular pattern of exploiting it.

Canalization and Genetic Assimilation

This section will deal with two related questions: (1) How does a phenotypic adaptation to stress—an acquired characteristic—get assimilated into the genotypes of the deme? This was Lamarck's question and one which is still a concern of evolutionists. (2) How is it that the members of a species resemble each other structurally and functionally during all stages of their development and at maturity?

In 1902, James Mark Baldwin, the psychologist and evolutionist, proposed an intriguing answer to the first question. He accepted natural selection as a major factor in evolution and proposed two others—*social transmission* and *organic selection*. Social transmission is cultural learning—what one generation learns and teaches to the next. Baldwin assumed that social transmission occurs more frequently and readily in the higher than lower organisms, reaching its peak in man. The notion was not invented by Baldwin, but he incorporated it into his theory. The process of organic selection, however, seems to have been originated by him. In any case, it has come to be known as *the Baldwin effect* (Mayr 1963). The essence of the Baldwin effect is as follows: when an environmental stress occurs, certain individuals learn ways of coping with or adapting to the stress, whereas other members do not and die. The individuals who survive reproduce (natural selection), and through social transmission their offspring learn the acquired characteristic. Thus, certain individuals are kept alive until an appropriate congenital variation (Baldwin's phrase, probably meaning mutation) occurs. When it does occur, it transforms the acquired characteristic into an inherited one. "The species will therefore make progress in the same directions as those first marked out by the acquired modifications, and will gradually 'pick up' by congenital variation the same characters which were at first only individually acquired" (Baldwin 1902, p. 138).

What should be noted about Baldwin's explanation (which is generally discounted today) is that it is anti-Lamarckian. Lamarck would have assumed that over the course of many generations the changes brought about by social transmission would automatically become "congenital." Implicit in Baldwin's reasoning was the idea that in order for the phenotypic character to become congenital, something congenitally *new* had to be added to the system. This is an intuitively appealing assumption. In fact, the idea that you can get an acquired characteristic genetically assimilated without the introduction of new genetic material (or mutations) seems implausible. But is it? Consider the following four facts about genotypes and phenotypes:

1. Nearly all members of a species have different genotypes.

2. Yet, nearly all members of a species bear a close resemblance to one another.
3. The phenotype is a product of the genotype and the succession of environments encountered. Hence, the same genotype could lead to a variety of phenotypes, the extent of this variability being determined by the norm of reaction of the species.
4. Unlike Mendel's peas, all phenotypic characteristics of sexually breeding species are probably influenced by the joint action of many genes (Mayr 1963).

When these facts are considered together, the assumption can be that there is substantial genetic variability among members of a species which is not expressed, i.e., it is suppressed in the phenotypes. Stated another way, there may be a lot of "inconstancy" underlying species "constancies" (Fraser 1961). Thus, it may be hypothesized that the genetic assimilation of acquired characters need not come from the introduction of new genetic variation, but rather from the unlocking or freeing up of already existing but suppressed genetic variation in a species.

Is this type of genetic assimilation possible? Yes—not only is it possible, but probable, as the research of Waddington and his students has shown. Support of this view requires the demonstration of at least three things:

1. The existence of a relatively constant or invariant characteristic which is relatively resistant to selection pressures or moderate environmental stress.
2. The release of phenotypic variability of this character, i.e., the appearance of new characters following a strong environmental stress.
3. The capability of applying selection pressures to the new characters so that they become assimilated into the genotype of the species, i.e., the characters appear in the offspring without the environmental stress.

The first major studies were performed by Waddington and are summarized in his 1960 and 1968 papers. In this research he chose for study the wing pattern of a species of the Drosophila fly. Three facts are significant.

1. The wing pattern is essentially invariant in the species, with over ninety-nine percent of normally reared flies having wings which are characterized by the presence of several long veins and several short veins (crossveins) connecting them (see Figure 4).
2. This wing pattern is known to be controlled by several major genes and several minor genes.
3. When flies with abnormal wings are bred, the offspring develop normal wings.

Waddington exposed the flies in their early stage of development to intense heat—an environmental stress. Following the heat shock, many of the surviving flies developed abnormal wings with one or more crossveins missing (see Figure 4 on p. 34). When the abnormal flies were allowed to breed and their offspring were not subjected to heat shock, over ninety-nine percent of them developed the normal wing pattern. However, when offspring of the abnormal flies were subjected to heat shock at the early stage of development, many of them developed the crossveinless wing pattern. When the abnormal flies of this generation were allowed to breed and their offspring were heat shocked, an even higher percentage of the offspring developed the crossveinless wing pattern. When this procedure was carried out for many generations, almost all the flies eventually developed the abnormal wing pattern. Moreover, when these flies were allowed to breed and their offspring were not heat shocked, a high percentage of them developed the abnormal wing pattern.

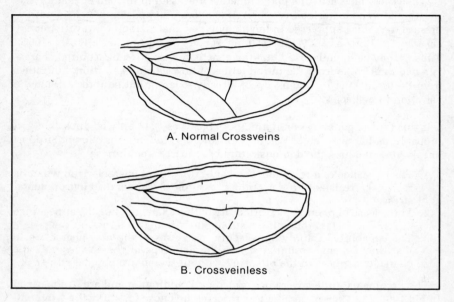

A. Normal Crossveins

B. Crossveinless

Figure 4

Hypothetical examples of normal and abnormal wings.

Thus, all three required conditions for demonstrating the genetic assimilation of an acquired characteristic were met. The normal crossvein wing pattern is nearly invariant in the species. This pattern cannot readily be changed by selection procedures, i.e., breeding the flies with abnormal wings prior to the sequence of heat shocks failed to produce an abnormal pattern. Finally, a continued environmental stress and selection for a new characteristic produced by the stress, i.e., crossveinless wings, led to the acquisition of the new characteristic in an unstressed environment.

This phenomenon is explained by Waddington as an example of the process of canalization, which works somewhat as follows: the genotype of an individual contains a set of instructions for the potential interactions of the developing phenotype with the environment. Owing to environmental or genetic differences, there are aspects of development which will vary across individuals of a species, such as rate of growth, size and shape of various bodily structures, specific coloration of skin or hair, and certain behavioral and physiological functions. There are other aspects of development, however, that are relatively invariant or constant across individuals despite environmental or genetic differences, such as sequences of growth, pattern of anatomical structures, e.g., two eyes and one nose, and certain behavioral or physiological functioning, e.g., the sucking reflex and temperature regulation. Both aspects of development are under the control of a number of genes, but the constancies are said to be canalized. By this we mean that the development pathways of the phenotype (in Waddington's terminology, *chreods*) are resistant to moderate genetic and environmental stresses which might deflect development away from those chreods. In a sense, at each point in development, for all members of a species, and for a variety of phenotypic characteristics, a set of targets is aimed for, and despite underlying genetic variability, genetic processes operate together to ensure that the targets will be hit. This is a very active process in which genes compensate for, or collaborate with one another to ensure that phenotypic development will reach those targets, by whatever route is necessary.

Waddington (1957) depicts canalization processes in development as a ball (the phenotype) rolling through a set of valleys (see Figure 5 on p. 36). The deeper the valley, the greater is the canalization, and the more difficult it is by either environmental or genetic stresses to move the ball out of the particular valley (chreod) into another one. At some points in development, where many potential pathways intersect, the phenotype undergoes a rapid change and is susceptible to moderate genetic or environmental stresses. As you will see in the next chapter, the varied effects of thalidomide on infants can be explained by this example.

How does the concept of canalization explain the heat shock experiment? Figure 6 on p. 37 depicts the hypothetical relationship between genotype variability for crossveins and phenotype variability for crossveins for offspring reared in a normal range of environments. The top half of the figure shows that ninety-nine percent of all normal flies have genotype variability scores between three and seven, with an average score of five. The curve in the lower half of the figure indicates that crossveins are canalized for genotype variability scores in this range, i.e., irrespective of the underlying genetic variability between three and seven, the phenotype will develop into a number three. For our purposes, assume that a phenotype of three is a wing with normal crossveins, and a phenotype greater than three is at least partially crossveinless. Let's further assume that in a heat-shocked environment a certain percentage of flies with genotype variability of five, six, or seven will develop crossveinless wings. When these flies are bred, a higher percentage of the offspring will have genotype variability scores greater than five than the original population. When the procedure of heat shock followed by selective breeding of crossveinless flies is repeated a great number of times, the genotype variability scores will keep moving to the right, until many of the flies will have scores greater

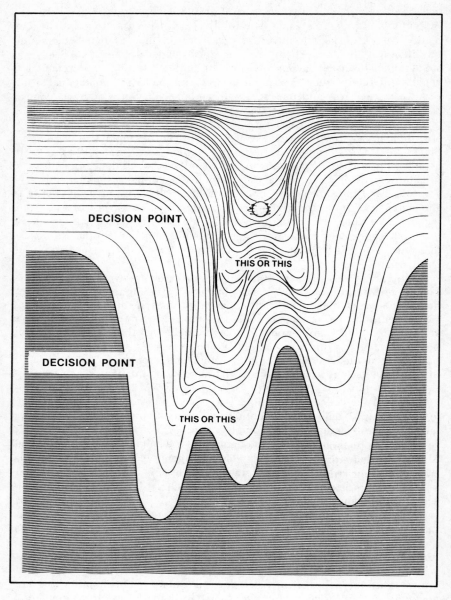

Figure 5

The epigenetic landscape. The rolling ball represents the development of some canalized characteristic. At each "decision point" the characteristic is required to move onto one of at least two divergent pathways. As development proceeds along one of those pathways, the more difficult it becomes to move it onto the alternative pathways (Drawn by Alex Fraser).

than seven. As can be seen from the curve, in normal environments genotype scores greater than seven lead to phenotype scores greater than three, and hence to crossveinless wings.

As we have indicated, canalization processes operate to resist genetic and environmental stresses in order to ensure that the phenotype will develop along certain chreods. However, canalization is not an all or nothing affair; characteristics vary in the degree to which they are canalized. An elegant set of

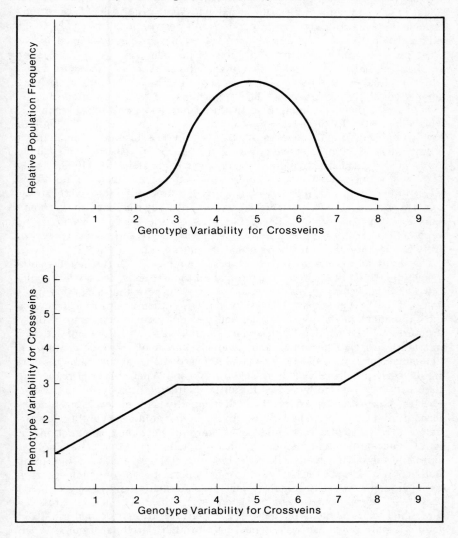

Figure 6

Hypothetical relationship depicting canalization of wing pattern.

experiments by Fraser and his colleagues (summarized by Waddington 1962) demonstrates this point. Fraser chose for study hair growth of the mouse. Three types of hair were examined: the primary facial whiskers, the secondary facial whiskers, and the hair coat covering the body. There is virtually no variability within the species of mouse he used in either the primary or secondary whiskers, the latter almost always being equal to nineteen. When mice with secondaries greater than nineteen were selectively bred, the offspring had nineteen. Thus, like Waddington's flies, the facial whiskers in normal genetic or environmental backgrounds were impervious to selective breeding.

Fraser then introduced a mutant gene, *Tabby*, into the colony of mice he was breeding. The *Tabby* gene primarily affects the hair coat, giving it a tabby appearance. This mutant gene also affects the number of secondary facial whiskers, freeing up the expression of a considerable amount of underlying genetic variability. The primary facial whiskers are relatively unaffected by *Tabby*. Fraser then selectively bred two lines of mice, one line for secondary whiskers greater than nineteen, and one for fewer than nineteen. Strength of canalization can roughly be measured by assessing the difficulty of changing a characteristic through selective breeding procedures. If a characteristic can be easily modified by selective breeding, e.g., eye color, then it is either weakly canalized or not canalized at all, and if it is extremely difficult to modify by selective breeding, then it is heavily canalized. Fraser found that hair coat was weakly canalized, secondary whiskers were moderately canalized, and primary whiskers were heavily canalized. Figure 7 on the next page shows the hypothetical relationship between genotype variability and phenotype variability for the three different types of hair follicles.

The results of these experiments suggest the following: If the members of a species are reared in environments normal for their species, i.e., environments to which the species evolved and adapted, they will resemble each other in all stages of their development. That is, the *pattern* of their anatomical structures and the pattern of the physiological and psychological functioning of these structures will be similar. That is canalization. Nearly all the complex land animal species, e.g., the reptiles and mammals, have evolved in such a way that all members of a given species are reared in nearly identical environments during the early prebirth stages of their development. When this environment is disturbed, e.g., the mother takes the drug thalidomide or develops German measles, then a stress is produced which frequently leads to developmental abnormalities. For the period after birth for the higher animals, evolution has operated to canalize structures and behavioral and physiological functions in both the developing and mature organisms to help ensure that certain crucial aspects of the environment will be in the normal range, e.g., lactation in the mother and sucking by the babies. However, sometimes the young offspring are reared in abnormal environments, develop abnormally, and have a reduced Darwinian fitness. Sometimes a persistent environmental or genetic stress occurs which deflects many of the young organisms off their normal canalized pathways onto other pathways which lead to high Darwinian fitness. When this occurs, the new canalized characteristics become genetically assimilated into the deme.

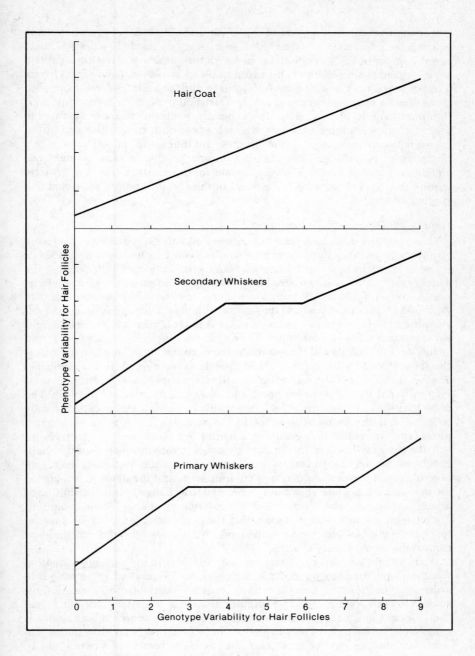

Figure 7

Hypothetical relationship depicting different degrees of canalization of hair follicles.

It is the working assumption of this book that almost all of the phenotypic constancies or invariances observed in species which reside in a normal range of environments, i.e., environments to which the species evolved and adapted, are canalized characteristics. This assumption encompasses behavioral characteristics as well as physiological ones, and includes humans as well as nonhumans. It is a strong assumption, but it is consistent with experimental findings. In humans and in the higher species generally, evolution has also operated to permit great phenotypic plasticity which leads to both similarities and differences between members of the species. In the realm of behavior, then, phenotypic plasticity and not canalization may produce a close resemblance among members of a deme. Hence, evidence for canalization of behavior would require that the behavior be widespread in the species and not restricted to a single deme.

The Five Major Factors In Evolution

The preceding discussion can be summarized and extended by considering evolutionary processes or factors as a whole. Evolution has been described as an experiment in design, the design being a collection of individuals—the deme—residing in given environments, having a particular set of characteristics. As Waddington (1968) points out, there is substantial indeterminancy in evolutionary processes because they operate on the epigenetic system—the developing individuals of the deme—and yet it is genotypes which are transmitted to succeeding generations. Thus, phenotypes are weeded out and genotypes are inherited. If the sequence of environments of later generations is similar to that of the earlier ones, then the later phenotypes will very probably be similar to those of the earlier ones. If the later sequence of environments is very different from the earlier ones, a number of outcomes are possible. The deme may die out; the norm of reaction, which includes learning capacity, may be great and the deme will adapt to the new sequence of environments; phenotypic variability locked up by canalization processes may be released and the deme will adapt to the new sequence of environments; and certain genotypes having low fitness in the old sequence of environments may have high fitness in the new sequence of environments and the deme may adapt to the new sequence. The last two outcomes lead to a change in the distribution of alleles in the deme and hence reflect an evolutionary change. Some evolutionary changes are sufficiently marked that the deme emerges as a new species, reproductively isolated from members of other demes who did not undergo comparable evolutionary changes.

We have just touched on three important ideas—genetic variability, natural selection operating on phenotypic variation, and reproductive isolation. In order for evolution to occur, there must be genetic variability. There are three sources of this variability. The original source is mutations, an additional source is changes of the chromosomes, but the major source of variability is genetic recombination. In its simplest terms, a mutation is an error in the process of producing germ cells which leads to the production of a new allele. In Figure 3 on p. 30, if a mutation occurred in the D type gene, a third allele would be created—D_3. Geneticists have determined that almost all mutations, if expressed in the phenotype, have harmful effects on that individual in any environment. Although mutations are relatively rare occurrences, all humans, owing to their large number of genes, are carriers of several mutant genes. Thus, every time an individual reproduces there is a high likelihood that he or she will transmit mutant genes to the offspring. If two individuals have the same mutant gene, e.g., a brother and a sister, and mate, it is likely that the mutation will be expressed in the phenotype, which as we said above will probably have harmful effects. This suggests that there is genetic "wisdom" in incest taboos, a topic which will be discussed in a later chapter.

The second source of genetic variability—changes in chromosome number and structure—is a very complex subject, and we will treat it only briefly here. It is useful to think of chromosomes as being closeknit packages of genes. Man has forty-six chromosomes, and each species has a characteristic number. During the production of germ cells, errors affecting the chromosomes sometimes occur. Sometimes these errors lead to the production of a germ cell with an additional chromosome, as in Down's Syndrome in humans. Sometimes these errors lead to a rearrangement of the genes that comprise a given chromosome, and sometimes a gene or group of genes is eliminated. As with genetic mutations, chromosomal changes generally have harmful effects.

Genetic recombination, the third source of genetic variability, occurs when two individuals mate—the genes get recombined in new ways. Excluding chromosomal mutations, each human can produce up to 2^{23} different types of chromosomal combinations, i.e., in the production of germ cells, the twenty-three pairs of homologous chromosomes randomly line up and divide into two germ cells, each containing twenty-three chromosomes. This means that for a given pair of parents there are 2^{46} possible combinations of chromosomes for each offspring, which is more possibilities than the total number of people who have ever lived on the earth. Moreover, each human chromosome contains thousands of genes, which increases the number of possible genetic combinations by many thousands of orders of magnitude. The particular genetic combination—the genotype—gives a potential for the development of the phenotype. The way in which an individual actually develops is a function of the particular combination of genes he has and the particular sequence of environments he encounters in his development. This is a very complicated affair because the phenotypic effects of any gene or collection of genes may vary as a function of the other genes in the genotype. This variation of gene effects also places a constraint or limitation on the process of genetic recombination because some combinations aren't viable, e.g., the mother miscarries or the offspring dies before sexual maturity.

The fourth major factor, natural selection, acts on the characteristics of individuals and operates at all stages of development of the phenotype. The ultimate measure of natural selection is the extent to which an individual's genes influence the future gene distribution of the deme. This is generally assessed by noting the individual's reproduction rate relative to the other members of the deme—his Darwinian fitness or selective value. An individual who dies before reproducing generally has zero Darwinian fitness, and an individual who reproduces less than the average of the deme generally has low fitness. There are cases, e.g., social insects whose worker class doesn't reproduce at all, where individuals have high fitness. Without the worker class, who have genotypes highly similar to the queen's, the colony (deme) would die out. This type of phenomenon also occurs in human societies where brothers or sisters don't reproduce but aid in the high reproduction rate of their siblings or other close relatives. Darwinian fitness refers to the contribution of a given genotype in a given environment, hence an individual with high fitness in one environment may have low fitness in another.

Dobzhansky (1962) and Stebbins (1971) describe the three different recognized kinds of natural selection—stabilizing selection, directional selection, and disruptive selection. When the environment is relatively constant for long periods of time, natural selection operates to keep the population genetically constant. This is called stabilizing selection. Stabilizing selection does not mean that all individuals are alike genetically, but rather that the distribution of genes remains relatively constant from generation to generation. Implicit in stabilizing selection is the notion that a particular gene distribution of a population is optimally adapted to a given environment. Hence, stabilizing selection is a conservative force which weeds out detrimental mutants and other hereditary weaknesses. In man, for example, stabilizing selection has operated over the past 250,000 years to keep average brain size at about 1350 c.c. The shape of man's pelvis has apparently gone almost unchanged for about one million years, an even more dramatic example of stabilizing selection.

Directional selection occurs when the environment to which a species has been adapted changes in a given direction. When this occurs, certain types of individuals who had average or low Darwinian fitness in the old environment come to have high Darwinian fitness in the new environment. Directional selection has operated in cases of progressive warming or cooling of the environment, introduction of new predators into the environment, and migration into a new territory by a population of a given species. A good example of directional selection is the immunity to insecticides built up in a population of insects. In directional selection the distribution of genotypes changes from generation to generation. In the early part of man's evolution, for example, the genotype underlying increased brain size and complexity progressively changed for more than one million years.

Disruptive selection can occur in either of two ways. In the first, a relatively homogeneous population becomes subjected to different selection pressures in different parts of its natural habitat. In the second, small subpopulations of the homogeneous population, each having slightly different gene distributions, become isolated from one another. This, in turn, may lead to a differential response to the same environment. The principal effect of disruptive selection is to convert the deme's stable homogeneous gene distribution into two or more heterogeneous gene distributions. Disruptive selection often leads to the creation of races or subspecies.

In general, selection pressures are greatest in times of crisis, and the particular crisis affects the particular phenotypes selected for. Selection pressures are strongest at the borders of a species' habitat. It is typically at the borders that the greatest variability of genotypes within a deme is found. On occasion, individuals less well adapted to the typical habitat of the deme will be well adapted to an adjacent habitat. This may well have been the case when man's ancestors moved out of the forests and into the plains.

The fifth major factor, reproductive isolation, operates with natural selection to guide populations in certain directions. Reproductive isolation is produced by a variety of *isolating mechanisms* (Mayr 1963). Isolating mechanisms are biological characteristics with at least a partial genetic basis which prevent the interbreeding of populations that are actually or potentially able to live in the same area. Sterility and geographical isolation are not necessarily the only methods for achieving reproductive isolation (Mayr 1963). Mayr maintains that for sexually breeding animals the most important type of isolating mechanisms are *ethological*, referring primarily to the different behaviors different species of animals engage in during courtship.

The way the five factors interact to produce a new species can be summarized by the following sequence of evolutionary stages suggested by Stebbins (1971). In the first stage, a given species inhabits a particular environment in such a way that no deme of the species is spatially isolated from any other deme. In the next stage, one or more demes of the population migrate to particular, differentiated parts of the environment which tend to spatially isolate those demes from others in the population. In the third stage, there is complete spatial isolation of at least one deme from the rest of the population so that there is no interbreeding between that deme and the remainder of the population. In the fourth and final stage, different gene recombinations and gene and chromosome mutations operate in the isolated deme to produce isolating mechanisms. Hence, a new species is formed. Once the isolating mechanisms have developed, the new and the old species can live in the same environment and yet not interbreed. If they do come to reside in the same geographical area, natural selection will operate to increase the distinctiveness between the two species, becauses if two species occupy the same niche it is likely that one of the species will become extinct.

This brings to a close a highly abbreviated summary of evolutionary theory. Now we turn to a related and persistent concern of geneticists and psychologists, a theory of development. The theory which will be sketched out in the next chapter will use evolutionary theory in several ways. First, it is based on the evolutionary writings of Herbert Spencer. Second, it is heavily influenced by genetics and embryology. Third, the concept of canalization plays a central role in it. As has been indicated in this chapter, evolutionary processes operate on the epigenetic system, and hence, at all points in development. Thus, although it is the sexually mature who reproduce, an individual must have "passed muster" prior to that time to be given the opportunity to do so. This implies that the design of a species encompasses individuals at all points in their development. The theory which will be presented provides a framework with which to look at the course of this development.

SUMMARY

Evolutionary theories, as opposed to "Divine Creation," were invented during the nineteenth century. The first major theorist was Lamarck, who in 1809 presented a comprehensive view which included the now disreputed mechanism of the inheritance of acquired characters through their "use and disuse." The widespread acceptance of evolution did not come until after Darwin in 1859 and Spencer in 1855 presented their views. Both included the Lamarckian mechanism in their theories, but it was Darwin who recognized and wrote about the importance of the mechanism of natural selection. From the time of Darwin's and Spencer's important publications until about 1900, the major problem that researchers and theorists struggled with was the identification of the hereditary mechanism. With the rediscovery of Mendel's (1866) work in 1900 by de Vríes and Johannsen, the search focused on genes. Two opposing camps of evolutionists emerged after this time: those who believed that evolution could be explained solely by natural selection, and those who believed that it could be explained solely by genetic mutations. Lamarckianism at this point came into disrepute.

About 1935 a synthesis of these two camps started to appear in the published literature. In this view, it was recognized that natural selection by itself could not be the cause of evolution, in that it is not the cause of genetic variation between members of a species. It was also recognized that although mutations were the original source of genetic variations, their effect is almost always neutral or harmful, and hence they could not play more than a small role in evolution. The modern synthetic theory of evolution resolves these problems in the following way. It states that in order for evolution to occur there must be genetic variability. Mutations of genes and mutations of chromosomes are the two minor sources with respect to evolutionary processes, and the major source is genetic recombination. Genetic recombination occurs when two individuals mate. In humans there are 2^{46} possible combinations of chromosomes for each offspring, which is more possibilities than the total number of people who have ever lived on the earth. Each particular combination leads to a particular sequence of phenotypic characteristics in the particular sequence of environments in which the individual matures.

Natural selection, which is a weeding out process, acts on the phenotype at all stages in the individual's development. The ultimate measure of natural selection is the extent to which an individual's genes influence the future gene distribution of the population to which the individual belongs. This is called *Darwinian fitness*. Reproductive isolation operates with natural selection to guide populations in certain directions. Reproductive isolation is brought about by the existence of isolating mechanisms, which prevent the interbreeding of populations that are actually or potentially able to live in the same area.

Two other major points were made in the chapter. The first is that evolution can be described as an experiment in design, or a trial-and-success experiment. The evolutionary designs are certain genotypes which lead to certain clusters of phenotypic characters in particular environments. When a given design (genotype) is successful, it leads to greater reproduction relative to other genotypes of the particular population in the particular environments. Thus, the successful design is propogated in the species. When the sequences of environments change, the design may become inappropriate.

The second remaining major point is that nearly all important invariancies or constancies seen in members of a species are canalized. Canalization is a set of genetic processes which buffer the developing individual against minor abnormal genetic or environmental influences, in order that certain developmental targets will be attained. It is an active process in which genes compensate for, or collaborate with one another to ensure that the targets will be hit. These targets may be anatomical, physiological, or psychological.

Chapter 3

EMBRYOLOGY AND DEVELOPMENTAL THEORY

In this chapter we will attempt to both familiarize the reader with some aspects of human embryology, one of the three major concerns of evolutionary theory and genetics, and to develop an overview of a theory of psychological development.[1] The latter will be accomplished in part by showing the relationship between embryological development and psychological development.

Starting with Herbert Spencer, an influential group of psychological theorists have assumed that the postnatal development of individuals can best be construed and understood as analogous to an embryological process. This is a very simple, yet very powerful and intuitively appealing idea. After all, it is obvious to everyone that development doesn't stop at birth; in fact, most development appears to occur after birth.

The major difficulty with this idea, however, stems from the fact that embryological processes—prenatal processes—are investigated primarily from the view of the anatomical development of individuals, and postnatal psychological development deals with behavior, or how the anatomical structures function. It is possible that the principles underlying structural development are very different from those underlying functional development. In any case, Spencer put forward the idea, and many succeeding developmental theorists, some independently of Spencer, adopted it, such as James Mark Baldwin, Sigmund Freud, Arnold Gesell, Heinz Werner, Jean Piaget, and Erik Erikson.

What does it mean to consider psychological development as analogous to an embryological process? Developmental theorists have answered this question

---

[1] Some of the ideas in this chapter were first elaborated in an unpublished working paper written by the author and Sheldon White entitled "The Spencer Themes."

in three ways—ways in which prenatal anatomical development can also be conceptualized. They are:

1. Development is keyed to the level of maturation and the concurrent environmental influences.
2. Development proceeds by increasing differentiation and hierarchical integration.
3. Development proceeds by stages.

Underlying these concepts is the fundamental idea that the genotype sets the potential for development. For example, although development is keyed to the level of maturation and the concurrent environmental influences, the way an individual reacts to those influences is largely determined by his genetic code.

ASPECTS OF HUMAN EMBRYOLOGY

There are essentially three components to embryological development: growth, *morphogenesis*, and differentiation (Torrey 1971). Growth is an increase in mass which is brought about during the prenatal period by cell multiplication, followed by the growth of individual cells. Morphogenesis refers to the development of new forms or shapes, which is typically accompanied by growth and differentiation. Prenatally, the most salient types of morphogenesis are the formation of layers (the skin), tubes (blood vessels), and the folding or bending of parts of the embryo or fetus (the brain). Differentiation refers to the diversification or specialization of individual cells which is manifested in primarily three ways. First, the cells become morphologically distinct, i.e., they become different in either size, shape or internal architecture. Second, the cells become behaviorally differentiated, i.e., they develop specialized functional capabilities such as the transmission of electrical–chemical impulses by nerve cells, contraction by muscle cells, and secretion by gland cells. Third, the cells become chemically differentiated, i.e., the chemical constitution within cells becomes different for different groups of cells. Torrey (1971) and Waddington (1962) believe that this third type of differentiation is probably the basis for understanding how the first and second types of differentiation are produced. But what determines how a cell will become chemically differentiated?

As Koestler (1967) has indicated, embryological development occurs within a hierarchy of environments, each environment producing its own unique influences, all of them, however, having an effect on the activity of the genes of any given cell. This hierarchy can be described as follows:

1. the genes themselves in the nucleus of the cell;
2. the cytoplasm surrounding the nucleus;
3. the membrane of the cell, which encloses the cytoplasm and nucleus;
4. membranes of other cells with which a given cell is in contact;
5. the extracellular fluids in which the cell is immersed.

The significance of this concept is that in mammals not all the genes of a given cell are active at any one time, and what primarily determines which genes get activated and which get suppressed are the various environmental influences acting at the time. The particular state of these various environments, including the intracellular environments, sets limits and provides opportunities for certain types of chemical differentiation to occur. In short, the environments, which in part were produced by gene activity, constrain the future development of any cell or group of cells.

Apparently this is only part of the story. As Waddington (1962) points out, the level of maturation or "competence" of the cells places limits on both the actual and potential influence of the environment to produce certain types of cell differentiation. Waddington suggests that a later type of development, e.g., the formation of the lens of an eye, may depend upon cells having previously proceeded through particular developmental episodes. Stated another way, once a given developmental path has been taken, which produces a given level of maturation, a particular set of alternative ways of cell differentiation becomes possible; but after this level of maturation has been reached, other sets of alternatives are precluded.

What has been implied in this discussion is the fact that the whole process of embryological development involves an orchestration by the entire genotype. This has been referred to before as a "collusion of genes" or canalization. Growth, differentiation, and morphogenesis follow given chreods, some of which are heavily canalized, some moderately so, and some only weakly so. But without this canalization, it would be impossible to build from a single cell a complex, integrated organism comprised of billions of cells, no two exactly alike, yet all but the germ cells containing the identical genetic information. Moreover, this epigenetic system is so finely tuned that the occurrence of a single gene mutation has the potential of making the entire process discordant and the organism nonviable.

With this overview in mind, we are now prepared to examine one phase of human embryology—the first seven weeks of prenatal life. This phase has been chosen for study primarily because by the end of this time the beginnings of all the major internal and external anatomical structures are present in the embryo (Moore 1973). Figure 8 on pp. 50–51 (from Moore 1973) summarizes many of the salient developmental events of this phase. The following discussion is keyed to this figure.

Fertilization of the ovum by a sperm forming a zygote occurs in the uterine tube. The zygote divides (undergoes *cleavage*) about thirty hours after it is formed, forming two daughter cells, or *blastomeres*. By the third or fourth day, after three more divisions have occurred, a solid ball of sixteen blastomeres called the *morula* has formed. By the fourth day, the morula has entered the uterus, and fluid from the uterine cavity has entered the morula, creating a cavity within it and converting it into a *blastocyst*. The cells continue to divide, and on about the sixth day the blastocyst starts to implant itself into the lining—the *epithelium*—of the walls of the uterus. By the end of the first week, the blastocyst is partially implanted into the walls and the first germ layer of the embryo—the *embryonic endoderm*—has begun to differentiate from the rest of the cells.

By the eighth day, the embryonic endoderm, along with the other cells within the blastocyst, become transformed into a bilaminar disc, composed of embryonomic ectoderm and embryonic endoderm. Moore suggests that the bilaminar disc can be envisioned as the contact points of two balloons being pushed together. One balloon contains the primitive yolk sac, and the other, the amniotic cavity. The lacunae, which form in the placenta on about the ninth day, are isolated spaces into which secretions are diffused from the mother. By about the twelfth day, the blastocyst is completely implanted within the walls of the uterus and a utero-placental circulation has been established with the lacunar network. On about the twelfth day, a new layer of cells, the extraembryonic mesoderm, forms within the blastocyst, and isolated cavities called coelom form within this mesoderm. By the thirteenth day, primary villi begin to form on the extraembryonic mesoderm. These villi will eventually develop into blood vessels. By the fourteenth day, the isolated coelom spaces have fused, forming a cavity which surrounds the amnion and the yolk sac. Also at about this time a portion of the embryonic endoderm thickens, called the prochordal plate. This is the future site of the head of the developing embryo. The bilaminar disc is now known as the embryonic disc.

By about the fifteenth day, a thickening linear band of cells of the embryonic ectoderm starts to form, the primitive streak, terminating at the primitive knot. Cells migrating from the primitive streak form the third embryonic germ layer, the embryonic mesoderm, creating a trilaminar embryo. The primitive knot gives rise to the notocord which runs through the embryonic mesoderm, giving the developing embryo stability. The notocord also induces the differentiation of adjacent embryonic ectoderm into nerve cells, the neural plate. By about the nineteenth day, the midline portion of the neural plate starts to fold, forming the neural fold and a neural groove, which will eventually become the nervous system of the embryo. Also at this time isolated spaces, embryonic coelom, start to form in the embryonic mesoderm. These spaces fuse shortly afterwards and eventually give rise to the body cavities, e.g., that containing the heart and lungs. On about the twentieth day, pairs of somites start to form in the embryonic mesoderm. Eventually forty-two to forty-four pairs will develop and give rise to the skeletal system.

The fourth through seventh weeks are known as the embryonic period. It is during this critical period of development that the organism is most susceptible to environmentally produced congenital defects. During the fourth week, the shape or morphology of the embryo changes from a disc to a cylinder, produced by a folding in both north-south and east-west directions, and by the formation and growth of the neural tube. The neural tube is formed by the fusion of the neural fold around the neural groove. The neural tube is fused at this time along positions opposite the somites, but is open at the ends at positions called the anterior neuropore and posterior neuropore. The brain, eyes, and ears (the otic depression is a primordial inner ear) will form near the anterior neuropore, and the terminal end of the spinal cord will form at the posterior neuropore. The branchial arches start to form at about the twenty-fourth day. They will eventually develop into the jaws and associated nerves, muscles, and cartilage of the face, throat, jaws, and ears.

The morphological changes during the fifth week are not as marked as those of the preceding week. During the fifth week, the head grows tremendously,

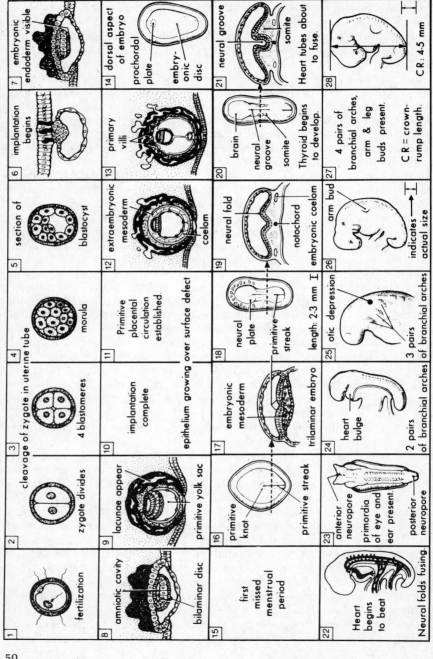

1 fertilization

2 zygote divides

3 cleavage of zygote in uterine tube

4 morula

5 section of blastocyst

6 implantation begins

7 embryonic endoderm visible

8 amniotic cavity / bilaminar disc

9 lacunae appear / primitive yolk sac

10 implantation complete

11 Primitive placental circulation established.

12 extraembryonic mesoderm / coelom

13 primary villi

14 dorsal aspect of embryo / prochordal plate / embryonic disc

15 first missed menstrual period

16 primitive knot / primitive streak

17 embryonic mesoderm / trilaminar embryo

18 neural plate / primitive streak

19 neural fold / notochord / embryonic coelom

20 brain / neural groove / somite / Thyroid begins to develop.

21 neural groove / somite / Heart tubes about to fuse.

epithelium growing over surface defect

length: 2-3 mm

22 Heart begins to beat / Neural folds fusing.

23 anterior neuropore / primordia of eye and ear present / posterior neuropore

24 heart bulge / 2 pairs of branchial arches

25 otic depression / 3 pairs of branchial arches

26 arm bud / indicates → actual size

27 4 pairs of branchial arches, arm & leg buds present. / CR = crown-rump length.

28 CR: 4-5 mm

50

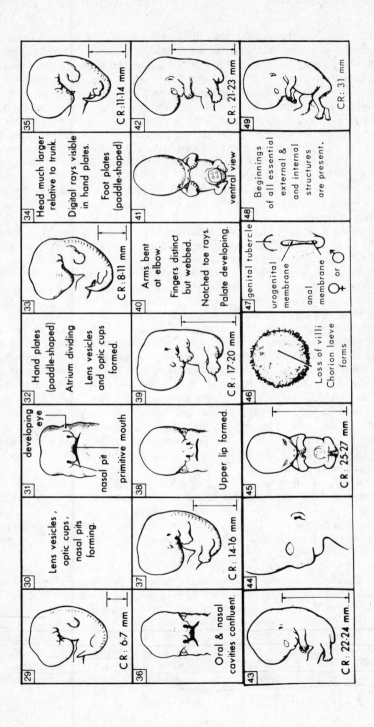

Figure 8

The first seven weeks of prenatal life (From Moore 1973).

primarily owing to the growth and differentiation of the brain. The future hands, the *hand plates*, differentiate considerably, forming *digital rays* which will eventually become fingers. One of the major chambers of the primitive heart, the *atrium*, starts to divide during this period, eventually forming the auricles. The development of the eye involves a highly articulated set of inductions which can be described as follows. First, the differentiation of the forebrain from adjacent neural areas is induced by the notocord and related mesoderm. Once the forebrain is developed, part of it is secondarily induced by adjacent mesoderm to differentiate into an *optic cup*, which appears as an indentation in the forebrain. The optic cup then induces the adjacent ectoderm to thicken and form a *lens vesicle*, which will eventually become the lens of the eye. The lens vesicle and the optic cup look like a ball in a cup. Finally, after the fifth week, the lens induces the overlying tissue to differentiate, forming the cornea of the eye.

During the sixth week, the *crown-rump length* (the sitting height of the embryo) doubles. The major external morphological changes involve the limbs, and the nose and mouth regions. On the thirty-sixth day, the mouth and nose cavities run into one another, but with the formation of the palate and the lips, these two cavities become somewhat distinct. The limbs grow considerably, *toe rays* (future toes) form at about the thirty-seventh day, and *notches* (indentations) appear between the rays by about the forty-second day.

During the seventh week, the crown-rump length increases another eight to ten millimeters. The limbs lengthen and become morphologically more distinctive. The eyelids can be seen, the neck region becomes relatively distinct, and the fingers and toes are highly differentiated. Although gonadal development first becomes apparent during the fifth week, and morphological changes as well as cell differentiation continue thereafter, by the end of the seventh week there is no apparent external distinction between males and females, as indicated for Day 47 in Figure 8. Finally, the placenta starts to undergo some external changes during the seventh week, resulting in the loss of villi from the *chorion* (the outer covering of the baby sac), and the chorion becomes smooth, i.e., *chorion laeve* forms.

Much of the preceding discussion on the temporal changes which occur during embryonic development is summarized and expanded in the spatial configuration shown in Figure 9 on the next page. In this figure, encompassing the entire prenatal period, the terms *paraxial, intermediate,* and *lateral plate* refer to differentiated parts of the embryonic mesoderm; otherwise the figure is self-explanatory.

We will now turn to a discussion of environmentally induced, or *teratogenic,* congenital defects. As we have indicated, embryological development is a well-orchestrated or canalized process. One of the major concepts of canalization is the idea that development follows certain chreods, and that critical periods, or, in Waddington's term, "epigenetic crises," exist in which the developing organism moves from one chreod onto another, e.g., the induction of the neural plate from embryonic ectoderm and the formation of the ear. During these periods the organism should be relatively susceptible to teratogenic effects, which deform the developmental process. Once development has moved

onto the new chreod, however, these same teratogenic stresses should have little distorting effect. The times of epigenetic crisis are analogous to the times of

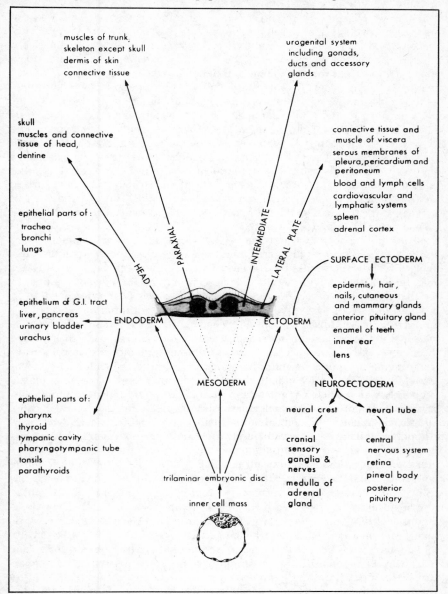

Figure 9
Summary of developmental changes during prenatal period (From Moore 1973).

improvisation in jazz, and the times when development has successfully moved onto the new chreod are analogous to the periods when everyone is playing the written score.

It may be inferred from the preceding description of the first seven weeks of human embryology that development consists of a sequence of these critical periods. If the concept of epigenetic crisis is a valid one, then two related sets of phenomena should be observed. In the first, for a given epigenetic crisis, e.g., the formation of the ear, there should initially be a time period in which a given teratogen has no effect. This should be followed by a period in which it has a pronounced deforming effect. And finally, once the crisis is passed, but the anatomical structure is not completely formed, the teratogen should have little effect. In the second set of phenomena, the effects of any given teratogen should be linked in time to the temporal sequence of epigenetic crises. For example, if the heart starts to develop before the arms, which in turn start to develop before the teeth, then a given teratogen administered at the heart epigenetic crisis should affect the heart but not arms or teeth. If administered at a later time, it should affect the arms, but not the heart or teeth, and if administered at a still later time, it should affect the teeth, but not the heart or arms. How do the empirical data fit these expectations?

Saxén and Rapola (1969) and Moore (1973) summarize a variety of laboratory and naturalistic studies with birds, amphibians, and mammals, including humans, which bear on these issues. They state that there are three stages of development with respect to teratogenic susceptibility in all species studied. In the first stage, which corresponds to the first two weeks after fertilization in humans, teratogens basically have one of two effects: either prenatal death, or an initial defect followed by complete regeneration, i.e., the offspring are normal. In the earlier part of the second stage, which corresponds to the third through seventh weeks after fertilization in humans, teratogens almost always lead to some congenital defect in some anatomical structure. In the later part of this stage, which corresponds to the eighth through tenth weeks, teratogens frequently lead to some congenital defect. It is during this stage of human embryology that all the major anatomical structures are being formed and become distinctive. In the final stage, after the tenth week in humans, teratogens usually do not lead to congenital defects, the major exception being the nervous system.

As Saxén and Rapola point out, teratogens have their effect by interfering with the normal way in which the genetic code "instructs" a cell to be chemically differentiated. The two primary ways this occurs are through the inhibition or speeding up of gene activity. These dysfunctions frequently have the effect of "splitting" or making two where there should have been one, or of severely diminishing the size of an anatomical structure. It is infrequent for teratogens to start gene activity before the normal starting time, or to extend gene activity beyond the normal stopping time. There are basically three factors which determine whether a teratogen will interfere with the normal process and produce a congenital defect: the specific teratogen used, the quantity of the teratogen used, and the time in development in which it is applied, i.e., whether or not the development of the structure is in a critical period. Critical periods are somewhat flexible in the sense that they can be partially extended by increasing the quantity of the teratogen.

The preceding ideas about critical periods are summarized and amplified in Figure 10 on p. 56 (from Moore 1973). This figure summarizes the effects of a variety of teratogens on human embryology. The three stages of teratogenic susceptibility can be clearly seen, as well as the time-linked effect of taratogens on the various anatomical structures. Figure 11 on p. 57 (from Saxén and Rapola 1969) shows a more detailed analysis of these phenomena. It relates the type of congenital defect produced by thalidomide to the period in pregnancy in which the drug was taken. For example, thalidomide taken during the thirty-eighth through forty-second days of pregnancy produced the defect of marked diminishment of the thumb, but taken during the forty-sixth through fiftieth days, it produced an extra bone in the thumb. Taken as a whole, the results shown in Figure 11 are very striking, and indicate just how finely tuned the developmental system is.

PSYCHOLOGICAL DEVELOPMENT

In this section an attempt will be made to synthesize the ideas of a number of theorists to give an overview of human psychological development. This will be done by amplifying the three embryological themes noted in the introduction of this chapter, and by showing the parallels between embryological development and psychological development. The primary importance of such an overview is that it provides a framework in which to understand the development of any major aspect of human behavior, e.g., language and motor skills.

The basic idea in the preceding discussion of embryological development was that phenotypic development is part of an epigenetic system. This means that development involves a highly constrained set of interactions between the instructions contained in the genotype, the current characteristics of the phenotype, which include its competence or maturation, and the current environmental influences acting on the genotype. The fact that development is constrained implies that phenotypic targets or templates are "sought" for at each stage in development, and when reached, frequently make succeeding stages in development possible.

We saw that embryological development involves a progressive reorganization of the cell tissues, moving the phenotype from a single fertilized cell to a bilaminar disc, to a trilaminar disc, to a cylinder, and so on. This reorganization is guided by the sought-for phenotypic targets, and proceeds by increasing cell and morphological differentiation and increasing morphological integration. For example, not only do optic cups and lens vesicles form, but the two anatomical structures become subordinated to, or hierarchically integrated into, an eye. As you can see in Figure 9 on p. 53, these phenomena of progressive differentiation and integration appear throughout the entire course of embryological development. It is assumed that psychological development occurs in analogous ways.

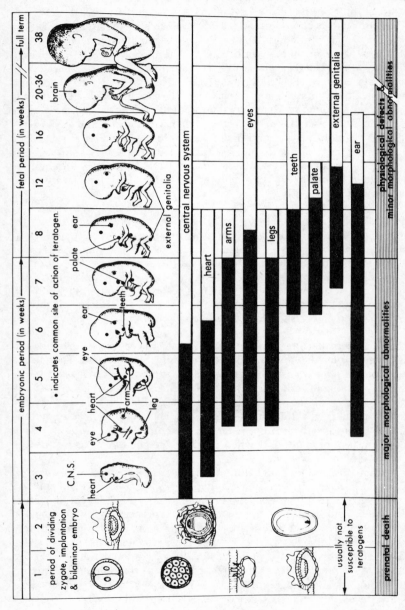

Figure 10

Schematic illustration of the sensitive or critical periods in human prenatal development. Dark shading denotes highly sensitive periods; light shading denotes less sensitive periods (From Moore 1973).

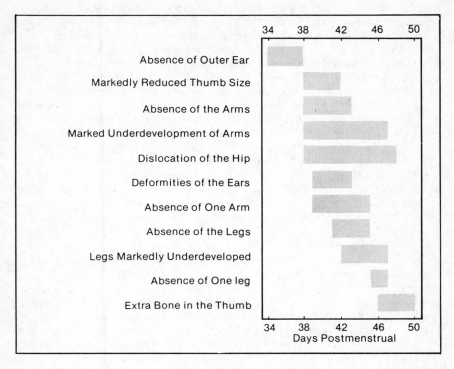

Figure 11

The type of malformation produced by Thalidomide in relation to the stage in pregnancy at which the drug was taken by the mothers (From Saxén and Rapola 1969).

We also pointed out that embryological development occurs within a hierarchy of environments which changes with changes in the maturation or stage of development of the particular cell tissue. The particular set of environments interacting with particular genes induce the phenotype to develop in genetically preprogrammed ways. This interacting system of environments, maturation, and genetic programming is so finely orchestrated that normal development follows fixed or invariant sequences. One analogy frequently used to describe this developmental invariancy is that of a sequence of crossroads, where in order to get to C, you must have taken A first, and then B. When these observations are generalized to encompass psychological development, Lorenz's (1972) position is adopted. That is, environmental induction continues to operate throughout postnatal development, keyed to the individual's level of maturation, which produces invariant sequences of psychological functioning.

Finally, we noted that development is a canalized process in which there are times of progression along highly stable chreods which are generally unaffected by abnormal environmental influences (teratogens), and times of relatively unstable critical periods (relative to the chreod times) in which development can be markedly affected by teratogens. During the critical periods, the organism is undergoing rapid development of some anatomical structure. The critical periods may be either short or long depending upon how long the structure is undergoing this rapid change, e.g., it is very lengthy for brain development. Critical periods may also be slightly extended by increasing the quantity of the teratogen. Abnormal environments primarily have their effects by inhibiting development, or by speeding it up once the critical period has been entered. Rarely do teratogens start a developmental sequence prior to the normal onset of the critical period. When these observations are generalized to include psychological development, one should expect to find the existence of critical periods, but owing to the relatively long time spans involved in human development, their duration is lengthy. Moreover, attempts to speed up behavioral development would meet with little success if the individual was not ready for the environmental influences. The last two issues raised—critical periods and environmental influences—will shortly be discussed.

Interactionist Hypothesis

The *interactionist hypothesis* is a shorthand way of stating the theme that psychological development is keyed to the level of biological maturation and the concurrent environmental influences. Perhaps the most important aspects of this view are the ideas that the anatomical structures intimately connected with psychological functioning are progressively reorganizing throughout life, and that this reorganizing leads to a progressive reorganization of behavior, provided the individual experiences the appropriate environmental stimulation. For example, it is known that at birth the human brain is very immature, and that it undergoes tremendous changes in size, complexity, and organization in the next six to ten years, at which time the adult level is approximately reached. Closely connected with brain maturation are changes which occur in the hormonal system, the most obvious being puberty. These maturational changes make possible, and are probably necessary conditions for, a host of psychological changes, e.g., walking, speaking, catching a ball, figuring out spatial relationships between objects, and heterosexual involvement. Spencer (1870) writes:

> Those who contend that knowledge results wholly from the experience of the individual, ignoring as they do the mental evolution which accompanies the ontogenous development of the nervous system, fall into an error as great as if they were to ascribe all bodily growth and structure to exercise, forgetting the innate tendency to assume the adult form. Were the infant born with a full size and completely constructed brain, the position would be less untenable. But as the case stands, the gradually increasing intelligence displayed through childhood and youth, is more attributable to completion of the cerebral organization, than to individual experiences. . . . Doubtless, experiences received by the individual furnish the concrete materials for all thought. Doubtless the organized and semiorganized arrangements existing among the cerebral nerves, can give no knowledge until there has been a presentation of the external relations to which they correspond. And doubt-

less, the child's daily observations and reasoning aid the formation of the involved nervous connections that are in the process of spontaneous evolution. . . . But saying this is quite a different thing from saying that its intelligence is wholly produced by experience.*

The term "interactionist hypothesis" also underlines the crucial idea that maturation level and environment are interactive and not additive, i.e., a given environmental influence has different effects on behavior at different levels of maturation. Instructing a child to kick a moving soccer ball when he is three years old and uncoordinated will give very different results from instructing him when he is eight years old. Another obvious example is sex education, which will mean very different things to children before and after puberty.

What has also been emphasized is that development is part of an epigenetic system, which means, among other things, that the progressive reorganization of anatomical, physiological, and psychological systems is brought about by the genetic program and the environmental influences. Markedly abnormal environments produce abnormal anatomical and physiological development, which in turn produce abnormal psychological development. For example, Riesen (1958) has shown that unless mammals are exposed to light during the early part of infancy, degeneration of nerve cells underlying vision will occur, producing profound visual defects. Also, markedly abnormal environments may produce abnormal psychological development without having disturbed in any noticeable way anatomical or physiological development, e.g., Harlow's socially isolated monkeys.

Perhaps we have placed too much emphasis on abnormal development. As Waddington and Piaget have pointed out, the epigenetic system is a canalized system which ensures that moderately abnormal environmental influences will be buffered, and that anatomical, physiological, and psychological development will proceed normally. For example, in the realm of psychosexual development, Freud (1949) envisions the maturing child as moving through a series of phases in which the maximum erotic pleasure received from stimulation is more or less localized in certain parts of the body. When a child is in the "oral" phase, for example, stimulation of the lips or mouth gives the child more pleasure than stimulation elsewhere. When the child moves out of this phase, through the joint action of neural maturation and his experiences, the location of maximum erotic pleasure shifts to another part of the body. However, the speed with which it shifts and the success of the shift is contingent upon the nature of the child's experiences.

As another example of canalized development, in the realm of intellectual development (Piaget and Inhelder 1969, Piaget 1970), a large number of abstract abilities seen among European and American children start to emerge at around the age of seven, e.g., conservation of number and understanding classification. Piaget calls the psychological organization underlying these new abilities "concrete operations." Children who possess this organization will frequently experience external events differently than those who have not

---

*Herbert Spencer, The Principles of Psychology, 2nd ed., vol. 1 (London: Williams and Norgate, 1870), pp. 469–70.

yet developed these operations. For example, when in one of Piaget's experiments on number conservation, a row of cups and a row of saucers are lined up, one exactly above the other, both the preoperational and operational children indicate that there are an equal number of cups and saucers. However, when the cups are spread further apart, such that the row of cups is longer than the row of saucers, the preoperational children now say that there are more cups than saucers, whereas the operational children say that there are still an equal number of cups and saucers.

It has been noted that "critical periods" and periods of "readiness" are part of the canalization process. Thus far there have apparently been no planned experiments on critical periods for human psychological development. However, at least one set of unplanned experiments has unfortunately been carried out dealing with the development of attachment behavior. The observations were made of orphaned infants raised in foundling homes who were infrequently held and "mothered." The critical period for attachment occurs between the ages of six weeks and six months (Bowlby 1969). Those infants who received little mothering and holding during this age span developed abnormally and had a higher mortality rate than those who received more normal levels of contact during this time period.

Readiness refers to a time interval in which certain environmental stimulation will have an optimum effect. The classical experiment on readiness in humans is that by McGraw (1935) on stair climbing. One of two normal twins, Johnny, was given extensive training in stair climbing, beginning at an age prior to the age when children normally climb stairs. Jimmy, his brother, was untutored. Johnny showed steady improvement in stair climbing, but at some later point Jimmy spontaneously began to climb stairs, and in a relatively short period of time improved to the ability level of his brother. Hence, the early training for Johnny was given at a less optimal time than his maturational schedule dictated, i.e., when he was not "ready" for it.

Scott (1968), one of the leading students of mammalian socialization, believes that critical periods are prevalent throughout development. We will close this section by quoting his views:

> . . . a critical period is one in which rapid organization of some kind is taking place. While this is going on, it is easy to change the nature of the organization. However, organization in itself has a tendency to produce stability. *Therefore, any period in life when rapid organization is taking place is a critical period*, since the changes which are easily and often accidentally produced at that time become a fixed and relatively permanent feature of the stabilized organization (Scott 1962). In the case of primary socialization, the young animal is organizing its first social relationships.

> By extension we can reason that *any period in life when a major new relationship is being formed is a critical one for determining the nature of that relationship*. Such a period would occur in later life during courtship and mating and the resulting formation of the first sexual relationship, and we have already seen an example of a critical period in the formation of a relationship by the mother sheep for her offspring. Such a period should

occur in any mammal when the young are born. The period of primary socialization is an unusually critical one in that it may indirectly affect the formation of these later relationships.*

Development Leads to Increasing
Differentiation and Hierarchic Integration

Werner (1948) refers to this theme as the "orthogenic principle." It is a theme which characterizes the theories of all the psychologists mentioned at the beginning of the chapter. According to Werner, increasing differentiation of psychological functioning makes perception and thought more *discrete* and less *syncretic*, more *articulated* and less *diffuse*. Syncretic thinking fuses ideas, perceptions, or feelings which can be, or are in reality, separate, e.g., in a dream a character becomes both one's brother and father. As another example, the young child fails to separate the properties of an object from what he does to it or how he feels about it. It's as if the properties he attributes to it are inherent in the object, e.g., the cracked plate is angry. When perception and thought are discrete, the various functions or contents are singled out and made more specific. The child understands that the anger is not a property of the plate, or that the difficulty he has in pronouncing a word is not an inherent property of the word. In diffuse thinking or perception, the child doesn't separate the parts from the whole. For example, when a child's father shaves off his beard, the child believes his father is a different person; or the child may be unable to identify the similarity between a red truck and a green one because for him, all the parts in each truck are blended together. In articulated thinking, the child can identify the separate parts which comprise the whole, and he understands that the parts and the whole are distinct entities. With increasing maturity, syncretic thinking and diffuse thinking do not disappear; rather they tend to diminish in frequency relative to discrete and articulated thought. The psychoanalytic defense mechanism of projection—attributing your own feelings to another—is an example of syncretic thinking, and stereotypes and over-generalizations ("all politicians are bad") are examples of diffuse thinking.

Simultaneously with increases in differentiation, the child is progressively able to coordinate or hierarchically integrate his perceptions and thoughts. He comes to perceive relationships where none had previously existed for him. For example, he not only is able to distinguish the parts from the whole, but he is also able to see the relationships between them, and to distinguish the relevant from the irrelevant. Not only is he able to separate his feelings and actions from those of others, but he is able to understand the relationships between them, e.g., "I'm angry with you and acted nasty and now you're angry with me." Werner speaks of this increasing hierarchical integration as an increasing centralization in which the higher mental functions—those that are

---

*J. P. Scott, *Early Experience and the Organization of Behavior* (Monterey, Calif.: Brooks/Cole Publishing, 1968), p. 142. By permission of Brooks/Cole Publishing Company.

phylogenetically more recent—become dominant over the lower ones. For example, the growing child comes to use language to help direct and integrate his behavior. This increasing hierarchization makes perception and thought more *flexible* and less *rigid*, more *stable* and less *labile* (Werner 1948). With increased flexibility, one can choose from a number of alternatives to reach a goal, solve a problem, or understand a poem. In rigid thinking, there is generally "only one way." Rigid is not to be confused with stable. In stable thinking, one may identify the same pattern of alternatives on different occasions and choose from among them; in labile thinking, one doesn't identify the pattern, but rather a different alternative on each different occasion. In essence, "there's only one way," but it's a different "one way" each time. Again, with increasing maturation the more primitive ways of thinking and perceiving do not disappear, but the more advanced ways become more dominant.

These increases in differentiation and hierarchic integration also lead to more adequate conceptions of space and time. The world of the young child is essentially in and of the present. His plans involve activities which may occur within minutes or an hour. He can only be aware of sequences which have a narrow time span, and he does not understand the ideas of "tomorrow" or "yesterday." With increasing development, the child becomes able to coordinate and represent both past and future events, and to plan activities taking past, present, and future into account. Regarding spatial concepts, in early infancy the only objects which exist for the child are those with which he has visual or tactual contact. At a later period, he develops the concept of the permanent object, and still later he develops the ability to represent distant objects which are hypothetical, i.e., which he has not perceived. Thus, with increasing development, the size of the spatial world increases, as does the complexity of spatial relationships which the child can represent.

One of Werner's last published descriptions of this theme (1957) is the following:

> According to this principle, a state involving a relative lack of differentiation between subject and object is developmentally prior to one in which there is a polarity of subject and object. Thus the young child's acceptance of dreams as external to himself, the lack of differentiation between what one dreams and what one sees as is found in psychosis . . . all of these betoken a relative condition of genetic primordiality compared to the polarity between subject and object found in reflective thinking. This increasing subject-object differentiation involves the corollary that the organism becomes increasingly less dominated by the immediate concrete situation; the person is less stimulus-bound and less impelled by his own affective states. A consequence of this freedom is the clearer understanding of goals, the possibility of employing substitutive means and alternative ends. There is hence a greater capacity for delay and planned action. The person is better able to exercise choice and willfully rearrange a situation. In short, he can manipulate the environment rather than passively respond to the environment. This freedom from the domination of the immediate situation also permits a more accurate assessment of others. The adult is more able than the child to distinguish between the motivational dynamics and the overt behavior of personalities. At developmentally higher levels, therefore, there is less of a

tendency for the world to be interpreted solely in terms of one's own needs and an increasing appreciation of the needs of others and of group goals.*

Development in Stages

Almost all the psychologists mentioned in this chapter describe the behavior of developing individuals as moving through a sequence of stages. A stage is seen as a period in psychological development in which a major reorganization takes place. This reorganization is manifested both qualitatively, e.g., the individual solves problems in new ways, experiences new feelings, or perceives new relations, and quantitively, e.g., his success in solving a particular problem or class of problems increases tremendously. Postulating the existence of stages in no way implies that psychological development is discontinuous, just as the postulation of stages in anatomical development did not imply that embryological development was discontinuous. Rather, during the continuous processes of growth and development, the individual moves along new pathways which lead to progressive anatomical and psychological reorganization.

The idea of stage progression can perhaps most readily be understood for quantitative changes. If one notes over an extended period of time the behavior of any growing child in response to a problem, he will generally find relatively continuous improvement in that behavior, e.g., learning to walk, learning to read, learning to play soccer. The list is endless. In each case, however, three periods or phases in this improvement can usually be seen:

1. The child has close to zero probability of succeeding with the problem.
2. He frequently succeeds and frequently fails.
3. He succeeds with the problem almost all the time.

Clearly the child who succeeds nearly all the time, e.g., walks without falling, is in a different stage of development, for that problem at least, than a child who has rarely or never succeeded with the problem.

Let's extend this discussion to classes or groups of problems. Anyone who has observed a child for long periods of time will note that the preceding three phases describe the child's success in solving what appear to be, on an *a priori* basis, related kinds of problems, e.g., problems involving fine motor control and problems in which the child has to "figure out" things in his head. That is, the child at some point in his development becomes able to solve a certain class of problems which prior to that time he was unable to solve. Within this class, some problems are mastered quickly, others more slowly, and some, perhaps, very, very slowly. Nevertheless, the child shows some progress with all of them and eventually masters nearly all of them. A child who is able to solve a certain class of problems is in a different stage of development than one who can't solve them, even though the first child's progress was continuous.

Our previous discussions have indicated that these developmental stages are canalized, i.e., they will inevitably occur for normal individuals raised in a

*H. Werner, "The Concept of Development from a Comparative and Organismic View," in *The Concept of Development*, ed. D. B. Harris (Minneapolis: The University of Minneapolis Press, 1957), p. 127. Reprinted by permission of the University of Minnesota Press.

normal environment. Moreover, it is likely that many behavioral changes are linked to the growth and functioning of the brain. The relatively slow maturation of the cortical areas underlying language do correspond in a rough way to the slow development of language abilities. Similar parallels have been found for the development of motor abilities. Unfortunately, we know little about these linkages. When the "stages of brain maturation—stages of psychological development" relationship is better understood, no doubt it will be complicated. However, it is not difficult to envision that psychological capacities change in determined ways as the organization of the brain changes in determined ways.

What we have been saying is that stages of development are a reality and not merely a convenient description of the progress in development. These stages take time to develop, and they are identified when major changes in the organization of thought and perception have completed themselves and present a certain coherence or unity. All the theorists who emphasize stages indicate that the earlier stages provide the necessary base for the development of the later stages, and are hierarchically integrated by the later stages. For example, before a child can walk, he must first have mastered the ability to move his legs in an alternating fashion, and before he can run, he must first have mastered the ability to stand without falling and to move himself on only two legs.

The number of stages identified varies with both the breadth and domain of the class of problems one is concerned with, e.g., sexual, social, cognitive, motor. For example, Lenneberg (1966) identifies five stages of language development, from no language under one year of age to nearly fully established language at about age five. The psychoanalyst Erikson (1963) identifies eight stages of social development (or psycho-social crises), from birth (the "oral-sensory" stage in which the major psychological issue is basic trust versus mistrust), to old age (the "maturity" stage in which the major psychological issue is ego integrity versus despair). In the broad realm of cognitive development, four stages have been observed which reflect the increasing ability of the child to deal with abstractions. Spencer (1870) referred to the four stages as:

1. "presentation," in which the child can deal with only his sensations;
2. "presentation-representation," in which the child can deal with relationships between his sensations and representations of the objects which produced those sensations;
3. "representation," in which the child can deal with relationships between representations of objects or events which he has experienced;
4. "re-representation," in which the child can deal with the hypothetical or with abstract symbols.

These stages are described in the following passage.

An infant, gazing, grasping all it can, and putting to its mouth whatever it lays hold of, shows a consciousness in which presented feelings greatly predominate. An urchin, pulling to pieces his toys, building car-houses, whipping his top, gathering flowers and pebbles and shells, passes an intellectual life that is mainly perceptive—presented feelings are here being associated with represented feelings, forming knowledge of the properties and actions of things around; and what goes on of higher representation, as in the dramatizing to which dolls and sets of miniature tea-things minister, is limited to actions observed in the household. In the boy and in the savage there is greater excessiveness of representation; but still representation that passes is not much beyond those wider, concrete experiences which larger spheres of activities have disclosed . . . representations are practically limited to the transactions of individuals. Only as maturity is approached do we find in the few of the civilized such higher degree of representation, here passing into representation, as that which groups particular mode of human action under general truths.*

Piaget's description of the four stages of mental development closely parallels Spencer's. The first stage, that of sensory-motor intelligence, is one in which the child's knowledge of the world is motor knowledge. Technically speaking, sensory-motor intelligence consists of cognitive structures corresponding to sensory-motor patterns of behavior. The child knows as much of the world as he can outline by differentiated motor activities. In the second, preoperational stage, there is an internalization of actions, imagery, and intuitional thought, a first level of symbolic representation of the world. In the third stage, concrete operations, the child organizes the internalized actions into systems which permit deduction and reasoning, but only about concrete phenomena—real configurations of events in the child's experience. Space, time, and causality are understood. Finally, in the stage of formal operations, the system of systems appears—through which reasoning develops into the realm of the hypothetical. The adolescent can reason about purely formal ideas that do not correspond to his experience.

The ages associated with these particular stages of cognitive development cannot be given unequivocally, primarily for two reasons: (1) the various theorists offer slightly different demarcation points, and the demarcation points seem to be somewhat fluid, and (2) the empirical research does not support the assertion of universal, fixed, age-related stages. The particular individual, family, and culture have marked effects on the age at which a particular stage of development will become manifest. As a rough guide, the sensory motor period ends at about age two, the preoperational period at about age seven, and the concrete operational period at about age twelve. Hence, for normal children we should not expect concrete operations to appear at age two, or for the first time at age fifteen.

The two major implications of this theme are that during development certain classes of behavior should undergo transformation or become manifest at about the same time, and that the order in which certain classes of behaviors appear should be relatively constant. For example, different abilities indicating that the child is in the stage of concrete operations should appear at about the same time, and the ability seen in the period of concrete operations should not appear before classes of preoperational behavior. In other words, children's cognitive attainments can be ordered on an ordinal scale, i.e., the stages should occur in an invariant sequence.

---

*Herbert Spencer, The Principles of Psychology, 2nd ed., vol. 2 (London: Williams and Norgate, 1872), p. 518.

This discussion brings the present chapter and the first section of the book to a close. Perhaps the most important ideas that should be carried forward are that evolutionary processes "designed" all aspects of human development from conception to death, and that part of this design was the creation of canalization processes which operate to ensure that in a normal range of environments, genetically normal individuals will develop in specified ways. In the next section of the book, an attempt will be made to determine the nature of part of this design by examining human and primate phylogeny.

SUMMARY

The starting point of this chapter was the assumption that the postnatal psychological development of individuals can best be understood as analogous to an embryological process. Embryological development occurs within a hierarchy of environments, each producing its own unique influences, and all having an effect on the activity of the genes of any given cell. The whole process of embryological development involves an orchestration by the entire genotype—canalization. The three components of embryology—growth, differentiation, and morphogenesis—follow given developmental paths, some of which are heavily canalized, some moderately so, and some only weakly so. Without this canalization it would be impossible to build from a single cell a complex, integrated organism comprised of billions of cells, no two exactly alike, yet all but the germ cells containing the identical genetic information.

We then examined in some detail the first seven weeks of prenatal life, and showed how the canalization concept helped us to understand environmentally induced congenital defects. One of the major ideas of canalization is that development follows certain chreods; and that critical periods exist in which the developing organism moves from one chreod to the next. During these critical periods the organism is relatively susceptible to abnormal environments, which deform the developmental process, and produce defects. Once development has moved onto the new chreod, however, these same abnormal environments have little distorting effect.

We then discussed three ways in which psychological development is analogous to embryological development. The first way is called the interactionist hypothesis, which states that development is keyed to the level of biological maturation and the concurrent environmental influences. One important aspect of this theme is that the anatomical structures intimately connected with psychological functioning are progressively reorganizing throughout life, and that this reorganizing leads to a progressive reorganization of behavior, provided that the individual experiences the appropriate environmental stimulation. This theme also implies that the same environmental influences will have different effects on behavior at different levels of maturation. In extreme cases, such as critical periods, these differential effects may be very pronounced.

The second way of conceptualizing psychological development is that with increasing maturation individuals become increasingly differentiated and hierarchically integrated in their functioning. An example of the former is the ability to make distinctions between one's subjective experiences and the objective external situation. Increasing hierarchical integration is reflected in the progressive ability to find relationships between events or experiences where none had previously been found, and the progressive ability to distinguish the relevant from the irrelevant.

The third way of construing psychological development is that it proceeds through a sequence of stages. Although development is continuous, age-related periods exist in which major reorganizations take place. For example, the individual solves problems in new ways, experiences new feelings, or shows a marked improvement in his ability to perform certain activities. The number of stages identified varies with both the domain and breadth of the psychological issue one is concerned with, e.g., sexual, social, cognitive, motor. Further, for each issue there are no fixed ages at which each reorganization occurs; however, the sequence of stages should be the same for all individuals.

Part Two
PHYLOGENY

Chapter 4

THE PALEOANTHROPOLOGICAL RECORD

OVERVIEW

In the next four chapters an attempt will be made to describe important psychological or behavioral aspects of the nature of man's design produced by evolutionary processes. By "design" we mean the nature of the epigenetic system of the species in relation to the patterns in which the species exploits the environment. In order to describe this design, several related lines of data will be considered:

1. the paleoanthropological record of human and nonhuman primates, which includes bones, teeth, and artifacts
2. neuropsychological research, which deals with brain-behavior relationships
3. nonhuman primate socialization, which deals primarily with common behavior patterns observed in contemporary Old World primates
4. hunter-gatherer socialization, which deals with common behavior patterns observed in contemporary hunter-gatherer societies.

The basic reasoning behind this selection of data goes somewhat as follows. In order to assert that man has a particular design (behavioral or other), it is necessary not only to show continuity with the past, but also conservatism. Continuity and conservatism in prehistoric times can only be assessed by examination of the paleoanthropological record. If it was demonstrated, for example, that man's major anatomical structures had undergone marked changes every 10,000 years, then one would be on shaky ground in identifying a design. However, if marked conservatism were found, i.e., little change over hundreds of thousands of years, one would be on firmer ground in attempting to identify a design. Similarly, if marked evolutionary discontinuities appeared in the primate record, they could justify the argument that there is little to gain in comparing man with the other primates. In a sense, continuity is evidence of conservatism.

Hence, the starting point in attempting to describe psychological aspects of man's design must be the paleoanthropological record. What is the nature of this record and what are its limitations? Basically, it contains only bones, teeth, and artifacts, and all that can be reconstructed from the bones and teeth are the skeletal and dental systems with their supporting musculature. Frequently, many crucial bones and teeth are missing and the reconstruction must be hypothetical. There is no record of any other anatomical structures, nor is there any record of the way any of these structures functioned. Hence, in order to make inferences about either the nature of the missing structures, or the way an anatomical structure functioned, it is necessary to examine living species. (A similar argument can be made regarding the artifacts.)

Perhaps the major limitation of the paleoanthropological record from our perspective is that it is relatively mute about the behavior or activities of early man and his ancestors. Evolutionary theory tells us that the essence of an adaptive design is that it produces effective interaction with the environment. The individuals who were most effective in their interactions with the environment generally reproduced more than those less effective, and thus contributed more genes to the offspring of the succeeding generations. These offspring tended to develop anatomical structures which resembled those of their parents, and these structures probably functioned in the same way in interactions with the environment as did those of their parents. If an anatomical structure did not lead to effective interaction, it was not selected for and eventually "dropped." Thus, it can be assumed that the existence of either progressively changing or long-standing anatomical structures in the paleoanthropological record indicates that they were necessary for effective interaction with the environment. What was the nature of this interaction? Again, the answer must lie in an examination of living species, but which ones?

Evolutionary theory guides us in answering this question. First, man is an Old World primate who maintains a ground-living or terrestrial adaptation. Given the conservatism of evolutionary processes and epigenetic systems, this implies that other Old World primates should be examined, especially those who are closely related to man or who maintain a terrestrial adaptation. These species and man share a common heritage and common structures. Thus, an examination of their behaviors and the nature of their interactions with the environment should aid us in determining some aspects of man's design. Second, man evolved as a hunter-gatherer, and ninety-nine percent of all human generations have lived as hunter-gatherers. It is only in the last 10,000 years that substantial numbers of people have left this mode of adaptation. Some people today, however, still maintain the hunter-gatherer adaptation. If it is assumed that these people maintain an adaptive mode similar to that of our prehistoric ancestors, then other important aspects of man's design can be determined through an examination of their activities.

To summarize, there is an intimate connection between anatomical structures and physiological and psychological function. The paleoanthropological record is essentially mute about this connection. Thus, in order to determine the nature of this connection for species who lived in prehistoric times, it is necessary to examine contemporary species whose anatomy is similar to their ancestors and who reside in an environment similar to their ancestors. In addition, in order to make statements about the design of a species, it is necessary to show that its anatomical structures have been either highly stable, or have progressed in a given direction over long periods of time.

We will start this examination by focusing on selected anatomical adaptations of the placental mammals, then the nonhuman primates, and then man. In the discussion of man's evolution, we will also emphasize the development and use of tools. We will continue this examination of anatomical adaptations in the next chapter, which focuses on the brain.

THE FOSSIL RECORD AND FOSSIL DATING

The study of paleoanthropology has been likened to the solution of a complicated jigsaw puzzle. More accurately, it is an attempt to simultaneously solve a large number of jigsaw puzzles without knowing which pieces go with which puzzles. One doesn't even know whether there is a puzzle to go with a given piece. The theory of evolution is the synthesizer which gives guidance to solving these problems. It states that certain groups of animals are related to each other, in the sense that they had the same common ancestor, and that they do (for living species) and did (for extinct species) differ from one another because of the different environments in which they evolved and to which they adapted. Hence, genetic-ancestral links are assumed to have existed, and the task of the paleoanthropologist is to find them.

The primary data for the paleoanthropologist are fossilized teeth and bones, and tools made of stone or fossilized organic materials. Sometimes the only information available on an extinct species is a single jaw containing a few teeth. From this scanty evidence, the paleoanthropologist attempts to reconstruct the entire body of the individual and to make inferences about his behavior. These reconstructions and inferences are frequently hotly contested by the experts, but they can be made by comparing them with other extinct species or with living species, and through rough knowledge of the environment in which the individual lived. For example, meat eaters have different types of teeth than vegetable eaters, and quadrupedal animals (who walk on four limbs) have different pelvic and foot bones than bipedal animals (Campbell 1966).

There are very large gaps in the primate fossil record (in contrast to that for the horse, which is relatively complete), which exist for primarily three reasons (Leakey 1961). First, there is the influence of chance. If the paleoanthropologist doesn't happen to be at the right place at the right time, he will not dig up or stumble upon the sought-for fossils. Second, there is the small number of fossil hunters and their location preferences. Most studies are restricted to several key sites in Africa, the Middle East, and Europe. There is some digging in Asia, but much less than in the other areas. Not only has this led to gaps in the record, but it also restricts the conclusions to the locations worked in. A useful analogy would be studying only New York and Cincinnati to learn about the contemporary American way of life. The third reason involves the conditions under which fossilization occurs. Basically, forests are poor areas for fossilization, whereas wet plains, rivers, and lakes are better because burial in mud leads to good preservation, and the rate of burial owing to rapid sedimentation is higher in wet areas than in forests. Hence, animals which lived near rivers and lakes are more likely to have become fossilized than those who lived in forests. Since most of the evolution of man's ancestors probably occurred in forests, part of the fossil record is irrevocably lost.

There are basically two techniques for dating fossils, one which gives a relative date and can be used almost anywhere, and another which gives a precise date, but can be used only infrequently (Longwell and Flint 1955). The first and oldest technique involves examining the strata or sedimentary layers in which fossils have been found and noting the various types of plant and animal remains therein. Because evolution moves in only one direction, each broad time span has certain types of plants and animals associated with it. The first appearance of a species is a starting point, hence the relative age of fossils from different regions can be compared. Further, unless there is contrary evidence, the top layers are more recent than the lower ones. Geologists are able to determine in a rough way the length of time it took to lay down a given layer. Thus, by adding up the layers, one can determine an approximate age. The second technique involves various radioactive dating procedures which give absolute, rather than relative time. The well-known radiocarbon dating technique is applicable for fossils not more than about 40,000 years old. The uranium decay technique, which covers time spans of millions of years, is generally only applicable with igneous rocks. Conditions associated with the production of igneous rocks, however, are poor conditions for fossilization. Keeping these limitations in mind, we now move on to the fossil record itself.

PLACENTAL ADAPTATIONS

The paleoanthropological record suggests that mammals evolved from reptiles approximately 200 million years ago during the age of the dinosaurs. The reptiles were dominant during this time, with mammals having a very minor role. These mammals were probably not placentals, but more closely allied to the marsupials, e.g., opposum, and the monotremes, e.g., platypus. The evolution of the placentals occurred at about the same time or shortly after the extinction of the dinosaurs, approximately 100 million years ago. The first placentals were probably small, ground-living insect eaters, the ancestors of the mammalian order Insectivora. It is assumed that these animals are the basic stock from which approximately twenty-five mammalian orders evolved (Simpson 1949).

Both Hulse (1963) and Campbell (1966) argue that greater flexibility in changing environments was the key to the adaptative success of the mammals and especially the placentals. In contrast to contemporary reptiles, who become quite torpid in cold weather and who have little tolerance for very hot weather, the mammals are able to maintain relatively constant activity levels under a wide variety of temperatures.

Campbell identifies four main complexes of interrelated anatomical and physiological characteristics which made it possible for the mammals to have greater ecological boundaries than reptiles. These involve temperature regulation, food utilization, reproduction, and central control of behavior. In mammals, the internal temperature remains relatively constant despite great changes in the external temperature. This *homoiothermy* was made possible by the evolution of a temperature-regulating mechanism in the brain (the hypothalamus), the evolution of hair, and the development of subcutaneous fat beneath the outer layers of skin.

The changes involved with food utilization allowed the placentals to make use of a greater variety of food resources than were available to the reptiles. It is very important to note that flowering plants evolved with the mammals. These plants had fruits and seeds and were not as tough as the earlier plants. The major characteristics of the placental food adaptation were as follows: The teeth became differentiated into canines, incisors, premolars, and molars. The different types of teeth permitted different functions such as grasping, tearing, chewing, and grinding. Chewing and grinding, for example, released the full nutrient value of certain foods, such as nuts and seeds, which swallowing whole generally does not produce. An upper palate evolved which further separated the nose from the mouth, and hence further separated the activities of eating and breathing. Jaws became strengthened and their movements more varied, and a new enzyme was added to the saliva which aided in digestion.

Two major types of changes occurred in the placentals related to reproduction. These involved *viviparity*—the growth of the fertilized egg within and nourished by the mother (rather than by yolk) until an advanced state of development, and parental care of the young after birth. Some of the physiological concomitants of viviparity were the development of the placenta, the estrus cycle, and "heat" in females, which attracts males to copulate. *Homo sapiens* is apparently the only species of placental mammal in which the females do not come into heat, but rather are sexually receptive throughout the entire estrus cycle. Unfortunately, it cannot be determined from the fossil record when this adaptation occurred. Although parental care of the young occurs in birds and some fishes and reptiles, it is only in the mammal that milk glands are found and the young are nursed. This placental adaptation involves an extended period of parental care of the young, which is especially pronounced in man.

Lastly, the evolution of placentals was accompanied by an increase in size of the cerebral hemispheres and, relative to the reptiles, a higher degree of central nervous system (CNS) control over behavior and internal functioning. The earliest placentals had highly developed olfactory lobes and a relatively larger cortex than the reptiles. We will consider these changes in greater detail in the next chapter.

PRIMATE EVOLUTION AND ANTHROPOID ADAPTATIONS

The primates are essentially tropical and subtropical animals. This diverse *order* started to differentiate or radiate from the insectivores approximately sixty million years ago. Their initial adaptation was for life in the trees, with most contemporary species maintaining this adaptation. Le Gros Clark (1959), one of the major contributors to our understanding of primate evolution, identifies the following evolutionary trends as the defining characteristics of the primates:

1. The preservation of a generalized structure of the limbs with a primitive pentadactyly (five digits on the extremities - HDF) and the retention of certain elements of the limb skeleton (such as the clavicle) which tend to be reduced or to disappear in some groups of mammals.
2. An enhancement of the free mobility of the digits, especially the thumb and big toe (which are used for grasping purposes).
3. The replacement of sharp compressed claws by flattened nails, associated with the development of highly sensitive tactile pads on the digits.
4. The progressive abbreviation of the snout or muzzle.
5. The elaboration and perfection of the visual apparatus with the development to varying degrees of binocular vision.
6. Reduction of the apparatus of smell.
7. The loss of certain elements of the primitive mammalian dentition, and the preservation of a simple cusp pattern of the molar teeth.
8. Progressive expansion and elaboration of the brain, affecting predominantly the cerebral cortex and its dependencies.
9. Progressive and increasingly efficient development of those gestational processes concerned with the nourishment of the foetus before birth.*

The living primates, endpoints of millions of years of independent evolution, are classified by Romer (1966) into four suborders:

1. the Lemuroidea, which include the lemurs and tree-shrews and live in the Old World tropics
2. the Tarsiodea, which includes only one genus, the tarsiers, who live in the Asian tropics
3. the Platyrrhini, which include all the New World monkeys
4. the Catarrhini, which include the Old World monkeys, apes, and man.

In the older, and perhaps more familiar classification, the lemuroids and tarsiods are referred to as prosimians, and the platyrrhines and catarrhines as anthropoids.

The paleoanthropological record (see lower half of Figure 12 on p. 75) indicates that the first primate suborder to evolve from the tree-shrew-like insectivore animals (basal insectivore stock) were the Lemuroidea, who are represented today by tree shrews, lorisoforms, and lemurs, and who live in the Old World tropics. In general, contemporary lemuroids are small, long-snouted arboreal animals who may possess one or more claws rather than fingernails. In overall appearance they are midway between monkeys and lower mammals. About fifty million years ago the next primate suborder, the Tarsiodea, dif-

---

*W. E. Le Gros Clark, *The Antecedents of Man* (Edinburgh: Edinburgh University Press, 1959), p. 43. Reprinted by permission of Edinburgh University Press.

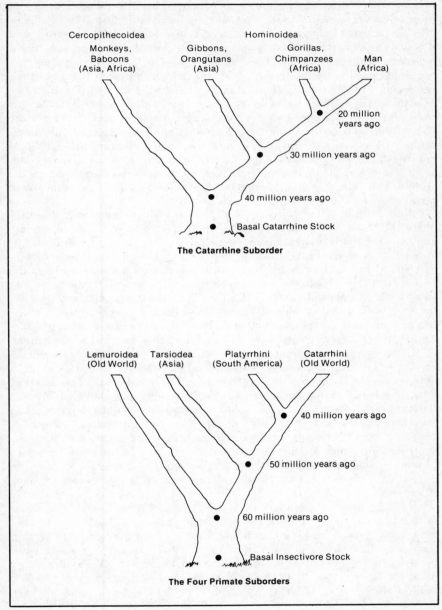

Cercopithecoidea   Hominoidea

Monkeys, Baboons (Asia, Africa)   Gibbons, Orangutans (Asia)   Gorillas, Chimpanzees (Africa)   Man (Africa)

20 million years ago

30 million years ago

40 million years ago

Basal Catarrhine Stock

The Catarrhine Suborder

Lemuroidea (Old World)   Tarsiodea (Asia)   Platyrrhini (South America)   Catarrhini (Old World)

40 million years ago

50 million years ago

60 million years ago

Basal Insectivore Stock

The Four Primate Suborders

Figure 12

Evolution of the Primate Suborders and of the Catarrhine Super-Families. The dates reflect the approximate time at which a major evolutionary differentiation occurred.

75

ferentiated out of the basal primate stock. In Figure 12 this basal stock is represented by the branch of the tree connecting the Lemuroidea to the Tarsiodea. There is only one living genus of the tarsiod suborder, the tarsiers, who live in the Asian tropics. They are very small arboreal animals who appear midway between the lemuroids and the monkeys. It is believed that neither the lemuroids nor the tarsiods have undergone substantial evolution since their emergence fifty to sixty million years ago (Le Gros Clark 1959). The final two primate suborders, the Platyrrhini and Catarrhini, differentiated from the new basal primate stock (represented by the branch connecting the Tarsiodea to the Platyrrhini and Catarrhini branches) about forty million years ago.[1] The platyrrhines are the New World monkeys, and the catarrhines include the Old World monkeys, apes, and man. All of the platyrrhines today retain an arboreal adaptation, whereas, obviously, some of the catarrhines have returned to the ground. The living New World and Old World monkeys differ anatomically in many ways, e.g., in their dentition, skulls, and tails.

Before describing the top half of Figure 12, which represents the early phases of man's evolution, it will be helpful to give an overview of the taxonomy of the living catarrhines shown in Table 1 on p. 77. As we indicated in Chapter 2, taxonomic categories are in part based on Linnaeus' technique of describing the similarities between various groups of animals. Perhaps the primary difference between contemporary taxonomy and Linnaeus is that today we have an evolutionary perspective. Thus, the taxonomic category a living species is placed in depends upon the evolutionary reconstruction of the line of which that species is a member. This is not always an easy thing to do because species undergo change over time, and most species have become extinct. As you move from left to right across Table 1, the taxonomic categories become smaller and reflect more and more specialized adaptations. As you move up or down on Table 1, the taxonomic categories not only indicate different collections or patterns of anatomical or behavioral characteristics, but also different starting points in evolution, e.g., the hominoids resemble each other more than they do any of the cercopithecoids, and the two superfamilies had different ancestors. As you can see in Table 1, the catarrhines are categorized into two superfamilies, which are further subdivided into three families, and which in turn are further subdivided into eighteen genera. For the family Hominidae, there is only one living genus, *Homo*, and only one living species of that genus, *H. sapiens*.

Returning now to the top half of Figure 12 on p. 75, you can see that about forty million years ago the catarrhines differentiated into two superfamilies, the cercopithecoids and the hominoids. Moving along the hominoid branch, the lines leading to the gibbons and orangutans differentiated from the basic hominoid stock about thirty million years ago. The modern gibbons and orangutans live in Asia, and both maintain an arboreal adaptation. About twenty million years ago in Africa, the separate lines leading to the contemporary

---

[1] This discussion does not attempt to accommodate the facts concerning continental drift. For example, it is believed that Africa and South America separated sixty-five million years ago.

Table 1

The Catarrhini Suborder of the Living Primates

Superfamily	Family	Genus	Common Name
Cercopithecoidea (Old World Monkeys)	Cercopithecidae	Macaca	Macaque
		Cynopithecus	Black Ape
		Cercocebus	Mangabey
		Papio	Baboon, Drill
		Theropithecus	Gelada
		Cercopithecus	Guenon
		Erythrocebus	Patas Monkey
		Presbytis	Common Langur
		Pygathrix	Done Langur
		Rhinopithecus	Snub-nosed Langur
		Simias	Pagi Island Langur
		Nasalis	Proboscis Monkey
		Colobus	Gueraza
Hominoidea (Apes and Man)	Pongidae	Hylobates	Gibbon, Siamang
		Pongo	Orangutan
		Pan	Chimpanzee
		Gorilla	Gorilla
	Hominidae	Homo	Man

gorillas, chimpanzees, and man differentiated. It is at this point in time that the hominid family can first be identified. It is not clear from the fossil record whether these first hominids were arboreal or terrestrial; however, it does appear that they lived in forests and were vegetarians (Campbell 1966, Hulse 1963, Le Gros Clark 1959, Pilbeam 1972).

The primate arboreal adaptation brought with it four broad anatomical-functional changes underlying brain function (which will be discussed in the next chapter), vision, touch and grasping, and posture and locomotion (Campbell 1966, Hulse 1963, Le Gros Clark 1959, Pilbeam 1972). With the ascent into the trees, smell became secondarily important to vision. Living high above the ground was dangerous. Literally one false step could mean serious injury or death. Among contemporary gibbons, for example, it is estimated that about one-third of the adults have suffered at least one broken bone (Pfeiffer 1972). Those who survived and reproduced had to be able to see well beyond the noses on their faces. The fossil record indicates that the following changes in the visual system occurred in the primates:

1. enlargement of the eyes, which increased sensitivity to light
2. enlargement of the cortical areas underlying vision
3. movement of the eyes to the center of the face, which allowed for stereoscopic vision
4. relative reduction of the cortical areas underlying smell.

Examination of contemporary anthropoids indicates that all have color vision; however, New World and Old World monkeys have different types of color vision (DeValois and Jacobs 1971), and all have excellent visual acuity and light sensitivity. There is essentially no difference in visual perceptual ability among the hominoids, and in general, little difference among the Catarrhini (DeValois and Jacobs 1971).

The changes in the structure and function of the anthropoid hand were even more dramatic than those involved with vision. The insectivore's relatively immobile paw with five claws was replaced by a hand with very sensitive fingertips, each finger and thumb having a fingernail. The hand became prehensile—it could grasp objects or limbs of trees by wrapping the fingers around them—and the thumb became opposable—it could touch one or more fingers. In short, the mobility of the hand increased markedly. It became an instrument for exploring the environment, for powerfully grasping and holding onto things, and for making finely controlled movements. Hands of a variety of contemporary primates are shown in Figure 13 below.

The changes in anthropoid posture and locomotion are a bit more complicated to describe. Basically, the successful ascent into the trees required greater mobility in all the limbs compared to the insectivores, and it produced a shift toward a more erect posture. With the exception of man and the gibbons, all the anthropoids are primarily quadrupedal. However, the anthropoid mode of movement of swinging through the trees—brachiation—is often accomplished by using only the forelimbs. This movement, in contrast with other four-legged mammals, encourages a certain independence between the legs and the

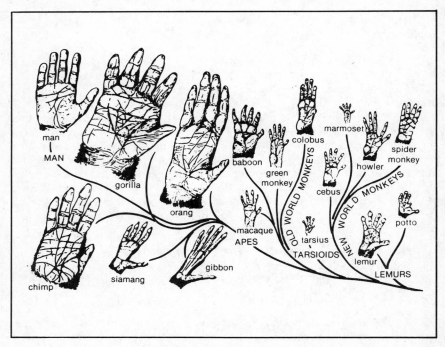

Figure 13
The hands of selected primates (From Alland 1967).

forelimbs. As a consequence, most anthropoids periodically walk bipedally (on two limbs). Full bipedal walking required additional structural changes, and the basic complex of anthropoid characteristics paved the way for them.

CLIMATE, HOMINID EVOLUTION, AND HOMINID ADAPTATIONS

The hominid family started to evolve about twenty million years ago. The geological record indicates that in the period from about three million to twenty million years ago, in contrast to the last three million years, the climate was relatively unvaried in the tropical and subtropical regions. About three million years ago, worldwide temperature and climate started to fluctuate, and have continued to do so until the present time (Hays and Berggren 1971). These fluctuations were most pronounced during the latter half of the Pleistocene geological epoch, which started approximately two million years ago, and ended 10,000 years ago at the beginning of the "Recent" epoch. In the shorter, *glacial* times of the cycle, lasting thousands of years, temperature dropped and precipitation increased. In the longer-lasting *interglacial* times, temperature increased and precipitation decreased. These fluctuations had very different effects in different geographical regions. In the temperate and arctic zones, glaciers frequently formed when the temperature decreased and precipitation increased. These glaciers grew and spread, covering most of Europe, for example, and all of Canada. A tremendous amount of water was locked into these glaciers, and worldwide sea level dropped hundreds of feet. During the interglacial times, the ice melted to produce large rivers and lakes. In the tropical and subtropical zones, the temperature decreased only a little during the glacial periods, but the amount of rain increased markedly, forming large rivers and lakes. During the interglacial periods, again, little temperature change occurred, but the large lakes and rivers diminished in size and small ones dried up.

The paleoanthropological record (e.g., Leakey 1961, Pfeiffer 1972) indicates that the early hominids lived and evolved in the tropical and subtropical zones. Towards the middle of the Pleistocene, about three-quarters of a million years ago, the hominids moved into the temperate zones of Europe and Asia (Campbell 1972). However, during the glacial times most of the land in these zones was uninhabitable, forcing the early men south. In the tropical and subtropical zones, an enormous amount of land was habitable during the glacials, much more so than during the interglacials, when the sea level rose and deserts were created. During the interglacials, the competition for water and food among the early hominids must have increased tremendously. Without doubt, those who were skillful with tools had a better chance of surviving and reproducing than those less skillful. During the interglacials, those who had the opportunity to move north probably did so. Large rivers and lakes abounded there and game was probably relatively more abundant than in the south. However, the move into the temperate zone produced new stresses—regular, recurring, seasonal climate changes. Keeping warm during the winter was a new problem. Once again, the skillful toolmakers were probably more successful than the less skilled. In short, the Pleistocene was a time when the old modes of adaptation were severely challenged, and evolution was encouraged (Leakey 1961).

Let's return now to the beginnings of hominid evolution, about twenty million years ago. As you can see in Figure 14 below, the basal hominoid stock out of which the first hominids, the ramapithecines, emerged were forest-living apes called dryopithecines. The major research on the genus Ramapithecus was done by Simons (1964). Here is a case where a few teeth and a few jaws can successfully be stretched a long way. Simons' technique involved comparing Ramapithecus fragments with those of a contemporary, Dryopithecus, and with the succeeding hominids, Australopithecus and Homo. Simons' analysis showed that the shape of the mandible—the part of the lower jaw that carried the teeth, the size of the canines and incisors, and the shape of the molars —more closely resembled the hominids than the apes. Other anthropologists concur with Simons' view, e.g., Campbell (1966), Howells (1973), Pilbeam (1972), and classify Ramapithecus as a hominid and as a probable ancestor of Homo. Both Howells and Pilbeam believe that the ramapithecines ate foods growing on the forest floor, such as seeds and roots, that they were primarily ground-living as opposed to tree-living, and that they had a stronger tendency than the apes to walk bipedally. The adaptation of this genus must have been

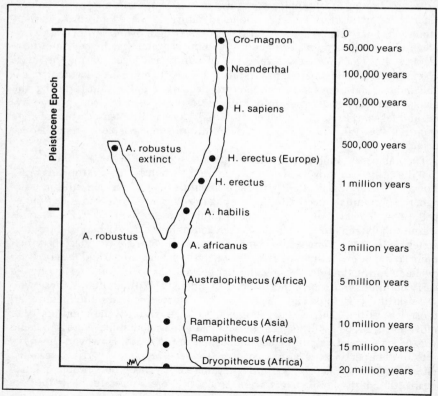

Figure 14

Evolution of the hominid family. The tree is drawn on a logarithmic time scale.

very successful because the fossils found in India dating about ten million years ago are extremely similar to those found in Africa dating about fourteen million years ago.

From Ramapithecus to the next hominids, the genus Australopithecus, there is about a five million year gap in the hominid fossil record. It is assumed that some species of Ramapithecus evolved into the australopithecines, and that other ramapithecines, if there were any, became extinct. The fossil evidence dates the existence of Australopithecus from about five million years ago in southern and eastern Africa, and the coexistence of at least two species of this genus, A. africanus and A. robustus, from about three million years ago. Undoubtedly, these two species occupied different environmental niches, A. robustus being a vegetarian, and A. africanus being an omnivorous hunter-gatherer, feeding on vegetables, scavenged meat, and small animals which they hunted. Recent evidence suggests that A. africanus occupied dry environments, somewhat akin to grassy areas and open savannas, whereas A. robustus fossils are associated with wet climates and perhaps wooded areas (Howells 1973). Structurally, A. africanus was smaller, had smaller jaws, smaller teeth, and a more rounded cranium than A. robustus. Both species were clearly bipedal, but the fossil evidence indicates that they had a less efficient gait than Homo, and probably walked in a jogging fashion. The hands of both species closely resembled those of Homo, although their thumbs were relatively shorter, and the angle between the thumb and index finger was smaller than in Homo. This implies that their thumb was not as fully opposable as man's—probably a requirement for precision toolmaking. Like Ramapithecus, the australopithecines were smaller than Homo, A. africanus weighing between forty and seventy pounds and measuring between three and three and a half feet tall, and A. robustus weighing between eighty and one hundred forty pounds and measuring between four and four and a half feet tall. They had small brains (brain size will be discussed in the next chapter), and heads shaped more like an ape than a man. Hence, with the exception of their overall size and shape of their head, the australopithecines structurally resembled Homo, and there is little question that one of the species was the ancestor of man.

Although there is some dispute as to whether the australopithecines made tools, the most recent evidence indicates that A. africanus did (Howell 1972, Oakley 1972). Toolmaking dates back approximately 2.6 million years. The earliest types are called pebble tools and can readily be made by taking a fist-sized stone and hitting it against another stone to yield a sharp edge. Pebble tools were probably used for cutting and perhaps for hunting small animals (see Figure 15 on p. 82).

Approximately 1.75 million years ago, near the beginning of the Pleistocene, the A. africanus line dropped out and was replaced by a species named A. habilis (Howell 1972, Oakley 1972, Pilbeam 1972, Tobias 1970).[2] Virtually all

---

[2]The recent discovery by Richard Leakey (reported by Howell 1973) of a very large-brained hominid dated at 2.6 million years ago indicates that at an earlier time in parts of Africa the A. habilis line and the A. africanus line coexisted. Leakey's findings have not been readily integrated by other paleoanthropologists, e.g., Howells (1973).

paleoanthropologists believe that *A. habilis* was the immediate ancestor of early man—the genus Homo. *A. habilis* and *A. robustus* coexisted for about

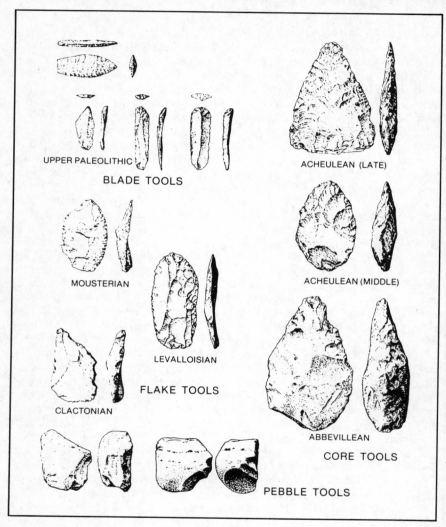

Figure 15

Tool traditions of Europe. The earliest tools are depicted on the bottom of the figure, and the later ones on the top. With the exception of the blade tools, the other tools are shown from the side and edge views. The "core" tools consist of a piece of stone from which a few flakes have been chipped. The "flake" tools consist of the flakes from the original stone, which are further refined. "Blade" tools are made from flakes with nearly parallel sides. Tool traditions are named for the site where the tools of a given type were discovered (From Washburn 1960).

three-quarters of a million years, whereupon, about one million years ago, *A. habilis* was replaced by (evolved into) *Homo erectus. A. robustus* and *H. erectus* continued to coexist for approximately half a million years until *A. robustus* became extinct (Howell 1972).

The fossil evidence indicates that in dental structure, hand structure, brain size, height (about four to four and a half feet tall) and the structures underlying walking, *A. habilis* was about midway between *A. africanus* and *H. erectus*. It is generally agreed that *A. habilis* was a hunter of small animals and a gatherer of vegetables and fruits. These hominids bore little resemblance to apes, unlike *A. africanus*. Regarding tool manufacture, it appears that during the early and middle phases of the evolution of *A. habilis*, a variety of pebble tools were made, and during the later phases they also made primitive core tools resembling the Abbevillean traditions shown in Figure 15 on p. 82 (Pilbeam 1972).

There is little dispute among paleoanthropologists that *H. erectus* was a man, and the direct ancestor of our species, *H. sapiens*. As far as we can determine from the fossil record, with the exception of the shape of the head and size of the brain, there is essentially no difference between the size and shape of the anatomical structures of the two species. Brain size in some races (subspecies) of *H. erectus* overlapped the lower end of the range of normal brain size for *H. sapiens*. This increased brain size of *H. erectus* was reflected in their great variety of precision tools, their use of fire, and their building of shelters (which allowed them to live in cold climates). It is believed that they cooperatively hunted large game and had butchering sites where they used their various tools to cut up and distribute their kill. During the early evolutionary phases of *H. erectus*, tools were made in the Abbevillean and Clactonian traditions (see Figure 15), but in the later phases Middle and Late Acheulean and Levalloisan types were also made (Leakey 1961, Pilbeam 1972). In short, the *H. erectus* hunter-gatherer adaptation was a fully human one, and *one that persisted for about one million years essentially unchanged.*

Looking back over the description of man's ancestors from *A. africanus* to *H. erectus*, it is clear that there was a progressive increase in man's size which stabilized at five foot eight inches tall. Went (1968) has forcefully argued that this size increase was one of man's crucial adaptations. A successful adaptation is always the result of the interaction of a number of forces. For example, Went points out that if a man seven feet tall used a club proportionate in size to his body, and struck something with it, the blow would have four times the force of a club swung by a man five foot eight inches tall. The latter person's swing, however, would have twice the force of that swung by a man five foot tall, and twenty-five times the force of that swung by a three-foot tall person. For a hunter using clubs and spears to bring down animals, especially large ones, size is crucial. However, a man seven foot tall would require much more food than one five foot eight inches tall, and if the giant fell while running after game, he would have a much higher probability of getting injured. Went calculates that a six-foot tall person who falls hits the ground with twenty to a hundred times the force of a small child learning to walk, and one-thirty-second the impact of a giant twelve feet high. One safe way to increase height (and size) is to use quadrupedal locomotion, as gorillas and elephants do; however, all the advantages of bipedal locomotion, including the ability to carry and swing clubs, would be lost.

The fossil evidence indicates that the first races of H. sapiens emerged about a quarter of a million years ago. As far as we can determine, their tools and artifacts at this time were of the same level of complexity as those of H. erectus. Approximately 75,000 years ago, a race of H. sapiens appeared in Europe, the Neanderthals. From the fossil record it appears that their brain size was slightly larger than that of modern man. The Neanderthals made very complex tools of the Mousterian type (see Figure 15 on p. 82), buried their dead in ritualistic ways, and apparently stored food.

Approximately 35,000 years ago, "modern man" (Cro-Magnon man) appeared in Europe, completely replacing and absorbing the Neanderthals. Man's physical evolution appears to have ceased at this time. Lieberman (1973) has convincingly argued that the human fossil evidence concerning the vocal tract is consistent with the view that the Cro-Magnon men were more adept speakers than the Neanderthals, and that this superior communication ability made them more adaptive than the earlier race of men. Between 35,000 and 10,000 years ago, the last changes in tool manufacture occurred. Small blade tools called microliths appeared which were frequently used for arrowheads and as parts of harpoons (see Figure 15). Spears and eventually sickles were used. Bones were used for pins, fishhooks, and spearthrowers. The Cro-Magnons made exquisite paintings on cave walls, fashioned small sculptures out of stone, made jewelry, and decorated their clothes. In short, there was little to differentiate these people from contemporary hunter-gatherers (Braidwood 1967).

There is good evidence that about 10,000 years ago, on the hilly flanks of high mountain ridges of what is today Iran, Iraq, Turkey, Syria, and Israel, certain groups of people were settled in permanent villages and engaged in farming and domestication of goats and pigs. It was a very short step from an intensive collecting and hunting adaptation, which apparently earlier characterized these people, to the farming way of life. When wild grains are plentiful and grow year-round in given locations, and where game is bountiful year-round, it is convenient to settle into permanent villages, which is probably what these people did. The farming model of subsistence spread rapidly throughout the Old World, and by about 5,000 years ago it had apparently become a typical mode of living nearly everywhere. In the New World, where man migrated approximately 30,000 years ago, a parallel cultural development occurred, and domestication of animals and plants started about 5,000 years ago.

The next major adaptational shift occurred between 5,000 and 5,500 years ago, when cities emerged on the alluvial land of the lower Tigris, Euphrates, and Nile rivers. It is with the formation of cities that we start getting the extremes in specialization of activities in man as opposed to those of the village farming community or the hunting-gathering society. It should be pointed out that despite the great spread of village farming communities and cities throughout Europe, Africa, and the East, there were always areas on the globe in which the hunter-gatherer form of life was still maintained and is maintained today (Braidwood 1967).

Table 2

Summary of Some Major Characteristics of Hominid Evolution

	Years ago	Size	Tools	Diet and Method of Obtaining Food	Locomotion
H. sapiens Cro-Magnon	35,000	5'8"	Blade tools	Omnivorous: gathering, hunting large game	Advanced bipedal
H. sapiens Neanderthal	75,000	5'8"	Mousterian Flake	Omnivorous: gathering, hunting large game	Advanced bipedal
H. erectus	1,000,000	5'6"	Advanced Core, Flake	Omnivorous: gathering, hunting large game	Advanced bipedal
A. habilis	1,750,000	4'-4'6"	Primitive Core	Omnivorous: gathering, hunting large game	Bipedal
A. africanus	3,000,000	3'-4'	Pebble tools	Omnivorous: gathering, hunting small game	Inefficient bipedal
A. robustus	3,000,000	4'-4'6"	None	Omnivorous: gathering, scavenging	Inefficient bipedal
Ramapithecus	14,000,000	Unknown	None	Vegetarian	Quadrupedal

Chapter 5

BRAIN FUNCTION AND EVOLUTION OF THE BRAIN

OVERVIEW

We stated in Chapter 1, following the views of Lorenz, Piaget, and Waddington, that evolutionary processes are fundamentally involved with the acquisition of information or knowledge about the environmental niche of the species. In general, the greater the knowledge that members of a species have about the environment in which they will develop, the more effective will be their actions in that environment, and hence, the greater will be their chances of surviving and reproducing, i.e., the higher will be their Darwinian fitness.

There are at least six interrelated characteristics or components involved with the "acquisition of knowledge" used in its evolutionary sense. Individuals must possess a system which:

1. receives information, e.g., patterns of light
2. identifies information, e.g., it's a dog
3. stores information, e.g., stores in the memory some representation of that dog
4. operates on or elaborates information, e.g., that dog is four times larger than any other dog seen before
5. makes decisions (which need not be conscious) about information, e.g., that dog is dangerous
6. acts on the decisions made about the information, e.g., run like hell.

In lower animals, such as Lorenz's protozoa described in Chapter 1, some aspects of this system may be genetic, e.g., the information concerning whether the environment is noxious or not is stored in the genotype. However, in the higher animals, such as the vertebrates, these systems involve the functioning of anatomical structures which were "designed" to acquire information or knowledge, e.g., in primates, eyes with rods and cones to receive color information, brains to identify, store, operate on, and decide about information, hands and legs to act on the information.

Restricting our discussion to the higher animals, the anatomical structures which comprise a knowledge acquisition system of a given species can roughly be divided into two categories: those which are evolutionarily conservative, and hence are found at a number of different phylogenetic levels, e.g., prehensile hands, eyes, certain structures of the brain; and those which are phylogenetically new and reflect the particular adaptation of that species, e.g., prehensile tails of certain New World monkeys, the anatomical structures underlying bipedal locomotion, and certain structures in man's brain. It is important to point out that the nature of these phylogenetically new species-specific adaptations depends in part upon the nature of the phylogenetically old adaptations on which they are built. For example, the knowledge acquisition systems underlying cooperative hunting are different for wolves and man owing to the different phylogenetic histories of these species. Thus, in order to understand the particular adaptation or design of a species, it is necessary to specify both the phylogenetically old and the phylogenetically new aspects of its knowledge acquisition system. This is exactly what was done in part of the preceding chapter regarding the evolution of anatomical structures which received information, and anatomical structures which acted on information. For information reception, we saw that a binocular visual system and hands with sensitive fingertips were phylogenetically old in primate evolution; and for acting on information, we saw that prehensile hands were phylogenetically old, and bipedal locomotion was phylogenetically new.

In the previous chapter, owing to the complexity of the subject matter, we eliminated any discussion of the evolution of the primary anatomical structure of man's knowledge acquisition system—the brain. This omission may have given the false impression that the factors operating on the evolution of the brain were different than those operating on the evolution of man's other anatomical structures. Just as all the components of knowledge acquisition are interrelated, e.g., information reception is obviously related to information identification, all of the anatomical structures comprising a knowledge acquisition system are interrelated, and moreover, they evolved and became canalized together. Man has spoken language because of the anatomy of his vocal tract *and* his brain, and those individuals who could speak had higher Darwinian fitness than those who spoke less well. Thus, speech became canalized in man's epigenetic system. Man evolved as a precision toolmaker because of the anatomy of his hand *and* his brain, and those individuals who made and used tools had higher Darwinian fitness than those who were less skilled at these tasks. Thus, highly developed motor skills became canalized in man's epigenetic system. Man evolved as a cooperative hunter of big game because of the anatomy of his digestive tract, his size, his utilization of large tools, *and* his brain, and those individuals who had a particular social structure, processed particular kinds of information, and engaged in cooperative hunting had higher Darwinian fitness than those who did not. Thus, the structures and functions underlying cooperative hunting became canalized in man's epigenetic system.

Returning now to the opening theme of this chapter, we stated that the greater the knowledge that members of a species have about the environment in which they will develop, the more effective will be their actions in that environment. In man and the other higher animals, the brain is the chief anatomical structure involved with the acquisition of this knowledge. Writing in a similar vein about man's cerebral cortex, the neuropsychologist Roger Sperry (1952) has stated:

> Cerebration essentially serves to bring into motor behavior additional refinement, increased direction toward distant, future goals and greater overall adaptiveness and survival value. The evolutionary increase in man's capacity for perception, feeling, ideation, imagination and the like may be regarded not so much as an end in itself as something that has enabled us to behave, to act, more wisely and efficiently.*

METHODS OF STUDYING BRAIN EVOLUTION

There are basically three interrelated techniques used to study the evolution of man's brain: the study of fossil remains, the comparison of brains of living species (comparative neuroanatomy), and the study of brain-behavior relationships (neuropsychology). Used alone, each of these techniques has serious drawbacks, but used in combination, some clear evolutionary trends can be established and tentative conclusions about man's evolution can be stated.

There are no brains in the fossil record, but there are parts of skulls, usually crushed, and occasionally natural *endocasts*. An endocast is a filling in the endocranial cavity of the skull, with the skull serving as the mold for the filling. In living animals, most of the endocranial cavity is filled with the brain. A natural endocast consists of the sediment which has filled the endocranial cavity of an uncrushed skull. Where the fossilized skull has been crushed, there are no natural endocasts, but artificial ones can be made after the skull has been pieced together. There is a fair amount of guesswork in piecing a fossilized skull together because many parts are usually missing, and no one knows exactly how the intact skull looked. Thus, both natural and especially artificial endocasts give at best a rough estimate of brain size. Where natural endocasts have been found, an additional piece of information can sometimes be inferred—the surface markings on the cortex of the brain. These surface markings are useful in determining which parts of the cortex have undergone the greatest changes during the course of evolution (Holloway 1968, Jerison 1973).

Turning to comparative neuroanatomy, the anatomy of each living species reflects what is phylogenetically old and what is phylogenetically new for that species. Each species is unique anatomically owing to its unique history and unique adaptive niche. Thus, in making assessments about the evolution of man's brain, it is unwise to assume that the brain of a "lower" primate

---

*R. W. Sperry, "Neurology and the Mind-Brain Problem," *American Scientist* **40** (1952): 299. Reprinted by permission, *American Scientist*, journal of Sigma Xi The Scientific Research Society of North America, Inc.

accurately represents the brain of one of man's ancestors, even if the brain of the living primate is the same size as the fossil brain. For example, australopithecine brain size was approximately the same as that of living chimpanzees, yet it is extremely doubtful that their brains were identical. It is a little safer, however, to make assessments by averaging a number of species at the same phylogenetic level, e.g., the Old World baboons and monkeys, thus suppressing what is unique in each species. What is to be gained from this procedure? As noted in the preceding paragraph, the fossil record yields very little information about the surface markings of the cortex of the brain, and nothing at all about the structures under the surface. Thus, any evolutionary changes which have occurred below the surface are completely obscured in the fossil record. By comparing the brains of living primates, one gains some understanding of the surface markings of the endocasts, as well as a great deal of information about the probable evolutionary changes in deeper structures of the brain (Stephan and Andy 1970, Stephan 1972).

The primary ingredient missing from both the study of the fossil record and comparative neuroanatomy is information concerning the significance of the various evolutionary changes which have occurred in the hominid brain. The basic way that the significance of a change (or lack of change) is assessed is by determining the function of the anatomical structure under consideration. For example, unless it was known that the olfactory bulbs mediate the perception of smell, knowledge of a change in their relative size during hominid evolution would have little meaning. Likewise, the opposability of man's thumb can be evaluated by making reference to the function of the thumb in precision toolmaking. Thus, an understanding of brain-behavior relationships is crucial to an understanding of the adaptive value of the changes observed in brain evolution.

Information from the fossil record and comparative neuroanatomy concerns the absolute or relative changes in the size of parts of, or all of the brain; information from neuropsychology concerns the functional relationships between the brain and behavior. Guidelines are needed to help us understand how these two types of information can be synthesized. Jerison (1973) has provided a solution to this problem, which he calls the "principle of proper mass." He describes this principle as follows:

> The mass of neural tissue controlling a particular function is appropriate to the amount of information processing involved in performing the function (Jerison's italics). This implies that in comparisons among species the importance of a function in the life of each species will be reflected by the absolute amount of neural tissue for that function in each species. It also implies that, within a species, the relative masses of neural tissue associated with different functions are related to the relative importance of the functions in the species.*

According to this principle, evolutionary increases in a structure underlying a given function, e.g., spatial understanding, imply that that function became

---

*H. J. Jerison, *Evolution of the Brain and Intelligence* (New York: Academic Press, 1973), pp. 8–9.

increasingly important in the progressive adaptation of that species. Jerison reminds us, however, that the principle of proper mass also implies that, all things being equal, brain size should be related to body size, Thus, in hominid evolution we saw a progressive increase in body size in the Australopithecus-Homo line, which should have been accompanied by a progressive increase in brain size.

How does one determine whether an evolutionary increase (or decrease) in the size of the brain reflects only an increase in body size or an increase over and above increased body size? The technique evolutionists have used is called an *index of cephalization* (Jerison 1973, Stephan 1972, Tobias 1970). When applied to primates, the index of cephalization uses a formula[1] which expresses the extent to which a particular brain structure, or the brain as a whole, has increased or decreased *relative to* that of a typical basal insectivore—members of the mammalian order Insectivora who have apparently undergone little change over the past sixty million years, such as shrews and hedgehogs. In other words, the formula predicts what the brain of a shrew or hedgehog would be like if the shrew or hedgehog had the same body size as a prosimian, a monkey, a chimpanzee, and a man. For example, although man's olfactory bulbs are larger in an absolute sense than those of a hedgehog, the index of cephalization shows that *relative to* body size, man's olfactory bulbs are one-fiftieth the size of a hedgehog's. That means that if during the course of the evolutionary line leading from the basal insectivores to man, brain size increased only in proportion to body size, man's olfactory bulbs would be fifty times larger than they currently are.

To summarize, three interrelated techniques are used to understand the evolution of man's brain—the study of fossil remains, comparative neuroanatomy, and neuropsychology. From the fossil remains, inferences can be made about changes in overall size of the brain, and to a limited extent, about changes on the surface of the brain. From comparative neuroanatomy, inferences can be made about changes which have occurred in deeper structures of the brain. And from neuropsychology, inferences can be made about the functional or adaptive significance of these changes. The principle of proper mass guides us in assessing this significance, and the index of cephalization helps us determine whether the changes in brain size were proportional to the changes in body size.

THE FOSSIL RECORD

Increased Brain Size

Perhaps the most striking aspect of hominid evolution from *A. africanus* to *H. sapiens* has been the almost explosive growth of the brain. As we indicated in the last chapter, with the exception of brain size and the shape of the face and neck, there has been essentially no change in man's anatomical structures

---

[1]The index of cephalization formula is: $E = .03P^{2/3}$, where E is predicted brain size and P is body size. The constant .03 assumes that the relationship between predicted brain size and body size is the same as that for basal insectivores. The constant 2/3 applies to all phylogenetic levels, and not just to the basal insectivores.

over the past million years. Table 3 shows the means and ranges of brain size of some contemporary genera of the hominoid superfamily, as well as the extinct hominids of this superfamily. For the extinct members, the sample size (N's) consists of all the fossil remains for which a good estimate can be made (Tobias 1970). The fossils of the *H. erectus* subspecies Pithecanthropus were found in Java, and are dated earlier than the subspecies Sinanthropus, whose remains were found in China. Three general points should be made about this table. First, within any given evolutionary line, body size and brain size are related. In the line from *A. africanus* to *H. sapiens*, body size increased, but not in a linear fashion; hence, some of the increased brain size reflects this increase in body size. Second, an examination of the fossil record of brain size plotted against time suggests that the growth of the hominid brain from *A. africanus* to *H. sapiens* was almost linear (Pilbeam 1972). That is, there are apparently no jumps in brain size in man's evolution, but rather the record is one of steady increase over three million years. Finally, within a species, variations in brain size within the normal range *generally* have little meaning. A human with a large brain may or may not be more intelligent than one with a small brain. For example, Walt Whitman had a cranial capacity of 1282 c.c., and Daniel Webster a cranial capacity of about 1900 c.c. (Tobias 1970). However, Van Valen (1974) pointed out, following a review of the literature which related external head measurements to intelligence, that the correlation between human brain size and intelligence may be as high as .30. For predicting intelligence from brain size, a correlation of .30 is essentially no help, but from the view of natural selection operating on an important phenotypic characteristic, a correlation of .30 is substantial, and can completely account for the increase in hominid brain size seen in the fossil record.

It is generally assumed that within a given evolutionary line in which increased brain size has occurred, the increase was the major contributor to the successful adaptation of the species. The key problem in understanding the relationship between brain size and adaptation has been to translate brain size into other units which might reflect this increased adaptability. Ideally, these

Table 3

Hominoid Cranial Capacity (c.c.)

	Mean	Sample Range
A. africanus	494 (N=6)	435 - 540
A. habilis	656 (N=3)	633 - 684
Homo erectus (Pithecanthropus)	859 (N=6)	750 - 975
Homo erectus (Sinanthropus)	1043 (N=5)	915 - 1225
Homo sapiens (modern man)	1350	1000 - 2000
Hylobates (Gibbons)	89	87 - 130
Pan (Chimpanzees)	394	320 - 480
Gorilla (Gorillas)	498	340 - 752
Pongo (Orangutans)	411	295 - 475

Source: Philip V. Tobias, *The Brain in Hominid Evolution* (New York: Columbia University Press, 1970), pp. 52–53. Reprinted by permission of the publisher and the author.

units should quantify the different levels of adaptability at the different stages in evolution.

Jerison (1963, 1973) has attempted such an analysis. He reasoned as follows. Two classes of nerve cells underlie the structure and function of the brain: those dealing with sensory-motor, vegetative, and self-preservation and procreation functions, which are related to body size, and those dealing with adaptive functions or behavioral plasticity, which are unrelated to body size. He assumed that the more cells of the latter type that a given species has, the greater is its "extra" information-processing capacity. The major problem, then, is determining for a given species the number of nerve cells (neurons) related to body size, and the number related to "extra" information-processing capacities. Jerison's starting point is that the *relationship* between brain size and total number of neurons is constant within the mammals, living and extinct, i.e., there is a specific number of neurons per cubic centimeter of brain. There is some question about this, e.g., Holloway (1968), but others agree that it is not a bad starting point, e.g., Tobias (1970). He then assumes that the number of neurons related to body size can be determined by first computing with the index of cephalization the brain-to-body-size ratio of the contemporary basal insectivores, and then applying this ratio to other species. Underlying this assumption is the idea that the brain of these primitive mammals is largely involved with vegetative, procreative, and self-preservative functions, and very little with extra information-processing capacities. Thus, for each species of interest, living and extinct, a computation is made of the predicted brain size if the brain of that species were comparable to those of basal insectivores and was only involved with basic functions. By subtracting this number from the actual brain size, the number of extra neurons can be estimated for each species.

The results of Jerison's analysis as modified by Tobias (1970) are shown in Table 4. For comparison purposes, the number of extra neurons of the gorilla and chimpanzee are presented. Looking at the first row, if the chimpanzee brain were comparable to those of shrews and hedgehogs, it would contain about .9 billion neurons. It is relatively much larger, however, and contains

Table 4

Estimates of "Extra Neurons" in Selected Hominoids
(In Billions)

	Total Number of Neurons	Number of Body-Size-Related Neurons	Number of Extra Neurons
Chimpanzees	4.3	.9	3.4
Gorillas	5.3-5.7	1.8-2.1	3.5-3.6
A. africanus	5.0	.7	4.3
A. habilis	6.2	.8	5.4
H. erectus	6.6-8.0	.9-1.0	5.7-7.0
H. sapiens	9.5	1.0	8.5

Source: Philip V. Tobias, *The Brain in Hominid Evolution* (New York: Columbia University Press, 1970), p. 111. Reprinted by permission of the publisher and the author.

about 4.3 billion neurons, 3.4 billion of which are used for increased information processing. As you can see from this table, in the early stage of hominid
evolution there is relatively little difference in extra neurons between A.
africanus and the contemporary great apes; however, in the stage of A. habilis
there is a substantial difference. This difference in number of extra neurons
increases over the course of evolution, reaching its peak in H. sapiens. Unfortunately, what cannot be determined from this table, nor from the fossil record,
are the structures in the brain which have undergone the greatest evolutionary
change. What can be assumed is that the increase in extra neurons was due to
both the expansion of structures involved with the elaboration of old functions,
e.g., identification of visual information, and the creation of new structures
involved with new functions, e.g., decision making through the utilization of
language. Jerison (1973) believes that the increase in extra neurons seen in
man's evolution was primarily a response to his increasing reliance on higher
cognitive capacities, such as language, imagery, and higher order Gestalt
perception.

Brain Size and Rate of Maturation

It is quite clear from the evolutionary record that hominid brain size approximately tripled from A. africanus to H. sapiens, where it stabilized. It is extremely
doubtful that brain size itself was selected for in evolution—a big brain in and
of itself just sits there—but rather the individuals with bigger brains (and by
implication, more complex brains) must have been more adaptive in their
interactions with the environment than those with smaller, less complex
brains. That is, certain types of individuals had at least slightly higher survival
and reproduction rates than other individuals, and the former types had at least
slightly more complex brains than the latter.

Evolutionary processes operate at each point in development, from conception until death. Based on what is known about growth and development,
bigger-brained adults must have been bigger-brained infants. Relative to their
smaller-brained cohorts, they either had a higher survival rate in infancy and
childhood, or a higher reproductive rate as adults, or both. Bigger-brained
infants by and large had bigger-brained parents, who by virtue of their more
complex brains may have been more adept at assuring the survival of their
offspring than parents with less complex brains. Bigger-brained children,
relative to those with smaller brains, may have been more adept at learning
what was required for survival, and hence may have had higher survival rates.
Thus, assuming no difference in number of offspring actually produced between bigger-brained and smaller-brained adults, the difference in either child
care or children's adeptness at learning led to a higher survival rate of offspring
for the bigger-brained individuals.

An evolutionary invention, however, is always a compromise, as we indicated in our discussion of man's increased body size. In order to produce adults
with bigger brains, bigger-brained infants had to be produced, and in order to
do the latter, women with larger birth canals had to be produced so that their
bigger-headed babies could be born. Larger birth canals require a pelvis which

is less conducive to fast running in humans, and hence is somewhat maladaptive. Another way to get bigger-brained babies is to bring them out while their brains are in a relatively immature state. But a baby with an immature brain is a relatively helpless baby who requires a tremendous amount of care from his mother. In any case, relative to the other primates, human babies have immature brains at birth. The adaptive advantages which went with large, complex brains must have been great, because both compromises—large birth canals and highly immature-brained babies—were produced during the course of man's evolution.

There is another compromise which went along with increased brain size —an increased period of infancy and childhood. It is assumed by anthropologists, based in part on the fossil record, but primarily on comparisons within the primate order, that during hominid evolution, rate of maturity consistently decreased (e.g., Hallowell 1963, Washburn and Moore 1974). The standard explanation of this slowing down in maturation is that an increased period of childhood was required because there was increasingly more to learn, i.e., *A. habilis* children had more to learn than *A. africanus* children, and so on up the ladder. A less subjective explanation is that the larger and more complex the adult brain is, the longer it takes to get all the connections made between the nerve cells of the brain. The human brain contains about ten billion neurons and each neuron may have more than 16,000 connections with other neurons (Cragg 1967). This is a phenomenal wiring job, and it takes a lot of time to complete. In order for an individual to take on an adult role in society, he has to have all the required anatomical equipment. Thus, evolutionary processes operated to delay sexual maturity until the wiring of the brain was essentially completed.

There is no direct evidence to confirm the preceding argument that in hominid evolution *(A. africanus-H. sapiens)*, rate of sexual maturity was inversely related to adult brain size. Indirect support of this argument can be seen, however, when rate of maturation and adult brain size are compared across Catarrhini species. We assume that within the catarrhines, the time it takes to complete the wiring job of the brain is approximately proportional to the number of neurons (inferred from brain size) involved, and that this time determines the approximate amount of time it takes to reach sexual maturity. Support for this argument is given in Figure 16 on p. 95, in which adult brain size and age of puberty of each species are averaged across males and females. In general, males mature later, have bigger bodies, and bigger brains. As Figure 16 shows, species with larger brains generally take longer to reach puberty, although this relationship is not simple. The most interesting inconsistency involves the gibbons, whose rate of maturity is much slower than both the macaques, who have an equivalent brain size, and the Savanna baboons, who have larger brains. This suggests that the brain size-rate of maturation relationship may be different for the hominoids and the Old World monkeys.

It can be stated from the fossil record that it took approximately three million years for the hominid brain to increase from about 400 c.c. to 1300 c.c. If the rate of maturation of *A. africanus* was about the same as that of the four living nonhuman hominoids shown in Figure 16, then it may be inferred that the pre-adolescent period increased five or six years in three million years. This is an average increase of less than one day per generation; hence, there was nothing dramatic in the short run about the progressive hominid delay in sexual maturity.

HUNTER-GATHERER ADAPTATIONS AND AN OVERVIEW OF MAN'S THREE BRAINS

As we stated in the previous chapter, hominid evolution is characterized by an initial descent from the trees to a ground-living, vegetarian mode of subsistence, then to an omnivorous subsistence with meat gotten partly by scavenging, then to an omnivorous subsistence with the meat of small animals gotten through killing with simple stone tools, and finally to an omnivorous subsistence with the meat of large animals obtained through cooperative hunting with sophisticated stone tools. The last phase is the time of man, the genus Homo, which lasted for approximately one million years.

There are at least three behavioral characteristics which distinguish the last phase of the hunter-gatherer adaptation from the adaptation of carnivorous

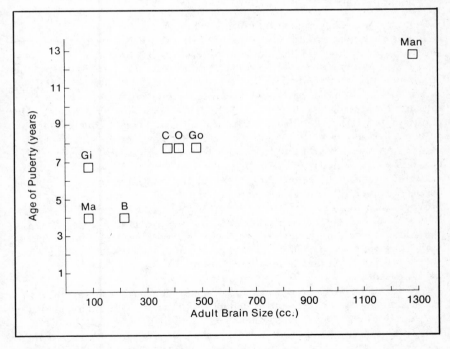

Figure 16

The relationship between brain size and age of puberty in selected Catarrhini: Gi = Gibbons; Ma = Macaques; B = Savanna Baboons; C = Chimpanzees; O = Orangutans; Go = Gorillas (From Campbell 1966, Harrison and Montagna 1969, Jay 1968, Jolly 1972, Tobias 1970).

pack-hunting animals such as wolves and dogs. First, unlike man, these carnivores are almost exclusively meateaters, which implies that the amount and type of subsistence-related information they must acquire is much more limited than that required by man. When man became a meateater, he didn't stop being a vegetable eater. Second, unlike man, these carnivores place great reliance on olfactory cues in acquiring spatial information. They know where they are in great part by the scents (information) they have placed on trails (Peters 1973). Man, on the other hand, relies on visually based representations or memories of the environment for knowing where he is and where he has been. What is on the road for wolves must be in the head for man. Finally, man makes and uses tools, whereas the pack-hunting carnivores don't. Sophisticated tool manufacture and tool use require the following psychological characteristics:

1. highly refined motor skills
2. knowledge of the appearance and function of particular tools
3. the ability to envision manufacturing possibilities from the raw material
4. the ability to instruct others and to be instructed in tool use and tool manufacture.

From the preceding description of the behavioral differences between carnivorous pack-hunters and human hunter-gatherers, it is safe to assume that there are substantial neuroanatomical differences between the two groups. Man's brain is not simply that of a pack-hunter who walks erect. Instead, he required a different kind of brain to process more and different kinds of information than that of pack-hunters. An omnivorous diet and tool manufacture and tool use also distinguish man from the other advanced primates. In addition, unlike the other primates, man evolved as a cooperative hunter and gatherer. This is not to imply that other primates never eat meat, never make and use tools, or never hunt cooperatively, but rather that these behavioral characteristics do not play more than a very minor role in their adaptation. Thus, it is safe to assume that there are substantial neuroanatomical differences between man and the other primates.

What do the fossil record and comparative neuroanatomy show? Basically, both methods of comparison confirm the preceding assumptions. The way these assumptions are confirmed, however, is very interesting. In the discussion which follows, some of the neuroanatomical differences between man and the carnivores and other primates will be briefly discussed, and then brain evolution and brain function will be treated more fully.

As with the changes produced in other anatomical structures, evolutionary processes acted in a conservative manner on the brain—the phylogenetically old structures were modified to some extent, and phylogenetically new neural structures were added to the old. Paul MacLean (1962, 1970, 1973), one of the leading students of the evolution of the brain, has conceptualized this "adding on" process as shown in Figure 17 on p. 97. In this conception, the brain of higher mammals is viewed as consisting of three interconnected, basic components: a reptilian brain, an old mammalian brain or limbic system, and a new mammalian brain or neocortex. The reptilian brain is phylogenetically the oldest, dating back to the evolution of the reptiles, and it provides the basic foundation for the nervous system. Apart from the relative size of the various substructures of this brain, there is little distinction between the reptilian brains of the advanced mammals. In terms of function, this brain component is largely involved with alertness, consciousness (when connections are severed between the reptilian brain and the more recent "brains," the individual is not killed, but becomes permanently unconscious), with the crude processing of sensory inputs and motor outputs, and with a variety of vegetative functions such as digestion, breathing, and body metabolism.

Evolution of the early placental mammals about 100 million years ago brought about the addition of a second brain, the limbic system. This second brain added on new sensory and motor organizations and exerted certain controls over the first brain. The limbic system is found in the great limbic lobe which surrounds the brain stem. It contains a true cortex—the old cortex or

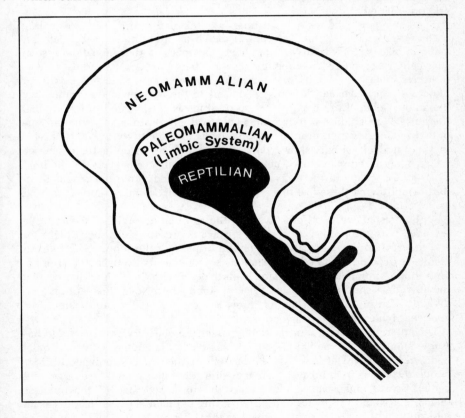

Figure 17

Diagram of hierarchic organization of three basic brain types, which, in the evolution of the mammalian forebrain, become part of man's inheritance. Each type has distinctive structural and chemical features. Man's counterpart of the paleomammalian brain comprises the so-called limbic system which has been found to play an important role in emotional behavior (From MacLean 1967).

cingulate gyrus. Like the reptilian brain, but unlike the new mammalian brain, the limbic system is a stable evolutionary feature, as shown in Figure 18 on p. 99. As you can see in Figure 19 on p. 100, it is depicted as a structurally and functionally integrated system with three main subdivisions: the amygdala division, the septum division, and the anterior thalamus division (MacLean 1962, 1970). These subdivisions are connected to each other, to the cingulate gyrus, and to another subcortical structure, the hippocampus. The amygdala and septum divisions in primates have been relatively stable phylogenetically, whereas the thalamic division and the hippocampus have become progressively larger in primate evolution, reaching their maximal size in man. All three subdivisions of the limbic system, the cingulate gyrus, and the hippocampus have connections with the hypothalamus, a structure which has major importance in integrating behavior systems involved in self-preservation and procreation.

The amygdala subdivision is primarily concerned with behaviors dealing with self-preservation, such as eating, searching, fighting, and self-defense. Wild monkeys, for example, who have had part of the amygdala system surgically removed become docile after the operation, pick up and eat objects indiscriminately, and fail to defend themselves when attacked. Dominant monkeys who have had this operation fall to the bottom of the dominance hierarchy. Some of these experimental findings are duplicated in the clinical literature. Case studies of individuals with epileptic lesions (a particular type of brain damage which produces spontaneous nerve activity or "discharges") in the amygdala subdivision report feelings during an epileptic discharge which include hunger, thirst, nausea, cold, warmth, terror, fear, foreboding, and sadness. Some of the automatisms (uncontrolled, often unconscious activities) following these feelings are eating, drinking, running, and screaming as if afraid.

As contrasted with self-preservation, the septum subdivision seems to be involved with the preservation of the species in areas such as social behavior and procreation. In male cats, stimulation of parts of the septum subdivision results in grooming and sexual reactions seen in courtship behavior. In monkeys, stimulation in this subdivision leads to penile erection. It is of interest that the amygdala subdivision seems to exert some control over the septum subdivision, for in the experiments in which the amygdala subdivision was removed, hypersexuality was one result.

The anterior thalamic subdivision bypasses the olfactory apparatus and has connections, via the medial dorsal nucleus of the thalamus, with the frontal neocortex areas. Electrical stimulation within this third subdivision elicits sexual responses in monkeys, such as penile erection, seminal discharge, and genital scratching. MacLean interprets the increased size of the anterior thalamic system in primates and its bypassing of the olfactory apparatus as an indication that in social-sexual behavior, there has been an evolutionary shift in emphasis from olfactory to visual influences.

What has thus far been described is an evolutionarily stable, structurally and functionally integrated system which mediates oral, genital, and aggressive behavior. MacLean and others, e.g., Magoun (1969), have spoken of this system

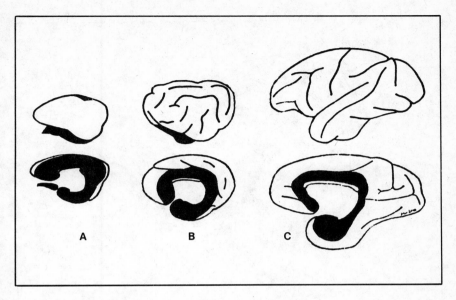

Figure 18

Lateral and medial views of brains of rabbit (A), cat (B), and monkey (C) drawn roughly to scale. This figure illustrates that the limbic lobe (dark shading in medial view) is found as a common denominator of the cerebrum throughout the mammalian series. Surrounding the brainstem, the limbic lobe contains most of the cortex corresponding to that of the paleomammalian brain. The greater part of the neocortex, which mushrooms late in evolution, occupies the lateral surface (From MacLean 1954, 1967).

as the emotional and motivational system. It is the neuroanatomical system involved with reward and punishment. Other functions of the limbic system which have been particularly important in human evolution are those involved with empathy, memory, and emotional language. These will be discussed in the next section of the chapter.

The third brain, the new mammalian brain or neocortex, is a late development in placental mammals which reaches its maximum size in the primates. Analogous to the limbic system, the neocortex added on new sensory and motor organizations and exerted certain controls over the second brain. Figure 20 on p. 101 represents the lateral view of one cerebral hemisphere of the human neocortex (the one involved with language) with some of the major areas and "landmarks" noted. In appearance, it is relatively the same as that of the higher primates. All of the major areas of the neocortex have connections with lower structures in the brain and connections with each other. Although the brain underwent marked growth from the australopithecines to *Homo sapiens*, the growth was much greater in the neocortex than in the older parts of the brain. The neuropsychological evidence suggests that the functioning of the human brain also became increasingly differentiated or specialized during the course of evolution (Diamond and Hall 1969, Herrick 1956, MacLean 1970).

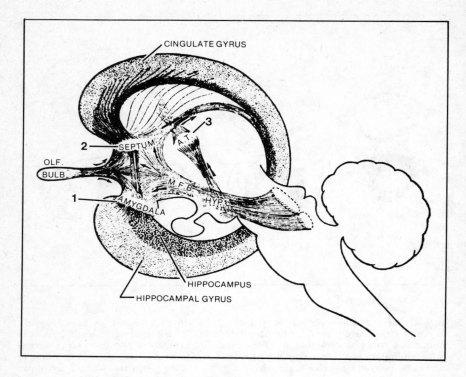

Figure 19

The limbic system comprises the limbic cortex and structures of the brainstem with which it has primary connections. This diagram shows the ring of limbic cortex in light and dark stipple and focuses on three pathways (1, 2, and 3) that link three main subdivisions of the limbic system. See text for functional significance. Abbreviations: A. T., anterior thalamic nuclei; HYP, hypothalamus; M.F.B., medial forebrain bundle; OLF, olfactory (From MacLean 1967).

The discussion which follows is based primarily on the research of Critchley (1953), Geschwind (1972), Milner (1970), Penfield and Roberts (1959), and Sperry (1972). In general, primate brain sensory inputs are transmitted from the receptors through the thalamus to the "primary projection" areas (this is not true for smell). The primary projection area for vision is in the occipital lobe (noted in Figure 20 on p. 101 as "visual sensory"); the primary projection area for touch, proprioception, muscle sense, and skin sensation is in the parietal lobe immediately adjacent to the central sulcus; the primary projection area for audition is in the temporal lobe; the olfactory bulbs (not shown) are the primary projection areas for smell; and the primary projection area for taste is immediately below those for touch and skin sensation in the parietal lobe. Stimulation in these areas produces sensations which correspond to the sensory modality projected there, and damage to these areas produces losses in the corresponding sensory modality. For example, damage to the auditory area

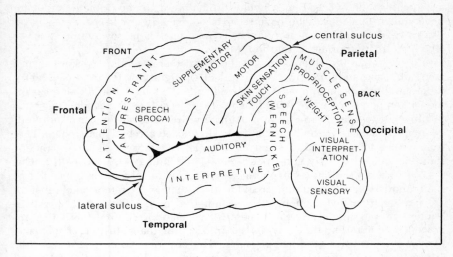

Figure 20

The left (dominant) hemisphere of man showing various areas. Complex memories ("flashbacks") are evoked by electrical stimulation of the area marked "interpretative." There are two areas concerned with speech, one more anterior (Broca's area) and the other lying between the areas connected with the main receptor systems (Wernicke's area) (From J. Z. Young 1971).

impairs the ability to make timbre discriminations, to localize sounds, and to discriminate sequences of notes. As another example, when the visual area is destroyed, form or pattern perception is lost.

The area immediately in front of the central sulcus is the primary motor area (noted in Figure 20 as "motor"). This area has been very carefully mapped in man and other primates, and its relationships to specific muscle groups are highly localized. Electrical stimulation in this area produces specific movements, and damage there produces specific paralyses. The area immediately in front of it, the "supplementary motor" area, is not as highly localized. It is apparently involved, however, with the inhibition and coordination of motor acts (Penfield and Roberts 1959, Milner 1970).

Speech and language areas are located in the left cerebral hemisphere in right-handed individuals, noted in Figure 20 as Wernicke's area and Broca's area. These will be discussed further in a subsequent section of this chapter. The remaining areas in all four lobes are called either interpretive areas or association areas. Their primary functions are to elaborate either sensory or motor information and to coordinate information received or initiated in the various substructures of the brain. Although in proportion to the rest of the cortex, the association and interpretive areas are very large, relatively little localization of function can be attributed to them. It is known, however, that important aspects of spatial orientation, spatial localization, and spatial conceptualization are generally localized in the parietal lobes (Critchley 1953). The frontal lobes appear to be involved with attention and the representation and organization of acts. Experiments with both nonhuman primates and man have shown that those who have received damage in the frontal lobes have difficulty in dropping inappropriate behavior, i.e., they persevere in responses which are inappropriate to solution (Milner 1970).

In man, unlike the other primates, the two cerebral hemispheres are asymmetrical in size and function (Geschwind 1972), signifying the increased brain differentiation just mentioned. Geschwind and others have found that areas in the left temporal lobe underlying language are larger than corresponding areas in the right temporal lobe. In approximately ninety-seven out of a hundred people, language functioning is controlled by the left cerebral hemisphere. The right cerebral hemisphere has only a minimal capacity for language understanding, and apparently none for speech (Geschwind 1972, Sperry 1972). On the other hand, the right hemisphere is more highly developed than the left for spatial understanding and nonverbal ideation, such as the retention of music.

To summarize this section, man's adaptation or design as a cooperative hunter of large animals and a gatherer of vegetation required the ability to process both more and different kinds of information than either other cooperative hunting species or other primates. The chief anatomical structure for information processing is the brain, and it was assumed that the different information requirements would be reflected there. As with other anatomical structures, however, brain evolution was a conservative process. The brains of all the recent mammals, including pack-hunting carnivores and primates, are built on the same plan consisting of three major interconnected components: a reptilian brain, an old mammalian brain (the limbic system), and a new mammalian brain (the neocortex). The first two brains are very stable in an evolutionary sense, but the neocortex underwent tremendous changes in primate evolution in general, and man's evolution in particular. In the next two sections, the roles of the limbic system and the neocortex in man's hunter-gatherer adaptation will be explored in more depth.

THE LIMBIC SYSTEM

Studies of comparative neuroanatomy (e.g., MacLean 1973, Stephan and Andy 1970, Stephan 1972) indicate that as one moves from the basal insectivores to the prosimians to the anthropoids in primate evolution, the olfactory bulbs, which underlie smell, show a progressive decrease in relative size, and the hippocampus and thalamus show a progressive increase in relative size. These changes are most marked in man. The size decrease in the olfactory bulbs had particular significance for man because alternative structures of the brain had to be called upon to handle the information which, in the basal insectivores and pack-hunting carnivores, was mediated by the sense of smell. In the latter animals, the sense of smell plays an important part in social interactions between members of the species, and as we have already mentioned, with memory. Two of the structures in the limbic system intimately involved with primate social interactions and memory are the thalamus and the hippocampus. Two aspects of social interaction—emotional language and empathy—and one aspect of memory—internal inhibition—will be discussed in this section. In the next section another aspect of memory will be taken up—memory consolidation.

When the primates ascended into the trees, they became increasingly depen-dent on audition (and vision) as a source of communication. Each species developed a repertoire of sounds which communicated information about the environment and the emotional state of individual members. In man, an additional source of auditory communication evolved—language—along with new neocortical structures to support it. Man never lost the old neuroanatomi-cal structures, however, but intermeshed the old with the new. The old neuroanatomical structures are part of the limbic system. Robinson (1972) has summarized the research dealing with these structures.

When rhesus and squirrel monkeys (Old World and New World species, respectively) are electrically stimulated in a variety of regions in the limbic system, they vocalize. These vocalizations are essentially identical to those that the monkeys normally emit, as determined by sound analysis, the responses of other monkeys, and the impressions of human observers. Moreover, there are no sounds emitted naturally that are not emitted after electrical stimulation. Attempts to evoke sounds or inhibit sounds by stimulating areas of the monkey brain which roughly correspond to the human neocortical areas involved with language production have met without success. On the other hand, electrical stimulation of the human limbic system does produce vocalization analogous to that of the monkey—largely emotional sounds. Robinson suggests that human speech is mediated by two systems: the limbic system which governs the emotional aspects of speech, and the neocortical system which primarily governs the linguistic aspects of speech. Both systems normally work together, hence speech reflects both emotional and linguistic content.

We will now turn to another aspect of social interaction—empathy. As MacLean (1970, 1973) has pointed out, the thalamus subdivision of the limbic system, which bypasses the olfactory bulbs and has connections with the prefrontal cortex, showed great evolutionary change in the primates, and especially in man. The thalamus subdivision which receives extensive inputs of visual information is intimately involved with socio-sexual behavior. MacLean and his colleagues have shown with squirrel monkeys, for example, that surgical destruction of parts of this system produce marked changes in visually based genital displays. The bypassing of the olfactory bulbs and the strong connec-tions with the prefrontal cortex, which is involved with planning and foresight, suggest to MacLean that the thalamic subdivision plays an important role in planning for one's own social activities and the activities of others. This ability to plan for others requires empathy, or the capacity to take the view of another. MacLean argues that underlying this capacity is our ability to see others with feeling, or to "transform the cold light with which we see into the warm light with which we feel." Thus, empathy involves a combination of our feeling system, the limbic system, and our planning and foresight system—the pre-frontal cortex. It will be argued in a later chapter that the evolution of this ability—empathy—was crucial to the success of man's adaptation as a hunter-gatherer.

Now we turn to a discussion of the role of the hippocampus in the develop-ment of internal inhibition. We rely primarily on the excellent summaries of this research by Douglas (1967) and Kimble (1968). Internal inhibition is a concept first coined by Pavlov (1927), which refers to a brain process which actively suppresses or inhibits behavior. The process is activated and strengthened by nonreinforcement, i.e., the withholding of unconditioned stimuli or, in everyday parlance, rewards or punishments. In the typical Pavlovian situation, an animal is conditioned to salivate to a tone by presenting the tone paired with food a number of times. Following the stable anticipatory (to the food) salivation to the tone, the food is withheld, i.e., the tone is nonreinforced. Eventually the animal stops salivating to the tone. When reinforcement is reintroduced, it is more difficult to condition the animal than it was originally, which is evidence for the action of internal inhibition.

Another example of the action of internal inhibition is the phenomenon of habituation. When a novel stimulus is presented to an individual without reinforcement, a whole set of responses are activated which orient the individual to the stimulus. When the stimulus is repeatedly presented, these responses eventually drop out and become suppressed, i.e., habituated. Another example of internal inhibition is seen in the passive avoidance conditioning procedure. Food is placed in a given location and a hungry animal is repeatedly given access to it. Then the location is electrified so that the animal receives a shock if he goes to that place. Eventually the animal learns to avoid that location, i.e., he builds up internal inhibition.

In these and a number of other experimental paradigms, internal inhibition is seen to operate on the suppression of learned and unlearned responses which are made in response to certain stimuli or situations. In a sense, when internal inhibition doesn't operate, the behavior perseveres. The adaptive function of internal inhibition prevents the individual from getting locked into situations where rewards are not forthcoming or where punishments are. The neuropsychological literature indicates that the hippocampus is the structure primarily involved with the development of internal inhibition. This research shows that when the hippocampus is surgically destroyed, internal inhibition either fails to develop, or develops very slowly. No other brain structures have been shown to have these effects in any consistent way.

This section may be summarized as follows. In primate evolution, the auditory modality became particularly important as a means of communicating emotional information. Experimental studies with monkeys and man indicate that the neuroanatomical structure which mediates the expression of this information is the limbic system. The two sub-structures of the limbic system which underwent the greatest growth in human evolution are the thalamus and the hippocampus. The former, through its connections with the prefrontal cortex, is involved with man's ability to empathize with others, and the latter structure is involved with development of an important aspect of memory —internal inhibition.

THE NEOCORTEX

In this section we will discuss the role of the neocortex in relationship to four major behavioral aspects of the hunter-gatherer adaptation: motor skills, language, attention and memory, and spatial understanding. As we have indicated, the fossil record shows that man's brain approximately tripled in size from *A. africanus* to *H. sapiens,* and comparative neuroanatomical studies show that some of this growth occurred in structures of the limbic system. What about the neocortex? Not surprisingly, the growth there was phenomenal. Using the index of cephalization, Stephan and Andy (1970) found that relative to the basal insectivores, the prosimian neocortex increased on the average by a multiple of about 15; the anthropoid neocortex, including the apes but excluding *H. sapiens,* increased on the average by a multiple of about 40; and man's neocortex increased by a factor of 156. (Man's hippocampus, by comparison, increased by a factor of 4.) Given the fact that in man 99 percent of the cerebral hemispheres are comprised of the neocortex (Stephan, Bauchot, and Andy 1970), it is safe to conclude that the phenomenal growth in the hominid brain was primarily of the neocortex.

Given that the human neocortex expanded so greatly in evolution, the principle of proper mass tells us that it is important to determine which neocortical regions increased the most. By this principle, the functions associated with the regions which showed the greatest expansion, were increasingly important in human adaptation. Using the comparative neuroanatomical method in a study of the total surface area of the cerebral cortex (new and old cortex) in a series of primates from the macaques to man, Blinkov and Glezer (1958) reached the following conclusions. As one progresses in this series of primates:

1. the relative size of the frontal, temporal, and inferior parietal (the part involved with language) neocortex increases
2. the relative size of the primary motor area of the brain remains relatively constant; however, as Woolsey (1958) has shown, the regions underlying the production of speech (e.g., mouth, tongue, jaws) and those for the fingers and hand are proportionally much larger in man than in the other primates
3. the relative size of the occipital neocortex, which is essentially related to vision, and the old cortex associated with the limbic system decreases.

On the basis of an examination of other data which includes fossil endocasts, Holloway (1968) concludes, however, that man's cerebral cortex showed a relative increase in size only in the temporal and inferior parietal areas, and not in the frontal areas. Some of these relationships may be seen in Figure 21 on p. 106.

What is the significance of these findings? It turns out that the neocortical regions which showed the greatest change and growth in hominid evolution, as compared to the neocortex of other primates, are the regions involved with motor skills, language, attention and memory, and spatial understanding. (The relationship between the prefrontal cortex and empathy has already been discussed.)

As Luria (1970) has emphasized, any complex form of human behavior, such as voluntary movement, depends upon the activities of a number of regions in the brain. Luria's clinical research has dealt primarily with patients who have suffered some damage, usually caused by bullets, to various regions of the brain. By noting the relationship between the site of the brain damage and the nature of the psychological deficit produced, inferences can be made about normal functioning of the brain. Luria's conclusions about voluntary, skilled motor behavior can be summarized as follows. There are at least five neocortical regions involved (see Figure 20 on p. 101).

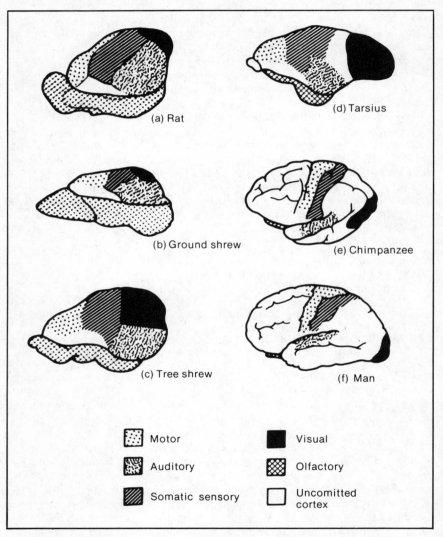

(a) Rat

(d) Tarsius

(b) Ground shrew

(e) Chimpanzee

(c) Tree shrew

(f) Man

Motor

Visual

Auditory

Olfactory

Somatic sensory

Uncomitted cortex

Figure 21

Mammalian brains, to show variations in the proportions devoted to different activities. The comparison can only be rough because important parts are often concealed. The area devoted to olfaction is much reduced in primates. The area marked "uncommitted cortex" is not related to particular sensory or motor functions. It includes the parietal association areas and much of the frontal and prefrontal lobes (From J. Z. Young 1971).

1. the primary motor area, which directs the activity of the particular muscle groups involved with a given movement
2. the proprioception and muscle sense areas, which continuously receive sensory feedback from the muscles and joints involved in the movement
3. an area surrounding the boundary of the parietal and occipital lobes, which is involved with the way the movement is organized in space
4. the supplementary motor area, which serves to link together the various components of a skilled act
5. the prefrontal area, which is involved with the planning and organization of movements.

When one of these areas is damaged, the individual loses part of his capacity for performing skilled motor activity, e.g., damage to the parietal-occipital area renders the individual unable to precisely locate his movements in space, although the component parts of the skill are left relatively intact. As you can see from Figure 21 and the preceding discussion, all of these regions underwent tremendous growth in hominid evolution.

Turning now to language and Figure 20 on p. 101, comparative neuroanatomy indicates that man evolved three new neocortical structures underlying language: Broca's area, Wernicke's area, and the angular gyrus (a portion of the neocortex at the border of the temporal, parietal, and occipital lobes, but not indicated in the figure). As we have noted before, these structures are localized for right-handed people in the left cerebral hemisphere, and they have a number of connections with the emotional language regions of the limbic system. On the basis of a rather extensive examination of the neurological literature, Geschwind (1972) presents the following model (which we have simplified) of language behavior for persons with normal hearing. Broca's Area functions to control the musculature involved in speech. A person with damage only in Broca's Area has difficulty talking, but has no impairment in understanding spoken or written language. Wernicke's Area is involved with both understanding spoken language and speaking meaningfully. A person with damage only to Wernicke's Area will fail to understand another's speech, and will be unable to generate meaningful speech. His ability to speak, however, will be unimpaired. The angular gyrus is involved with the visual-spatial aspects of speech, e.g., understanding and producing written language. Damage there will result in the inability to read or write with comprehension, but the person's ability to understand spoken language and speak will be unimpaired. If the connections between these areas are damaged, the language abilities become disconnected. For example, if the connections between Broca's Area and Wernicke's Area are destroyed, leaving the two areas intact, the person can talk clearly, but without meaning, and he can understand spoken language.

Let's turn now to the interrelated functions of attention and memory. Penfield (1959) has argued that little, if any, learning and memory can occur without attention. Attention involves a focusing of mental activity, which depends in great part on the nature of incoming information from the external world and the activity levels of reptilian brain and limbic system structures. Attention and habituation have a particularly close linkage—we stop attending to, or habituate to, incoming information once it loses its novelty and meaning.

A loss of novelty or meaning implies that a memory of the information has been built up and stored. As far as we can determine from the neurological literature, e.g., Penfield (1969), Pribram (1969), there is no single neocortical locus of attention; rather, neuroanatomical structures mediating attention seem to be widespread. On the other hand, two neuroanatomical structures—the hippocampus and the temporal neocortex—have been identified which mediate the consolidation of memory. Memory consolidation is the process by which temporary memories become more permanently stored.

Milner (1968, 1971) has summarized much of the neuropsychological research bearing on this issue, most of which deals with the performance of patients who have had one or more regions of their brains removed in an attempt to control epilepsy. Basically, the findings show that the left temporal neocortex and hippocampus play an important part in the learning and memory of verbal materials, but not in the learning and memory of visual materials or of music. The right temporal neocortex and hippocampus have the opposite effects. For example, patients whose right temporal lobe has been removed, thus eliminating the hippocampus and neocortex, have an extraordinarily difficult time recognizing photographs of faces they have recently seen. In short, they couldn't readily consolidate this visual information (Milner 1968). In one unfortunate case, both temporal lobes were removed, sparing the auditory and speech areas. This man has completely lost the ability to remember for more than a few minutes any new information received. His memory for events which occurred prior to this operation is apparently normal.

Finally, we turn to spatial understanding. Critchley (1953), Luria (1970), Sperry (1972), and others have shown that the parietal neocortex underlies spatial perception, orientation, and understanding. Sperry's work, in particular, has demonstrated that the right parietal lobe (the lobe not involved with speech) is superior to the left one in mediating these abilities. Spatial abilities are central to an extremely large number of human activities, e.g., skilled movements, writing, reading, finding one's way, remembering the locations of things, and no doubt they have been important in man's adaptation. An example of laboratory research dealing with this issue is that of Semmes, Weinstein, Ghent, and Teuber (1955). They asked patients with different types of traumatic brain injury and normal control subjects to follow routes indicated on maps. The subjects were brought into a room on which nine large red spots were placed on the floor, forming a 3 x 3 matrix. They were given a "map" which identified a particular path to be followed from one spot to the next, and so on. The number of errors they made in following each route were noted. The basic findings were that patients with parietal neocortex damage performed substantially lower than either the normal controls or patients with nonparietal damage, and no statistically reliable difference was found between the latter two groups.

This section may be summarized as follows. In the evolution of the human brain, the structures which underwent the greatest growth were those of the neocortex. Within the neocortex, the regions whose size increased the most· were the interpretive or association areas of the temporal, parietal, and frontal lobes. In addition, new structures underlying language appeared. The principle of proper mass implies that the functions which these regions mediate must have been progressively important in human evolution. Neuropsychological research indicates that the functions most intimately involved with these "new" regions are motor skills, language, attention and memory, and spatial understanding.

GROWTH AND MATURATION OF THE
HUMAN BRAIN AND NEOCORTEX

In Figure 22 on p. 110 the relative growth of the brain from birth to maturity is shown in terms of the percentage of postnatal growth occurring each year to age twenty. It is contrasted with growth curves for three other anatomical structures of the body. As you can see, relative to the body as a whole (noted as "general") and the reproductive organs, brain growth is extremely rapid, reaching ninety percent adult size by about age six. As we said in a previous chapter, growth and maturation are not synonymous; thus, the fact that the human brain is nearly fully grown at age six does not imply that it is functioning at ninety percent adult capacity at that time.

Blinkov and Glezer (1968), two leading students of the brain, point out that the relative rate of growth for three major subdivisions of the human brain—the brain stem, the cerebellum, and the cerebral hemispheres—is different during the period from birth to one year, but from age one to maturity, their relative increase in brain weight is approximately the same. In the cerebral cortex, which comprises ninety-nine percent of an adult human's cerebral hemispheres, the regions which underlie language (and the corresponding regions on the opposite hemisphere) grow by a factor of nine from birth to maturity; the frontal lobe grows by a factor of eight, the association areas in the temporal lobe by a factor of seven, and the primary projection areas for vision, audition, touch, proprioception, and the muscle sense (the somatosensory cortex) grow by a factor of five (Blinkov and Glezer 1968).

Conel (1939-67), whose work is summarized in eight volumes, studied the nerve cells in histological preparations of the brains of children aged from birth to six years old. He used nine criteria, e.g., cell differentiation, degree of myelination (this is related to how rapidly nerve impulses are transmitted), to assess the relative maturity of different regions of the cerebral cortex. Where Conel, Blinkov, and Glezer make parallel statements about a given region, they are in general agreement. The following is a highly abbreviated summary of Conel's findings (see Figures 20 and 21 on pp. 102 and 107 for identifying the various locations mentioned).

Frontal lobes   From birth to approximately fifteen months of age, the primary motor area is the most highly developed region of the cerebral cortex. This area continues to mature until the age of four, whereupon its growth tends to stabilize. Within the primary motor area, the functional regions corresponding to the hand, shoulder, arm, and trunk mature the fastest, followed by the regions corresponding to the head, and lastly by those regions corresponding to the lower extremities. The remaining regions of the frontal lobes continue to mature from birth to age six. The relative state of maturity of these regions is inversely related to distance from the primary motor area. Hence, the association areas are the last to reach maturity, and are not mature at age six.

Primary Projection Areas   This grouping includes the somatosensory cortex, the visual areas, and the auditory areas. From birth to one year, the somatosensory cortex is the most highly developed, followed by the visual areas and the auditory areas. From fifteen months to four years, the somatosensory cortex, the visual areas, and the primary motor areas are at approximately

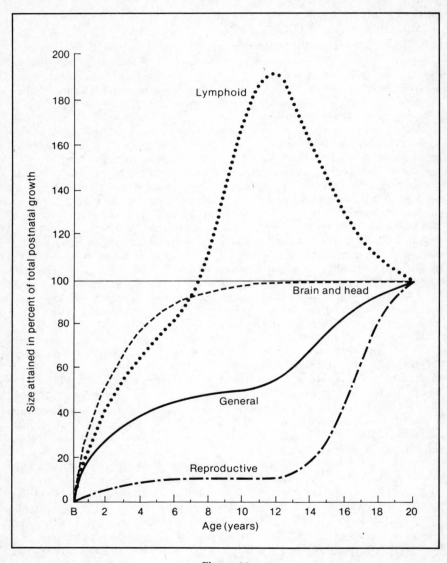

Figure 22

Growth curves of different parts of the body, plotted as percentage of total gain from birth to age 20 (From Tanner 1962).

the same level of maturity, all greater than the auditory area. From age four to six, all three primary projection areas continue to mature, and at age six all are at approximately the same level of maturity. Within the somatosensory cortex, the relative rate of development of the different functional regions corresponds to their counterparts in the primary motor area.

Association Areas   In general, throughout development the association areas closest to the primary projection areas are more mature than those further away, but less mature than the primary projection areas themselves. The association areas show continuous maturation during the period studied, i.e., birth to six years. The regions underlying language (and the corresponding regions in the other cerebral hemisphere) at the junction of the temporal, parietal, and occipital lobes show the slowest rate of maturation.

The preceding discussion indicates that the brain of the young infant is very undeveloped, but that it subsequently undergoes rapid growth and maturation. By the age of six, brain size is nearly ninety percent adult size. This rapid development reflects both increased maturation in each region of the brain, and increased functional connections between the various regions of the brain. Blinkov and Glezer suggest that most of the growth after age six is based on nutritional demands, as opposed to organizational changes, although Conel's work implies that organizational changes after age six may be substantial. The relative rate of maturation of the various regions of the cerebral cortex indicates that those underlying higher mental processes, including language, planning, empathy, spatial understanding, memory consolidation, and highly controlled skilled movements, lag considerably behind those regions underlying both the reception of stimulation and the initiation of simple movements.

SUMMARY

The data just presented suggest that the evolution of the human brain can be described as follows. First, the basic structures which evolved in the reptiles and early placentals were maintained and somewhat enlarged in the further adaptations of the hominid line. The maintenance of these structures in hominid evolution suggests that they are strongly canalized, and that some of the behaviors they mediate may also be strongly canalized. The increase in the size of the hippocampus and thalamus of the limbic system relative to those of other primates reflects an adaptational advance. We noted that the functioning of the hippocampus underlies both the reduction of maladaptive behavior perseverance through the development of internal inhibition, and memory consolidation. The thalamus is intimately involved with empathy.

Second, the human brain underwent marked growth from *A. africanus* to *H. sapiens*. This was interpreted as reflecting a great increase in neurons or nerve cells underlying information processing capacities. This view is supported by comparative neuroanatomical data, which indicate that the growth of the neocortex—the new mammalian brain—was almost explosive in man's evolution. Third, it was argued that this tremendous growth in the brain was the primary cause of a slower rate of sexual maturation. It was noted that there is a strong correspondence between adult brain size and age of sexual maturity in the Old World primates. Fourth, the relative growth of the neocortex in human evolution was apparently greatest in the temporal, parietal, and possibly frontal lobes. This differential growth is in the areas of the brain underlying language ability, nonverbal ideation, spatial understanding, memory consolidation, skilled movements, and planning abilities. Fifth, it was found that the neocortical areas which grew the most in the evolution of man's brain are approximately the areas which mature the slowest in human infants and children. Finally, the functioning of the brain became increasingly differentiated or specialized during hominid evolution. Among the primates, the human brain is the only one which is asymmetrical in size and functions. This specialization may allow for more optimal use of the brain.

Chapter 6

CATARRHINE SOCIAL ADAPTATIONS

OVERVIEW

Following are some of the major ideas discussed in the preceding chapters. Evolution is an experiment in design which operates on the epigenetic system of individuals of a deme. The design is coded in the genotype, but the "experiment" is carried out by the developing phenotype in a given sequence of environments. Successful designs lead to the production of individuals with high Darwinian fitness, and unsuccessful designs to individuals with low fitness. Owing to the fact that epigenetic systems have limited plasticity and are not readily susceptible to change, evolution is conservative, operating on the principle, "If it works, keep it if you can, modify it if you have to." Thus, in any evolutionary line, e.g., the catarrhines, there should be a high degree of phenotypic similarity between different species in that line. In the previous two chapters we saw this to be the case for the anatomical adaptations of the catarrhines—the Old World Monkeys, apes, and man.

One point emphasized in these chapters was that the primary reason for the evolution of any given catarrhine anatomical structure or set of structures was that they led to effective action in the environment. Stated another way, the phenotypic characteristics selected for in the catarrhines were behavioral, and the anatomical structures which mediated those behaviors are the structures seen in the paleoanthropological record. Anatomical structures which just "sit there" by and large have little survival or reproductive value. It was noted, however, that in order to infer how any anatomical structure had previously functioned, a comparative approach had to be taken in which the behavior of different living species was observed. For example, in the chapter on the brain, it was seen that the limbic system is a phylogenetically conservative set of

113

structures which mediate primate behaviors involved with self-preservation and preservation of the species.

Although in theory the comparative approach is applicable to the investigation of all relationships between anatomical structures and behavior, in actual fact the available data are limited in both number of primate species used and number of behaviors observed. For example, we know in a general way that the limbic system is involved with social relationships between members of the same species, but we know neither to what extent nor how it is involved in determining either the specific social organization of that species or the general social characteristics of a group of related species. Both Hamadryas baboons and the closely related Anubis baboons form very tight social units, but those of the former are single male "harems," and those of the latter are multi-male, multi-female groups. Although it is assumed that neuroanatomical similarities underlie the social cohesiveness common to both species, and that neuroanatomical differences underlie the behavioral differences, no one has demonstrated (or even attempted to demonstrate) what these neuroanatomical similarities and differences are.

Observations by a large number of anthropologists and primatologists (individuals who study nonhuman primates) have indicated that the primates are intensely social animals, and they have argued that in order to understand a major component of human evolution—the primate design—the primate social adaptations must be understood. In the present chapter we attempt to gain such an understanding by using the comparative method. In this method, a set of catarrhine species, including man, is selected, and common elements of their social adaptations are identified. It is assumed that these common elements comprise part of the conservative aspects of man's evolutionary design. These social adaptations are indirectly linked to the evolutionary record and to anatomy. (We have already shown the evolutionary and anatomical connections between these species.) Owing to the fact that there is no paleoanthropological record of social adaptations, nor are there data directly relating particular anatomical structures to particular catarrhine social adaptations, no firm statements can be made about when the catarrhine social adaptations emerged.

CANALIZATION OF BEHAVIOR AND LEARNING

Canalization is one of the most fundamental concepts discussed in this book. It has been described as a set of processes of the epigenetic system which ensures that development will follow certain paths or chreods. Thus, canalization produces phenotypic constancies in a species. Certain characteristics may be heavily canalized, i.e., very resistant to environmental or genetic stresses, others moderately canalized, and still other characteristics weakly canalized. Presumably characteristics which have high adaptive value for a species are heavily canalized; however, there is no research bearing on this issue. Moreover, although the behaviors of a species have been described as being central to their adaptation, there has been no canalization research dealing with behavior. All that exists in the research literature is a large number of studies dealing with a small number of apparently insignificant anatomical characteristics.

Despite this lack of data dealing with the canalization of behavior, we will assume from now on that where behavioral constancies exist within a species, those behaviors are canalized. Why make this assumption? It makes theoretical sense—based on what is known about evolutionary processes and epigenetic systems, it couldn't be otherwise. It is well to repeat our quotation from Lorenz (1972) on this point. He says:

> Ethology has . . . demonstrat(ed) irrefutably that all behavior, exactly like all bodily structure, can develop in the ontogeny of the individual only along the lines and within the possibilities of species—specific programs which have been mapped out in the phylogeny and laid down in the code of the genome.*

It should be pointed out, however, that it would be difficult to argue for the existence of canalization of behavior if there were no underlying neuroanatomical constancies. The structures of the brain mediate behavior, and these structures were "designed" to mediate particular kinds of behavior in particular environments, i.e., those in which the species evolved and adapted. The demonstration of these neuroanatomical constancies within the human species, and those between humans and other primates, has already been accomplished in our sections on human embryology and paleoanthropology.

When we discuss canalization of behavior, just as when we discussed canalization of anatomical structures, we are not implying that the behavior (or anatomical structures) will be developed or acquired no matter what happens. Rather, if the individual develops in environments which are in the normal range for his species, if he has had experiences typical for his species, then the behavior will be acquired. In principle, this is no different from the acquisition of anatomical characteristics as discussed in the section on human embryology, e.g., depending upon the sequence of environments experienced by embryonic ectoderm, it will be induced to develop into either the lens of an eye, the neural tube, or simple skin.

Given that canalized behaviors are acquired as a function of experience, what is the relationship between canalization of behavior and learning? Learning was earlier defined as a set of functions or processes which progressively organize the individual's future sensory experiences or motor activities, or both. These functions are set into motion when the individual interacts with his environment, enabling the individual to better coordinate his behavior with the environment. By this definition, all canalized behaviors are learned, but not all learned behaviors are canalized. That is, if the behavior is inevitably acquired by normal individuals raised in environments normal for the species, then it is canalized, e.g., learning to speak a language; but if it is not inevitably learned, e.g., playing the piano, then it is not canalized.

---

*Konrad Z. Lorenz, "The Enmity Between Generations and Its Probable Ethological Causes," in *Play and Development*, ed. M. W. Piers (New York: W. W. Norton, 1972), p. 65.

Three independent groups of researchers using different terminology have reached similar conclusions concerning the relationship between phylogeny and the acquisition of behavior. They are: a group of ethologists interested in the study of instincts, e.g., Hinde (1966), Bowlby (1969); a group of anthropologists interested in social learning of primates, e.g., Hall (1968), Washburn and Hamburg (1965); and a group of experimental psychologists interested in conditioning of "lower" mammals, e.g., Garcia and Koelling (1966), Rozin and Kalat (1971), and Seligman (1970). Bowlby and Hinde distinguish between behavior which is "environmentally stable" and that which is "environmentally labile." A behavior which is environmentally stable—instinctive behavior—is acquired behavior influenced little by variations in environments which are in the normal range of a species, e.g., attachment behavior in primates. Noninstinctive behavior—environmentally labile behavior—does vary with normal variations in the environment, e.g., piano playing. Instinctive behavior is not necessarily the same stereotyped behavior for all members of a given species; rather, it is behavior which is somewhat idiosyncratic from individual to individual. However, the behavior follows some pattern which can be clearly discerned, and in a majority of cases it leads to a result which is beneficial to the individual or to the species.

Washburn and Hamburg's (1965) position is similar, and is stated as follows:

What is inherited is ease of learning rather than fixed instinctive patterns. The species easily, almost inevitably, learns the essential behaviors for its survival. So, although it is true that monkeys learn to be social, they are so constructed that under normal circumstances this learning always takes place. Similarly human beings learn to talk, but they inherit structures that make this inevitable, except under the most peculiar circumstances.*

What distinguishes canalized from noncanalized acquired behavior, then, is *not* whether it is learned or unlearned, but rather the ease and inevitability with which it is learned.

Finally, we briefly consider the views of the experimental psychologists. The focus of their research has been on species-specific predispositions to learn to associate particular kinds of stimuli with particular kinds of responses. Garcia and Koelling (1966) have written about this predisposition as "belongingness," and Seligman (1970) as "preparedness." That is, for a given species, it is relatively easy to train individuals to make particular responses to certain stimuli (the stimuli and responses "belong" together, or the species is "prepared" to form the connections), but it is relatively difficult to train individuals to make those particular responses to certain other stimuli.

One of the classic experiments is that of Garcia and Koelling. In their experiment, rats were given an opportunity to drink saccharine-flavored water from a drinking tube. Whenever they drank this water, bright lights flashed and a loud noise sounded. During these sessions, the rats were also X-irradiated.

---

* S. L. Washburn and D. A. Hamburg, "The Study of Primate Behavior," in *Primate Behavior: Field Studies of Monkeys and Apes*, ed. I. De Vore (New York: Holt, Rinehart and Winston, 1965), pp. 5–6.

This makes rats sick, but typically the illness does not set in for at least one hour after the radiation. In Pavlovian terms, the saccharine-tasting water, the bright lights, and the loud noise were conditioned stimuli, and the nausea produced by the X-irradiation was the unconditioned response. Following the experimental session, the animals were tested for their aversion to saccharine, bright lights, and noise. Garcia and Koelling found that the rats had acquired an aversion to the saccharine, but *not* to the bright lights and noise. Thus, saccharine taste and nausea "belonged" together, whereas bright lights, noise, and nausea did not.

In a second experiment using rats as subjects, Garcia and Koelling paired bright lights, noisy sounds, and saccharine-tasting water with electric shock to the feet. In this experiment, the rats acquired an aversion to the bright lights and loud noise, but *not* to the saccharine-tasting water. Thus, bright lights, noise, and shock-induced pain belonged together, whereas saccharine and pain did not.

One final example from the primatology literature should help sharpen the distinction between canalized and noncanalized behavior. As we mentioned earlier, the Hamadryas and Anubis baboons are closely related species with different social organizations—the Hamadryas invariably form one-male harems (see Figure 23 on p. 118), and the Anubis invariably form multi-male, multi-female groups. The male Hamadryas keeps his females in close proximity by giving any straying female a light bite on the neck, which produces some pain but inflicts essentially no damage. When the female is bitten, she immediately rushes back to join the other members of the harem. There is no comparable behavior in Anubis groups. Kummer (1971) introduced some Anubis females into Hamadryas groups, and they were immediately "claimed" by males and coerced into harems. The Anubis females eventually learned to stay close to the males in order to avoid being bitten. However, the frequency with which they strayed from the males was much greater than that seen in Hamadryas females. Thus, what is readily, inevitably, and strongly learned by Hamadryas females, i.e., canalized, can be learned by Anubis females, but in the Anubis it is not canalized.

WHICH PRIMATES TO COMPARE?

The focus of this chapter is identification of those aspects of man's primate heritage which deal with his social adaptations. The initial problem we face in attempting to do this involves the question, which nonhuman primates should be compared to man? Four criteria have been taken into consideration in answering this question:

1. degree of neuroanatomical similarity
2. evolutionary distance between the species, i.e., time separating their divergence from a common ancestor
3. similarity of their adaptive environments
4. similarity of the environments in which the behaviors are observed.

Regarding the first of these criteria, the closer the resemblance of nonhuman and human primate brains, the greater is the likelihood of common canalized

Figure 23

Artificial feeding of a hamadryas troop leads first to crowding; this, in turn, makes the males uncertain about the integrity of their harems. While rival males threaten each other, their females line up in the "attach shadows" of their respective owners (From Kummer 1971).

behavior characteristics. We have seen that the closest similarity in brain size, and presumably structure, is between man and the chimpanzees, gorillas, and orangutans. Regarding the second criterion, we have seen that man is more closely related to the gorillas and chimpanzees than he is to any of the other primates. Regarding the third, however, man is closely allied to primates who evolved as terrestrial gatherers, such as baboons, gorillas, and macaques. The chimpanzee, although terrestrial, is a gatherer of arboreal fruits, and the orangutan is essentially an arboreal animal. Environment determines the selection pressures exerted on a developing species, and it must be assumed that closely related species who have undergone similar selection pressures should develop similar modes of adaptation. The fourth criterion indicates that we should compare human hunter-gatherers living in their natural habitat with nonhuman primates living in their natural habitat. Thus, people living in cities or farms should not be compared with nonhuman primates living in the wild, nor should nonhuman primates living in cages be compared with human hunter-gatherers. (There is some question about the comparability of people in cities and primates in zoos, but we won't be dealing with it here.)

These criteria indicate that comparisons should be made among the following catarrhine species: man, gorillas, chimpanzees, baboons, and macaques.

These species and man evolved in the warm zones of Africa, and in all cases but man the members of these species continue to live in warm zones, i.e., roughly between the Tropic of Capricorn and the Tropic of Cancer.

GENERAL CHARACTERISTICS OF SELECTED CATARRHINES

The primary catarrhine adaptation is for life as a member of a group. These species have evolved so that the group provides the framework for (1) subsistence activities, (2) protection, (3) reproduction, and (4) socialization of the young. In each of these species there is a nearly continuous association of members of all ages and both sexes throughout the lifetime of each individual. In all cases the offspring are typically born singly and are relatively helpless at birth, and they are highly dependent on the adults for a considerable period thereafter. Socialization starts shortly after birth. If the social development of certain maturing members of the group is abnormal, then as adults they will not be able to contribute to the four vital functions of the social group just mentioned. Natural selection has operated and continues to operate in such a way that individuals who are appropriately socially developed contribute to all four vital functions of the group, and those who are not appropriately socially developed become peripheral members of the group. This is a negative feedback system involving genes and behaviors. In a stable environment, animals who have a genetic structure such that their social development will be normal develop into normal individuals and reproduce, thus continuing their genes in the population gene distribution. Those whose genetic structure is such that they do not readily develop into normal adults reproduce less or do not reproduce at all, and hence their genes are diminished in the gene distribution.

There is another major aspect of catarrhine social adaptations common to all these species, reaching its maximum importance in man—the formation of culture or tradition. The essence of tradition is the acquisition of new behaviors (or knowledge) which is transmitted across generations. Thus the young of each generation can build their adaptations on what was acquired in previous generations. Primatologists have only recently begun to look at this phenomenon, but those who have looked have clearly seen it, e.g., Kawai (1965), Kummer (1971). In order to study the formation of tradition, the group must be observed for more than one generation; however, most studies of primates in the wild have been carried out for less than two years. Kawai's study is one of the exceptions. In 1952 at the Japan Monkey Center, a new food was introduced to the Japanese macaques (*Macaca fuscata*)—sweet potatoes. They were thrown on the sandy beach near the forest where the monkeys normally foraged. Although the potatoes were appealing food, the sand which stuck to them was not. About a year after this new food was introduced, one of the two year old females was seen carrying a sandy sweet potato to the water, washing off the sand in the water, and then eating the potato. The habit gradually spread throughout the group over a number of years (the adult males were the last to adopt the habit), and at the present time the potato-washing tradition is a well-established part of this culture, including socialization of infants by their mothers.

There are several common characteristics in the social organization of these selected catarrhines, including man. First, all the species form into subsistence groups, i.e., groups which hunt and/or gather together and whose members are well-known to each other. The size of the basic subsistence group and the population density varies both across and within a species, depending on the relative availability of food and the amount required for each individual in the group. In general, the population density is higher for the smaller species, which require less food than the larger ones, and is higher in the forests than in the plains. Table 5 shows the typical subsistence group sizes, population densities, and habitats for our selected species.

The two baboon species identified are two of the most widely studied baboon species, and in terms of their social behavior, two of the most interesting. For convenience, all of the Macaca species have been grouped together. The first column, Mean Subsistence Group Size, refers to the following: for man, the average number of men, women, and children in a variety of habitats who form a hunter-gatherer grouping; for the gorilla, chimpanzee, savanna baboon, and macaques, the number of animals who are apparently recognizable to each other and who utilize the food resources in a given area in common; and for the hamadryas baboon, the average size of the social group which maintains a close proximity to each other while gathering food. For the hamadryas baboon, many subsistence groups occupy a given home range and utilize the resources in common. The characteristics of the social organization of these groups will be discussed in Table 6 on p. 122. The next column, Population Density, is self-explanatory. In general, when a given species occupies a forest area, the population density will be higher than when that same species occupies a savanna or desert area. The last column, Habitat, indicates that with the

Table 5

Some Catarrhine Population and Habitat Characteristics

	Mean Subsistence Group Size	Population Density: Number of Individuals Per Square Mile	Habitat
Man (Homo sapiens)	25	1.0	Terrestrial: Varied
Gorilla (Gorilla gorilla)	13	3	Terrestrial: Forest
Chimpanzee (Pan troglodytes)	60	21 (Forest)	Terristrial - Arboreal: Forest
Savanna Baboon (Papio cynocephalus)	40	20	Terrestrial: Forest, Savanna
Hamadryas Baboon (Papio hamadryas)	5	6	Terrestrial: Desert, Savanna
Macaques (Macaca)	30	450 (Forest)	Terrestrial: Varied

Source: Alison Jolly, *The Evolution of Primate Behavior* (New York: The MacMillan Company, 1972), Table 12.

exception of the chimpanzee, all of the species mentioned are terrestrial as opposed to arboreal. This column further indicates that the typical environment of the gorilla and chimpanzee species is the forest; whereas for the baboon, the macaques, and man, the range of environments is extremely varied. In the cases of the baboons and macaques, unlike that of man, the exploitation of new environments has led to the evolution of new species within those genera.

A second common feature is that all these catarrhine species subsist primarily on fruits or other vegetation (this statement does not apply to hunter-gatherers living in temperate or cold zones). Most of the catarrhines will periodically eat insects, and the baboons and chimpanzees have been observed capturing and eating meat; but in all cases, meat eating plays a small part in their diet. For hunter-gatherers in warm zones, meat eating is a crucial part of the diet, but accounts for only about twenty percent of the caloric intake (Lee and DeVore 1968).

A third common feature is that all the groups are seminomadic and nonterritorial. They are seminomadic in the sense that they stay in a "home range" which they exploit for food and protection from predators, but they build no permanent sleeping sites within it. They may return to particular sleeping cliffs, trees, or shelters several nights or weeks in a row, but they invariably move on to another location within the home range. They are nonterritorial in the sense that they do not defend the boundaries of their home range against nongroup members of the same species. When different groups meet at their common boundary, they either ignore one another or move away from one another. Fighting between different groups is rare (Jay 1968, Kummer 1971). The gibbons, who are not in our selected species, are apparently one of the few territorial anthropoids.

A fourth common feature is that in all these species the core of the social unit is the mother-infant dyad. As we have noted, infants are born singly and are relatively helpless at birth. They are carried by their mothers throughout much of the infancy stage of development, and during this time are rarely out of sight of their mothers. In all these species, the mother-infant dyad is one of the group's centers of attention, especially for childless females. In some catarrhine species, the mother readily allows others to hold her infant, e.g., humans and chimpanzees; but the macaques and baboons hesitate to do so. In all cases the adult males in the group immediately approach the mother-infant dyad in times of danger. Thus the cry of "women and children first" apparently has a strong biological base (Jay 1968, Kummer 1971, Poirier 1973).

Perhaps the major distinguishing feature of these catarrhine groups is the characteristic social organization of the subsistence group. There are four major types, as you can see in Table 6. For human hunter-gatherers, the typical social unit is the husband, his wife, and their children. Several families of this sort comprise a subsistence group. At times during the year, certain families form a subsistence group and share what is gained from hunting and gathering, and at other times during the year these families split up and join other families to form other subsistence groups. For the gorillas, savanna baboons, and macaques, the subsistence group and the social unit are the same. What should be noted, however, is that in general, there are approximately two or three times as many adult females in their social unit as there are adult males. The greatest disparity between the size of the subsistence group and the basic social unit is in the chimpanzees; their most stable and distinct social unit is the mother and her one or two offspring. Of all the species listed in Table 6, it is only in the chimpanzees and man that an adult female will frequently be seen alone. Although chimpanzees will form temporary social groupings (groups whose members stay in close proximity to each other for one or more days) consisting of either males, males and/or females of certain ages, or many females and their offspring, the only stable unit for the chimpanzee is the adult female and her offspring. The social unit for the hamadryas baboon is the one-male harem. The hamadryas baboon is particularly interesting. Owing to the relative scarcity of food, the various harems are widely separated from each other during the daytime; however, owing to predator pressures, the social units gather to sleep together in either cliffs or treetops in the evening. Even at night, the basic social group maintains its identity, sleeping in close proximity to each other.

To summarize, our selected catarrhine species are omnivorous in their food habits, with meat accounting for only a minority of their caloric intake, and they live in small subsistence groups which are comprised of adult males, females, juveniles, and infants. They are terrestrial, with the exception of the chimpanzee, who lives somewhat of an arboreal existence, but all are seminomadic and nonterritorial. Usually one infant is born at a time, with the temporal spacing between infants related to the rate of maturation. Usually an adult female does not have another infant until the previous infant is able to feed and transport himself. In all these catarrhine groups, the infant is in either close physical contact or close proximity to the mother.

In all the species, great attention is paid to the mother-infant dyad. They are the center of attention and receive a good deal of social contact from other adult females and juveniles. Although the extent of contact between adult males and infants varies within these primate species, in times of threat, the adult males in the subsistence group immediately approach the mother-infant dyad.

One of the basic distinguishing characteristics of these species is the composition and size of the basic social unit. In chimpanzees the basic unit is the mother and her one or two most recent offspring; in the gorillas, savanna baboons, and macaques, it is a very large collection of intimately related adult males, adult females, juveniles, and infants; in the Hamadryas baboons, it is the one-male harem; and in man, it is the monogomous family.

Table 6
Social Organization of Selected Catarrhines

Man	One male/ One female/ offspring
Gorilla	$\geq$ Two males/ $\geq$ Two females/ offspring
Chimpanzee	One female/ One or two offspring
Savanna Baboon	$\geq$ Two males/ $\geq$ Two females/ offspring
Hamadryas Baboon	One male/ $\geq$ Two females/ offspring
Macaca	$\geq$ Two males/ $\geq$ Two females/ offspring

SOCIALIZATION, MATURATION, AND LEARNING

Ideally, the process of catarrhine socialization leads to the production of individuals who will contribute to the viability of the group. In order to do this, individuals must not only survive, but they must also aid in the protection of the group against predators, reproduce themselves or provide opportunities for others to reproduce, and help maintain the stability of the group. The route to becoming a contributing member of a group involves learning the answers to a number of questions, some of which are:

1. Food: what can be eaten, what can't be eaten, what's desirable, where and when can food be eaten?
2. Protection: which species are dangerous, which are not, who in the group can be sought for protection, where is the best place to hide?
3. Reproduction: who can be mated with, when, how is it accomplished?
4. Group Identity: who is part of the group, who can be approached for play and/or affection, from whom should a safe distance be kept?
5. Role: what is appropriate behavior for infants, juveniles, adolescents, adults; what is appropriate behavior for males, females, mothers, fathers?

Shortly after an infant is born into a catarrhine group he starts to learn the answers to these questions. The answers aren't static, however, because what is expected of an individual depends in great part upon his/her sex and stage of development. For example, an infant can safely pull the hair of a dominant male, but a subadult male had better not do so. Infants can nurse on their mothers' breasts, but juveniles cannot. Thus, much of what an individual learns during catarrhine socialization has to be continuously tested and verified by him, especially during the period preceding adulthood.

Catarrhine socialization involves an extensive period of learning, and the nature of what is learned varies with the sex and stage of development of the learner. What is so striking about this entire process is the similarity in the way it is accomplished in our selected catarrhine species, i.e., the process appears to be canalized (Jolly 1972, Kummer 1971, Poirier 1973). In the discussion which follows, we will first describe in a general way the nature of catarrhine stages of development. Then we will discuss in a more detailed way some of the major learning issues in each stage of development, the primary individuals involved with the learning, i.e., the socializing agents, and some of the major behaviors learned.

Table 7 presents the rates of maturation and the longevity of these primates. The age ranges reported for the different stages of maturation are for the males of the species. They are averages, and there is substantial individual variability within each species. In all these species the females complete the subadult stage approximately two years earlier than the males of the same species. The period of infancy refers to the stage of development in which the offspring is primarily dependent on the mother for food, transportation, and protection from other members of the social group. The behavior of infants is benignly tolerated by older members of the group. The juvenile period refers to the stage in development in which the offspring have achieved a fair amount of independence from the mother and are primarily oriented towards other juveniles

Table 7
Rate of Maturation and Longevity of Selected Catarrhines (In Years)

	Infant	Juvenile	Subadult	Adult
Man	0-6	6-13	13-18	18-70
Gorilla	0-3	3-8	8-11	11-35
Chimpanzee	0-3	3-8	8-11	11-35
Savanna Baboon	0-1½	1½-4	4-8	8-28
Hamadryas Baboon	0-1½	1½-4	4-8	8-28
Macaca	0-1½	1½-4	4-7½	7½-27

in play groups. Juveniles are frequently treated very roughly by individuals other than the mother. One of the demarcation points for entry into the juvenile stage is when the offspring is no longer carried by the mother. The subadult stage is frequently very brief for females, but it is rather extensive for males of some of these species. It is entered when the individual reaches puberty. In this stage the individuals are rather independent of one another, and play diminishes markedly. The adult stage is entered when the individual is full grown and fully matured. As you can see from Table 7, the relative duration of the four stages of maturation is approximately the same in all of these primates. The most obvious and important trend in this table is that the period of maturation is quickest in the monkeys, next quickest in the apes, and slowest in man.

Table 8 shows some developmental stages of infancy for rhesus macaques, chimpanzees, and man. The times are approximate and reflect the number of weeks or months after birth when the particular class of behavior is first observed. As you can see, the pattern of development is remarkably similar for the three species, and the unfolding of these behaviors is clearly related to the rate of maturation for these species.

Infancy

As we have indicated, the mother-infant dyad is the core of the group. In all the selected catarrhine groups, the mother is the primary socializing agent of the infant. She nurses her offspring, protects him from others in and out of the group, shows him which foods to eat, which not to eat, and attempts to gain for her infant (this need not be done consciously) a smooth entry into the group. During the earliest period of infancy, the infant either clings to the underside of his mother, or is held by her. At a later stage, the infant either walks next to his

Table 8
Stages of Development During the Infancy Period

	Rhesus Macaque	Chimpanzee	Man
Social "smile"	1 week	1 month	2 months
Reach for objects	1 month	2 months	4 months
Fear calls (fear of stranger)	3 months	5 months	9 months
Aggressive threat	6 months	10 weeks	18 months

Source: Alison Jolly, *The Evolution of Primate Behavior* (New York: The MacMillan Company, 1972), Figure 146.

mother, or is carried by her, typically on her back, or in humans, at her side. At still a later point in infancy, the infant transports himself, but stays in close proximity to his mother and comes to her at any sign of danger or tension (Jolly 1972, Van Lawick-Goodall 1968).

Weaning appears to be one of the most traumatic aspects of infancy. It usually occurs about midway between birth and the onset of the juvenile stage of development. In general, males are weaned earlier than females, and first-time mothers seem to have more difficulty weaning than second (or more)-time mothers (Poirier 1973). What is so important about weaning is that it starts to produce some degree of independence in the infant, but in a protective atmosphere. When the mother weans her offspring she doesn't prevent him from staying close, nor does she stop protecting him.

The learning of sex roles is initiated in the period of infancy. Although shortly after birth the members of a group inspect the genitals of the newborn, e.g., "it's a girl!" (Poirier 1973), it is not until later in infancy that differential treatment of males and females occurs. This differential treatment is, no doubt, partly attributable to the differential behavior of male and female infants. The males are generally more aggressive, more active, and more playful. They are likely to stray further from their mothers than the females (Kummer 1971, Poirier 1973). Mothers, in turn, tend to act more aggressively towards the male infants, and as we noted above, to wean them earlier.

There is another aspect of role identification which appears to have its roots in infancy—social status. The research dealing with this topic in nonhuman primates has primarily been with terrestrial baboons and monkeys, but it has yielded consistent results (Jolly 1972, Poirier 1973). In a nonhuman primate group, social status in its most general sense refers to the "supplanting" ability of a member (Kummer 1971). For example, if there is a desirable sleeping place or eating place and one individual is using it, another individual with higher social status will supplant the first, typically by just walking over to the desired location. The lower social status individual allows himself to be supplanted by getting up and leaving. Recent research shows that infants of high status mothers tend to develop into high status adults, and infants of low status mothers tend to develop into low status adults. Although the specific child care practices which lead to high and low adult status have not been identified, noticeable differences in the behavior of infants of low and high status mothers have been observed. The former tend to be more easily frightened and spend more time with their mothers than the latter (Poirier 1973).

Perhaps the major event in the socialization of an infant is the formation of a social bond with his mother. This initial bonding, attachment (Bowlby 1969), or "mother love" (Harlow, Gluck and Suomi 1972) forms the basis for all subsequent social relations that the maturing individual has within his group. Attachment is not just a phenomenon restricted to infancy. Once an individual becomes attached to his mother, he maintains this bond throughout childhood, and frequently into adulthood.

There are two main characteristics of attachment behavior: (1) the child maintains proximity to his mother and actively restores this close proximity if it is changed, and (2) the attachment behavior is specific to the mother (or to the mother surrogate, and on occasion to one other individual also). Attachment behavior is a characteristic of the infant and should be distinguished from the mother's caretaking behavior which maintains the proximity of the mother to the infant. The two classes of behavior are obviously related, forming an interdependent system.

In humans, attachment behavior takes the following form. In a family setting, most infants respond differently to the mother than they do to others by four months of age. That is, they smile and vocalize more readily to her than to others, and follow her with their eyes. In some cases it has been shown that infants as early as four months of age show differential crying when the mother leaves, and by six to nine months of age, most infants display this behavior. The major way an infant who does not crawl maintains close proximity to his mother is by crying. It is fortunate that mothers, or the primary caretakers, are so structured that the crying of their infant impels them to maintain a close proximity to the infant. When the infant starts to crawl, at about nine months of age, he maintains close proximity to the mother by following her. It has generally been found that when the infant can crawl, his crying decreases in response to the mother's absence. During the child's second and third years of life, attachment behavior is apparently just as strong as during the end of his first year. After the child's third year of life, attachment behavior drops off markedly, but still plays a role throughout childhood. One of the major factors affecting attachment behavior is alarm or threat. When a child is frightened, attachment behavior becomes very intensive—the child hurries to and clings to his mother. This phenomenon leads to a very interesting paradox which most of us have observed. When a child is punished by his mother, the child seeks comfort from her and is frequently seen clinging to her.

From an evolutionary point of view, one of the most fascinating things about attachment behavior is that at about the time when the infant starts to crawl —the time of great potential danger for the infant—the fear of strangers develops. As we have just seen, a child's attachment behavior becomes most intense when he is frightened or alarmed. Hence, any inclination the young infant has to move away from his mother will probably very quickly put him in a fearful situation which will drive him into the arms of his awaiting mother.

The phenomena we have described and the order of their occurrence have been observed in our catarrhine species in both the field and the laboratory. Harlow and his colleagues have been studying attachment behavior for approximately fifteen years with rhesus macaques in the laboratory (they call this behavior "mother love"). Harlow et al. (1972) summarize some of the major findings of this research as follows:

> In these experiments, we were able to demonstrate that activities associated with the breast, including nursing, were variables of importance secondary to good, soft bodily contact, and we believe that human breasts were put there by God for more than aesthetic purposes. Furthermore, rocking motion was a positive variable of value, and temperature was a variable with impact. Hot, or at least warm, mothers were cheerfully chosen over others, and cold mothers were adversive. An infant upon contacting an ice-cold mother

designed by Suomi fled screaming in horror and never returned to the mother over a 30-day period.*

The other side of the attachment coin is loss, and there are striking parallels between the human and nonhuman primates. The basic human phenomena, originally called "anaclitic depression" by Spitz, have been summarized by Bowlby (1969). When a child between the ages of six months and approximately three years has been separated from his mother for periods ranging from a week to three months, the following behaviors have been observed. Initially the child enters a stage which Bowlby identifies as protest. During this time the child makes strong attempts to get to his mother. He appears very acutely depressed and is frequently seen crying and throwing himself about. This phase may last for a few hours to one or more weeks. The second phase, despair, typically follows the protest phase. In this phase the child doesn't actively seek his mother, but he cries often. He is withdrawn and inactive, and appears to be in a stage of deep mourning. The phase of despair lasts a variable length of time and is followed by a phase called detachment. In this phase, which lasts the longest, the child shows more interest in his surroundings and in other people. However, he appears to no longer care for anyone. This phase continues until the child is returned to his mother and his normal environment.

Hinde (1971) has summarized much of the comparable data for nonhuman primates (primarily macaque monkeys). The typical experimental situation involves monkeys living in a group situation with the mothers forceably separated from their infants when the infants are approximately six months of age. In some experiments, the separation was six days and in other experiments, approximately one month. Upon the initial separation, the infants became extremely distressed. Following this, they became very inactive, spending a lot more time than usual sitting, and playing far less than usual. Following this, the activity level and other social indicators of normalcy increased for these infants; however; their behavior did not quite reach that observed during the preseparation period. When the mother was returned to the home cage after either six days or one month, the infants immediately clung to her. In some cases the clinging dropped out after a few days, but in other cases it persisted for several months after the separation.

The Juvenile Stage

During this stage of development, same-sex peers become a major socializing force on the maturing individual. Although the juvenile still maintains close bonds to his mother, and to a lesser extent to his siblings, he becomes much more oriented to his peers than was the case during infancy.

There are marked differences at this stage in the activities of juvenile males and females, and in the way adults treat them. The females, much more so than

---

*H. F. Harlow, J. P. Gluck, and S. J. Suomi, "Generalization of Behavioral Data between Nonhuman and Human Animals," American Psychologist 27 (1972): 709–716.

the males, stay near their mothers (who now have a new baby), and the females are much more interested in infants and infant care than the males. The more active, aggressive males are apt to be treated much more roughly by the adults than are the females. In short, sex role identity is greatly enhanced during this period.

Returning now to peer socialization, the major activity seen during the latter half of infancy, other than sleeping and eating, and through all of the juvenile period, is peer play (Bruner 1972, Dolhinow and Bishop 1970, Harlow 1971). Play drops off markedly during the subadult stage, and in adulthood, with the exception of mothers with infants, it is relatively infrequent.

Although it is extremely difficult to describe precisely a play activity, e.g., "playing" with one's food, and although there are species-specific play activities, there are a large number of common play activities seen across the primates. Some of these are: running and jumping, chasing, mounting (for humans this might involve one child mounting another person for a horseback ride), threat behavior, wrestling, and grooming (how many of you have had the experience of a three year old combing your hair?). Although play activities are known for their variety and lack of a stereotyped quality, trained observers and some parents can readily identify them with a fair degree of reliability. One of the chief characteristics of play is its repetitiveness—specific acts and gestures, sometimes in new sequences, sometimes in old ones, are repeated over and over again. For example, A will chase B, B will stop, threaten A, then chase A; A will then stop and perhaps chase B and mount him, and so on. The game can go on endlessly (Dolhinow and Bishop 1970).

Even though play appears to be a strongly motivated behavior, its occurrence is somewhat tenuous. Play occurs in familiar situations which are free of tension and danger. For example, when a predator is present, or fighting breaks out in the social group, play stops, and if the individual is young, he typically will run to his mother. In an environment which is conducive to play, however, it may continue for hours on end (Dolhinow and Bishop).

Peer play is intimately involved with the potential contribution an individual will make to the viability of the group. It accomplishes this through three types of activity: protection, reproduction, and group integration. We will consider these one at a time. Regarding protection, Dolhinow and Bishop state:

> Consider for example, young monkeys dashing at high speed in trees, chasing one another, making what appear to be hazardous jumps, running with alarming speed out onto the smaller branches, and falling to the ground. The observer may well wonder why this happens when it seems so risky. If the observer also sees escape behavior in a serious fight among adults, then it is possible to see how important the practice in youth may be. The ability to escape from an attacking adult or from an attacking predator may mean the difference from serious damage or death, and safety.*

*P. J. Dolhinow and N. Bishop, "The Development of Motor Skills and Social Relationships Among Primates Through Play," in Minnesota *Symposia in Child Psychology,* ed. J.P. Hill (Minneapolis: University of Minnesota Press, 1970), p. 169.

In human hunter-gatherers, the ability to run quickly, jump, and climb a tree, or to accurately throw a spear or shoot an arrow, has the same survival characteristics as those seen in the preceding quote for nonhuman primates. Related to this, Bruner (1972) has argued that many of the cognitive and manipulative skills an individual acquires are first tested out and extensively practiced during the juvenile stage.

The major source of data for the relationship between play behavior and reproduction is the work of Harlow and his colleagues. The basic laboratory situation Harlow studied involved a comparison of adult sexual behavior in two groups of animals (Harlow and Harlow 1962). In one group, the individuals were raised with their mothers but were not allowed to play with their peers. In the other group, individuals were raised with surrogate mothers, and allowed only twenty minutes a day to play with their peers. Harlow found that individuals who were allowed to play with their peers appear to have normal sexual behavior as adults, whereas in those raised with only their natural mother, either abnormal sexual behavior or no sexual behavior as adults was observed. Hence, animals who didn't play didn't reproduce. Because all nonhuman primates raised in the natural environment have peers to play with, and at least in the earliest stages of infancy have a mother to nurture them, we have no way of verifying Harlow's work outside of the laboratory. Using retrospective data, however, it might be possible to confirm Harlow's research with humans. That is, one could identify groups of individuals who are and who are not having sexual problems and make comparisons concerning the nature and frequency of play relationships they had as infants and juveniles.

Finally, it is in large part due to peer play that individuals form bonds with other members of their group (Harlow 1971 refers to this as "peer love"). It is crucial to the survival of the group that individuals be able to identify one another, to communicate with one another, to interact with one another, and to be motivated to be near one another. Group solidarity is not just an ideal, but a necessity for survival. In the play situation, juveniles are allowed the opportunity to test out a variety of social activities and to be "taught" by the responses of their peers whether or not these activities are socially acceptable, e.g., biting, pulling another's hair, hugging, kissing. There is some suggestion that dominance and aggression relationships also get their initial start during this time (Poirier and Smith 1973). Poirier and Smith suggest that if the individual has not mastered the appropriate social behaviors by the end of the juvenile period, he will probably be ill-equipped to take on the adult roles required by the group.

The Subadult and Adult Stages

The onset of puberty is the demarcation point for the beginning of the subadult or adolescent stage. There are tremendous differences in the sex roles of males and females at this time. In general, in all the selected catarrhine species, the females become pregnant near the beginning of this stage, and following the birth of their first offspring there is little to differentiate their behavior from that of females in the adult stage. For the males, however, the subadult stage is typically one in which they have a low status, peripheral role in the group (Jolly 1972, Kummer 1971). This may be seen in Figure 24 for the Hamadryas baboon. For Savanna baboon troops, a similar picture is seen when the troop is on the move—the subadult males are literally positioned on the periphery, whereas the females, infants, juveniles, and adult males are in the center. In human hunter-gatherers, the peripheral role of subadult males is generally more psychological than physical. Basically, they have little to say in the planning or organizing activities of the group.

The initiation of the subadult female into motherhood is apparently a smooth one (Poirier 1973). As Poirier has pointed out, females prepare for the maternal role from late infancy on. They stay close to their mothers and other adult females, show great interest in infants, and usually handle them, i.e., "babysitting" is common to all the selected catarrhines. The laboratory research of Harlow and his colleagues (e.g., Harlow, Harlow, Dodsworth, and Arling 1966) has shown that infants raised without mothers or without peer play develop into abnormal mothers, treating their offspring with active hostility. Thus, learning to become a normal mother is easy and inevitable for catarrhines raised in groups, but the social experiences typical of group living are necessary conditions for this learning to occur.

Figure 24

Hamadryas baboons huddling in one-male groups on a cool morning. The subadult male "follower" on the left is associated with the group in the foreground but excluded from the huddling (From Kummer 1971).

The route to adulthood for males is very different than that for females. For the females, who almost invariably become mothers, there is little difficulty in taking on the adult roles which start in adolescence. For the males, there are many hurdles to becoming a fully integrated, reproducing adult. This is especially true for the monkeys and baboons, who almost literally have to fight their way in, and less so for the apes and man. Underlying full integration into the group for most of the male catarrhines is the acquisition of social status, which, as we will see in the next section, is intimately linked to agression and dominance.

One of the primary functions of adulthood for males and females is reproduction. Another is teaching or modeling appropriate behaviors to the young. An obvious question is, reproduce with whom? In human societies, there are some universal incest taboos which help to answer this question, i.e., the mother-son, father-daughter, and brother-sister taboos. Are there similar taboos for the nonhuman catarrhines? Some attention has been given to this topic in recent years for macaque and chimpanzee groups. Data bearing on this issue requires a longitudinal study lasting many years, and such studies have not been carried out for the baboons or gorillas. The data which are available have been summarized by Itani (1972), Jolly (1972), and Pilbeam (1972).

The basic finding of these studies is that it is a rare event for a male to copulate with his mother, even though he remains in the same subsistence group, copulates with other females, and there are no barriers to casual copulation; however, it is a common practice for fathers to copulate with their daughters, and brothers to copulate with their sisters. Hence, of the three major human incest taboos, only the mother-son taboo appears to be canalized in nonhuman primates. This does not imply that the human brother-sister and father-daughter incest taboos are not canalized. One fact of particular interest concerning the mother-son incest taboo is that it plays a substantial role in Freudian theory of human development. Recall that in this theory the resolution of the Oedipus complex—giving up the mother as a sexual object—is a major stage in the child's development. The macaque and chimpanzee data suggest, on the other hand, that this urge to copulate with mother is not a very strong one at all.

AGGRESSION

In recent years, a substantial number of researchers have written about the central role of aggression in the primate adaptations, e.g., Bernstein and Gordon (1974), Kummer (1971), Lorenz (1966), Washburn and Hamburg (1968). Aggression is apparently a necessary condition for maintaining stability within the group and protecting the group from the outside. Washburn and Hamburg state:

> ... in Old World monkeys and apes aggression is an essential adaptive mechanism. It is an important factor in determining interindividual relations; it is frequent; and successful aggression is highly rewarded. It is a major factor in intergroup relations, and the importance of aggression as a species-spacing mechanism means that aggression is most frequent between

groups of the same species. Both within groups and between groups aggression is an integral part of dominance, feeding, and reproduction. Biological bases of aggressive behaviors is complex, including parts of the brain, hormones, muscles-teeth-jaws, and structures of display; successful aggression has been a major factor in primate evolution.

Man inherits the biological base, modified by the great development of the social brain and language. Aggression may be increased by early experience, play, and the rewards of the social system. The individual's aggressive actions are determined by biology and experience.*

As we have indicated, males are more aggressive than females, and this difference becomes manifest in infancy. Experiments have shown that the male sex hormone, testosterone, is significantly involved with aggressive behavior. For example, female vertebrates treated with testosterone early in their development exhibit certain male physiological characteristics and act in a more aggressive fashion than untreated females. Hence, it is not surprising that in general, males within a species act much more aggressively than do females of that species (Marler and Hamilton 1966). As we indicated in Chapter 5, the neural basis of aggressive behavior is in the old mammalian brain, the limbic system, which has undergone relatively little change during the course of primate evolution. However, the form that aggressive behavior takes in humans is culturally influenced and neocortically mediated.

The primary function of aggression between different groups of the same species is to ensure adequate space for each group. For our selected group of primates, including hunter-gatherers, meetings between different groups of the same species range from friendly behavior, in which members of the two groups mix, to fighting. For gorillas, chimpanzees, and hunter-gatherers, meetings between different subsistence groups are typically either friendly, or the groups ignore one another, with the latter behavior predominating. In macaques and baboons, the typical reaction is avoidance. Fighting between different groups of gorillas, chimpanzees, and hunter-gatherers has rarely been observed, and its occurrence in macaques and baboons is related to population density. Where there is a small overlap of home ranges between the different subsistence groups, fighting is rarely observed. When it does occur under these circumstances, it is usually of very brief duration and no one gets seriously hurt. For rhesus macaques living in the city (known as temple rhesus macaques), where there is a considerable overlap of home ranges between different subsistence groups, fighting is frequently seen and sometimes it is very violent (DeVore 1965, Jay 1968, Jolly 1972).

There are three alternative ways aggression is handled within a group (this generally applies to adult males, for whom within-group aggression is such a crucial matter). In the first way, adult males will not tolerate each other's presence and fighting will be intense and relatively continuous. The species who handle aggression in this manner have apparently not developed inhibit-

---

* S. L. Washburn and D. A. Hamburg, "Aggressive Behavior in Old World Monkeys and Apes," in *Primates*, ed. Phyllis C. Jay (New York: Holt, Rinehart and Winston, 1968), p. 478.

ing mechanisms to control it. One species showing this characteristic is the Patas monkey, who is not among our selected catarrhines (Kummer 1971). Although adult male gibbons tolerate each other in all-male groups, when adult females are involved, the males become extremely intolerant of each other and fight for sole "possession" of the females and the territory (Jay 1968).

In the second way, which characterizes the baboons and macaques, there is an intense amount of aggression, but it is highly ritualized, taking the form of avoidance and threat (Jolly 1972, Kummer 1971). In these groups a dominance hierarchy is formed, with the most aggressive being at the top. Within-group fighting is rare, and when it occurs usually no one gets permanently injured.

In baboons and macaques, the most dominant animals attract the most attention and have first priority to estrus females, food, and nesting places. The most dominant animals maintain the integrity of the group in that the other members of the group continuously orient their behavior to them. Dominance within a group is typically maintained by threat. Conflict within a group is avoided by the actions of the less dominant, who look at and keep away from the dominant members. In general, adult males are the most dominant members of a group, and within this subgroup there is a fairly clear-cut dominance hierarchy. Next in dominance are certain of the subadult males and adult females. Last come the juveniles and the infants.

The third way of handling aggression is the way of the gorillas and chimpanzees (Kummer 1971). Although a dominance hierarchy can be observed in these groups, there is relatively little within-group aggression, and low dominant males are not prevented from eating choice food or mating with females in the presence of more dominant males. As with the baboons and macaques, within-group aggression is typically handled by avoidance and threat.

What is the human way? The data are paradoxical. When human hunter-gatherers are observed, within-group aggression is most similar to that of chimpanzees and gorillas, except that it is rare for a hunter-gatherer subsistence group to have a dominance hierarchy (Lee and DeVore 1968). In these groups, there is no leader as such; rather, some individuals may be leaders in hunting, others in art making, and others in religious activities. When conflict occurs, it is common for the entire group to become involved in settling the dispute. Violent conflicts would destroy the close working relationships required by the group. If the conflict becomes too severe, however, one of the members involved in the conflict will take his family and shift over to another subsistence group. Because the shifting of families among subsistence groups is the norm for these societies, this mode of avoiding conflict is perfectly acceptable.

When human city dwellers are observed, on the other hand, within-group aggression is most similar to that of baboons and macaques, where there are strong, clear-cut dominance hierarchies. Analogies between monkey societies and human urban societies are not completely appropriate, however, because there are few, if any, subsistence groups living in cities. Thus, it is difficult to determine what is within-group aggression, and what is between-group aggression. Nevertheless, the paradox is present, and should be explained. One suggestion, following Turnbull (1972), is that the development and maintenance of inhibitory mechanisms which suppress aggression and dominance require the existence of the close interdependencies which hold hunter-gatherer groups together. In cities, these close interdependencies don't exist, and hence, the inhibitory mechanisms either fail to develop, or if they do, they are not maintained.

SUMMARY

Canalized behavior has been defined as behavior which is easily and almost inevitably learned by individuals raised in environments in which their species were "designed" to operate. There are classes of canalized behaviors which are shared by species who have a common evolutionary history, and other classes of canalized behaviors which are relatively unique to a given species and which reflect its unique evolutionary adaptations. In this chapter, the former behaviors were discussed for a group of catarrhine species to whom human hunter-gatherers have a close affinity. In the next chapter, the hunter-gatherer behavioral adaptations or design will be discussed.

Four common characteristics of social organization were observed for the selected group of catarrhines:

1. they all form into subsistence groups whose members are well-known to one another
2. within each group the mother-infant dyad is the core of the social unit
3. all groups subsist primarily on fruits or other vegetation
4. all groups are seminomadic and nonterritorial.

For all the selected catarrhines, the linkage of socialization, maturation, and learning was very similar. Infancy is a period in which offspring form their first affectional bonds through attachment processes. Infants stay in close proximity to their mothers during this time, even after weaning has occurred. Sex role identification becomes manifest during the latter part of this developmental stage, and play becomes a major socializing activity. During the juvenile stage, clear-cut sex role differences emerge, and other than eating and sleeping, peer play is the predominant activity. The second affectional bonds are formed during this time, which Harlow refers to as "peer love." In the subadult stage, the females enter the center of group life and become mothers, whereas the males become peripheral members of the group. Finally, in the adult stage, the males become fully integrated into the group, reproducing and contributing to group stability, typically through the establishment of dominance hierarchies.

Finally, the central role of aggression in primate societies was discussed. We pointed out that within human hunter-gatherer groups, aggression and dominance relations are similar to those which exist in gorilla and chimpanzee groups, but in cities, the baboon and macaque dominance relations are more likely to be observed.

Chapter 7

HUNTER-GATHERER SOCIAL ADAPTATIONS

OVERVIEW

Man has been described in many ways: as the toolmaking animal, as the political animal, as the symbol-making animal, as the knowing animal, as the ethical animal, as the cultural animal (Dobzansky 1962). He is all these and more; however, as we saw in the previous chapter, the fundamental way in which man must be described is as a member of a group. Following the analyses of Hallowell (1963), G.H. Mead (1934), Simpson (1949), and Waddington (1960b), one key to understanding the form human group life took, including some of the preceding characteristics, is the idea of "reciprocal obligations." In the hunter-gatherer group, like other catarrhine groups, group identity and cohesiveness, i.e., knowing who are members of one's group and having social bonds with them, are essential characteristics of survival. The basic distinction between human and nonhuman groups is that for the latter, individual members by and large are not reciprocally obligated to one another. Simpson (1949) writes about these ideas as follows:

> Man is much the most knowing or thinking animal, as our predecessors rightly recognized in bestowing on him the distinctive qualification of *sapiens*. Man is also the responsible animal. This is more basic than his knowledge, although dependent on it, for some other animals surely know and think in a way not completely inhuman, but no other animal can truly be said to be responsible in anything like the same sense in which man is responsible.*

---

*G. G. Simpson, *The Meaning of Evolution* (New Haven: Yale University Press, 1949), p. 310. Reprinted by permission of Yale University Press.

Man's responsibility or reciprocal obligations to other members of his group frequently leads to behavior which is viewed as virtuous or morally right. At the base of these actions, however, is group survival. Turnbull (1972), one of the leading students of hunter-gatherer societies, evaluates these behaviors as follows:

> . . . hunters frequently display those characteristics that we find so admirable in man: kindness, generosity, consideration, affection, honesty, hospitality, compassion, charity, and others. This sounds like a formidable list of virtues, and so it would be if they *were* virtues, but for the hunter they are not. For the hunter in his tiny, close-knit society, these are necessities for survival; without them society would collapse. It is a far cry from our society, in which anyone possessing even half these qualities would find it hard indeed to survive, yet we are given to thinking that somehow these are virtues inherent in man.*

Thus, the ability to form reciprocal obligations, like other behavioral capacities or processes, evolved in man and became part of his evolutionary design because it led to more effective activity in the environment. As Turnbull indicates, the "virtues" which accompany reciprocal obligations are easily and inevitably learned in the normal range of environments, which is consistent with our previous discussions about the canalization of behavior. However, like all other canalized phenotypic characteristics, if individuals are not reared in normal environments, reciprocal obligations and the accompanying virtues may not develop normally.

A hunter-gatherer group can be viewed, then, as comprised of an interrelated set of reciprocal obligations, with each individual being responsible to many others in the group because of what they have done for him, and they, in turn, being responsible to him because of what he has done for them. Let's consider several examples. The old members of a group, who no longer have the stamina for hunting or gathering, have acquired special knowledge of the home range which they share with the middle-aged members. The old also care for the children of the middle-aged and aid in tool making. The middle-aged protect the elderly and provide food for them. Middle-aged men become reciprocally obligated to one another through cooperative hunting and food sharing. Middle-aged women become reciprocally obligated to one another through cooperative gathering and food sharing. Middle-aged men and women become obligated to one another through a variety of husband-wife reciprocities, such as sexual fidelity, food sharing, and child care. The list goes on, encompassing events which occurred in the past, as well as those which will occur in the future.

What is it about man, but not the other catarrhines, that allows him to form reciprocal obligations? Mead (1934) believes that there are two necessary conditions: self-awareness—the ability to objectively view one's self or reflect

---

*Colin M. Turnbull, *The Mountain People* (New York: Simon & Schuster, 1972), p. 31.

upon one's self, and empathy—the ability to take the other's point of view. Self-awareness gives an individual the ability to be aware of his own actions in a given situation and of the subsequent reactions of others. Empathy gives an individual the ability to predict how he would react if he were in the other's situation. In order to be reciprocally obligated, it is necessary to be aware of the potential effects your actions will have on others, and to act in ways, as a consequence, which would be satisfying to yourself if you were in the other's place.

Are other catarrhines capable of self-awareness? There is an interesting set of experiments which suggests that some are, at least in a rudimentary form (Gallup 1968, 1970). In these experiments, the typical situation involves placing a mirror in front of an individual subject and noting that individual's behavior. Basically, two classes of responses have been observed: those which indicate that the individual treats the mirror reflection as that of another member of his species, e.g., the subject performs a variety of "social" responses to the image which are typically made to another member of his species; and those which indicate that the subject treats the reflection as his own reflection, e.g., he grooms himself or inspects parts of his body using the mirror for guidance.

The former class of responses is taken to signify the absence of a body self-concept, and the latter the presence of a body self-concept (Gallup 1968). In Gallup's 1970 paper, macaques did not demonstrate the presence of a body self-concept, whereas chimpanzees did. In one experiment, for example, the animals were made unconscious, and their foreheads were marked with a red dye. Upon awakening and looking in the mirror, the chimpanzees touched and examined their foreheads, whereas the macaques did not.

Are other catarrhines capable of empathy? There is apparently no psychological research dealing with this issue. The neuropsychological research summarized in the chapter on the brain suggests that in at least a rudimentary form, the great apes may have this capacity. Recall that the thalamic subdivision of the limbic system underwent the greatest growth in primate evolution, reaching its maximum size in man. MacLean maintains that this subdivision, with its connections with the prefrontal cortex, is involved with the mediation of empathy. Given that the great apes have such relatively large brains, including relatively large frontal lobes, it's possible that they are capable of empathy.

When did self-awareness, empathy, and reciprocal obligations emerge in human evolution? Possibly these characteristics date back to *H. erectus*, and perhaps earlier. This hunch is based on the early existence of a division of labor between males and females, as evidenced by the hunting of large game, and the assumed sharing of meat and vegetation by members of the group. It is hard to conceive of such a complex food distribution system without reciprocity.

Given that a key to understanding man's social adaptations is the idea of reciprocal obligations, the glue which holds the group together, what about the other descriptions of man's evolution mentioned in the opening paragraph of this chapter? A consensus is starting to emerge concerning them. Almost all evolutionists, e.g., Campbell (1966), Dobzansky (1962), Holloway (1972), Pilbeam (1972), Waddington (1960b), consider at least some of the following behavior patterns as having been crucial elements in man's adaptation:

1. cooperative hunting
2. food sharing
3. tool manufacture
4. husband-wife reciprocities
5. symbolic communication
6. rule giving and rule following.

This list is supported by the fact that these behavior patterns are characteristic of almost all contemporary hunter-gatherers, and evidence for some of them is found in the paleoanthropological record. Following a brief discussion of assumptions about canalization and a short description of contemporary hunting and gathering societies, these six characteristics will be discussed in some detail.

ASSUMPTIONS ABOUT CANALIZATION

We have defined canalization of behaviors in terms of their inevitable ease of learning in the normal range of environments, and we infer canalization from the widespread existence of the behaviors in question. Although all of the preceding behavior patterns can be seen in at least some city dwellers and some farmers, it is appropriate that they be discussed in relation to contemporary hunter-gatherers, who most closely resemble our ancestors in terms of their environmental niche, group structure, technology, and subsistence activities. In short, it is more likely that the hunter-gatherers reside in the normal range of environments for our evolutionary adaptations than do either city dwellers or farmers.

Since fewer than .01 percent of mankind currently live as hunter-gatherers, how do we know that they aren't aberrant and live in an aberrant environment? Does it make sense to place our bets on them in terms of identifying and inferring canalized behavior patterns? At least two assumptions need to be made. First, that the behavior patterns identified in contemporary hunter-gatherers are not very different from those of our preagricultural ancestors. This is the working assumption of most anthropologists interested in the evolution of man. It also seems to make sense to a number of paleoanthropologists interested in preagricultural man. In fact, some of the problems in the paleoanthropological record are cleared up when this assumption is made (Pfeiffer 1972). Further, the early existence in man's evolution of some of these behaviors can be readily inferred or noted from the paleoanthropological record, e.g., tool manufacture, cooperative hunting, use of symbols.

The second assumption is that the central nervous system has gone essentially unchanged in man (including nonhunter-gatherers) from preagricultural times to the present. Many geneticists make a similar assumption when they state that man's evolution during the past 40,000 years has been primarily cultural rather than genetic, e.g., Mayr (1963), Stebbins (1971). There is some indirect evidence to support this second assumption. As we pointed out in Chapter 5, brain size stabilized approximately 250,000 years ago; however, we have no way of determining whether the structure of the brain stabilized then. Another line of indirect evidence is that the behaviors under consideration are seen in a number of different races of man in extremely different environments which are more or less geographically isolated. Although we cannot say with certainty when the different racial stocks diverged, it is safe to assume that it occurred well over 40,000 years ago (Darlington 1969). It is difficult to see how common behavior patterns could exist in these different racial groups without a common cultural environment and an essentially identical brain structure underlying them.

In short, the strategy adopted in the present chapter is to examine the anthropological record of contemporary hunter-gatherer societies, identify and discuss the classes of behavior patterns they share, extrapolate backwards in time concerning man's adaptation, and infer that these behaviors are induced or canalized—man learns them because he was designed to learn them. Before discussing these behavior adaptations, it would be useful to give an overview of the contemporary hunter-gatherers. Our summary is based on material contained in four collections of essays and research articles dealing with contemporary hunter-gatherers: Biccieri (1972), Cohen (1968a, 1968b), and Lee and DeVore (1968).

CONTEMPORARY HUNTER-GATHERERS

In general, anthropologists indicate that the present day hunter-gatherers live in the least accessible and least desirable places on earth. However, prior to the arrival of widespread agriculture, just the opposite was the case. It is estimated, for example, that two-thirds of the Eskimos living in preagricultural times lived south of the Arctic Circle. Today, the African Bushmen and Australian Aborigines are largely confined to desert areas, whereas in preagricultural times, probably a very tiny percentage of these people were desert dwellers. Hence, contemporary hunter-gatherers live under almost the least optimal conditions for survival, which places a severe test—perhaps a boundary condition—on this mode of adaptation.

The primary subsistence activity of most contemporary hunter-gatherers is gathering. In the warm climates, i.e., within plus and minus 40° of the equator, hunting generally provides only about twenty to forty percent of the diet, the rest coming from gathering. It is only in the cold climates, where there is sparse vegetation, that hunting and fishing become the primary subsistence activities. Since man evolved and adapted in the warm climates, and most of the human population lived in these climates in preagricultural times, it is relatively safe to assume that hunting has generally been a secondary, but important, subsistence activity. Some writers believe that fishing is a relatively late adaptation, and hence was not a factor in man's evolution.

In hunter-gatherer groups, there is a subsistence-related division of labor. In general, the women and young children do the gathering, and the men do the hunting. However, in some cultures women and children do participate in group hunting activities, and in some societies men do some of the gathering. Hence, in the warm climate areas, women generally provide the overwhelming majority of food for the group.

We have stated that under present conditions the hunter-gatherer mode of subsistence is placed under a severe test. Up until recently, it was generally believed that modern hunter-gatherers were continuously on the verge of starvation. In the past ten years some anthropologists have provided data on this issue. First, in Africa, the health of hunter-gatherers is at least as good and frequently better than that of their neighboring cultivators. Second, the typical hunter-gatherer in warm climates usually spends not more than twenty to twenty-five hours a week in subsistence activities. This leaves him (or her) a tremendous amount of time for games, visiting, resting, and other leisure activities. Far from being on the verge of starvation, the hunter-gatherers have been described as the original "affluent society" (Lee and DeVore 1968).

Man's basic social unit is the family, several families comprising the basic subsistence group. However, the composition of the subsistence group is fluid, generally consisting of a small number of core families who reside in a given area throughout much of the year, who are joined by several other families who may stay with the group for periods of months or years. There is no evidence of territoriality, i.e., the subsistence group does not prevent nongroup members from entering and utilizing the area. Further, there is no evidence of land ownership with inheritance rights. Rather, the family or families with the greatest longevity in a given area are in a ritual sense the "keepers" of the area and the guardians of the totems. In times of limited availability of food, which are usually seasonal, the group may split into its family components, each family moving to an area which contains enough food to support it. When the food supply becomes more ample, the families rejoin their subsistence group.

Although it was once believed by many anthropologists that members of a hunter-gatherer subsistence group are always related through the father, recent evidence has indicated that this is not the case. However, the members of a subsistence group are generally all related to one another. In some cultures, they are related primarily through the father, in others, primarily through the mother, and in still others, through either relative. The latter situation is perhaps the most adaptive, in that it readily allows for fluidity of size—a necessary response to seasonal variations in food supply—and variations in the overall distribution of the population in its geographical range.

Population size of hunter-gatherer groups remains very stable from generation to generation, probably at about thirty percent of the actual carrying capacity of the environment (Lee and DeVore 1968). This is interpreted by anthropologists as a protection against ecological crises. The typical methods of population control are long periods of lactation, which in some cases keeps the woman infertile, birth control, the killing of one twin, and systematic infanticide. Some anthropologists have suggested that the incidence of infanticide in preagricultural times may have been fifteen to twenty percent. In the warm climates, there is little evidence of desertion of the aged as a means of population control.

Lee and DeVore (1968) point to several other basic features of warm-zone hunter-gatherer societies. First, because these people move around a lot, they have very little personal property. This constraint on property keeps differences in accumulated wealth between members of the groups at a minimum. In many cultures, in fact, highly prized items are rarely kept by any individual for more than a short time, but are passed on to other members of the group. Second, the absence of territoriality and the variations of food supply lead to a fair amount of seasonal visiting between groups, which of course is an important adaptation for survival. Third, frequent visiting decreases the likelihood of desire for a permanent attachment to and control of any natural resource. This makes it very easy for conflicts to be resolved by one family moving to another area. With permanent attachment to a given area of land, this separation might be difficult and conflicts might frequently lead to violence. We have only to look at our contemporary industrial society to see the validity of this hypothesis.

CANALIZED BEHAVIOR PATTERNS

Before discussing these behaviors in detail, a few general points should be made about them. First, although these behaviors will vary by culture and environment, they are universal almost without exception in warm-zone and cold-zone hunter-gatherer societies. Second, all of them bear directly on subsistence activities, though not exclusively so. Third, the development of all these behaviors has strong roots in infancy and childhood. Perhaps critical periods exist for their normal development or manifestation; only limited data exist on this point, however. Fourth, all involve behaviors dissociated from the present or from immediate biological needs (at times, food sharing is an exception). Campbell (1966) sees this as one of the key human attributes. For example, human cooperative hunting involves planning for the future; sharing of food often involves carrying it long distances to a home base, and so on. This dissociation from the here-and-now is a point made by developmental psychologists from Spencer to Piaget concerning the growth of intelligence. Finally, and probably most important, all these behaviors have been greatly elaborated during the course of evolution, sometimes to the benefit of mankind, e.g., the production of art and music (symbolic communication), and sometimes to man's detriment, e.g., wars (cooperative hunting).

Cooperative Hunting

Although hunting is a secondary subsistence activity for warm-zone hunter-gatherers, animal food is a prized commodity. Not only is it tasty and high in protein content, it is an alternative food to plants, which can and must on occasion provide the majority of food intake. If early man had been almost exclusively herbivorous, as are the rest of the primates, not only would his adaptation have been restricted to places containing extensive vegetation, but his existence would have been more fragile than it apparently was. Although other primates hunt, and hunt cooperatively, there is good reason to believe that they could not make a go of it if they had to occasionally depend on meat for survival. For them, meat is "dessert," but for hunter-gatherers, it is frequently the entire dinner.

At least three anthropologists, Washburn and Lancaster (1968) and Laughlin (1968), believe that hunting was a major integrator of human activity and a major shaper of human adaptation during the course of evolution. To quote Laughlin is particularly instructive:

> Hunting is the master behavior pattern of the human species. It is the ongoing activity which integrated the morphological, physiological, genetic, and intellectual aspects of the individual human organisms and of the population who compose our single species. Hunting is a way of life, not simply a "subsistence technique" which importantly involves commitments, correlates, and consequences spanning the entire bio-behavioral continuum of the individual and of the entire species of which he is a member.*

Laughlin views hunting as a sequence of at least five behavior complexes, all involving substantial and extensive learning in childhood and adolescence. They are:

1. scanning the environment for information relevant to locating game
2. stalking and pursuing game
3. immobilizing the game, typically by killing or trapping
4. retrieving the game
5. making maximal use of the game.

Basic to these complexes are a "habit of observation" and a thorough and systematic knowledge of animal behavior. Laughlin implies the existence of a critical period in childhood for success in hunting. He points out that the only successful kayak sea otter hunters in the world are the Aleuts and the Koniags. Much of their success, according to Laughlin, is clearly traced to behavioral and physical training in childhood. Laughlin points out an interesting relationship between the development of weapons technology and knowledge of animal behavior. Hunter-gatherers have incredible knowledge about animals, and the equipment they use to kill their quarry requires accuracy for only short distances, usually under thirty feet. The subsequent development and use of sophisticated, long-range weaponry may have had the effect of diminishing the knowledge hunters have of animal behavior.

Kaplan (1973) has pointed out a related characteristic which has permitted man to be a successful hunter—his ability to create and use "cognitive maps" or internal representations of information contained in the spatial and temporal (seasonal) environments which he utilizes. This is not to imply that other animals do not utilize cognitive maps, but rather that in man's evolution this ability was particularly significant. Kaplan has identified four components or aspects of cognitive maps:

1. information concerning where one is and where others are, or the identification of the current situation
2. information concerning what is likely to happen next, or prediction
3. information concerning whether the possible outcomes will be good or bad, or evaluation
4. information concerning the possible courses of action.

---

*W. S. Laughlin, "Hunting: An Integrating Biobehavior System and Its Evolutionary Importance," in *Man the Hunter*, eds. R. B. Lee and I. DeVore (Chicago: Aldine Publishing, 1968), p. 304. Reprinted by permission of Aldine Publishing.

It is obvious that the information contained in these components requires a long period of learning, as well as a high degree of intelligence and maturity. Hence, it is no surprise that children and adolescents have only a secondary role in hunting.

The paleoanthropological record confirms the antiquity of the hunting of large animals. Not only does this type of hunting require the skills and behavior sequences noted by Laughlin and Kaplan, but it also requires cooperation and hence reciprocal obligations. From observation of contemporary hunter-gatherers, it is clear that this cooperation was primarily between adult men. Although male-male "cooperativeness" is seen among certain nonhuman primates, e.g., in defense against predators, hunting by chimpanzees (Teleki 1973), and dominance cliques in baboon troops (Jay 1968), these activities are generally infrequent and do not characterize the majority of adults of these other species. Washburn and Lancaster stress the importance and newness of this evolutionary event among the primates (although they do note its occurrence in wolves and wild dogs). It led to a new social organization in which the division of labor between men and women was intensified, and in which other male-male primate behavior patterns had to be modified. For example, a dominance hierarchy as seen in nonhuman primates doesn't exist in hunter-gatherer societies. Rather, a reciprocity is found which allows almost all men to find mates and families to readily visit among other subsistence groups.

One of the major effects of the intensified division of labor was in the nature of child training. Boys of necessity had to be trained to be cooperative hunters, and girls to be mothers and gatherers. From what is known about the relationship between genetics and behavior and the differential effects of male and female sex hormones on behavior, e.g., Broverman, Klaiber, Kobayashi, and Vogel (1968) have presented evidence that hormonal and physiological differences are the basis for sex differences in human cognitive abilities, it is not a great leap to assume that this intensified division of labor may be canalized. Girls may more readily learn female adult sex roles than boys, and boys may more readily learn adult male sex roles than girls. Sex-differentiated child-training techniques capitalize on this difference.

Although the underlying anatomical and physiological changes which made cooperative hunting possible are not known with certainty, three changes appear as necessary preconditions. First, cooperative hunting requires a kind of docility between the male hunters, i.e., a reduced aggressiveness. There is good indirect evidence, briefly summarized by Washburn (1960), that the anatomical structures underlying aggressiveness did change during the course of human evolution. Further, the data summarized in Chapter 5 suggest that in humans there is a greater degree of cortical control over the "aggression centers" in the limbic system than there is in nonhuman primates. Second, cooperative hunting requires extensive planning. Research on brain-behavior relations indicates that the human has the best structures for this—the language areas and the frontal lobes. Third, human cooperative hunting requires the ability to extract and store a large amount of spatial and temporal information. As we noted in Chapter 5, the parietal and temporal lobes—the structures underlying these abilities—underwent marked growth during man's evolution, and are relatively larger than those of other primates.

Tool Manufacture and Tool Use

Although the existence of widespread tool use in the animal kingdom has been documented (Hall 1968), and limited tool manufacture has been reported for the chimpanzee (Van Lawick-Goodall 1968), human tool manufacture is by far the most extensive. Further, no other animals have been found to manufacture tools whose sole function is to aid in the manufacture of other tools. The paleoanthropological record indicates that hominid tool manufacture dates back more than two and a half million years; hence, we are dealing with a phenomenon that antedates the hunting of large game,

Washburn (1960) argues that the use and manufacture of tools is perhaps the most crucial behavior involved in human evolution. This behavior was supported by, and in turn enhanced through natural selection, the following structural changes:

1. changes in the pelvis and foot, producing more efficient bipedal locomotion
2. changes in the hand, producing more effective manipulative skills
3. changes in the sensory cortex and motor cortex, giving the thumb and hand increased representation
4. changes in the frontal lobes and association areas of the brain, allowing for increased planning ability and finer aesthetic judgements
5. a slowing of the rate of fetal brain maturation so that the head of the baby could get through the birth canal.

Effective tool making involves a highly developed set of motor skills, an aesthetic sensitivity (Washburn 1970), and high intelligence (as contrasted with nonhuman primates). These same criteria are also necessary for certain motor skills which have a less ancient history, e.g., creative painting and piano playing. The development of these abilities starts in childhood and is not completed until adulthood, if this development is ever completed. Bruner (1972), in discussing the developmental aspects of tool use and tool manufacturing in hunter-gatherer societies, makes at least two important points. First, that the use and manufacture of tools are intimately tied to play, as are other important human activities. It is in the play situation that the child can practice his incipient skills and test them out in new combinations. Second, that formal instruction in tool making and tool use is infrequent, and essentially never occurs outside the situation in which the activity is to be employed. Rather, the child typically learns by observation and imitation.

Food Sharing

The sharing of meat is a widespread activity among the carnivores, and occurs among chimpanzees following a successful "hunt" (Teleki 1973). In the latter case, the sharing is among those in the vicinity of the kill. As Washburn and Lancaster (1968) point out, human food sharing is quite different from that of carnivores or chimpanzees. Among humans it includes nonmeats, e.g., fruits, vegetables, and nuts, as well as meats; it involves those who are not in the vicinity of the hunting or gathering; and it involves a division of labor. Among the nonhuman primates, essentially the only food sharing which regularly occurs is between the mother and her young infant. Once the infant has been weaned, he or she becomes almost completely independent of the mother for subsistence. Human food sharing involves both sexes and members of all age groups, and hence is intimately connected with reciprocal obligations.

Food sharing is closely related to hunting and tool making. Large game is usually butchered at the site of the kill and the useful products are carried back to the home camp. The paleoanthropological record indicates that butchering sites existed several hundred thousands of years age (Pfeiffer 1972). Both butchering and carrying require tools, and containers must be used to carry nonmeat products to the home camp. They must be large and lightweight, or they wouldn't be practical.

When small game is killed, it is frequently eaten on the spot and not shared. However, large game is always brought back to camp and distributed, usually under an elaborate set of guidelines: first to the immediate family, then to the parents or in-laws, then to those who have supplied game most recently, finally to the remainder of the camp. The amounts distributed are decided upon with great care. One major sign of conflict is failure to share with a given individual or family. When this occurs, the individual and his family who were "snubbed" will usually leave the camp and join another subsistence group.

Two of the extremes on the food sharing continuum are represented by the Guayaki of Paraguay and the Paliyans of India (Bicchieri 1972). For the Guayaki, the majority of food is obtained through hunting. However in this society, the hunter is prohibited by taboo from eating the game he has killed. He can give some to his wife and children, but not to his parents. Hence, each Guayaki man is almost completely dependent on other men in his subsistence group for survival. Among the Paliyans, for whom about eighty percent of the food comes from gathering, food sharing is at a minimum. In this society, individual economic autonomy is stressed, although limited cooperative hunting and honey gathering activities do exist. It is not rare in the Paliyan society for husband and wife to remain economically independent, sharing no food with each other for weeks at a stretch.

The sharing of food is an example of the more widespread phenomenon of sharing all resources. It is perhaps the most important because it goes to the heart of subsistence, and hence survival. However, the survival of the subsistence group as a social unit is dependent on many types of sharing and reciprocal obligations. We have already mentioned the passing around of prized possessions. Child care is also a shared responsibility of the group, as is education of the young.

There are only limited data bearing on the question of how children in these societies learn the sharing ethic. Beyond the observations that infants prior to weaning are greatly indulged, and adulthood is a period in which all adults are expected to conform to the social standards of the group, no other broad generalizations can be made. In some societies, such as the Bushman, little pressure is placed on the child or adolescent to conform to social norms. However, for the Guayaki, the sharing ethic is urged upon even three year olds (Bicchieri 1972). As indicated before, young children and adolescents are frequently with adults. Their games generally mimic the adult roles they will one day play, and they are encouraged to imitate their parents and "successful" members of the group. Hence, they acquire the sharing ethic primarily through games, observation, and imitation to the extent that this ethic is manifested by the adults of the group.

Husband-Wife Reciprocities

"Husband-Wife" reciprocities are widespread in the animal kingdom. They characterize many species of birds, carnivores, some nonhuman primates, and man (Wickler 1972). Marriage and marriage rituals are human, cultural ways of augmenting this pair formation which is the initial requirement of husband-wife reciprocities. In the human species, the pairs would form, as they do in other species, without the rituals. In Wickler's fine book summarizing familial relationships, he indicates that at least three common behaviors are found in the monogamous situation:

1. brood tending or care of the offspring
2. sexual relationships between the partners
3. behaviors related to brood tending or reproduction which inhibit aggression between partners.

Presumably when any of these aspects is eliminated, e.g., the children "leave the nest," the bond is weakened.

Campbell (1966) hypothesizes that similar to the Hamadryas baboon, the human family evolved as a response to varying food supply in the open plains. In times of scarcity, no small geographical region can supply food for more than a single human family. The structure of the human family differs from that of the Hamadryas in at least two important ways. First, the Hamadryas family in the evening always stays close to other members of the troop; whereas the individual human families in some hunter-gatherer societies are periodically isolated from each other for months. Second, in the Hamadryas, the single adult male-single adult female plus offspring family is very infrequent; whereas in man, this is the typical family (Whiting 1968). In fact, polygamy is not permitted in some hunter-gatherer societies.

A cooperating, sharing adult man-adult woman dyad and their offspring is the minimum viable social unit capable of surviving and reproducing. Some of the major husband-wife reciprocities are: sharing of food with the implied division of labor, mutual care and education of their children, giving appropriate respect and treatment to in-laws, and sexual fidelity. The permanence of first marriages varies from society to society. In some, the young men and women go through several marriages in quick succession; whereas in others, e.g., those where the marriage ritual is very elaborate and expensive, first marriages tend to last. In all societies, however, marriages made when the husband and wife are in their late twenties or early thirties usually last until one of the partners dies.

In general, the question whether or not one should marry is not asked in hunter-gatherer societies. All young men and young women are expected to marry, to raise families, and to care for their parents when the parents are too old to fend for themselves. Further, full adulthood is generally accorded only to those who have married. Hence, a large number of forces are operating in a subsistence group to make and keep the family a cohesive unit.

Symbolic Communication

Behaviors in this category include language, the arts, rituals, and myths. The oldest of these is probably some form of spoken language, which may have arisen as long ago as one million years (Hockett and Ascher 1964), and the most recent is written language, which dates back only about 5,000 years (Braidwood 1967). Many anthropologists, e.g., L. White (1959), Campbell (1966), consider the evolution of language as central to man's cultural and traditional development. In addition, Campbell emphasizes the importance of language in maintaining group cohesiveness and stability as it relates to the codification of laws and the development of religion.

In light of these considerations, we will restrict our discussion to language behavior. Further, in order to understand language as it relates to homologous nonhuman behaviors, it is most useful to view it as a communication system. Hockett (1960) and Hockett and Ascher (1964) identify four design features of communication systems which are characteristic of all the known spoken languages in the world, and which distinguish human language from primate "call systems." These features are identified as "displacement," "productivity," "traditional transmission," and "duality of patterning."

The design feature "displacement" refers to the fact that human language can refer to objects and events distant in time and space, e.g., the past and the future. This feature is apparently lacking in the communication system of other primates, which is primarily of the here and now. The design feature "productivity" is related to "displacement." It refers to the ability to make new statements, never heard or said before, that are nonetheless understood by the listener. These statements are comprised of old words in new combinations.

The design feature "traditional transmission" refers to the fact that the detailed aspects of any language—the words—are learned, although the capacity to learn a language is probably genetically determined. It is not clear how big a part traditional transmission plays in other primate communication systems. The design feature related to this, "duality of patterning," refers to the fact that the extraordinarily large number of words in a language are made up of a relatively small number of apparently meaningless sounds, called phonemes, combined in different ways. The same phonemes used in different combinations have discrete and different meanings, e.g., tack, cat, and act. This feature is shared by none of the other primate communication systems.

Hockett asserts that the first of these design features to emerge in human language was productivity—the combination of old words into new patterns. It is of interest that in language learning children go through a stage where productivity is absent. Their first major breakthrough is in recombining the words they have learned. The last design feature to be acquired in man's evolution was probably duality of patterning. This feature only becomes a necessary aspect of a communication system when it becomes extremely complex. With only several hundred words to learn, duality of patterning would probably not be necessary. Recent research with chimpanzees indicates that they can be trained to use American Sign Language, and hence are capable of handling the design features of productivity, displacement, and traditional transmission (Gardner and Gardner 1969). Since American Sign Language does not employ phonemes, it is not clear whether chimpanzees are capable of duality of transmission.

The research of Lenneberg (1966, 1967), which will be discussed in greater detail in the next section of this book, fits in very well with the present view that human language learning is canalized. Lenneberg makes the following points. First, progress in language acquisition from birth to about four years of age is closely related to progress in the motor functioning of the child both within and across cultures. The latter, almost all would agree, is largely under genetic control. Second, the maturational schedule for the milestones of language acquisition seen in the normal child is generally preserved, but occurs at a slower rate in mentally retarded children. Again, this supports the notion of genetic controls. Third, children born deaf or blind, and normal-hearing children of deaf-mutes, develop more or less normal language understanding and utilization. This indicates that even under very abnormal environments, language acquisition will occur.

Finally, there appears to be a critical period for "first language" acquisition, lasting from about two to twelve years of age. The supporting data Lenneberg presents are largely clinical observations of individuals who have suffered brain damage at different points in development. About half the children who received lateralized (on one side only) brain damage between birth and about twenty months of age developed language at the normal rate. The remaining half developed normal language, but a a slower rate. When lateralized brain damage occurs between about twenty-one months and three years, all language that the child has acquired disappears, but the child successfully reacquires language, passing through and repeating all the stages of language development. The occurrence of lateralized damage between three and ten years of age produces severe language deficiencies, but all the spoken language deficiencies generally recover. Damage between eleven and fourteen years of age generally leads to some permanent spoken language deficiencies. When damage occurs after age fourteen, and language deficiencies are present half a year after the injury, the deficiencies will be permanent.

Lenneberg explains these observations and the existence of a critical period by pointing to two related neural maturational processes—brain growth and lateralization of function. The onset of the critical period is thought to coincide with the attainment of about sixty percent of adult brain growth, and comes to a close when further brain growth is minimal. During this critical period, the two cerebral hemispheres gradually change from being equipotential with respect to function, to being lateralized in regard to function. At maturity, language is almost completely lateralized in the left hemisphere. However, prior to maturity, the right hemisphere can take over the language functions, and does so when certain areas of the left hemisphere are damaged.

The major anatomical changes in man's evolution which made language possible were:

1. changes in the sound-producing structures, allowing for greater phonetic variations, which, according to Lieberman (1973), attained their modern form in some races of *H. sapiens* about 300,000 years ago
2. changes in the teeth and mouth, which led to and supported the transfer of grasping and manipulating functions from the mouth to the hand
3. changes in certain association areas of the brain which mediate sound production and understanding.

Hockett and Ascher (1964) maintain that in a sense, bipedal locomotion was the necessary condition for all of these changes, and the manufacture of tools was a concomitant of the development of language.

Rule Giving and Rule Following

We have stated that the social structure which man evolved was a crucial aspect of his flexible adaptation. Two features of this structure or organization, as seen in the hunter-gatherers, are especially noteworthy. First, unlike nonhuman primates, human groups have flexible membership. Individuals and families frequently move from group to group with relative ease, a situation which apparently doesn't exist for the nonhuman primates. The chimpanzee may be an exception; however, humans who join other groups take the cooperative, sharing roles required of them in their new groups, whereas for the chimpanzee, there is apparently little cooperative behavior expected or required. When chimpanzees move to other groups, which is probably infrequent, their acceptance is indicated by their not being molested. Hence, the flexible membership of human groups is very different from the possible flexible membership of chimpanzee groups. Second, unlike the nonhuman primate groups, individuals and subgroups in hunter-gatherer groups frequently operate cooperatively at great distances from one another—out of sight, sound, and smell of other members of the group. This characteristic of man's social structure is seen to some extent in the pack-hunting carnivores, such as wolves and dogs, where one subgroup will go out and hunt and another subgroup will stay at the home base.

One reason these two features are so essential to the human adaptations is that both are intimately connected with eating and food-getting activities. Given that food gotten by hunting or gathering will be shared with other members of the subsistence group, it follows that the likelihood of having food is increased as the number of individuals or subgroups independently searching for food increases. If all the food seekers went together all the time, a string of bad luck could prove fatal to the group as a whole. As another example, in times of food shortage, families tend to split off from the main group and fend for themselves, rejoining the group when food becomes more plentiful. Again, if everybody stayed with the group during these hard times, everybody might starve. Flexible group membership is especially important when food is short in one region, but more plentiful in another. In these cases, individuals or families may join other groups who either have food, or who reside in a region where food is available. This situation apparently doesn't exist in nonhuman groups.

Thus, the ability to shift membership from one group to another, and the ability to engage in cooperative activities out of sight, sound, and smell of other members of the group appear to be very important human evolutionary adaptations. How did these adaptations come to be? We think the keys to understanding lie in man's language and the idea of "reciprocal obligations." Reciprocal obligations and language are integral parts of a human system of rule giving and rule following, and our hypothesis, consistent with those of Simpson (1949) and Waddington (1960b), is that it was the evolution of man as a lawgiver or ethical being which permitted many aspects of the human social adaptation to develop. Simpson (1949) writes about these ideas as follows:

> Man is a moral animal. With the exception of a few peculiar beings who are felt to be as surely crippled as if the deformity were physical, all men make judgments of good or bad in ethics and morals. All feel some degree of compulsion to value and promote the good, to condemn and eliminate the bad. It requires no demonstration that a demand for ethical standards is deeply ingrained in human psychology. Like so many human characteristics, indeed most of them, this trait is both innate and learned. Its basic mechanism is evidently part of our biological inheritance. The degree of development of this, in the individual and in society, as well as the particular form that it will take are conditioned by learning processes in the family and in the wider aspects of the social structure. Man almost inevitably acquires an ethic and this responds to a deep need in any normal member of the species.*

Thus, man is an ethical animal in that he is a giver and follower of moral rules, and as Turnbull (1972) suggests, his very existence depended on these characteristics. Other animals are ethical, and in ways shared by humans. Given any group of animals, theoretically their moral system can be determined by observing the behaviors of the members of the group. This is analogous to determining the rules governing language by observing the language as it is spoken. For example, in a Hamadryas baboon group, it is "unethical" for a female to stray too far from her mate, i.e., when she does, he runs after her and bites her. Similarly, in a savanna baboon troop, it is "ethical" or "moral" for the young male adults to rush to the perimeter of the troop when a predator is nearby, placing themselves between the predator and the other members of the troop.

In other words, the terms "ethics" and "moralilty" can be used to describe the normal interindividual and intergroup relationships that obtain in a group (primate or nonprimate) in a given environment, i.e., the social norms of a group. However, it is one thing to say that rules governing social interactions can be described, and another thing to say that the individuals themselves are conceptually aware of the rules, and that the rules are obligatory in the sense of "ought." The quality of knowing the ethical rules and the quality of their being obligatory appear to be the distinguishing characteristics of human from

---

*G. G. Simpson, *The Meaning of Evolution* (New Haven: Yale University Press, 1949), p. 294. Reprinted by permission of Yale University Press.

nonhuman ethics. People don't merely say, for example, "in our group, girls do not have sexual intercourse with their father," but rather, "in our group, it is wrong for girls to have sexual intercourse with their father." It could be argued that baboons do on occasion accept obligations to other members of their group. But were the young males who did not come to the defense of the group chastised? We doubt it. In any case, it is human rule giving and following which is of interest to us.

Ethical rules do at least the following three things for human societies:

1. they describe the typical behaviors of the different members of the group (by age, sex, social role)
2. they state what is obligatory from among these typical behaviors, which implies a statement of group ideals
3. they help to guide individuals' behaviors in new or ambiguous situations.

The latter is especially interesting because different members of a group may interpret the rules differently in these difficult situations, which in turn may lead to conflict.

Taken in its broadest context, then, the ethical nature of man evolved because it improved his competence in dealing with his social and physical environment. As Simpson (1949) stated, moral behavior is learned, but it is almost inevitable that it will be learned. This is canalization. To the extent that human societies resemble one another, then, the ethical rules acquired by individuals in different societies will be similar. However, this can be stated in the converse, i.e., to the extent that individuals are canalized to acquire the same ethical rules, important aspects of societies should resemble one another.

SUMMARY

The starting point in understanding man's social adaptations is the idea of reciprocal obligations. Human hunter-gatherers evolved in such a way that in a subsistence group, each individual develops an interrelated set of reciprocal obligations with many other members of the group. Fundamental to the development of reciprocal obligations are the capacities for individual self-awareness and empathy.

Reciprocal obligations are the glue which holds a group together, and to some extent, they serve as a framework in which to understand man's other social adaptations. Most evolutionists identify some or all of the following behavioral characteristics as essential to man's social adaptation: cooperative hunting, food sharing, tool manufacture and use, husband-wife reciprocities, symbolic behavior, and rule giving and rule following. Man acquires these characteristics in the normal range of environments because he was designed to learn them. The role of each of these characteristics in contemporary hunter-gatherer societies was discussed, as well as the possible causes for their emergence in man's evolution.

In the next and final section of the book, an attempt will be made to understand the relationships between man's evolutionary design and the socialization of children, i.e., the way in which children develop social competency. The evolution of man as a cooperative hunter, for example, is the result of millions of years of evolutionary processes acting on epigenetic systems. These processes acted in such a way that infants and children raised in the normal range of environments would acquire the social competencies to become cooperative hunters and gatherers. More generally, evolutionary processes acted on hominid epigenetic systems in such a way that at each stage of development, individuals would be fully integrated and contributing members of the basic subsistence group. This implies that at the adult stage, individuals will have acquired the hunter-gatherer characteristics described in this chapter. We now turn to an examination of the psychological literature which has greatest bearing on these issues.

Part Three
ONTOGENY

Chapter 8

MOTOR SKILLS
DEVELOPMENT

AN OVERVIEW OF SOCIAL COMPETENCY

The next and final five chapters of this book will deal with selected aspects of children's acquisition of social competency. The socially competent child generally develops into a socially competent adult, who in a hunter-gatherer society contributes to the stability of his or her group and to its genetic survival. As we have shown, in order for a hunter-gatherer to contribute to his group in these ways, he has to learn its language, learn how to make and use its tools, learn how to identify suitable animals or vegetation for food and how to pursue their "capture," learn to cooperate and share in these and other endeavors, learn to give and follow rules, and learn the appropriate roles for being a husband or wife and parent.

In our previous discussions of the paleoanthropological record and hunter-gatherer social adaptations, six broad psychological characteristics or aspects of social competency consistently emerged as crucial to an understanding of man's evolution and social adaptation: highly developed motor skills, language, highly developed attentional capabilities, highly developed memory capabilities, highly developed spatial understanding, and a highly developed moral "sense." We saw that each of these characteristics was intimately involved with at least one of the hunter-gatherer social adaptations, e.g., attention, memory, and spatial understanding with cooperative hunting; and we also saw that the region or regions of the brain which underlie each of these characteristics showed a progressive increase in size during the course of hominid evolution, e.g., the capacity for empathy—a component of moral behavior—is mediated by the thalamic division of the limbic system and the

153

prefrontal cortex, both of which underwent marked growth in man's evolution. Owing to the central importance of these characteristics in man's evolutionary design, then, the remainder of this book will focus on their development in normal children. In this way we believe that man's epigenetic system can be appreciated more fully.[1]

Given the importance of these psychological characteristics, it is highly unlikely that evolutionary processes would have left their development to chance, but rather that during the course of man's evolution they would have become canalized, i.e., genetically normal individuals raised in normal environments would easily and almost inevitably learn the behavior patterns associated with these characteristics. Further, canalization processes would ensure that individuals would develop along very similar paths or chreods, and move through the same sequence of behavior patterns during their maturation. These last statements should have a familiar ring to them. In our chapter on developmental theory, it was stated that postnatal psychological development can be seen as analogous to an embryological process, which implied the existence of both constancies and canalized invariant sequences of behavior. As we mentioned earlier, this is essentially the view of some of the major developmental theorists of this century, e.g., Arnold Gesell, Heinz Werner, and Jean Piaget. In an autobiographical memoir, Gesell writes as follows

> Huxley was right when he insisted that the study of embryology subtends the entire life cycle. The higher as well as lower orders of behavior were built by evolutionary processes, and they survive only through embryological (ontogenetic) processes however much they bear the final impress of acculturation. Learning is essentially growth; and even creative behavior is dependent upon the same kind of neuronic growth which fashions the capacities of the archaic motor system, in utero and ex utero. The performance of genius belongs to a hierarchical continuum because there is only one physiology of development. There is but one embryology of behavior.[*]

A selective review of research done in the six areas of social competency indicates that the learning that occurs in each appears to form an invariant sequence as a function of maturational level. Moreover, despite the fact that the learning which occurs is continuous, three sets of age ranges keep cropping up in which the learning seems either quantitatively or qualitatively different, suggesting that some major psychological reorganization is occurring. These are when children are one to two years old, five to seven years old, and nine to eleven years old. The first two age ranges correspond roughly to the end of the sensory-motor and preoperational periods of development respectively. The

---

[1] The six areas of social competency identified here fit very well with the areas of social competency identified by a panel of experts assembled in 1973 by the Office of Child Development of the U.S. Department of Health, Education, and Welfare. Their conclusions are summarized by Anderson and Messick (1974).

[*] Arnold Gesell, "Gesell Institute of Child Development" in *A History of Psychology in Autobiography*, Vol. 4, ed. E. G. Boring (Worcester, Massachusetts: Clark University Press, 1930), p. 139. Reprinted, New York: Russell & Russell, 1961.

third age range occupies the middle of the concrete operations period of development (Piaget 1970).

From an evolutionary perspective, what is significant about these age ranges? As we stated in Chapter 1, there are four possible explanations for the existence of a behavioral constancy:

1. the character has survival value at that point in development, e.g., the sucking reflex, fear of strangers;
2. the character does not have survival value at that point in development, but it is necessary in order to build another characteristic which eventually will have high survival value, e.g., the development of hand preference at age two which eventually leads to highly developed motor skills;
3. the character does not have survival value at that point in development, but it will eventually be combined with other characters, the combination eventually having high survival value, e.g., the variety of skills and knowledge acquired prior to puberty which can only be utilized by the sexually mature;
4. the character itself does not have survival value, but it is the outcome of a character which falls in one of the first three categories, e.g., the appearance of reflexes in infants which occur owing to the immaturity of the brain.

The last possibility is particularly important to consider because the brain mediates all of these areas of social competency and brain maturation continues throughout infancy and childhood.

Which of the four possible explanations applies to understanding these age-related shifts in learning? Although all the explanations are probably involved, the two which intuitively make most sense are the first, which deals with survival value, and the fourth, which deals with brain maturation. During the first age range, one to two, although the associative or elaborative regions of the brain are highly immature, the primary motor areas and primary projection areas for sensory inputs are not. It is possible that the wiring of the brain has reached sufficient maturity during this period to allow for new modes of processing information. This possibility receives some support from the neurological literature. Both Dekaban (1970) and Eichorn (1970) report that the electrical activity of the brain—the EEG pattern—as measured by the electroencephalograph, stabilizes (not at the adult level) just before one year of age, and Dekaban points out that almost all of the transitory reflexes associated with brain immaturity drop out by one year of age. From a survival point of view, the age range one to two is the time when the child becomes very mobile. This is in contrast to the first year of life, when he is almost constantly being held or carried. Hence, the child "needs" more adequate means of acquiring knowledge than he did between birth and age one. Some of the major psychological acquisitions occurring at this time which have high survival value are: using imagery, readily obeying instructions (this is in relation to younger children), and starting to speak in two-word sentences.

During the second age range, five to seven, the child has joined peer play groups, frequently out of sight of his mother. For a child living in a hunter-gatherer group, this is obviously a dangerous time, one which requires substantial increments in knowledge in order to ensure survival. It is during this age-range that the child acquires a relatively complete knowledge of the grammar of his language, a sense of guilt, thus internalizing the moral rules of his group, and a spatial understanding resembling that of adults. Regarding brain maturation, the research summarized in Chapter 5 suggests that despite some immaturity in the association areas, all the major connections between the various regions of the brain are being completed during this period. There is little change in myelination in most regions of the brain after age seven, although myelination does continue through adulthood. S. White (1969) briefly summarizes clinical research dealing with the age-related effects of traumatic injury, which suggests that some major reorganization of the brain occurs during this age range. For example, children blinded before age six rarely report visual memories, but those blinded after six do. Children who have had a leg amputated prior to age four rarely report having sensations from their amputated limb (this is the phantom limb phenomenon), whereas almost all those amputated after age eight do experience their phantom limb.

During the nine to eleven age range, the changes in social competency are primarily of a quantitative as opposed to qualitative nature—typically there is either a learning spurt during this period or a learning plateau. It is possible, however, that these phenomena are only characteristic of Western societies (the source of our data), where this age range is designated as the "prepubertal" period, and as a consequence, children receive different treatment than they did at earlier ages. There are two lines of thought, though, which suggest that the learning phenomena associated with this period are more general. First, brain maturation approaches adult levels, which means that the organization or wiring of the brain is nearly completed. This is reflected in both the size of the brain and in the pattern of electrical activity from the brain (Eichorn 1970). Eichorn reports that EEG patterns do change after this period, but certain patterns stabilize at an adult level at age ten. Second, the age of nine was noted earlier as the age when the great apes reach sexual maturity. We argued that rate of maturity is related to adult brain size, and that during the australopithecine stage of hominid evolution, brain size and presumably rate of maturation were comparable to those of the great apes. It is possible that certain hormonal or other maturational changes still occur at about age nine in humans which are carry-overs from this preceding stage of hominid evolution. These changes would have the effect of inducing some psychological reorganization. This speculation is consistent with the fact that epigenetic systems are very conservative, and that which has worked in the past will tend to be maintained in the future.

We can summarize as follows. Evolutionary processes operated to ensure that normal children reared in normal environments would develop into socially competent adults. Underlying this social competency is the acquisition of behaviors linked with six broad psychological characteristics: motor skills, language, attentional capabilities, memory capabilities, spatial understanding, and moral understanding. These behaviors are thought to be canalized, which produces both constancies and invariant sequences of psychological development, e.g., during infancy and childhood, three age-related stages reflecting differences in the way children learn were identified.

The existence of these stages was accounted for on the basis of survival demands and brain maturation.

There is another aspect of canalization of behavior which has not previously been discussed—motivation. Washburn and Hamburg (1968) have pointed out that if a behavior pattern is important in an evolutionary sense, the performance of that behavior will be pleasurable in and of itself, irrespective of whether it has immediate survival value, e.g., sex, eating beyond what is needed, making maps. In other words, a species is designed so that its members will be motivated to behave in certain ways because of the pleasure derived from those behaviors. In normal environments, these behaviors will usually be beneficial to either the individual or the species, but it is obvious that in abnormal environments, the behaviors may be harmful, e.g., eating too much sugar, which is extremely difficult to accomplish in a hunter-gatherer mode of subsistence.

Robert White (1959, 1960) considers motivation a directing function in learning, and views it as a crucial part of psychological development. The essence of his position is that all of us have an intrinsic motive or drive to deal competently with, or to have mastery over, our environment. He refers to this as "effectance motivation." When a child or adult succeeds in mastering something new, he receives pleasure from this accomplishment, or a "feeling of efficacy." Further, the nature of what an individual is striving to gain competence in changes in systematic ways with development. In his 1960 article, White shows the relationship between effectance motivation and the stages of psychosexual development proposed by Freud and Erikson. For example, in the oral stage, the major competence issues revolve around social play and manipulative skills; in the muscular-anal stage, they revolve around giving and receiving commands and motor skills.

White's view of the relationship between learning, competence motivation, and social competency anticipates much of what is described in this book, as you can see in this portion of the summary of his 1960 paper:

> The concept of competence subsumes the whole realm of learned behavior whereby the child comes to deal effectively with his environment. It includes manipulation, locomotion, language, the building of cognitive maps and skilled actions, and the growth of effective behavior in relation to other people (italics added). These acquisitions are made by young animals and children partly through exploratory and manipulative play when drives such as hunger and sex are in abeyance. The directed persistence of such behavior warrants the assumption of a motivation independent of drives, here called effectance motivation which has its immediate satisfaction in a feeling of efficacy and its adaptive significance in the growth of competence.*

MOTOR SKILLS: EVOLUTIONARY CONSIDERATIONS

The paleoanthropological record suggests that the convergence of three behavioral characteristics approximately 2.6 million years ago gave hominid

---

*Reprinted from "Competence and the Psychosexual Stage of Development" by R. W. White in M. R. Jones (ed.) *Nebraska Symposium on Motivation* by permission of University of Nebraska Press. © 1960 University of Nebraska Press, p. 137.

evolution a big push. These are: bipedal locomotion, stone tool manufacture, and an omnivorous diet. Australopithecine brain size at this time was approximately the same as that of the great apes, but following the confluence of these three characteristics, it started to increase at a rapid rate, tripling in approximately 2.3 million years. We also saw, based on comparative studies, that during this same time period the structures of the brain underlying skilled motor activity changed, giving increased sensory and motor representation to the hand especially. Along with these changes in the brain we noted changes in the shape of the hand, which attained a completely human status about one million years ago, and changes in the complexity and variety of tool making. Thus, there is no doubt that tool manufacture was a central feature of the human adaptation, and that the evolution of skilled motor activity involving the coordination of the eye and the hand was crucial to this adaptation.

A recent study by R. V. S. Wright (1972) gives us a new perspective on hominid tool manufacture and motor skills. In brief, using imitation as the basis for training, Wright taught a juvenile orangutan to make a flake stone tool from a core (we referred to this earlier as a "core" tool), and to use this tool to cut a cord in order to release the lid of a box, thereby gaining access to food. Wright first trained the orangutan in three sessions to use a stone tool to cut the cord: he would demonstrate the technique and then give the orangutan an opportunity to imitate. Unlike Wright, the orangutan held the stone pressed between his thumb and index finger. In seven more sessions, using the same technique of first demonstrating and then giving the orangutan an opportunity to imitate, the orangutan learned to flake a stone core using a hammer, take the tool just manufactured and cut the cord, thereby releasing the lid and allowing the food to be eaten. Figures 25 and 26 on pp. 159 and 160 depict two major aspects of the complete behavior sequence. As you can see in Figure 25, the orangutan has an advantage over humans in this process because he can hold the core with his prehensile feet while striking it with the hammer.

Let's consider the implications of Wright's study. Orangutans are almost completely arboreal animals with a brain size equal to that of *A. africanus*. It is highly unlikely that this species ever used stone tools, let alone manufactured them; carrying stone tools in trees would probably *decrease* survival value, not increase it. Hominid manufacture of core tools apparently did not occur until the evolution of *A. habilis*, who had larger brains than their ancestors. The Wright study indicates, however, that *A. africanus* had the capacity to make core stone tools long before they were actually made. If orangutans have this capacity, then the early australopithecines surely had it. What do we make, then, of the evolutionary changes in the brain and hand?

First, the changes which occurred in the hand and the related regions of the brain indicate that the ability to make highly skillful hand movements had positive selective value. As we stated in previous chapters, a selective advantage need only be slight for a characteristic to become widespread in a species. Second, the increase in brain size which occurred was probably in the association areas allowing for increased connections between the eye and the hand. In order to make stone tools, one must be able to coordinate one's hand movements with what is seen, and the more complicated the tool, the greater is the need for such coordination. Finally, *A. africanus* must have had two other

Figure 25

Abang hammering at the core. He steadies the board with his foot and with the back of the flexed wrist of his left hand (From Wright 1972).

characteristics of high selective value which were mediated by a particular brain size and structure. One of these characteristics is motivational in nature, and the other conceptual. Specifically, it is very likely that prior to the widespread occurrence of tool manufacture, a motivational base for object manipulation had evolved. The australopithecines must have enjoyed manipulating objects, and as a consequence, did so frequently, i.e., they must have acquired effectance motivation for object manipulation. Consistent with this assumption is the report by Van Lawick-Goodall (1973) that chimpanzee infants and juveniles frequently use twigs and branches in play, but baboon infants, who play with the chimpanzees, rarely do so. Thus, there are species differences in the extent of object manipulation, and in the australopithecines, the motivation underlying this characteristic was probably intense. What was the adaptive value of this motivation? There are several reports, summarized by Jolly (1972), that chimpanzees use tools for defense and for increasing dominance status. There is every reason to believe that early hominid tool use had at least these positive survival characteristics, and hence the underlying psychological capacities were selected for.

What about the conceptual base? Rumbaugh (1970) has pointed out that the essence of tool use involves a redefinition or reclassification of the function of materials, e.g., using a branch for hitting. Tool manufacture places additional conceptual demands on an individual in that he must have a plan for making

Figure 26

Preparing to cut the cord with a pushing cut. The loose end of the cord hangs down from the clamp (From Wright 1972).

and using the tool, i.e., he must perceive a need for the tool and have an idea of means-ends relationships, and he must have the capacity to delay using it, i.e., the tool made is typically carried to another place and used there. These capacities are present in at least a rudimentary fashion in the great apes, and possibly the monkeys (Rumbaugh 1970). The more extensive the material reclassification, the more elaborate is the plan, and the greater the delay in tool use, the greater are the conceptual requirements, and by implication, the greater are the brain size requirements. Those who had the requisite conceptual abilities were more likely to survive by virtue of their tool-making and tool-using skills than those who lacked them. Hence, these characteristics became widespread in the species. Thus, during the tool-making phase of hominid evolution, skilled motor behavior, effectance motivation, and conceptual abilities probably grew together, leading to increasingly more elaborate, more intensive, more enjoyable, and more generalized tool manufacture and use.

The remainder of this chapter will focus on children's learning of one aspect of these changes—motor skills involving the eye and the hand. The more conceptual aspects of children's learning will be investigated in subsequent chapters.

DEVELOPMENT OF REACTION TIME, TIMING, AND MOVEMENT TIME

Skilled behavior is an organized sequence of goal-directed, sensory-motor activities which are either guided or corrected by feedback, e.g., riding a bike, writing letters. The exquisite insect-catching abilities of mantisses and frogs lack this feedback component, and hence do not meet the definition (Bartlett 1958, Fitts and Posner 1967). This definition indicates that motor skills are intentionally performed and not reflexive, and that they are made up of more than one component. As Schiller (1952) and Bruner (1973) point out, however, the components of skilled behavior may be reflexive.

Almost all skilled movements involve postural, transport, and manipulation components (Smith and Sussman 1969). When we write, we maintain a certain posture in space, transport our hand by moving our arm from one position to another, and manipulate our hands and fingers at each location. All of these components are organized and responsive to a variety of feedback. Our posture is maintained through information extracted by sensory receptors which respond to gravitational forces. The movement and position of our arm are guided by information extracted by sensory receptors which respond to the position of our joints, the tension of our tendons and muscles (proprioceptive receptors), as well as by visual information. The feedback which guides our hands and fingers is both internal and external, static and dynamic. Proprioceptive information is internal, and while the hand is moving, it is dynamic or constantly changing. The letters we write provide external feedback, and are both dynamic and static, i.e., those which are written are static, while those in progress are dynamic.

The object of any skilled behavior is to accomplish a given task in an interaction with the environment. In the development of any skill we usually require external feedback, commonly referred to as "informational feedback" or "knowledge of results," to provide us with a measure of our success on the task and to help us correct our behavior. Once the skill is developed, internal feedback may be sufficient to guide and correct our behavior, e.g., performing a dive or a salute, or writing a letter of the alphabet.

By definition, then, all motor skills involve movement, and most motor skills involve sequences of movements. Bartlett (1958) points out that three time measures can be made in relation to these movements. The first is reaction time—the time elapsed between the signal to start the movement and the occurrence of the movement, e.g., the time that elapses between the perception that a baseball will fly over your head and your first movements backwards to correct this discrepancy. The second is the interval between successive movements in the sequence, e.g., the time between picking up a baseball and moving your arms to throw the ball to first base. Bartlett refers to this as "timing," and asserts that it is the most important aspect of motor skills. When the performance of a motor skill has the appearance of being uncoordinated or "jerky," it is probably because of faulty timing. The third is the movement time itself —how long it takes to perform each movement, e.g., the speed with which you move your arms down to pick up a ball.

In recent years, a fair amount of research has been carried out with adults on the factors involved in timing. Much of this research has been summarized by Schmidt (1968, 1971). He identifies three major factors or aspects involved in timing: the pattern of proprioceptive feedback from previous responses, the decay of proprioceptive feedback from previous responses, and preprograming of a sequence of movements. Evidence for the first factor comes from studies which varied the amount of proprioceptive feedback in each response of a sequence of responses. The hypothesis made was that the greater the proprioception, the greater would be the cues available to time responses. One way to vary proprioceptive feedback is to require a person to move a lever in a given sequence at given times and vary the force required to move the lever. In studies which have used this technique, accuracy of timing was found to be positively related to amount of proprioception. For the decay factor, the assertion is made that in performing a skill, the individual responds to the decaying memory of the proprioceptive feedback from the previous response. When the memory has decayed to a certain level, this serves as a cue for the next response. The typical example given is a diver performing a sequence of responses while in the air, with each movement timed to the decay of the memory of the preceding response. Evidence for the decay factor comes from studies which varied the tension, and hence the proprioceptive feedback, required to maintain a given response, e.g., holding a lever in a given position. It was hypothesized and found that the greater the tension, the greater was the ease in noting the decay, and hence the more accurate the timing. For the preprogramming factor, the assertion is made that there are situations where proprioceptive cues play essentially no part in the guidance of timing, but rather the sequence of movements is preset in the higher brain centers and "run off" as in a computer program. Evidence for preprogramming comes from observations of sequences of movements which are made too quickly for feedback to play a part, e.g., certain patterns in piano playing or speech. Some laboratory studies support the existence of this factor. As Schmidt points out, these three factors are not mutually exclusive. Rather, a given motor skill may involve the utilization of one or all of them, and further, in the learning and subsequent stable practice of a given skill, the relative contribution of these factors may change.

Given this theoretical background, it is important to determine how these three time-based components of motor skills develop in children. The first experiment deals with a comparison of simple reaction time (RT) with choice RT (Surwillo 1971). RT speed is generally considered to be a function of two separate activities—decision time and movement time. Decision time is the elapsed time between the onset of a signal and the beginning of a movement. Movement time is the time it takes for the movement to be completed. In Surwillo's experiment, movement time was of little consequence because the required movement was pushing a button. The subjects in this experiment were 110 children between the ages of four and seventeen. They were tested on two auditory RT tasks. In the first task, simple RT, ten high tones and ten low tones were presented at variable times ranging from ten to twenty-five seconds apart. The children were instructed to press a button as rapidly as they could to turn off the tone. In the second task, choice RT, they were instructed to press the button as rapidly as they could, but only when the high tones were presented. Two response measures were computed for each subject, for each task: mean RT, i.e., the interval between tone onset and button pressing, and RT standard deviation, which is a measure of how variable the child's performance was from trial to trial, e.g., a large standard deviation means high variability.

For the simple RT task, speed of RT was approximately .75 seconds for the youngest children and .25 seconds for the oldest, with the greatest decreases occurring between ages four and nine. The correlation between age and RT was −.874. This correlation implies that an individual's speed of reaction is almost completely predictable from knowledge of his age. (A correlation of −1.0 means complete predictability, and a correlation of 0.0 means absolutely no predictability. The minus sign in this case means that as age increased, the duration of the response decreased, i.e., speed increased.) For the choice RT task, speed of RT was approximately 1.3 seconds for the youngest children and .35 seconds for the oldest, again with the greatest decreases occurring between ages four and nine. The correlation between age and RT for this task was −.861.

For the standard deviation measure, older children were much less variable in their performance than younger children. For the simple RT task, the correlation between standard deviation size and age was −.759, and for the choice RT task, the correlation was −.561. The latter correlation implies that the predictability between an individual's age and degree of his variability is moderate. As with the speed measures, the greatest decrease in variability occurred between ages four and nine. These results indicate that motor skills which require rapid and consistent decision making, e.g., catching or hitting a ball, will be exceedingly difficult for young children to master. Further, the performance difference between the youngest and oldest children was magnified as the decision became more difficult, i.e., on simple RT, the oldest children reacted three times as fast as the youngest, but on the choice RT, they responded almost four times as fast. What happens when RT involving coordination of the eye and hand is studied?

The next experiment, which relates in part to the preceding question, was performed by Connolly (1970). In his study, the subjects were six groups of people having average ages of approximately six, eight, ten, twelve, fourteen, and twenty-four years. To assess decision time, each person was tested on four card-sorting tasks which varied in the number of choices per card the person was required to make. In one condition, each deck of cards was comprised of twelve cards of one color and twelve of another. All same-colored cards were to be placed in the same location. Hence, each card involved two choices: left location or right location. In the second condition, the deck consisted of six cards of each of four colors, thus involving four choices per card. In the third condition, the deck consisted of four cards each of six colors (six choices). In the fourth condition, the deck consisted of three cards each of eight colors (eight choices). Movement time for each choice deck was assessed by giving each person a blank deck of twenty-four cards and asking him to sort the cards on successive trials as rapidly as he could into two, four, six, and eight piles. The time it took to sort the "choice" decks was assumed to be a function of decision time and movement time. By subtracting the sorting time of the blank deck from the comparable choice deck, a "pure" measure of decision time could be computed.

Figure 27 on p. 165 represents the major results of this experiment for decision time, reported in terms of the average time to sort each card. It is important to note that there was no systematic difference in the number of errors made by the different age groups; however, all age groups made more errors in the two-choice condition than in the other conditions. As you can see, in the two-choice situations, decision time for the adults was three times as fast as that for the six year olds, a finding comparable to that of Surwillo. It is interesting to note that as number of choices increased, decision time also increased, but the performance ratio between the older and younger children decreased. That is, unlike the Surwillo results, as the decision became increasingly more difficult to make, the decision times of the older children were slowed down relatively more than those of the younger children. One possible explanation of this discrepancy is that in the Surwillo experiment, the choice involved inhibiting or making a response, whereas in the Connolly experiment, a response was always made. Perhaps for young children the decision to "go" or "not go" is a more difficult one than the decision to "go left" or "go right." This explanation is consistent with a conclusion of S. White (1965) that the regulation of inhibition consistently improves with age, and is a major issue in development. Finally, as Figure 27 shows, decision time reaches a plateau at about age ten, with the performance of ten, twelve, and fourteen year olds being approximately the same.

Regarding movement time, there was a general increase in speed with increasing age, the youngest child averaging about .86 seconds per card, and the adults about .40 seconds. The number of choices required had essentially

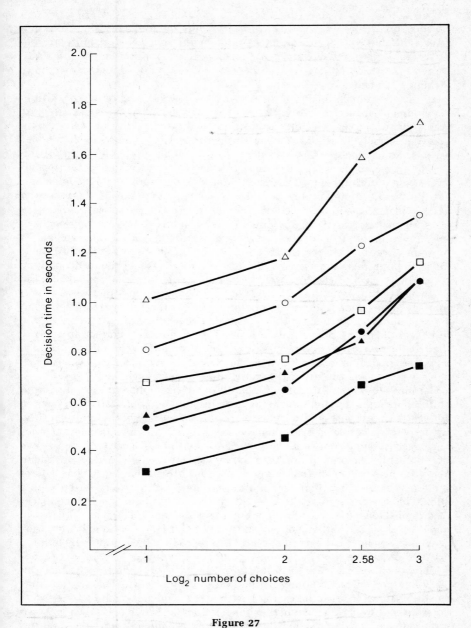

Figure 27

Decision time as a function of number of alternatives per card for the various age groups
(△ 6 years; ○ 8 years; □ 10 years; ▲ 12 years; ● 14 years; ■ adult) (From Connolly 1970).

no effect on performance for any age group. Thus, not only will young children have a difficult time acquiring motor skills requiring quick decisions, but also skills requiring quick movements. The six year old waiting for the pitcher to throw a ball takes a long time to decide to swing and a long time actually swinging the bat.

The last two experiments to be summarized in this section deal with the development of timing ability. Despite Bartlett's view that timing is the most crucial aspect of skilled motor behavior, and the acceptance of this view by many, extremely little research has been carried out on its developmental aspects. Rothstein's (1972) study deals with the ability of children to solve a timing problem. The subjects were four groups of boys with average ages of five, seven, nine, and eleven years. Their task was to learn to press a telegraph key the correct amount of time after their last key press. If the child pressed the key between 2.75 and 3.24 seconds after his last key press, he received a piece of candy; if he pressed the key outside of that interval, he received feedback informing him of the general direction of his error, i.e., too soon or too late. At no time were the children informed of the duration of the sought for timing interval, but rather they were to discover it on the basis of the feedback they received. Thus, consistently correct performance on the task required both the discovery of the target interval, and the ability to time one's responses to that interval. The major findings of this study were: the five year olds had an average number of 2.4 correct responses, the seven year olds, 7.2 correct, the nine year olds, 12.3 correct, and the eleven year olds, 11.3 correct. In general, the five year olds were more variable in their timing than the seven year olds, who were in turn more variable than the nine and eleven year olds. Thus, once again we see a plateau occurring in the nine to eleven age range.

Gardner's (1971) study deals with the ability of six, eight, and eleven year old children to duplicate rhythmic patterns of different lengths. Timing an interval between two responses or external events is a special case of rhythmic sensitivity. In playing a musical instrument or singing, not only must the correct notes be played or sung, but their duration and the intervals between successive notes must be accurate. If not, then the music may be discordant. One way to simplify the study of rhythm is to use a musical instrument in which neither the tone nor tone duration varies, e.g., tapping a drum or a table top with a stick. This is what Gardner did. The children in his study listened to sequences of rhythms, four, five, six, seven, or eight taps in length. The interval between any two taps was either one second or one-third of a second. After each sequence was heard, the child's task was to reproduce it accurately by tapping a pencil on a table top.

The major results were as follows. The six year olds were accurate about sixty-five percent of the time for the four-tap sequences. Their performance steadily decreased with increasing length of the sequence such that they were correct about twenty percent of the time for eight-tap sequences. The eight year olds were correct about eighty-five percent of the time for four-tap sequences, and fifty percent of the time for eight-tap sequences. The performance of the eleven year olds ranged from ninety percent correct for the four-tap sequences to sixty-five percent correct for the eight-tap sequence. Thus, like the Rothstein study, the older children performed better than the younger, but the performance difference between the two oldest groups was minimal.

When the studies in this section are considered as a whole, the following conclusions can be made. As children mature from age four to adulthood, they make faster movement decisions, more consistent movement decisions, faster movements, and their ability to time their movements becomes more accurate and consistent. The last statement is speculative because no complete data to support or refute it are available. For this age range, the period in which these shifts in performance are most marked is from age four to nine. Further, consistent with the view that some neural reorganization occurs during the nine to eleven age range, performance plateaus are consistently found in this period of development after which improvements are more gradual.

DEVELOPMENT OF VISUALLY GUIDED REACHING AND GRASPING

The final three sections of this chapter deal with three related aspects of the development of skilled tool use involving the coordination of the eye and the hand. They are: visually guided reaching and grasping, the complementary use of two hands, and visually guided tool use. Bruner provides a useful overview for conceptualizing the acquisition of these skills. He states

... a great deal of the orderliness in early skilled behavior comes from internal biological sources and is, so to speak, shaped but not constructed by the environment. The first orderly, skilled behavior is virtually "released" by appropriate objects in the environment, presented under appropriate conditions of arousal. A close examination of skill acquisition following this initial, preadapted stage suggests that a capacity for the appropriate construction of skilled action, designed to achieve intended ends, is operative. Skilled acts, to put it in simplest terms, are constructed by the serial deployment of constituent subroutines. The role of learning in the classical sense is to shape and correct these constructions to meet the idiosyncratic nature of particular instances of tasks encountered. Much of the task of "learning" to put constituent acts together for the appropriate attainment of intended objectives occurs in play, as we have argued. Learning, under the circumstances, deserves to be put into quotation marks, since under conditions of play there is no reinforcement for the sorts of sequences that will later appear in skilled behavior.*

The starting point in the child's acquisition of skillful tool use is learning to reach for and grasp the tool. Although this statement appears too obvious to mention, it turns out that visually guided reaching and grasping is a skill requiring many months for infants to acquire, and more importantly, the research bearing on this topic has significant theoretical implications for understanding motor skills development in general.

Perhaps the essential component of a voluntary visual-motor act is to put your limb where your eye "tells it" to go. What is the nature of the experiences an individual must have in order to acquire this ability? For a number of years

---

*Jerome S. Bruner, "Organization of Early Skilled Action," *Child Development* 44 (1973):9.

Richard Held and his colleagues have been carrying out an exciting line of research which is providing some answers to this question. In one experiment (Held and Hein 1963), pairs of kittens were the subjects. They were reared in the dark from birth for approximately ten weeks, at which time they were exposed to patterned light. One member of each pair, the "active" member, was placed in a harness which allowed him to walk and move relatively freely through a lighted room. The other "passive" member was placed in a "gondola" which allowed him to move his head, but not his legs. The gondola was hung in such a way that the passive kitten was moved as the active kitten moved, and thus was exposed to the same pattern of light as the active kitten. This is shown in Figure 28. Hence, the patterned light experience was essentially equivalent for each kitten, but one of them could voluntarily move around in the light, whereas the other could not. On subsequent tests of visually guided behavior, such as paw placement to a horizontal surface and blinking to an approaching object, all the active kittens but none of the passive kittens showed the normal visual-motor coordination. When the passive kittens were allowed two days of free movement in a lighted environment, they all subsequently showed normal sensory-motor coordination. Held and Hein con-

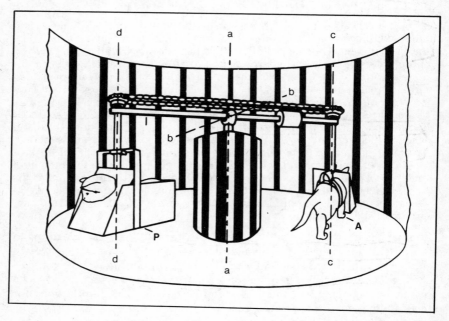

Figure 28

Apparatus for equaling motion and consequent visual feedback for an actively moving (A) and passively moved (P) kitten. The kitten, A, was free to move itself in both directions around the three axes of rotation, a-a, b-b, and c-c. The distance between c-c and d-d was 36 inches (From Held and Hein 1963).

cluded "that self-produced movement with its concurrent visual feedback is necessary for the development of visually guided behavior" (p. 875). But is this the complete answer?

A second experiment by Hein and Held (1967) showed that it was not. In this experiment, two groups of kittens were reared in the dark for four weeks, after which they were allowed free movement in the laboratory for six hours a day for twelve days. The kittens in one of the groups were each fitted during these free periods with a collar (see Figure 29) which prevented them from seeing their limbs and torso, whereas the other group did not have this restriction. For the remaining eighteen hours a day, all individuals were kept in the dark, but without any special collars. Following the twelfth day, the kittens were given two types of tests involving visually guided reach. In the first test, the kitten's body, hindlimbs, and one forelimb were held and the animal was carried downward towards a flat surface. All kittens in both groups extended their free limb towards the surface and made contact with it. In the second test, a similar procedure was carried out, except that the surface was cut in such a way as to form prongs. For this test the kittens were carried towards a prong on some trials, and towards the space between two prongs on other trials. Kittens reared without the collar made contact with a prong on ninety-five percent of these trials, but those reared with the collar made contact on fifty percent of the trials, or exactly by chance. Thus, the visually guided reaching of the restricted animals was markedly impaired. This impairment was not permanent, as demonstrated by the finding that after about eighteen hours of unrestricted movement in the light without the collar, their performance on this and related

Figure 29

Kitten wearing a collar that prevents sight of limbs and torso (From Hein and Held 1967).

tasks was normal. Hein and Held concluded that the development of normal, visually guided reaching requires extensive experience in seeing the voluntarily–produced movements of one's own limbs. Do the results and conclusions of this experiment apply to primates?

The answer is affirmative. Held and Bauer (1967) used stump-tailed macaques as subjects in an experiment in which they could freely move their limbs or any part of their body, but not see them. Within twelve hours after birth, the animals were placed in the special rearing apparatus which accomplished these restrictions (see Figure 30), where they lived for the following thirty-four days. Independent observations of monkeys reared under several laboratory conditions indicate that by one month of age, they can accurately reach for and manipulate objects. After day thirty-four, the specially reared animals were given the opportunity to reach for and manipulate small objects, including their nursing bottle, for one hour a day with one of their limbs. It took approximately twenty days of this procedure for them to develop proficient, visually guided reaching and grasping. At the end of this time, similar tests were run for the previously unexposed limb. After ten days of this procedure, the animals became proficient at visually guided reaching and grasping with the newly exposed limb. Held and Bauer reach the following conclusions:

> The results show that an infant primate initially fails to reach accurately for attractive visible objects with a limb that it has never previously viewed. Yet the animal demonstrates both its interest in the objects and its ability to control movements of eyes and head by orienting them to the target. At the same time, it shows the ability to control movement of its limbs and hands with respect to its body. Integration of visuomotor control of head movement and of nonvisual control of limb movement resulting in the ability to perform a visually directed reach appears to require the specific experience of viewing the moving hand. Sight of the moving hand enables the adult to adapt coordination of the eye and hand to the changes produced by optical rearrangement; likewise, sight of the moving hand perfects accurate visual control of reaching in the neonate.*

What about human infants? If the preceding results are general, then it might be inferred that conditions which slow down the opportunity for observing voluntary hand and limb movements should slow down the development of visually guided reaching and grasping, and conversely, that conditions which increase these opportunities should speed up visually guided reaching and grasping. The latter idea was tested by White, Castle, and Held (1964) and White and Held (1966). In these studies, the subjects were two groups of infants born and reared in an institution. All were judged to be physically normal. One group of infants was reared under the standard institutional procedures. That is, from approximately three weeks to four months of age, they stayed in a crib with sides covered by a white crib liner; they were fed and changed every four

---

*R. Held and J. A. Bauer, Jr., "Visually Guided Reaching in Infant Monkeys after Restricted Rearing," *Science* 155 (1971): 720.

hours; and they received a five-minute bath every morning. The second group of infants received "massive enrichment." For the first five weeks after birth they received an extra twenty minutes of handling each day. From the fifth week through the fourth month, the infants were placed on their undersides and the crib liner was removed after three of the feedings each day, permitting them to see the patterned visual surroundings. During this time period, a highly varied stabile was hung from the crib above their heads and arms, and multi-colored sheets and crib liners were substituted for the white ones normally used. Once a week the infants were given a battery of tests to observe their visually guided reaching behavior, as well as other behaviors.

The major results for the standard institutionally reared infants are shown in Figure 31 on p. 172. For each measurement, the horizontal bar indicates the range of ages for the first occurrence of the behavior, and the vertical slash indicates the group average (the median). In the "Piaget-type" reach, the child reaches towards an object near him, alternates glances between his hand and the object, and then touches the object. A "top-level" reach is a more advanced form of the Piaget-type reach. As you can see, the acquisition of visually guided reaching is a very slow process, taking about 145 days to accomplish. This is in marked contrast to swiping at objects, which takes about 65 days to accomplish. What about the massively enriched infants? For the first eight measures,

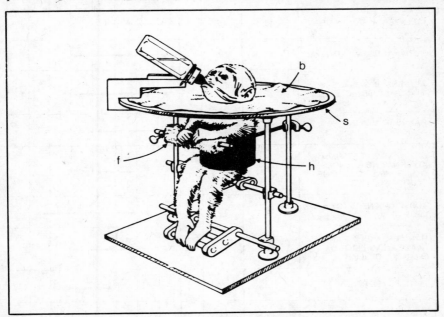

Figure 30

Apparatus for rearing an infant monkey without sight of its limbs. h, metal cylinder; f, fur-covered rod; s, plywood body shield; b, cloth bib (From Held and Bauer 1971).

i.e., "swipes at objects" through "hands to midline and clasp and oriented towards object," their rate of acquiring these behaviors was virtually indistinguishable from that of the other infants. However, for the Piaget-type reach and top-level reach, respectively, the massively enriched infants acquired these behaviors on average five weeks and seven weeks earlier. Thus, visually guided reaching was markedly sped up for these infants. Although it cannot be stated with absolute certainty that the crucial factor in these results was the increased opportunity to observe self-induced limb movement, the experimental manipulations, e.g., presence of the stabile, do indicate that such opportunity was a major factor.

The final research to be discussed in this section was carried out by Bruner (1970). His research starts where White and Held's ends, and deals with the early development of grasping, transferring, and storing objects. The subjects were five groups of infants aged four to five months, six to eight months, nine

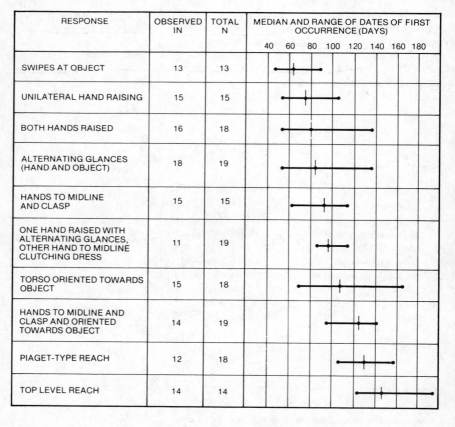

Figure 31

Development of visually directed reaching (From White, Castle, and Held 1964).

to eleven months, twelve to fourteen months, and fifteen to seventeen months. In the task employed, a small toy was presented in front of one of their hands. If the infant grasped it, a second toy was immediately presented to the full hand. If the child took the second toy, third and fourth toys were presented one at a time, midway between his hands. Four trials like this were run, two of which started with the right hand, and two with the left hand.

The major results were as follows. The four to five-month-old children had a very difficult time with this task. Some of them were unable to grasp the first toy, and many who could grasp it dropped it shortly afterwards, or when the second toy was presented. Those who held the first toy for more than a few seconds usually transferred the toy to their mouth. The six to eight-month-old children had a much easier time. All of them were able to grasp and hold two toys. When the second toy was presented, these children usually transferred the first toy to their other hand, but occasionally they transferred the first toy to their mouth. Only one of these children could handle three toys, and that occurred on only one trial. The performance of the nine to eleven-month-old children was similar to that of the six to eight-month-old children, except that about one-third of the older children could on occasion handle three or four toys. They did this by depositing one of the toys onto their lap or onto the armrest of the chair. The twelve to fourteen-month-old children had an easier time than the nine to eleven-month-old children. They handled an average of three toys per problem, only infrequently used their mouth, and they transferred the to-be-deposited toys to their lap or chair arm *in advance* of being presented with the third or fourth toy. The fifteen to seventeen-month-old children handled an average of 3.7 toys per problem, but in general performed much like the twelve to fourteen-month-old children.

These results indicate that grasping, transferring, and storing objects are gradually acquired sets of motor skills which near completion by one and a half years of age. Following the development of the ability to grasp and hold an object, the key age-related hurdles appear to be in transferring an object and storing an object. Once a child has learned to store objects, he rapidly learns to *anticipate* the necessity to do so. The latter ability starts to emerge at about one year of age.

DEVELOPMENT OF THE COMPLEMENTARY USE OF TWO HANDS

It is instructive to watch a person sharpen a pencil. First he will *reach* for the pencil with his preferred hand (usually the right one), *grasp* it, carry it to a pencil sharpener, *transfer* the pencil to his left hand, insert the pencil in the sharpener, and turn the handle of the sharpener with his right hand while simultaneously holding the pencil with his left hand. The turning and holding operation reflects the *complementary* use of two hands. The complementary use of two hands is almost always a necessary condition for hunter-gatherer tool manufacture, and it is frequently an important ingredient in tool use, e.g., using a bow and arrow. We saw in the previous section that the reaching, grasping, and transferring components of motor skills emerge only slowly in infancy, and are perfected during childhood. It should not be surprising to learn that the complementary use of two hands is an ability acquired even more slowly. Its development has an interesting human twist to it because unlike other primates, our brains and limbs are somewhat more specialized. In the discussion which follows, two studies will be summarized. They both cover much of the period of infancy and childhood.

The first study is by Bruner (1970). With the exception of the four to five-month-old infants, all the children in the previously described experiment were tested on a task which provided an opportunity for them to use both hands simultaneously and in a complementary fashion. In this task, they were presented with a box covered with a movable plastic lid, containing an attractive toy. The experimenters observed the behavior of the children in relation to the toy and the box. As expected, almost all the oldest children were always able to get the toy out of the box, whereas few of the youngest were able to do so. Of greater interest was the children's approach to the task. Four major classes of behavior were identified. The first, which Bruner calls "barrier banging," involves hitting the box. The frequency of this activity decreased from approximately two hits per trial at age six to eight months, to about one-third hits at age fifteen to seventeen months. The second, which Bruner calls "autonomous opening," involves opening and closing the lid without reaching for the toy. This behavior was also age-related, but in a more complicated way than barrier banging. In general, the two youngest groups had more autonomous openings than the two oldest groups. The third, which Bruner calls "one-handed reaches," involves sliding the lid up and grasping the toy with the same hand, leaving the other hand inactive. The six to eight-month-old children had the lowest number of one-hand reaches, and the nine to eleven-month-old children the highest. The final class of behaviors, called "partially complementary two-handed reaches," involves raising the lid with two hands, holding it open with one of them, and grasping the toy with the other. This behavior was rare in the six to eight-month-old children, and gradually increased with age, occurring in about one-third of the trials for the fifteen to seventeen-month-old children.

Thus, the ability to use two hands in a complementary fashion is a gradually acquired ability, which starts to emerge towards the end of the child's first year of life. However, once this ability has emerged, it competes with the old modes of behavior, e.g., one-handed reaches, and at a year and a half, it occurs on less than half the trials. Bruner reports that with increasing age beyond a year and a half, complementary two-handed behavior improves, becoming less of an effort and quicker.

There is apparently no recently published research covering the age range one and a half to six years which has systematically studied the complementary use of two hands. Related to this topic, however, is an important finding by Gesell and Ames (1947) that clear-cut hard dominance (handedness) emerges during the end of the child's second year of life. It might be assumed that the onset of handedness would be the basis for speeding up handedness preference in the complementary use of two hands. Is it? We now turn to a study by Bruml (1972) in an attempt to answer this question.

In Bruml's study, the subjects were children in kindergarten, second, and fourth grades, with average ages of approximately six, eight, and ten. They were given twenty-one tasks to perform, which were grouped into three categories. There were three complementary two-handed tasks which required the simultaneous use of both hands: threading beads, winding a thread around a spool, and applauding. There were thirteen "unimanual" preference tasks which required the child to perform a simple task with the hand of his choice, e.g., drawing a circle, touching his nose, picking up a ball, throwing a ball. Finally, there were five "differential" tasks which the child was asked to perform with each hand separately: squeeze a dynamometer to measure strength of grip, fill a pegboard, turn screws, tap with the index finger without aim for ten seconds, and for thirty seconds make dots in a number of small squares in a given order. The children were given all the tasks several times in two sessions separated by two weeks.

For the complementary two-handed tasks, handedness preference, or the stability of the division of labor, was determined as follows (for right-handed children): for the spool task, holding the spool in the left hand and winding the thread with the right; for the clapping task, moving the right hand to clap the left hand; and for the beads task, holding the thread with the left hand and pushing the bead onto it with the right hand. A similar age-related pattern of results was found on all three tasks. For the kindergartners, the percentage of children who performed stably, i.e., had a hand preference, on the three tasks ranged from twenty to forty percent; for the second graders, thirty to sixty-five percent; and for the fourth graders, fifty-five to eighty-five percent. Are these findings a function of change in hand preference?

For the unimanual preference tasks, two measures were reported: consistency of hand usage for a given task, and percentage of children who performed each task with their writing hand. The consistency scores within a session across all tasks and age groups ranged from seventy-seven to one hundred percent, and those between sessions ranged from forty to one hundred percent. There were no systematic differences between the different age groups. For the first session, the percentage of children who performed each task with their writing hand ranged from forty-seven to one hundred percent. Again, there were no systematic differences between the different age groups. Thus, changes in hand preference cannot explain the results.

On all the differential tasks, the older children performed better than the younger children, and with the exception of performance on the dynamometer, all groups of children performed better with their right than left hands. Importantly, the performance difference between the left and right hands remained relatively stable with increasing age.

These results indicate that the increase in handedness preference in the complementary use of two hands between the ages of six and ten cannot be explained in terms of an increase in hand preference per se (unimanual tasks), or a differential increase in skills between the left and right hands (differential tasks). Rather, it appears that a new component in motor skills, perhaps linked to increasing specialization in the brain, emerges and becomes increasingly consolidated during this age range.

To summarize, we can make the following statements about the experimental reports of this section and the previous one. First, the period of acquisition of mature, visually guided motor skills is a very long one. It starts at approximately four months of age with the infant's first attempt to reach an object, and is still maturing at ten years of age with the consolidation of hand preference in the complementary use of two hands. Second, the growth of visually guided two-handed skills consists of the following stages:

1. visually guided reaching at about four months
2. grasping and holding at about six months
3. anticipatory transfer of an object from one hand to another and the emergence of the complementary use of two hands at about one year of age
4. emergence of stable hand preferences in one-handed tasks at about two years of age
5. emergence of stable hand preferences in the complementary use of two hands at about six years of age.

Third, the easiest and simplest way to describe this development is that it moves towards more and more increased differentiation and hierarchical integration. These increases correlate with increased success and economy in performance. That is, as the child matures, he performs more accurately, with less effort, and frequently in a more specialized way. Finally, there is substantial plasticity in the rate at which these stages of development will emerge. Environmental influences can speed them up or slow them down, within limits. However, it is doubtful whether their order of appearance can be modified.

VISUALLY GUIDED TOOL USE: COPYING FIGURES

In the chapter on the brain, it was stated that voluntary motor skills involve the coordination of five neocortical regions (Luria 1970):

1. the primary motor area, which directs the activity of the particular muscle groups involved with a given movement
2. the proprioception and muscle sense areas, which continuously receive sensory feedback from the muscles and joints involved in the movement
3. an area surrounding the boundary of the parietal and occipital lobes, which is involved with the way the movement is organized in space
4. the supplementary motor area, which serves to link together the various components of a skilled act
5. the prefrontal area, which is involved with the planning and organization of movements.

When one of these areas is damaged, the individual loses part of his capacity for performing skilled motor activity, e.g., damage to the parietal-occipital area renders the individual unable to precisely locate his movements in space, although the component parts of the skill are left relatively intact. In a similar way, when any of these regions are highly immature, as in children, the individual lacks the full functional capacities of that region. The associative or integrative regions of the brain fall in this category; hence, planned organization of movements and their precise location in space should be particularly slow to develop.

All of these component processes and functions obviously apply to skilled tool manufacture, as in making flaked stones. However, there is an additional process here because the individual must visually assess his progress against some visual standard, whether "out there" or "in the head," i.e., the visual specification of the tool. When making flake tools, the core is prepared so as to meet certain visual specifications, and once the flake is knocked off, it in turn is worked on in order to attain certain other visual specifications. In making core tools, the core is unprepared, and the resulting flakes are generally not worked on.

What does copying figures have to do with all this? Basically, nearly everything. Copying a figure probably comes as close to meeting the psychological requirements of skilled tool manufacture as any other task short of tool making per se. For example, in order to copy a triangle, the child must accurately perceive the triangle, i.e., construct an image of it which encompasses its distinctive features, transfer this information to those locations of the brain which control fingers, hand, and arm movements, and move a pencil in ways which produce lines to match the parts of this image. As the pencil is moved, the child is receiving dynamic and static sensory information which he must accurately integrate, and on the basis of this information he must modify his movements in order to get the next sought-for visual, tactile, and proprioceptive feeedback, and so on, until the task is completed.

We will attempt to understand the factors underlying progress which children make in their attempts to master this type of problem by discussing several experiments carried out by Birch and Lefford (1963, 1967) and one by Rand (1973). In Birch and Lefford's (1967) experiments, children of ages five, six, seven, eight, nine, ten and eleven were given two types of tasks: visually discriminating forms and copying figures. In the form discrimination task, the children viewed a large card which contained twelve geometric shapes. Among them were an upright triangle, a vertical diamond, an inverted triangle, and an equiangular diamond. These were the four shapes used in the copying task. While viewing the large card, they were presented with a separate small card containing one of the twelve shapes and asked to point to the same shape on the large card. All twelve shapes were presented in this fashion. The two major results were: (1) the number correct increased with age, ranging from 10.9 at age five to 11.6 at age eleven; (2) the most typical errors made by the children aged five to eight involved confusing the two diamonds with each other and the two triangles with each other. For example, twenty-six percent of the five year olds chose the vertical diamond when presented with the equiangular one, and forty-eight percent of the five year olds chose the inverted triangle when the upright triangle was presented. These results indicate that the children studied have little difficulty in making discriminations between widely different shapes, but that the youngest children do have some difficulty in discriminating similar shapes.

On the figure-copying task, the children were tested in six different conditions with each of the four figures. Three of these were: tracing the figures, copying the figures freehand on a blank sheet of paper, and copying the figures on a sheet of paper which contained preprinted dots corresponding to the angles of the figures. In the last condition, all a child had to do to be correct was connect the dots with straight lines. The children's drawings were scored on the basis of five criteria: accuracy in the relative size of parts, accuracy in the vertical spatial orientation, accuracy in the horizontal spatial orientation, clearly defined angles, and straightness of lines. Thus, a child would receive a score of two if his lines were straight and his angles clearly defined, but he failed the other three criteria. The major results for these three conditions are presented in Table 9. The mean number of criteria (out of five) are shown for each age group which were adequately met for the two triangles and two diamonds.

As you can see from the table, under all drawing conditions with all figures there was an age-related improvement in accuracy, with the greatest change occurring between ages five and six, after which it became more gradual. This was especially pronounced for the diamonds conditions. In general, performance was far superior under the dot-connecting and tracing conditions than under the freehand copying conditions, with these effects being most marked when the diamonds were employed. Importantly, there was little performance difference between the dot-connecting and tracing conditions, which suggests that the difficulty found in the freehand copying condition is not attributable to drawing on blank space *per se*.

What do these results mean? The fact that the performance of the five year olds was very good with the triangles under the tracing and connecting conditions indicates that the difficulties they encountered in the other conditions are *not attributable* to lack of motor skills, i.e., directing the activity of particular muscle groups, linking the motor components together, and organizing the movements. The fact that all the children had difficulty drawing diamonds freehand, especially the five year olds, strongly suggests that *part of* the performance deficit lies in either localizing movements in space, or in assessing performance against a visual standard., The latter is essentially a

Table 9

Accuracy Scores in Copying Figures

Triangles

Age	5	6	7	8	9	10	11
Tracing	4.5	4.8	4.8	5.0	4.9	4.9	5.0
Connecting Dots	4.3	4.6	4.7	4.8	4.7	4.5	4.8
Copying Freehand	3.7	4.0	4.3	4.3	4.6	4.0	4.3

Diamonds

Age	5	6	7	8	9	10	11
Tracing	3.6	4.4	4.4	4.6	4.8	4.9	4.8
Connecting Dots	3.4	4.3	4.1	4.3	4.3	4.3	4.6
Copying Freehand	1.5	2.9	3.0	3.5	3.6	3.3	3.6

Source: Herbert G. Birch and Arthur Lefford, "Visual Differentiation, Intersensory Integration, and Voluntary Motor Control." *Monographs of the Society for Research in Child Development*, 1967, 32, Ser. no. 110.

perceptual discrimination problem. The following study by Rand (1973) allows us to rule out one of these two.

In Rand's experiment, the children were between three and five years old. They were initially tested on a discrimination task and freehand drawing task similar to those of Birch and Lefford. Following this the children were divided into three groups:

1. a group who received "visual analysis" training which was directed towards improving their ability to make visual discriminations
2. a group who received "drawing-rules" training, in which they were taught to make dots where corners of figures appeared
3. a control group who told stories and drew pictures.

Each group was then given another freehand drawing test and another discrimination test. The group who received visual analysis training performed much better on the post-training discrimination test than on the pre-training test, and better than the other two groups who showed no improvement over their initial pre-training performance. On the post-training freehand drawing test, however, none of the groups showed any improvement over their initial pretraining performance. These results indicate that increasing discrimination ability does not necessarily lead to increased copying ability; and hence, the superior performance of older as compared to younger children on copying tasks is probably not attributable to the superior discrimination ability of the older children.

During the performance of a freehand copying task, an individual must integrate information received from his touch, muscle, joint, and visual senses and attempt to locate in space his future responses on the basis of this integrated (or lack of integrated) information. Perhaps part of the difficulty young children have in freehand copying stems from their inability to accomplish such an intersensory integration. Stated another way, if the child can't compare what his hand and eye are separately telling him, then he will probably have trouble telling his hand where to go. One way of assessing how well children can integrate information from different sensory modalities is to present them with a stimulus through one sense modality and ask them to match it with a stimulus from another modality. This was essentially the procedure of Birch and Lefford (1963).

In their experiment, the same children as in the 1967 study were the subjects. The three modalities were visual, haptic, and kinesthetic. Haptic stimulation is a complex sensory input involving touch, muscle, and joint sensations, produced in this experiment by a child actively exploring an unseen object with his hand. Kinesthetic stimulation involves muscle and joint sensations, produced in this experiment by a child holding a stylus which the experimenter moved through a track on a board; thus, the child's arm was passive. The stimuli used were eight differently shaped blocks from the Sequin Form board, e.g., triangle, hexagon, cross. In the kinesthetic condition, the experimenter moved the stylus to correspond with the shape and size of the blocks. In the haptic condition, the child explored the block hidden behind a screen. On each trial the child was presented with two stimuli, each through a different sensory modality, and asked to respond "same" or "different". Two types of errors corresponding to two types of trials can occur: saying "same" when the two shapes are nonidentical, and saying "different" when they are identical. The percentage of errors for each condition is presented in Table 10.

As you can see from the table, relatively more errors were made when the children had to assess identical as opposed to nonidentical stimuli. This finding may be attributable to a response bias, however, since there were more than three times as many nonidentical as identical comparisons. Hence, correct performance usually called for the child to say "different," and children may have adopted the strategy of saying "different" when in doubt. Despite this caution, it should be noted that the youngest children in all conditions made on the average four times as many errors as the oldest children. In general, the five year olds experienced the greatest difficulty on these tasks, the six and seven year olds the next amount of difficulty, and with increasing age thereafter children had progressively less difficulty. Looking back at Table 9 on p. 178, comparable findings can be seen for the freehand copying of diamonds.

These findings suggest that young children generally experience substantial difficulty in integrating information from different sensory modalities. This inability should interfere with their freehand copying of figures when they must supply the visual image for locating their movements in space. In the tracing and dot—connecting conditions, they can rely primarily on the visual information supplied for them, and need not depend so heavily on kinesthetic feedback. Thus, the development of children's ability to copy figures is at least

Table 10
Percentage of Errors in Intersensory Integration

Judgments of Identical Forms

Age	Visual-Haptic	Visual-Kinesthetic	Haptic-Kinesthetic
5 years	14.4%	49.4%	49.4%
6 years	8.8	27.5	34.4
7 years	8.1	21.9	23.8
8 years	2.5	20.0	16.3
9 years	2.5	20.0	13.8
10 years	1.9	12.5	11.3
11 years	2.5	11.3	10.6

Judgments of Nonidentical Forms

Age	Visual-Haptic	Visual-Kinesthetic	Haptic-Kinesthetic
5 years	5.2%	10.2%	8.2%
6 years	3.9	9.3	6.2
7 years	4.1	8.7	6.2
8 years	2.5	6.4	4.6
9 years	2.0	5.2	3.0
10 years	2.1	5.4	2.7
11 years	1.2	2.5	1.6

Source: Herbert G. Birch and Arthur Lefford, "Visual Differentiation, Intersensory Integration, and Voluntary Motor Control." *Monographs of the Society for Research in Child Development*, 1967, 32, Ser. no. 110.

partly a function of their growing ability to precisely locate their movements in space; and precise localization depends at least partly on their ability to integrate sensory information from different modalities.

SUMMARY

This chapter may be briefly summarized as follows. There are three temporal aspects to voluntary skilled movements: reaction time, movement time, and timing. With increasing age, children make decisions faster and with less variability, make movements faster, and more accurately time the intervals between successive movements. The greatest changes in these components occur between the ages of four and nine.

The development of visually guided motor skills depends in part on the ability to perceive one's moving limbs. Conditions which speed up opportunities to do this speed up the acquisition of visually guided reaching and grasping. Children normally master both behaviors by six months of age, and by one year of age the child can anticipate the need to transfer objects from one hand to the other.

A key component of visually guided tool use and manufacture is the complementary use of two hands. Children start to acquire this ability at about age one and a half. Although stable hand preferences for grasping and using tools occurs by the end of the second year of life, stable hand preferences in the complementary use of two hands doesn't start to develop until about age six, and is not completely stabilized by age ten. Another key component in visually guided tool use and manufacture is the ability to precisely locate one's movements in space. Children of age five have great difficulty with tasks requiring this ability, and the difficulty they experience is partly attributable to their deficits in intersensory integration.

Chapter 9

LANGUAGE DEVELOPMENT

OVERVIEW

Although two chimpanzees have recently been taught the rudiments of human language—in one case Premack and Premack (1972) trained their young chimpanzee "Sarah" to use different color plastic shapes as words and to employ rules for spatially arranging the "words," and in the other case Gardner and Gardner (1969) trained their young chimpanzee "Washoe" to make limited use of the American Sign Language—it is quite clear that no species other than man normally utilizes humanlike language. In addition, in light of the fact that these chimpanzees acquire and use language exclusively through the visual modality, and that children acquire and use language primarily through the auditory modality, it is not clear what the chimpanzee data tell us about the evolution or development of language. In our earlier discussions on the evolution of man's brain and vocal apparatus, we saw that early man possessed three neocortical structures involved with the production or understanding of spoken language which differentiated him from the other higher primates—Broca's area, Wernicke's area, and the angular gyrus—and that man's vocal tract was progressively adapted for speech production, whereas that of the other primates was not. Thus, an understanding of language evolution or development requires an understanding of spoken language. That chimpanzees can learn highly symbolic acts testifies to their high level of conceptual abilities, but tells us little about man's language.

We speculated earlier, following Hockett and Ascher, that spoken language emerged about one million years ago with the evolution of *Homo erectus*. There really is no way to verify this speculation, and in fact, based on

182

Lieberman's (1973) analysis of Cro-Magnon and Neanderthal skulls, it may be that the contemporary form of language only became widespread about 40,000 years ago. It is possible that both views are correct. After all, brain size of *Homo erectus* does overlap the lower end of the distribution of normal brain size of *Homo sapiens,* and in almost all other ways there is little to distinguish between the two species. If it is difficult to state *when* language emerged in human evolution, then it must also be difficult to state *what role* it had in human evolution. The paleoanthropological record concerning man's cultural development provides few clues because it contains no sharp breaks which can be linked inevitably to the emergence of language; rather, the record tends to be one of gradual change.

One possible way to evaluate the role of language in evolution is through the comparative method. When the activities of human hunter-gatherers are compared with those of other primates and other social predators, such as wolves, one major distinguishing characteristic is that hunter-gatherers frequently operate at great distances from one another, i.e., out of sight, sound, and smell, and in a coordinated fashion, whereas the other species do so only infrequently. For example, the women may proceed in one direction to gather food, and different groups of men may move in other specified directions to hunt, all returning towards evening to share in their successes. One important role language may have had is to facilitate this future-oriented, long-distance coordination; in fact, it is difficult to envision this type of coordination without language. When the members of the other species are in sight, sound, and smell of each other in their normal social environment, their activities are frequently superbly coordinated, as in hunting, defense of the young, and maintaining harmony within the group. Hence, it is doubtful that the primary evolutionary push of language lay in regulating these nearby, here-and-now activities.

Whatever the initial role of language in man's evolution, once it became a stable characteristic, it came to have a life of its own. Until written language was invented about 5000 years ago, this independent life—this evolutionary "opportunity"—can only be speculated upon, but following Campbell's (1966) suggestion, it is highly likely that language contributed to group cohesion by making the creation of myths, rituals, and song possible. It augmented almost all of man's nearby, here-and-now activities, ranging from courtship to the initiating and settling of arguments. With the written word came additional opportunities and responsibilities. The quantity of knowledge which could be accumulated increased by many factors; laws could readily and publicly be codified; business transactions could easily be stored; and great myths, histories, and poems designed to answer great questions and stir men's hearts could be accurately recorded. But someone had to make and keep the records and someone had to teach others to do likewise. Eventually, literacy came to be not a luxury, but an obligation. Perhaps the turning point occurred with the invention of the printing press about 500 years ago. From the point of view of man's evolution, however, the time segment which encompasses written language is truly miniscule, and the time segment following the occurrence of widespread literacy is even smaller. As an interesting footnote to the last comment, the age at which children first have the necessary sensory-motor skills to write is many years after they have a good understanding of language and a fair ability to speak it.

In the discussion which follows, we will be concerned primarily with the ontogeny of the understanding, speaking, and utilizing of spoken language in normal children. Although the ontogeny of writing and reading skills is of great interest, and learning to read and write is frequently a source of great discomfort to some children and their parents, space limitations do not allow such a discussion.

What is meant by the phrase "spoken language?" In the simplest terms, a given spoken language is a collection of sounds, called phonemes, a set of rules for sequentially combining these sounds to form words ("morphemes"), a set of meanings for these words, a set of rules for combining these words into sentences, and a set of rules for relating sentences to meanings, i.e., the same words in different orders may have different meanings and different words in different sentences may have the same meaning. For any given language, linguists and psycholinguists are very confident about listing the phonemes and stating the rules for combining them into words. They are somewhat confident about stating the meaning of these words, but from that point on their confidence drops off markedly. It is highly unlikely that any native speaker can formulate any of these rules; rather, people speak in ways which indicate that their language is governed by rules (a "grammar"). The job of linguists and psycholinguists is to discover these rules and to determine how people actually use or misuse them. The job of the child is to learn the whole business. This is a phenomenal job, but one which every normal child accomplishes very success-fully. Once a child has accomplished this, he will have the ability to under-stand and speak an *infinite* number of sentences.

Prior to the early 1960s, only a handful of psychologists were actively involved in studying language development. Much of their research could easily be summarized, and in fact was summarized by Brown (1965). By the 1970s, however, the situation was quite different. Research in this important area is now written up faster than it can be summarized. As a consequence, the following discussion will be highly selective and will be based on the surveys of some of those most active in the field. Three broad areas will be covered:

1. the maturational control of language development
2. the child's first words and his development of an understanding of grammar
3. the development of the role of language in regulating the child's behavior.

MOTOR DEVELOPMENT AND LANGUAGE DEVELOPMENT

Some of Lenneberg's (1966, 1967) research will be summarized in this section. As we indicated in previous chapters, the starting assumptions are that language development is a canalized process which proceeds through a number of stages and is linked with brain maturation. In our brief discussions dealing with brain maturation and brain function, we stated that there are apparently three age periods in which major functional reorganizations occur, one to two years after birth, five to seven years, and nine to eleven years, and that the brain regions roughly corresponding to language understanding mature the slowest. Clearly there is no known one-to-one correspondence between a given level of brain maturation and a given stage of language development. For example, it cannot be said that a child starts using two-word phrases because a given region of his brain has reached a specified level of development. Thus, any evidence linking brain maturation with the nature of language development must be indirect. The indirect evidence we have selected deals with the relationship between motor development and language development in normal children and children with Down's Syndrome. Down's Syndrome is produced by the presence of an extra chromosome in the genotype and leads to, among other things, a sharply reduced level of intelligence. Lenneberg's basic argument is, given the assumption that motor development is under maturational control, that if the milestones for motor development and language development proceed in a nearly lock-step fashion, even if slowed down owing to mental retardation, then language development should also be under maturational control.

Table 11 summarizes some of the major developmental milestones of language and motor development in normal children. Several comments should be made about this table. First, the lock-step appearance of language and motor development should not be taken to mean that language development causes motor development, or vice versa. Both unfold under a maturational schedule, and there have been many documented cases with abnormal children in which one schedule has unfolded at a much slower rate than the other, e.g., children who start speaking at age three or four. Second, the table contains average ages, with some normal children moving along faster and some slower than the designated age-related milestones. Lenneberg asserts, however, that when development is slowed down or speeded up within the normal range, the language and motor milestones still covary. When children learn to run, they have also acquired the ability to use two-word phrases. Finally, the language environment to which the child is exposed apparently has little effect on the relationship between these two classes of milestones. Children from "primitive" societies and hearing children of deaf parents seem to show the same developmental patterns depicted in this table (Lenneberg 1967).

From the point of view of this argument, it is unfortunate that a table parallel to Table 11 cannot be constructed for children with Down's Syndrome. Lenneberg and his colleagues studied sixty-one Down's Syndrome children over a three year period who were living at home and being raised by their normal parents. The children were seen two or three times a year, and at each visit they were given a battery of tests. In general, a close positive relationship was found between IQ and language development, with some children never progressing beyond the stage in which only single words and two-word phrases were used. All the children below age fourteen made some progress on their motor and language development during the period of study. If motor development and language development are under maturational control, and if Down's Syndrome slows down the rate of maturation (as well as placing an upper limit on maturation), then three things should happen in a Down's Syndrome child:

1. the sequence of motor and language milestones should remain unchanged;
2. the various milestones should occur later in development relative to normals;
3. the time intervals between the various milestones should be proportionately longer.

This is exactly what was observed. For example, in normals, the time interval between sitting and putting words together is about thirteen months, and the apparent full establishment of language follows about twenty months later. In the Down's Syndrome children, if the interval between sitting and putting words together was about twenty-four months, then the full establishment of language did not occur until an additional sixty months had elapsed.

Table 11

Milestones in Language and Motor Development

Age	Motor Development	Language Development
12 weeks	supports head when in prone position	smiles when talked to and makes cooing sounds
16 weeks	plays with rattle when placed in hands	turns head in response to human sounds
20 weeks	sits with props	makes vowellike and consonantlike cooing sounds
6 months	reaches, grasps	cooing changes to babbling which resembles one-syllable sounds
8 months	stands holding on; picks up pellet with thumb and finger	increasing repetitions of some syllables
10 months	creeps; pulls self to standing position; takes side steps while holding on	appears to distinguish between different adult words by differential responding
12 months	walks when held by one hand; seats self on floor	understands some words; says mama, dada
18 months	can grasp, hold, and return objects quite well; creeps downstairs backward	has repertoire of between three and fifty spoken words, said singly
24 months	runs, walks up and down stairs	has repertoire of more than 50 words; uses two-word phrases
30 months	stands on one foot for about two seconds; takes a few steps on tiptoe	tremendous increase in spoken vocabulary; many phrases containing three to five words
3 years	tiptoes three yards; can operate a tricycle	vocabulary of about 1000 words; pronounciation clear
4 years	jumps over rope, hops on one foot	language apparently well established

Source: E. Lenneberg, *Biological Foundations of Language*, (New York: John Wiley & Sons, 1967), p. 225. By permission of John Wiley & Sons.

Table 12 shows some of the relationships between motor development and language development in the Down's Syndrome children observed by Lenneberg. The term "mostly babble" refers to the vocalization of syllablelike sounds, and the term "language developing" refers to the predominance of words and phrases in the child's vocalizations, and general absence of babbling. The numbers in the table refer to the number of children in a particular category. For example, fourteen children who mostly babbled, walked and ran; whereas thirty-nine children who walked and ran were developing language. As you can see from the table, language development and motor development are strongly related to one another. Lenneberg points out that the relationship between hand preference and language development is particularly interesting because both occur much later in children with Down's Syndrome than in normals, and yet the same relationship is seen in both groups.

Table 12
Relationship Between Motor Skills and Language in Children with Down's Syndrome

Motor Skills	Language	
	Mostly Babble	Language Developing
walk and run	14	39
toddle or less	7	1
dresses self	4	27
needs help dressing	17	13
feeds self well	11	35
feeds self poorly	10	5
right handed	6	23
ambidextrous or no determined handedness	12	14

Source: E. Lenneberg, *Biological Foundations of Language* (New York: John Wiley & Sons, 1967), p. 227. By permission of John Wiley & Sons.

To summarize, Lenneberg assumes that motor development is in large part under the control of the maturation of the brain, and asserts that language development is also. He argues that if it can be shown that the milestones for language development and motor development are linked together, or covary, then this constitutes indirect evidence that language development is under maturational control. He then shows that in fact the milestones do covary; and moreover, they covary for children with Down's Syndrome and normals in the same way. For children with Down's Syndrome, the sequence of milestones occur at a slower rate than for normals, and the intervals between the various milestones are proportionately longer for them than for the normals.

EARLY LANGUAGE UTILIZATION AND COMPREHENSION
As we stated in the "Overview," there is currently a vast amount of psychological research being carried out in the area of early language development. The two basic techniques being used are observational, i.e., noting

the spontaneous language use of children, and asking children to perform certain language-based activities, such as imitating sentences and following instructions. Typically both techniques are used in a given experiment, and the typical experiment which deals with a small number of children takes at least one year to complete. It is a very laborious process which is very boring for the researcher, less boring for the children's parents, and probably moderately interesting for the children who have little toleration for boring tasks. As a consequence, carrying out this research is highly dependent upon grimly determined researchers, cooperative parents who have little to gain by the research, and cooperative children who have nothing to gain. Probably owing to the fact that almost all the research in the United States has been carried out by white, middle-class psychologists, almost all the data collected there have been based on white, middle-class children. Fortunately, a fair amount of data have been collected in other countries with other racial-ethnic groups. Unfortunately, only some of these data are comparable to those of the American sample. We will relate the two sets of data where they can be related.

In order to be an effective listener and speaker, a child not only has to learn the words of a language and their meaning, but how to put the words together in specified ways so that he can understand the intentions of speakers and make his own language intentions understood. For example, "the ball hit the boy" has a very different meaning from "the boy hit the ball," although the two sentences are alike in all ways except word order. On the other hand, "the boy hit the ball" and "the ball was hit by the boy" have almost the same meaning.

One natural starting point in this discussion is the nature of the child's first words, and how well rate of subsequent language development can be predicted from the rate of acquiring these first words. As we have already noted, the average child starts using single-word utterances at about one year of age, builds up a working vocabulary of about fifty words during the next six to twelve months, at which time he starts to use two-word phrases. What kinds of words do children learn, what is the relative rate of acquisition of the different kinds of words, is initial rate of word acquisition related to subsequent language development, and how is rate of acquisition related to environmental influences?

Katherine Nelson's (1973) recent monograph provides tentative answers to these questions. In her study, eighteen white, middle-class children were regularly observed from the time they uttered their first comprehensible word at approximately one year of age, until they acquired a fifty word vocabulary at approximately twenty months of age. They were observed again at twenty-four and thirty months of age to assess their subsequent language development. Nelson classified these fifty words into the following five grammatical categories:

1. Nominals: words used to refer to animate and inanimate "things" in the world. They may be *specific nominals*, which identify categories in which there is only one member, e.g., "mommy," "Dizzy" (a pet), or *general nominals*, which identify all the members of a category, e.g., "ball," "doggie," "he."
2. Action Words: words that describe action, e.g., "go," "bye-bye"; demand

or accompany action, e.g., "up," "out"; or express or demand attention, e.g., "look," "hi."

3. Modifiers: words which refer to properties or qualities of events or "things," e.g., "big," "pretty," "allgone," "there," "mine."

4. Personal-Social: words which describe feelings or desires either initiated by the child, e.g., "please," "ouch," "want," or made in response to questions, e.g., "no," "yes."

5. Function Words: words that relate to other words and serve solely a grammatical function, e.g., "what," "where," "is," "to."

Table 13 shows the order of acquisition of these categories of words. As you can see, the overwhelming majority of the children's first fifty words are nominals. Of these, the acquisition of specific nominals decreases over time (the child learns "Mommy" and "Daddy" right away), and the acquisition of general nominals increases. Personal-social and function words are infrequent, comprising twelve percent of the words.

Table 14 analyzes the acquisition of general nominals. In commenting about these data, Nelson points out that the majority of the clothing words acquired were of those items which the child frequently and easily acted on, e.g., shoes, hat, socks, and that the majority of the household and furniture words acquired were of small items, e.g., clock, light, blanket. In general, the children failed to learn the names of things which just "sat there."

When Tables 13 and 14 are considered together, it may be concluded that the first fifty words generally refer to things which the child can act on, to things which move in some way, and to the child's own actions. This observation, of course, is consistent with the view that the child, during much of the period in which the first fifty words are acquired, is in the sensory-motor stage of development, when his knowledge of the world is based on action. Thus, during this period the child learns the symbols (words) for the knowledge he has already acquired through action.

Table 13

Percentage of Words in Each Grammatical Category

	Word Acquisition Order					
	1-10	11-20	21-30	31-40	41-50	Overall
Specific Nominals	24	12	14	12	9	14
General Nominals	41	45	46	60	62	51
Action Words	16	15	14	12	9	13
Modifiers	8	10	8	8	12	9
Personal-Social	5	13	11	4	4	8
Function Words	6	4	7	3	3	4

Source: Katharine Nelson, "Structure and Strategy in Learning to Talk," Monographs of the Society for Research in Child Development, 1973, 38, Ser. no. 149, p. 20.

In a subsequent paper, Nelson (1974) briefly reviews the literature dealing with children's word acquisition during their first two years of life, and summarizes the data as follows:

1. There is a small set of words that are learned at the outset by a large number of children. These consist largely of names for food, people, animals, and things that move or change in some way. The one outstand-

ing general characteristic of the early words is their reference to objects and events that are perceived in dynamic relationships; that is, actions, sounds, transformations—in short, variation of all kinds. This characteristic dynamic base results from principles utilized by the child rather than being adult imposed. Such a conclusion is supported by the obvious fact that the child selects from among those words spoken to him by adults those that he will use.

2. In addition, it has been widely observed by students of child language that when a word that expresses his meaning is not available, the young child from the very beginning of language acquisition will frequently invent one. Such productions must reflect the child's preexisting conceptual organization which does not always quite match that of the language community.

3. Once acquired, a word is usually generalized to other "similar" things. Similarity may be based on many different dimensions, of which the static perceptual dimension of shape or form is only one; others include function, action, or affect. Piaget, Leopold, and Werner and Kaplan among others have provided extensive examples of this early propensity for generalization, and Clark has recently analyzed some of the overextensions of word meanings found in early language diary studies. Bloom has suggested that there are stages of generalization reflecting the use of different cognitive principles at different ages, but the evidence for this hypothesis is, at present, slight. Furthermore, the child's meanings may also be underextended or simply "different from" adult meanings.*

Table 14
Semantic Categories of Early and Late General Nominals

	Words 1-10 (%)	Words 41-50 (%)
Animals	34	13
Food	23	30
Toys	15	2
Vehicles	9	4
Household Items	7	11
Clothing, Personal Items	6	15
People	6	2
Body Parts	—	17
Miscellaneous	1	6

Source: Katherine Nelson, "Structure and Strategy in Learning to Talk," *Monographs of the Society for Research in Child Development*, 1973, 38, Ser. no. 149, p. 30.

Returning now to Nelson's (1973) data, there was considerable variation in the rate at which these children learned to speak their first fifty words. Does a child who acquires these words rapidly also make rapid progress in later periods of language development? For example, does a child who learns his first ten words rapidly learn his first fifty words rapidly? Nelson took the following measures of language development for each child, and correlated each measure with every other measure:

---

*Katherine Nelson, "Concept, Word and Sentence: Interrelations in Acquisition and Development," *Psychological Review* 81 (1974): 269.

1. age at which the first ten words were acquired
2. age at which the first fifty words were acquired
3. number of new words per month
4. age at which the child spoke ten different two-word phrases (this and the preceding measures relate to ages younger than twenty-four months)
5. size of vocabulary at twenty-four months
6. average number of words spoken in each utterance at twenty-four months (MLU = mean length utterance)
7. how well children articulated phonemes at twenty-four months
8. MLU at thirty months
9. vocabulary at thirty months.

In general, all measures taken prior to twenty-four months of age were positively correlated with each other, ranging from .34 between number of new words per month and age at which children acquired their first ten words, to .86 between number of new words per month and age at which the first fifty words were acquired. Similarly, the measures taken at twenty-four months were positively correlated with those taken at thirty months. These positive correlations indicate that in the period between fifteen months and twenty-four months of age, and in the period between twenty-four months and thirty months of age, children who have progressed rapidly on one measure of language development have also made rapid progress on all other measures of language development. Similarly, children who have progressed slowly during these periods on one measure of language development have also progressed slowly on all other measures of language development.

What about the relationship between the two sets of measures? These correlations should indicate how well individual differences in later language learning can be predicted from rate of earlier language learning. For example, if we know that a child acquires his first fifty words very rapidly, can we predict that he will have a large vocabulary at thirty months of age? When the early measures were correlated with the measures taken at twenty-four months of age, there was moderately good predictability, with the correlations ranging from .26 between articulation and age of first ten phrases, to .73 between vocabulary and age of first fifty words. When the early measures were correlated with those taken at thirty months of age, there was very limited predictability, with the correlations ranging from −.02 between MLU and age of first ten words, to .36 between number of words per month and MLU. Hence, to answer the question raised at the beginning of this section, initial rate of word acquisition is not related to subsequent rate of language development.

Finally, how does rate of language development relate to the experiences the child has with his parents, other children, other adults, T.V., and contact with the outside world? Basically, none of the language measures taken at any age showed any systematic relationship with either the father's or mother's education level, with amount of time spent with the father, or with the number of other children they were in contact with. Also, the nature of the mother's talk to the child bore little systematic relationship to individual differences in language development. As you will shortly see, this last surprising result is found in another study dealing with very different groups of children. If these measures do not correlate with rate of language development, then what does?

Nelson identified four environmental factors which were moderately corre-lated with language development up to and including vocabulary and MLU at twenty-four months, but which were weakly correlated with MLU and vo-cabulary at thirty months. These were:

1. hours spent with other children each week (negatively correlated)
2. amount of T.V. watched (negatively correlated)
3. number of adults in contact with (positively correlated)
4. number of activities per week (positively correlated).

None of these factors were related to how well a child articulated. Nelson interprets these findings in terms of how much attention the mother and other adults give the child, and how much they interact with him—the more attention and interaction, the faster the early rate of spoken language acquisi-tion. However, by thirty months of age, these environmental influences, pre-sumably all within the normal range, lose their impact. This is reminiscent of the stair-climbing experiment of McGraw. You can temporarily speed up or delay psychological development by environmental influences, but the genetic schedule—the canalization process—takes over and overrides these factors.

The final study to be discussed in this section was carried out by Tizard, Cooperman, Joseph, and Tizard (1972). They were interested in assessing the effects of various environmental factors on the language development of young children reared in thirteen different English long-stay residential nurseries. About half the children were white, most were placed in the nurseries for adoption, and the mothers of virtually all of them were from the working class. About forty percent of the children were between two and three years old, thirty percent between three and four, and thirty percent between four and five. The average verbal and nonverbal intelligence scores of these children were at or above the norms for English children. None were mentally retarded.

Each of the children was given two tests which assessed his or her language development: one which evaluated ability to understand or comprehend the language used by others (language comprehension), and one which evaluated ability to use spoken language (language expression). The latter is similar to the measures Nelson (1973) employed with children two and a half years old. The test scores were averaged for each nursery, and the averages were corre-lated with several different measurements made on the staff members of each nursery. Three of the latter measurements are of particular interest:

1. amount of "informative staff talk," which is the extent to which staff members of a given nursery offer children explanations and ask for and give opinions and information to children
2. amount of "explanations with comments" by the staff, such as "stop it," "hurry up," followed by an explanation (this behavior is obviously very different from "informative staff talk")
3. amount of "active play with the children," which includes such activities as reading with discussion and building with blocks (reading to children without discussion is not included).

The results are very interesting. Like the findings of Nelson (1973), none of these measures was reliably correlated with language expression. That is, children from nurseries where the staff actively played with them spoke no better than children from nurseries where the staff didn't actively play with them, and similar findings were obtained for amount of informative staff talk and amount of commands with explanations. However, language comprehension was highly correlated with amount of informative staff talk (the correlation was .81), and moderately correlated with amount of active play (.68). Amount of explanations with commands was essentially uncorrelated with language comprehension. When these results are considered along with those of Nelson (1973), it may be concluded that the extent to which the primary caretakers interact with the child determines the early rate (two years or younger) at which he will use spoken language and his early and later ability (older than two years) to understand language. It is truly a puzzle why the factors which influence the language comprehension of older children don't affect their language utilization or expression.

EARLY DEVELOPMENT OF AN UNDERSTANDING OF GRAMMAR

In this section we will discuss the development of an understanding and utilization of grammar for children between the ages of two and five. Table 15 should help make the following discussion a little more understandable. The speech samples are from Adam, a child whose language development was studied by Roger Brown and his colleagues for several years.

It first makes sense to talk about whether a child is using grammatical rules when he starts using two-word phrases. As we indicated, children start using two-word phrases at about the time they have acquired a fifty-word vocabulary. This is apparently a universal phenomenon (Slobin 1971, 1972). In three children studied by Braine (1963), the cumulative number of different two-word phrases recorded in successive months was 14, 24, 54, 89, 350, 1400, and 2500 +. It's as if once children learn to put words together, a dam is opened and the phrases come flooding out. Moreover, the ways in which these pairs of words are put together is very systematic, and can be described as rule-based.

A language rule allows the child to communicate his semantic intentions to other people. The problem for the child is to learn some rules for conveying these intentions—in other words, to say what he knows. Schlesinger (1971) describes this problem in terms of the development of "realization rules"—rules of word order which allow a child to realize his semantic intentions into two-word, then three-word, and so on, phrases and sentences. The early two-word realization rules are simple and are derived from the more complex realization rules used by the older children and adults in a given language community. These rules are not consciously taught to the young child, but the child deduces them from hearing the language spoken.

Schlesinger describes eight realization rules which characterize almost all the semantic relations expressed in two-word English phrases which have appeared in the published literature. The list of semantic relations noted by Brown (1973) and Slobin (1972) expand Schlesinger's list. Brown states that eleven of these relations describe seventy-five percent of all two-word phrases used by children everywhere in their early stage of language learning. Hence, we are apparently dealing with a universal phenomenon.

Table 15
Samples of Adam's Speech

Child (28 months) MLU = 2.0	Adult
What dat . . . somebody pencil	Whose pencils are they?
Floor	Floor?
Where birdie go?	
Birdie	
Birdie up dere	
Birdie	
Read dat?	
Read dat?	Will you read it to me?
What inere?	
Hammer	Is that a hammer, Adam?
Hit hammer, mommy	

Child (35 months) MLU = 2.5	Adult
What his name?	His name
His name, Ursla?	I know his name
No . . . I don't know his name	
I don't know	
Can't come up, fellah (to a yo-yo)	
Going pick pick up	
Lemme do again	
Don't . . . don't hold with me	
Turning round	Yes, it is turning around
It's stop	It stopped?
What dat . . . feeled . . . like?	
What dat feeled like?	It feels like rubber, I guess.

Child (38 months) MLU = 3.5	Adult
I like a racing car	
D'you like some?	
I broke my racing car	Oh, did you used to have one?
Yes	
Look at dat one	
Like dis part broke	What part broke?
Dis part broke, like that	
It's got a flat tire	
What is dat?	
It's a what?	
He . . . his mouth is open	
What shall we shall have?	
Why he going to have some seeds?	
Why it's not working?	
You got some beads?	Yes

Source: Roger Brown and Ursula Bellugi, "Three Processes in the Child's Acquisition of Syntax," *Harvard Educational Review*, 34, Spring 1964, 133–151. Copyright © 1964 by President and Fellows of Harvard College.

A realization rule, then, specifies the word order in a given semantic relation. Following are Schlesinger's eight rules, examples of children's speech which conform to the rules, and an example of adult speech from which the rule was extracted. Thus, in the Agent + action rule, children rarely say "Come mama" when it is clear from the context that they are noting that their mother has come in; nor in the Action + object rule do they say "Sock see" when they see the sock.

1. *Agent + action:* "bambi go" "mama come" (Mama has come in.)
2. *Action + object:* "pick glove" "see sock" (I see my socks.)
3. *Agent + object:* "eve sandwich" "mommy book" (Mommy reads a book.)
4. *Modifier + head noun:* "big boat" "more nut" "my stool" (This is my stool.)
5. *Negation + X:* "no wash" "allgone shoe" "no down" (Don't put me down.)
6. *X + dative:* "Give mommy" "throw daddy" (Throw the ball to daddy.)
7. *Introducer + X:* "here book" "there ball" (There is the ball.)
8. *X + locative:* "go store" "book there" (The book is there.)

Brown (1973) indicates that until a child has an MLU of about 1.50, his speech is restricted to these forms of two-word phrases and to one-word utterances. As the child's average MLU increases from 1.50 to about 2.0, he starts using phrases of three or more words. The way in which children complicate their language during this period is very systematic, and is apparently the same in all languages that have been studied. First, children combine two of the realization rules to form three-word phrases without repeating the central term. For example, an agent + action relation "Adam hit" is combined with an action + object relation "hit ball" to form "Adam hit ball." Thus a child's language becomes hierarchical. The second way they complicate their language is by "expanding" a two-term relation. For example, "Daddy chair" is expanded into "sit Daddy chair." In all the languages studied, it appears that children in this stage of development expand primarily those types of relations grouped by Schlesinger under the "Modifier + head noun" rule.

Brown (1973) identified two other "invariancies" in early language development. The word "invariancies" is set off in quotations because one of the invariancies has been noted in only one study which dealt with only three children, and the other invariancy has only been noted in American children. Contradictory findings do not exist with other racial-ethnic groups, but comparable studies have not yet been carried out. The first of these invariancies deals with the relative rate of acquisition of fourteen functional morphemes in children who have average MLU's between about 2.0 and 2.5. Morphemes include roughly the meaningful words or parts of words in a language. The functional morphemes are those which primarily serve a grammatical function and are obligatory in certain sentence contexts. For example, noun and verb inflections—one boy, many boys, you stop, he stops—fall in this category, as do the articles *a* and *the*, the progressive auxiliary *be*, and the prepositions *in* and *on*. Some examples of obligatoriness are: In "I running" the auxiliary "be" is obligatory, i.e., "I am running"; in "give two book" the plural inflection "s" is obligatory, i.e., "give two books."

In Brown's study of three children, a functional morpheme was said to be acquired when in six consecutive sampling hours of a child's speech the child correctly used the morpheme in obligatory contexts ninety percent of the time. Brown notes that rate of acquisition was not a rapid, all-or-nothing affair; but rather, at some point in time, the children started using a given morpheme and gradually increased its frequency. Despite the fact that the three children started using two-word phrases at different ages, and acquired the fourteen functional morphemes at very different rates, the order in which they acquired these morphemes was virtually identical. The correlations of the order of acquisition between these children was approximately .86. Brown (1973) reports that a recent study by Jill and Peter de Villiers with twenty-one English-speaking American children is in almost complete agreement with his findings. Hence, the phenomenon is a general one.

During the period when the fourteen functional morphemes appear, a phenomenon well known to parents of young children also emerges which Slobin (1971) refers to as "regularization." Regularizations don't disappear when a child starts school at age five or six, but continue beyond that point. Basically, a regularization is a creative process of the child which involves his applying a grammatical rule to all relevant words, including irregular forms, sometimes incorrectly. The child is not imitating his parents, because when he regularizes his speech, he says things he has probably never heard. Some examples of regularization are: for the past tense—goed, comed, breaked, doed; for plurals—foots, feets, sockses. Another fascinating aspect of this process is that it has been observed that prior to regularization, some children correctly use the past tenses of the irregular verbs, sometimes for several months. Following their learning of one or two regular forms, they start saying the irregulars incorrectly.

The third invariancy noted by Brown has only been observed in the three children he and his colleagues studied. This invariancy deals with the grammatical complexity of the sentences children use. What is meant by grammatical complexity? Basically, this refers to the number of grammatical rules which have to be applied to a simple declarative sentence to generate another sentence, i.e., the more rules, the greater the complexity. The general finding is that the more complex forms of sentences are always preceded by the simpler forms, even when the child has already acquired the component rules of the complex form. We will consider two examples. The first deals with asking questions using "wh-words" (who, why, what, etc.). To do this correctly, a child must use two grammatical rules: "preposing the question words," i.e., placing the wh-word at the beginning of the sentence, and "inverting the subject and auxiliary." The sentence "Where can he ride?" successfully employs both rules, but the sentence "Where he can ride?" fails to invert the subject *he* and the auxiliary *can*. The former sentence is more complex than the latter. At a certain stage in development, children can prepose a question word in one sentence and invert the subject and auxiliary in another sentence, e.g., "can he ride in a truck," but he cannot use the two rules in the same sentence. Moreover, during this stage of development, children are frequently unable to imitate sentences containing both rules (Slobin 1971).

The second example is given by Brown, and deals with "tag questions." Tag questions are questions which typically involve a request for confirmation, e.g., "she'll be early, *won't she*," or "he's a smart fellow, *isn't he*." In English, these are very complex grammatically, whereas in some other languages, the speaker merely adds the same tag in all cases, e.g., in French, one adds "n'est-ce-pas." Consider the sentence "His wife can fly." To form the correct tag "can't she," the individual must use the following grammatical rules:

1. transform the subject into a third person, feminine, nominative case pronoun, i.e., "she";
2. make the tag negative by adding the contraction "n't" to the auxiliary "can";
3. make the tag interrogative by placing the auxiliary verb in front of the subject, i.e., "can't she" rather than "she can't";
4. retain the auxiliary of the predicate, i.e., "can," and delete the rest of the predicate, i.e., "fly."

In English one must fit the right tag to each declarative sentence, and there are an infinite number of declaratives that can be spoken. Someone who can use the preceding rules simultaneously can do this correctly in all cases. Brown reports that there is a stage in language development when the child has acquired all the necessary rules for generating a tag, but he cannot use them in the same sentence. This phenomenon is very similar to that observed by Piaget in the transition from concrete operations to formal operations. In the latter stage, children can coordinate inversion and reciprocity, whereas the concrete operational children can only utilize them separately.

The final question we will deal with in this section is "how does the nature of a child's experiences affect his learning of grammatical rules?" We can offer some negative and positive answers to this question. Brown (1973), and Brown, Cazden, and Bellugi (1969) have summarized much of the literature and offer the following negatives. First, from their systematic observations of parent-child interactions, it does not appear that children communicate better with their parents as their grammar improves. Thus, it cannot be argued that children are pressured to improve their grammar owing to poor communication. Second, and related to the first, when the data were examined for the effects of children's omissions of the obligatory functional morphemes, misunderstanding by the parents was rarely observed. Brown and his colleagues point out that many of these morphemes are apparently not even needed by the child to communicate effectively. Third, it appears from both laboratory research and inspection of the observational data that adult systematic expansions of children's incorrect sentences have no effect on children's learning, e.g., the child says "he come tonight" and the adult expands by saying "he will come tonight." Children learn equally well with and without the expansions. Fourth, there are stages in language development when the child occasionally uses both the correct and incorrect grammatical forms, e.g., in tag questions or wh-word questions. An examination of the observational data containing parent-child interactions reveals no differences in the communication effectiveness of the correct and incorrect forms. Thus, the child doesn't seem to improve his grammar to improve his communication. Finally, an examination of the observational data reveals that parents approve or disapprove of a child's utterance based upon the perceived truth value of it, and not on its grammatical form. For example, when one child expressed the idea that her mother was a girl and said "he a girl," her mother said "that's right," while another mother gave disapproval to the grammatically correct sentence "Walt Disney comes on, on Tuesday" because it was factually incorrect. Parents do occasionally correct pronunciation, "naughty" words, and regularized irregulars, but it is not clear that these corrections have any short-term or long-term effect. Thus, children are generally not punished for using poor grammar.

A recent study by Snow (1972) provides some positive answers. In Snow's experiment, middle-class mothers of either two-year-old children or ten-year-old children were the subjects. They and their children were brought into the laboratory and the mothers were asked to perform three verbal tasks:

1. make up and tell a story to your child;
2. instruct your child how to perform a particular way;
3. explain a physical phenomenon to your child.

The basic findings were that mothers talking to two year olds as compared to those talking to ten year olds (a) use shorter sentences, i.e., smaller MLUs, (b) use less grammatically complex sentences, e.g., their sentences contain fewer clauses and fewer compound verbs, (c) use sentences in which there are fewer words separating the subject and verb, and perhaps most importantly, (d) repeat complete sentences and paraphrase sentences much more often. Thus, children learning to speak hear a much simpler and more redundant spoken language than those for whom speech is well-established.

This section may be summarized as follows. At about the time a child has learned fifty words, he starts using two-word phrases. These phrases express his semantic intentions and obey a small number of grammatical rules. When a child expands these phrases into three-word phrases, he combines two of the grammatical rules in a hierarchical fashion. In the next stage of language development, children acquire functional morphemes, and the order in which these appear in their language is apparently invariant. During this stage "regularizations" also appear—words invented by children which they have not heard before, but which follow certain grammatical rules. As the child acquires more grammatical rules, he uses grammatically simple sentences prior to grammatically complex ones. Finally, the acquisition of a child's knowledge and utilization of grammar is apparently unrelated to how well he communicates with his parents or their approval or disapproval of correct or incorrect grammar. However, the grammar to which a young child is exposed is simple and redundant.

THE ACQUISITION OF GRAMMAR FROM AGE FIVE ONWARD

This section will primarily treat three interesting and important aspects of older children's development of grammatical understanding:

1. use of the passive tense
2. use of the verbs "ask" and "tell," which reflects knowledge of an exception to a grammatical rule called the "Minimal Distance Principle"
3. ability to detect sentence ambiguity.

These topics were selected because the research results are clear, and because they demonstrate the existence of language development beyond the onset of adolescence.

The use of the passive tense, e.g., "the ball was hit by the boy," instead of the active tense, e.g., "the boy hit the ball," though common in written materials, is very infrequent in normal spoken discourse, occurring less than five percent of the time (Palermo and Molfese 1972). Passive sentences are grammatically more complex than active, declarative ones, and in addition, they may be more difficult to understand due to semantic reasons, i.e., figuring out which noun is the subject and which is the object of the sentence. The latter problem is especially prominent when passive "reversible" as contrasted with passive "nonreversible" sentences are used. A reversible sentence is one which would be plausible if the action were reversed, e.g., "the girls were chased by the boys." The correct interpretation of this sentence is that the boys chased the girls, but it could be plausibly and incorrectly understood that it was the girls who were doing the chasing. In a nonreversible sentence, e.g., "the leaves were raked by the boys," it is not plausible to understand that the leaves were doing the raking. Active sentences may also be described as reversible or nonreversible, but it turns out that the semantic difficulty produced by reversibility is much smaller in active than in passive sentences (Slobin 1966, Turner and Rommetveit 1967).

In the Slobin (1966) study, the subjects were four groups of middle-class children with average ages of six, eight, ten, and twelve years, and one group of twenty-year-old college students. On each trial, either an active reversible, active nonreversible, passive reversible, or passive nonreversible sentence was read to them. Following this, a picture was shown and the subjects were to respond as quickly as possible by pushing either a "Right" button or a "Wrong" button indicating whether the picture accurately depicted the meaning of the sentence. Some of the pictures were accurate depictions, and some depicted a reversal between the subject and the object, e.g., if the sentence was "the dog chased the boy," the "reversed" picture showed the boy chasing the dog. The major findings for the reaction time (RT) data are as follows (Slobin does not report error data, but notes that they parallel the RT data). Under all conditions, the reaction time markedly increased between the ages of six and ten; the ten and twelve year olds performed similarly and faster than the younger children; and the college students performed the fastest. For all groups, RT to nonreversible sentences was faster than to reversible sentences, but this was much more pronounced for the passive sentences. In fact, passive nonreversible sentences were responded to nearly as quickly as active nonreversible sentences. Finally, for all groups, active reversible sentences were responded to more quickly than were passive reversible sentences.

The preceding pattern of results is strikingly confirmed by Turner and Rommetveit (1967), who used very different experimental procedures. In their experiment, the subjects were five groups of middle-class children with average ages of four, six, seven, eight, and nine years. Each child was tested on three different tasks, each task utilizing the four sentence types described in Slobin's experiment. In the first task, the imitation task, the child was asked to merely repeat the sentence uttered by the experimenter. In the second task, the comprehension task, a picture was presented to the child and two sentences were read, one accurately describing the picture, and the other reversing the action, e.g., "the grandmother washes the dishes," "the dishes wash the grandmother." The child was asked to indicate whether each sentence was an accurate or inaccurate description of the picture. In the third task, the production task, procedures similar to the comprehension task were used, except that the child was asked to repeat the sentence which accurately described the picture.

The major results were as follows. On the imitation task, with the exception of the four year olds, all groups performed essentially without error. On the comprehension and production tasks, the pattern of results was similar. In general, the nonreversible active sentences were the easiest, followed by the reversible active, then nonreversible passive, then reversible passive. By age six, subjects were responding correctly at least ninety percent of the time to the active sentences, but it was not until age nine that this occurred for the passive sentences. Finally, for the eight and nine year olds, performance with the passive nonreversible sentences was nearly identical to that with the active sentences. An analysis of the errors made indicates that nearly all stemmed from reversing the actor and acted-upon nouns, e.g., boys chasing girls rather than girls chasing boys. This is a semantic error which strongly suggests that the growth in understanding and use of the passive construction with age is in large part attributable to nongrammatical factors.

We now turn to a discussion of an exception to the Minimal Distance Principle (MDP), a relationship between noun phrases and a verb phrase. The sentence "I tell him where to go," which obeys the MDP, has two noun phrases, "I" and "him," and one complement verb phrase, "where to go." It is correctly interpreted as "I tell him where he should go." The sentence "I ask him where to go," which has the same two noun phrases and complement verb phrase, is an exception to the MDP, and is correctly interpreted as "I ask him where I should go." When the MDP is followed, the noun phrase (e.g., "him,") closest to the complement verb phrase (e.g., "where to go") is the subject of the complement verb phrase. In exceptions to the MDP, the subject of the complement verb phrase is the noun phrase farthest from the complement, e.g., "I" instead of "him."

The verb "ask" is unusual because sometimes it follows the MDP, e.g., "John asked Bill to play," and sometimes it doesn't, e.g., "John asked Bill where to go." When the verb "ask" follows the MDP, it can frequently be interpreted as roughly synonymous with the verb "tell," e.g., "John asked (told) Bill to play." When "ask" doesn't follow the MDP, however, it is always incorrect to use it as synonymous with "tell," e.g., "John asked Bill where to go" has a very different meaning from "John told Bill where to go." Owing to the unique grammatical characteristic of "ask" with respect to the MDP, it was hypothesized by C. Chomsky (1969) and Kramer, Koff, and Luria (1972) that older individuals should have more success in correctly interpreting exceptions to the MDP, and that the nature of the errors individuals make on these sentences should systematically vary with age.

In Chomsky's study, the subjects were forty middle-class children between the ages of five and ten, and in the Kramer et al. study, the subjects were six groups of middle-class individuals with average ages of nine, ten and a half, thirteen, fourteen and a half, fifteen and a half, and nineteen. In both experiments, two children were tested simultaneously. On each trial the experimenter requested one of the children to "ask" or "tell" the other child something, e.g., "Mary, ask Laura what time it is," or "Mary, tell Laura what time it is." Some of the experimenter's requests tapped the child's understanding of sentences which were exceptions to the MDP, and other requests, such as the two preceding examples, did not have this property. In all cases, the experimenter noted the nature of the child's response. For requests dealing with exceptions to the MDP, three patterns of performance were observed. In the first, children interpret "ask" as "tell," e.g., the experimenter says, "John, ask Bill which book to read" and John responds "read that book." In the second, children incorrectly obey the MDP, e.g., the experimenter says "Arthur, ask Nancy which comb to use" and Arthur responds "which comb do you want to use, Nancy?" In the third, children perform correctly.

The major results with respect to exceptions to the MDP were as follows. In Chomsky's experiment, only one child under age six and a half performed correctly, whereas two-thirds of the nine and ten year olds, and one-half of the seven and eight year olds did so. With regard to type of error, all of the children under six and a half who made errors interpreted "ask" as "tell." For the children older than six and a half who made errors, about one-half interpreted "ask" as "tell," and the other half incorrectly followed the MDP. In the Kramer et al. study, the proportion of individuals who performed correctly ranged from one-third for the nine year olds to two-thirds for the college students. Similar to Chomsky's findings, the younger children who made errors tended to interpret "ask" as "tell," and the older children tended to incorrectly follow the MDP. Although it is not clear why the comparably aged subjects of Kramer et al. performed more poorly than those of Chomsky, the results of the two experiments show clearly that the grammatical understanding necessary to correctly interpret exceptions to the Minimum Distance Principle doesn't start to emerge until about age six, and may not be fully acquired by age twenty. It is interesting to note that in a follow-up experiment carried out two years after initial data collection, Kramer et al. (1972) found that about one-half of the subjects who initially made errors were now successful. There was no systematic relation between age and improvement.

The final topic in this section deals with older children's ability to detect sentence ambiguity. This is a topic which has just recently begun to receive systematic treatment from a developmental perspective, and which, perhaps more than any other topic, goes to the heart of language function, i.e., communication. The experiment which we will discuss was carried out by Shultz and Pilon (1973). The thrust of their experiment was to evaluate how well children of different ages could detect four different types of sentence ambiguity—phonological, lexical, surface-structure, and deep structure. Phonological ambiguity is produced by different words having the same sounds, e.g., "the doctor is out of patience (patients)." When this sentence is *semantic*

heard, it is not clear whether the doctor is getting impatient, or whether his last patient has gone. The sentence can be made unambiguous by stating "the doctor has lost his temper." Lexical ambiguity is produced by the same word having more than one meaning, e.g., "he went lion hunting with a club." When this sentence is heard, it is not clear whether he intends to club the lion into submission, or whether he went with a group of fellow hunters. The sentence can be made unambiguous by stating "he went hunting with a group of friends." Surface structure ambiguity is grammatical ambiguity produced by the existence of two or more ways of grammatically relating or grouping the words in a sentence, e.g., "he sent her kids story books." When this sentence is heard, it is not clear whether the woman will receive "kids story books," or whether the woman's kids will receive story books. The sentence can be made unambiguous by stating "he sent the children some story books." Deep-structure ambiguity is grammatical ambiguity produced by different possible semantic intentions of the speaker leading to a sentence in which a single grouping of the words reflects these different meanings, e.g., "the duck is ready to eat." When this sentence is heard, it is not clear whether the duck will do the eating, or will himself be eaten. The sentence can be made unambiguous by stating "the duck is ready to eat the food."

The subjects in this experiment were four groups of middle-class children with average ages of six, nine, twelve, and fifteen. On each trial, they were read either one of the four types of ambiguous sentences, or an unambiguous but comparable sentence. The four ambiguous and unambiguous sentences just given as examples were used in the experiment, along with several other sentences of each type. After the child heard the sentence (either ambiguous or unambiguous), he was asked to tell the experimenter in his own words what it meant, i.e., to paraphrase it. If only one interpretation was given, the experimenter asked the child if the sentence had another meaning. Then the experimenter presented two pictures to the child which illustrated the two different meanings of the ambiguous sentence, and asked the child to point to the picture or pictures which depicted the meaning of the sentence. The child was also asked to justify his responses. Each child was given two scores, one for the paraphrase test, and one for the picture test, which indicated the percentage of ambiguous sentences he correctly detected, i.e., he understood that the sentences had two meanings. The authors assumed that the lower the level of linguistic development, the lower would be the percentage of ambiguity detected, and further, that the different types of linguistic ambiguity would systematically differ in ease of detection.

The major results were as follows, averaged across the paraphrase and picture tests. All subjects correctly interpreted all of the unambiguous sentences all of the time. For the ambiguous sentences, phonological ambiguity was easiest to detect at all ages, ranging from about twenty percent correct detections at age six, to about ninety percent at age fifteen. Lexical ambiguity was next easiest to detect, ranging from about ten percent correct detections at age six, to about eighty percent at age fifteen. There was essentially no difference in detectability between surface-structure and deep-structure ambiguity, i.e., the two types of grammatical ambiguity. Virtually none of the six and nine year olds detected grammatical ambiguity, i.e., they could only justify one meaning for the "ambiguous" sentences, whereas the twelve year olds had about fifty percent correct detections, and the fifteen year olds about sixty-five percent correct detections. These results clearly indicate that grammatical development lags behind phonological and lexical (semantic) development, and that children's acquisition of grammar is incomplete at age fifteen. These results, of course, fit very well with the other studies already discussed, and indicate that despite an early rapid development of grammatical understanding (prior to age five), this development proceeds beyond the onset of adolescence.

VERBAL REGULATION OF BEHAVIOR

The Soviet psychologist A. R. Luria (1960, 1969) has argued that one of the major functions of human language, from both an evolutionary and a developmental perspective, is regulating the behaviors of others and one's self. Verbal instructions are said to "regulate" behavior when the instructions can both *initiate* and *inhibit* activity. For example, when an infant is asked to hand you a toy, and does so, verbal regulation of behavior has not been demonstrated. In this case the instructions served only to initiate behavior—the production of inhibition by instructions did not occur, nor was it requested. However, if the same child is asked to "take the doll" while he is chasing a ball, and does so, then inhibition of behavior has been demonstrated.

Based on an extensive amount of research carried out by Luria and his colleagues, Luria has concluded that there are four age-related stages which children pass through in their acquisition of the ability of self-instruction to regulate behavior. In the first stage, from about one and a half to two and a half years of age, the verbal instructions of others can initiate the behavior of a child, but cannot readily inhibit it. The child's own speech to himself has no regulating effect on his behavior. In the second stage, from about two and a half to four years, the speech of others can have both an initiating and an inhibiting effect on a child's behavior. To a limited extent, his own speech starts to have a regulating function. He can readily instruct himself to initiate activity, but his speech to himself interferes with inhibiting activity, and in fact, tends to initiate it. In the third stage, from about four to five and a half, the child's own speech can both initiate and inhibit his activity, but the speech must be vocalized aloud. In the fourth stage, from about age five and a half on, subvocal speech, i.e., thinking in words, can regulate his behavior.

In a typical experiment carried out in Luria's laboratory, a child is seated at a table and a small inflated balloon is placed in his hand. The experimenter tells the child that when a red light is flashed he should say "press" and press the balloon, but when the green light is flashed he should say "No" and not press. For children in the first stage, typical performance involves inhibition to both lights; whereas for children in the second stage, typical performance involves pressing to both lights. The children in the third and fourth stages perform correctly. Luria's explanation of the performance of the second stage children, whom he believes are in a transitional stage, is as follows. When the child says "press," it has two effects which are consistent with each other—a semantic effect (press), and a generalized excitatory effect (press). When the child says

"No," it has two effects which are contradictory to each other—a semantic effect (don't press), and an excitatory or impulsive effect (press). Luria argues that at this stage in language development, the excitatory property of speech overrides the semantic one. When the experiment is changed and the child is told to say "Yes" to the red light and to press the balloon, and to say nothing to the green light and not to press, he learns to perform correctly. Thus, the shift from the second to the third stage involves the dominance of the semantic aspects of speech over its excitatory or impulsive aspects.

A number of researchers outside the Soviet Union have attempted to repeat and substantiate Luria's research findings, e.g., Jarvis (1968), Miller, Shelton, and Flavell (1970). These people have been especially interested in confirming the existence of the effects of self-instruction on the initiation and inhibition of behavior. One idea which seems crucial in Luria's conclusions is that two stages of development should exist, such that in the first, self-instruction will interfere with the inhibition of responding, and in the second, self-instruction will aid in the inhibition of responding. Both Jarvis (1968) and Miller et al. (1970) reasoned that if children in the former stage were instructed to say "don't press" to a green light to which they should not press, their performance would be interfered with, whereas if they were instructed to say nothing to the green light, their performance would *not* be interfered with. For children in the latter stage, however, performance under the "don't press" self-instruction should be as good as or better than performance under the silent condition.

In Jarvis' experiment, these ideas were tested with four groups of children with average ages of five, six, seven, and seven and a half years, and in the Miller et al. experiment, with four groups of children with average ages of three, three and a half, four, and five years. The basic findings of both experiments, which followed the typical Luria procedure, were (1) that the different kinds of self-instructions, i.e., silent to both lights, say "press" to red light and nothing to green light, say nothing to red light and say "don't press" to green light, had essentially no differential effects on performance as a function of age; and (2) that older children performed better than younger ones on both initiation (press) and inhibition (don't press). Since such a broad age span was tested in these experiments, an important detail in Luria's conclusions is called into question, i.e., the interfering aspect of self-instruction on inhibiting behavior.

The final study to be discussed in this section was carried out by Strommen (1973). As Strommen points out, the stages of development noted by Luria are based on research using relatively simple and highly repetitive tasks. This situation is very different from the one children encounter in their everyday lives, during which their parents or teachers ask them to do or not do a variety of things. Strommen reasoned that perhaps in a more complex task, the development of inhibition would be much slower than assumed by Luria, and that the regulatory rate of speech for children older than five and a half would be very different from that seen in Luria-type tasks. The situation Strommen used to test these ideas was the game of "Simon says." In "Simon says" the leader gives commands, sometimes preceded by the phrase "Simon says," e.g., "Simon says, hands on head," and sometimes preceded by nothing, e.g., "Clap your hands." The follower is supposed to perform the command when preceded by "Simon says" and do nothing, i.e., inhibit responding, when the leader does not say "Simon says." The parallels to Luria's tasks are clear—"Simon says" trials are analogous to trials in which the child should press, and "non-Simon says" trials are analogous to those in which the child should not press.

Strommen's subjects were four groups of children with average ages of four and three-quarters, five and three-quarters, seven, and nine years. Each child was tested for twenty trials, half of which were "Simon says" trials and half of which were not. Approximately one-third of the youngest children, and two of the five and three-quarter year olds could not understand the instructions to the game, and their data were eliminated. The major results were as follows. On the "Simon says" trials, virtually all of the children always responded correctly. On the inhibition trials, the four and three-quarter year olds made about eighty percent errors, i.e., failed to inhibit, the five and three-quarter year olds made about fifty-five percent errors, the seven year olds about thirty percent errors, and the nine year olds about five percent errors. Further, the two youngest groups showed no improvement over trials, whereas the older children did. Thus, despite the fact that verbal instructions had an equivalent effect at all ages on the initiation of activity, they had very different inhibitory effects. In fact, the two youngest groups performed as if they were in Luria's first stage of development.

When the studies in this section are considered together, it may be concluded that the verbal regulation of behavior proceeds through a number of age and task-related stages. In the first stage, the spoken language of others has an initiatory, but not inhibitory effect. In the second stage, it has both an initiatory and inhibitory effect, and self-instruction has a partially initiatory and partially inhibitory effect. In the third stage, self-instructions have almost completely initiatory and inhibitory effects. Based on Jarvis' and Miller et al.'s failure to find differential effects of covert (silent) self-instruction as a function of age, it appears that the third stage encompasses self-instructions spoken aloud or silently. Strommen's study underlines the task-related nature of these stages. As an interesting, relevant aside, it is commonplace for some people to "count to ten" when they feel very angry in the hope that their motor impulses will be checked. Does it work?

SUMMARY

This chapter may be briefly summarized as follows. Lenneberg's research correlating the major milestones in motor development and language development for normal children and children with Down's Syndrome strongly indicates that language development is a canalized process linked with the maturation of the brain. Children typically speak their first words at about one year of age, and acquire a fifty-word spoken vocabulary during the next six to twelve months, at which time they start using two-word "sentences." Although the early rates of acquisition of various measures of language utilization are highly correlated, they generally do not predict subsequent language abilities. The major environmental influence on early language acquisition, e.g., the first fifty words, appears to be the amount of interaction the child has with his primary caretakers; however, a child's subsequent spoken language seems to be unaffected by this factor. On the other hand, the amount of interaction a child has with his primary caretakers does have a marked effect on his early and later comprehension of language.

Between the ages of one and a half and five, the child's development of an understanding of grammar rapidly increases. At age five the child has learned most, but not all, of the grammatical rules of his language. The route by which he acquires these rules appears to form an invariant sequence, as would be expected for a canalized characteristic. Parents speak to their young children in a simplified and highly redundant manner, and the children, in turn, extract the grammatical rules from this language. Children's acquisition of grammar is apparently unrelated to how well they communicate with their parents, or whether their parents approve of correct grammatical usage and disapprove of incorrect grammatical usage. From age five through adolescence children show constant improvement in some aspects of grammatical understanding, e.g., the passive tense, sentence ambiguity. This improvement appears to be related to the complexity of the grammar, but it is also related to the child's semantic development.

Finally, spoken language is used to regulate one's own behavior and the behavior of others. Children appear to move through three age and task-related stages in the acquisition of these characteristics. In the first stage, the verbal instructions of others can initiate but not inhibit behavior. In the second stage, verbal instructions of others can both initiate and inhibit behavior, but one's own self-instructions can only partially inhibit and partially initiate behavior. In the third stage, one's own self-instructions can successfully inhibit and initiate behavior.

Chapter 10

DEVELOPMENT OF ATTENTION AND MEMORY

OVERVIEW

As we have stated in several different chapters, life processes can be seen as fundamentally involved with the acquisition of knowledge or information about the environment. In general, the greater the knowledge an individual has of his environment, the greater are the chances that his behavior will be effective from both a survival and a reproductive point of view. We stated that evolutionary processes produced two basic sets of mechanisms for the acquisition and transmission of knowledge: the hereditary mechanisms contained in the genotype, and the learning mechanisms, which ultimately depend on the genotype, but which must be understood in their own right.

In the chapter dealing with the brain, we indicated that there are at least six interrelated characteristics of a learning system involved with the "acquisition of knowledge." These are:

1. the reception of information
2. the identification of information
3. the storage of information
4. the operation on or elaboration of information
5. making decisions about information
6. acting on the decisions made about the information.

Although many anatomical structures are components of such a system, the chief anatomical structure is the brain. We saw during the last 2.3 million years of hominid evolution almost a tripling in brain size, most of which can be attributed to the massive growth of the necortex. This growth, however, was not equivalent in all regions of the brain; rather, it was disproportionately greater in the regions which mediate the psychological functions identified as "social competency." Two of these functions are attention and memory.

From the point of view of this chapter, attention and memory processes refer to aspects of the first four characteristics of a knowledge acquisition system just mentioned: the reception, identification, storage, and elaboration of information. Given the importance of attention and memory processes in such a system, it is clear that these processes must be involved with all varieties of learning, including motor skills, language, spatial understanding, and moral understanding. As Penfield (1969) has emphasized, there is essentially no learning without attention; and memory is a major component of all learning.

What is meant by attention and memory? A number of theorists have pointed out, e.g., Bartlett (1932), Neisser (1967), Norman (1969), that the two processes are so interdependent that often it is not clear when one is studying memory and when attention. An attentional process is defined as any process that determines which of the actual or potential environmental information gets selected for further processing. This definition combines the views of Norman (1969), who emphasizes the selective aspects of attention, and Gibson (1966), who emphasizes the exploration aspects. Hence, attentional processes include those which underlie how we orient our sensory receptors to the environment, how we identify information, how we explore the environment, and how we select information for additional processing, e.g., remembering the information, acting on it, elaborating on it, as with an unfinished tune. Attentional processes ultimately lead, then, to bringing certain sensory information into sharper focus.

A memory process is defined as any process which influences either which information stays in the system, how it is organized, or how it is retrieved. What is a memory? We will adopt Underwood's (1969) definition. He defines memory as an indiviudal's record of an event which consists of a collection of attributes. It is this collection of attributes which distinguishes one memory from another. In Underwood's paper, the major memory attributes identified are:

1. temporal (when in time an event occurred)
2. spatial (where in space it occurred)
3. frequency (how often it occurred)
4. modality (through which sensory modality the event was noted)
5. orthographic (this relates to various characteristics of words, such as number of syllables, initial letter, what other words it sounds like)
6. nonverbal associations (this includes such diverse attributes as images, feelings, and contexts associated with the event)
7. verbal associations (this includes words which are elicited by and associated with the event.

As Underwood points out, the particular attributes encoded will vary from individual to individual and, moreover, will change with development.

Memory processes and attentional processes work in tandem. Sensory information must be compared with the effects of previous information (memory) in order to be evaluated and selected for further processing. A remembered sensory event is different from an unremembered one, and a remembered painful sensory event is different from a remembered pleasant one. Unusual events are more attention-getting than commonplace ones, but how can we tell they're unusual unless we can make comparisons with what we remember? Research has shown (summarized by Neisser 1967) that these comparisons are made very rapidly, that many comparisons are made simultaneously, and that they seem to be made initially at a subconscious level (in Neisser's terminology, at a "preattentional" level).

What is remembered is constantly undergoing change, which implies that the outcome of attentional processes in a given situation will undergo change. For example, prior to your first psychology examination, you prepared by bringing to bear all your attentional strategies for study and all your memories of the kinds of questions your previous professors tended to ask. After the first test you noted that this professor likes tricky questions which involve obscure facts and footnotes. In preparing for the second test, these memories affected what aspects of the text you attended to. Note how attentional processes and memory interacted in this situation. Your memory affected what you attended to, and the information you attended to was probably differently remembered than the information not attended to.

What is important from a developmental perspective is that the nature of the attentional and memory processes is undergoing change as children mature. That is, the way in which children attend and remember differs at different stages of development. This idea, of course, is consistent with the observations previously made that the regions of the brain which in part underlie attentional and memory processes are among the slowest to reach maturity, and have not done so by age six. Perhaps the best way to conceptualize the nature of these developmental changes is that with increasing maturity, children's attentional and memory processes reflect increasing differentiation and hierarchical integration. As children get older, they become less dominated by the immediate stimulus situation and more able to select from and manipulate the environment. They become more planful and less reactive. They come to be able to make finer distinctions and to organize these distinctions in an integrated fashion. And they come to be able to discriminate the relevant from the irrelevant with respect to the task at hand.

In the remainder of the chapter we will discuss these and other aspects of attention and memory. In light of the fact that the research literature in these areas has mushroomed in the last decade, our discussion will be very selective. In the first section the topic will be the development of attention and memory during the first three years of life. The second section will deal with the development of attention from age three onward, and the third and final section will deal with the development of memory from age three onward.

ATTENTION AND MEMORY FROM BIRTH TO AGE THREE

How do you study attention and memory in an infant? Starting with the work of Fantz (1961, 1964), the answer to this question has been "primarily through looking time." Specifically, in most studies dealing with these topics, the assumption is made that if an infant is looking at a stimulus, as assessed by the apparent fixation of his eyes on it, then the infant is attending to that stimulus. What about memory? Here things get a little more complicated. The usual measure of memory is "habituation." Habituation is a process with two primary components: (1) the building up in memory of a representation or schema of external stimulation, and (2) the concomitant building up of inhibition which has the effect of suppressing responses to that stimulation (Magoun 1969, Sokolov 1960). The typical procedure for demonstrating habituation is to repeatedly present a particular stimulus to a subject and record his responses to it, e.g., looking time, change in heart rate. When the subject reduces his responding to the stimulation, it is assumed that he has "habituated" to it. That it is habituation and not fatigue producing the decrease in responding is demonstrated by presenting a novel stimulus and noting the partial or complete recovery of responding. If the subject does not habituate to the stimulus, it is usually assumed that he has not built up a memory of that stimulus. Thus, in order to assess the development of memory in infants, one uses changes in attention as a measure. The two typical measures used are decreases in looking time to a particular stimulus over repeated exposures of that stimulus, and a difference in looking time between a novel stimulus and an old stimulus.

The major findings will now be summarized. Between birth and about eight weeks of age, the infant is "captured" by stimuli. Infants in this age range fixate far longer at stimuli that move and have a high degree of black-white contrast than they do at static and low-contrast stimuli (Kagan 1970, 1972). When a stimulus is presented to children in this age range they typically fixate a small portion of its contour, as contrasted with exploring the entire contour (Salapatek 1973). By saying they are captured by stimuli we mean that they show essentially no evidence of habituation. That is, their looking time to a repeatedly presented stimulus does not decrease, nor do they show a preference to look at novel stimuli which are simultaneously presented with familiar stimuli (Fantz 1961, 1964, Wetherford and Cohen 1973).

The Wetherford and Cohen study illustrates several of these points, and also indicates that between the ages of six and eight weeks, infants develop a preference for familiar as opposed to novel stimuli. In their study, the subjects were four groups of infants with average ages of six, eight, ten, and twelve weeks. Following procedures developed by Fantz (1961), each infant was placed on his back so that his eyes were about ten inches from the stimulus material. Trained observers, out of the infant's field of view, noted the fixation of the infant's eyes by "reading" the reflections on his pupils. The stimuli, which were presented one at a time for fifteen seconds with an eight second interstimulus interval, were geometrical figures varying in shape and color. Seventeen trials were run. On the second, ninth, and sixteenth trials novel stimuli were presented, and on the remaining fourteen trials the same figure (the familiar figure) was presented. Thus, the degree of novelty to the new and familiarity to the old increased over trials.

The major results were as follows. For the familiar stimuli, the average fixation time of the six and eight-week-old infants (looking time) remained relatively constant across the fourteen presentations, but that of the ten and twelve week olds showed a systematic decline over trials. This suggests either that the younger infants failed to build up a memory of the familiar stimulus, and/or that they failed to develop inhibition. Which is it? To answer this question, performance to the familiar and novel stimuli is contrasted. For the six and eight-week-old infants, looking time to the novel stimulus relative to the familiar progressively decreased over trials, whereas the opposite was true for the older infants. Thus, older infants build up both a memory of the familiar and inhibition, which is demonstrated by their increased looking time to the novel and decreased looking time to the familiar. On the other hand, the younger infants build up a memory of the familiar, as evidenced by their decreased looking time to the novel, but fail to build up inhibition, as evidenced by their constant looking time to the familiar.

Between the ages of two months and one year, a variety of changes occur in both attention and memory. Infants show progressive improvement in their rate of habituation, as measured by decline in looking time and increased preference for fixating novel as opposed to familiar stimuli (Fantz 1964, Lewis, Goldberg, and Campbell 1969). In the Lewis et al. study, five experiments were conducted with children having average ages of three months, six months, nine months, thirteen months, one and a half years, and three and a half years. In their typical experiment, the infants were placed in a seat facing a light matrix located about eighteen inches away (see Figure 32 on p. 212). The mother sat near her child, but out of his view. The stimulus was the flashing on and off of the center light of the matrix for thirty seconds. There were four trials like this with thirty seconds between trials. The primary measure used was looking time to the flashing light as judged by two observers. The results averaged across all experiments indicate that the three-month-old infants showed no decrement in looking time, and that between the ages of six months and one and a half years the decrement in looking time (the increase in habituation) progressively increased. There was essentially no difference in performance between children aged one and a half and three and a half.

During the age range two months to six months, children prefer to look at patterned to unpatterned stimuli and photographs or drawings of faces to other kinds of patterned stimuli. Within this age range, however, there is apparently no relationship between age and preference for complexity (Fantz 1961, Fantz and Nevis 1967). During this period of development, children are acquiring a well-articulated schema or representation of the human face. The most marked improvement occurs during the fourth and fifth months of age (Caron, Caron, Caldwell, and Weiss 1973). In the Caron et al. study, it was shown that for four-month-old infants, the most salient feature of the face is the eyes, which are responded to as a structured unit, i.e., as a pair, located in the upper half of the face, horizontally arranged. However, infants of this age apparently have not formed a schema of the face configuration in which the eyes, nose, and mouth bear particular relationships to one another. For five month old infants, the mouth is as salient as the eyes, and the face configuration has emerged. Other research, summarized by Gibson (1969), indicates that the ability to recognize unique faces is well developed at six months of age, and that at seven months of age children start to demonstrate the ability to detect various facial expressions.

Between the ages of three months and one year, the amount of time children attend to (fixate) stimuli shows a progressive decrease. This phenomenon has been found for fixation to objects (Schaffer, Greenwood, and Parry 1972); as well as for photographs and drawings of human faces with normal and scrambled features (Lewis 1969) and three-dimensional masks of human faces with normal and scrambled features (Kagan 1970, 1972). These findings indicate that with increasing age, children are more able to readily extract the essential features of a stimulus in order to identify it. Kagan and Lewis suggest that this ability is mediated by the child's progressive development of schema for organizing and classifying information.

There is some discrepancy in the research literature concerning the relative attention-getting qualities of faces with normal features as contrasted with scrambled features. In Lewis' study (see Figure 33), three-month-old children tend to fixate regular and cyclops faces longer than the schematic and scrambled faces; six and nine-month-old children tend to fixate regular and

Figure 32

Schematic drawing of infant enclosure showing light matrix, observation windows on front wall, and Ss' seating arrangement for a child from 3 to 6 months of age (From Lewis, Goldberg, and Campbell, 1969).

schematic faces the most; and thirteen-month-old children show no differential fixation time. In Kagan's study (see Figure 34 on p. 214), children of four, eight, twelve, and thirteen months fixate scrambled and regular masks about the same amount, and both more than the blank face. It's possible that the differences in stimuli, e.g., two-dimensional versus three-dimensional, led to the different pattern of results in these two studies, but an explanation linking stimulus differences to response differences is not clear.

Finally, between the ages of one and three years, children progressively

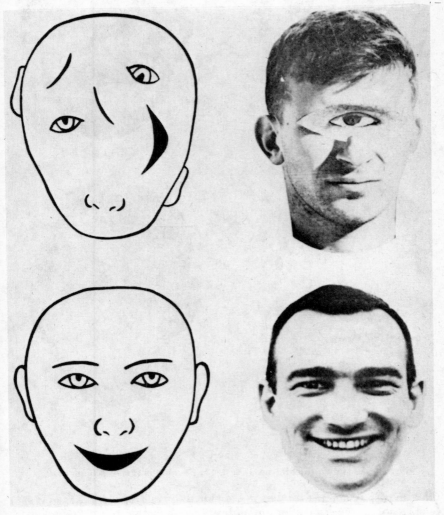

Figure 33

These four facial arrays were used as stimuli: scrambled (top left), cyclops (top right, schematic (bottom left), and regular (bottom right) (From Lewis 1969).

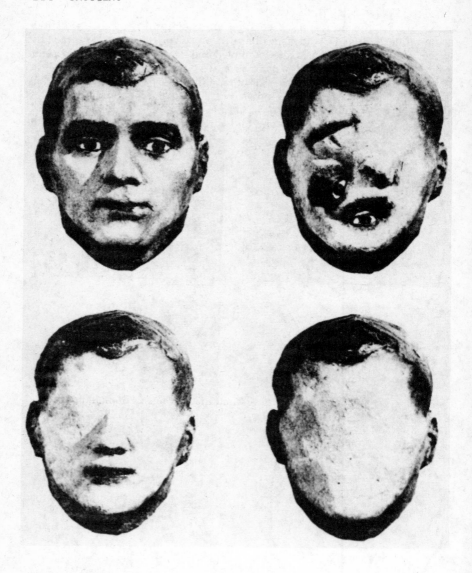

Figure 34

Clay masks shown to children at 4, 8, 13, 27 months (From Kagan 1970).

bring to ~~bear symbolic activities~~ in both attention and memory. Kagan (1970) refers to this as the acquisition and utilization of hypotheses. An "hypothesis," in his view, is "an interpretation of some experience accomplished by mentally transforming an unusual event to the form the child is familiar with. The 'form he is familiar with' is the schema." (Kagan 1970)* Kagan makes four assumptions linking hypotheses to attention:

1. that the activation of hypotheses requires increased attention to a stimulus;
2. that the more hypotheses are activated, the longer should be the attention;
3. that as children mature, they acquire and utilize more hypotheses in interpreting their experiences;
4. that moderately unusual stimuli will elicit more hypotheses than either highly familiar or highly unfamiliar stimuli.

Kagan and his colleagues offer two studies in support of this position. In the first study (Finley, Kagan, and Layne 1972), three groups of urban, white, middle-class American children and three groups of rural Mayan Indian children from Mexico with averages ages of one, two, and three years were the subjects. They were shown four paintings, similar to the four masks depicted in Figure 34 on p. 214, and a "free art form" which bore little resemblance to a human face. Each stimulus was presented singly, and the entire series was presented four times. The major results were:

1. the amount of fixation time, averaged across all stimuli, increased with age;
2. for the three year olds, the scrambled face received the most attention, whereas for one and two year olds, the normal and scrambled faces received an equal amount of attention;
3. for all age groups, the other stimuli received approximately the same lower amount of attention;
4. there were essentially no performance differences between the children from the different cultures.

In the second study, Kagan (1970) presented the four masks depicted in Figure 34 to groups of children with average ages of thirteen months and twenty-seven months. For the younger children, the regular and scrambled faces were fixated equally long, both more than the blank face, but for the older children, the scrambled face was fixated much longer than the regular face, which in turn was fixated longer than the blank face. As Finley et al. acknowledge, with the exception of the increased attention shown by older children to the normal face, which does not coincide with Assumption 4, the results of both studies are generally consistent with the "hypothesis" view of Kagan.

This section may be summarized as follows. Between birth and two months of age, infants are captured by stimuli with high contrast, moving stimuli being more attention-getting than static, low-contrast stimuli. Between six and eight weeks of age, they show an attentional preference for familiar over novel stimuli, but by ten weeks of age, the opposite is true. Between the ages of two months and six months, they show a progessive increase in rate of habituation, develop a well-articulated schema of the human face, and prefer attending to

---

* Jerome Kagan, "The determinants of attention in the infant," in *American Scientist* 58:303.

patterned rather than unpatterned stimuli and human faces rather than other patterned stimuli. Between the ages of three months and one year, their fixation time to stimuli progressively decreases, which indicates that they are becoming increasingly able to extract the relevant features of a stimulus in order to identify it. Between one and three years of age, they are progressively bringing to bear symbolic activities in both attention and memory.

DEVELOPMENT OF ATTENTION FROM AGE THREE ONWARD

Gibson (1969) describes the age-related changes in attention seen during childhood as the "optimization of attention." By optimization she means the following:

> . . . first, the tendency for attention to become more exploratory and less captive; second, the tendency for exploratory search to become more systematic and less random; third, the tendency for attention to become more selective; and fourth, the inverse tendency for attention to become more exclusive.*

It should always be kept in mind that attentional processes are rarely an end in themselves, but rather they are in the service of effective action in the environment. As children's exploratory activity becomes more systematic and organized, and as children become more able to select wanted information and exclude unwanted information, they increase the likelihood that the information which is brought into sharper focus will be the information they need for effective action.

In the "Overview" of this chapter, we linked attentional processes with aspects of the reception and identification of information. Thus, as attention becomes optimized, the information which is received should be the information which is more readily identifiable. In the preceding section we saw that during the first three years of life, children's attention becomes less captive and more exploratory, and that higher level symbolic activities start to come into play. Unfortunately, we know little from the published literature about the way children in that age range, especially the one and two year olds, go about exploring and selecting information. In great part this lack is attributable to two factors: the paucity of studies dealing with children in the age range of one to three years, and the difficulty in studying these processes with children who cannot use language effectively. In the present section these two factors are not operating and, as a consequence, we will be able to make some firm statements about the linkage between information reception and information identification. We will divide the discussion into two parts. The first will deal with how children of different ages orient to and explore the environment in order to extract certain information, and the second will deal with how children of different ages select for further processing information which they have received.

---

*Eleanor J. Gibson, *Principles of Perceptual Learning and Development* (New York: Appleton-Century-Crofts, 1969), p. 456.

Scanning and Exploration

In this section, four experimental reports will be summarized. Although the techniques employed in these experiments were different, the conclusions made were highly similar. In the first experiment, by Zinchenko, Chzhi-tsin, and Tarakanov (1963), the subjects were children between three and six years of age. They were given two tasks: (1) to familiarize themselves with some irregular shapes projected on a screen by visually exploring them, and (2) to attempt to recognize (identify) these figures when they were again projected on the screen. During both the familiarization task, which lasted twenty seconds per figure, and the recognition task, which lasted no more than fifteen seconds per figure, the children's eye movements were recorded.

The major results for the familiarization task were as follows. The three year olds explored the figures with relatively few eye movements, averaging 1.2 movements per second. Further, most of the points they fixated were near the center of the figure; rarely did they move their gaze along the outline which would give them the maximum shape information. An example of their behavior is shown in Figure 35 on p. 218. The four year olds averaged 2.4 eye movements per second; however, as with the three year olds, few of these movements were along the contours of the figures. The five year olds performed similarly to the four year olds, averaging 2.3 eye movements per second, and rarely fixating the contours; however, unlike the four year olds, they very carefully explored one distinctive part of the figure. The performance of the six year olds was very different from those of the other children. They averaged 4.0 eye movements per second, and moved their eyes almost exclusively around the outlines of the figure. An example of their behavior is seen in Figure 35. A control experiment was conducted in which these children were asked to follow with their eyes a pointer moving along the outline of the figure. No difference in performance was found between the various age groups; hence, the performance differences seen in the familiarization task cannot be attributed to sensory-motor deficits in the younger children.

In the recognition task, the three year olds made about fifty percent errors. Their average number of eye movements was 3.5 per second, and unlike any of the other age groups, they frequently fixated on points outside of the figure. This can be seen in Figure 35. The four year olds made about thirty percent errors. Although they spent less time per figure in the recognition task than the three year olds (approximately 4.5 seconds versus 9 seconds), their average number of eye movements per second was 3.1. Hence, they fixated fewer points than the three year olds. The five year olds averaged 3.3 eye movements per second, fixating at only a few points of the figure, and spending about as much time scanning the figure as the four year olds. The five year olds, however, made no recognition errors. The six year olds also made no errors, spent less time than the three year olds scanning the figure, and averaged 2.7 eye movements per second while doing so. An example of their behavior can be seen in Figure 35.

Zinchenko et al. drew the following conclusions from these results. First, during familiarization there is a gradual improvement with age in the ability to orient to and isolate the relevant (for the task at hand) aspects of an external object. A child who doesn't explore contours can't readily encode contour and hence shape information. Second, with increasing age, the behavior in familiarization and recognition tasks becomes increasingly differentiated. The youngest children seemed to still be familiarizing themselves with the figures in the recognition task, whereas the oldest children explored only a limited part of the figure during recognition. Finally, on the recognition tasks, scanning behavior became more economical with increasing age. The figures

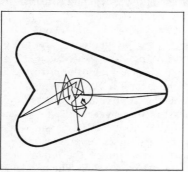

Trajectory of eye movements of three-year-old in familiarization with figure (20 seconds).

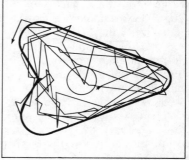

Trajectory of eye movements of six-year-old in familiarization with figure (20 seconds).

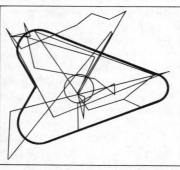

Trajectory of eye movements of three-year-old in recognition of figure (9 seconds).

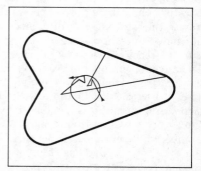

Trajectory of eye movements of six-year-old in recognition of figure (4 seconds).

Figure 35

Eye movements of a three year old and a six year old (From Zinchenko, Chzhi-tsin, and Tarakanov 1963).

contained a great deal of potentially redundant information, and the older children apparently could readily identify and use this redundancy during recognition.

In the second study, by Abravanel (1968), the subjects were normal children between three and fourteen years of age. In one condition they were asked to assess the length of a wooden bar by touch alone (they couldn't look at the bar), and to demonstrate this assessment visually by telling the experimenter to adjust the length of a tape measure so that it would equal the length of the bar. The lengths used varied from five centimeters to fifteen centimeters.

The major results of this experiment were as follows. With increasing age from three to seven, accuracy of performance (identification) markedly increased on all tasks. From age seven to fourteen, there was little improvement in performance. Of primary interest is the mode of tactual exploration used by the different age groups. The three year olds primarily engaged in what Abravanel calls "general palpation." This consists of clutching the bar, stroking it, and rotating it with the palms and fingers of one or both hands. Another exploratory activity which was common for this age group was cupping the ends of the bar with both palms and allowing it to rest there. By four years of age, the extent of general palpation markedly decreased. The four year olds still engaged in cupping the ends, but two new modes of exploration emerged —what Abravanel calls "ends to center" and "holds ends." In the former, the child slides his palms and fingers, or fingers alone, from one end of the bar to the center of it, and in the latter, the child passively holds the bar with his palms and fingers, or fingers alone. By five years of age, generalized palpation decreased even further, and essentially disappeared after this age. The five year olds cupped the ends as frequently as the four year olds, but their primary mode of exploration was holding the ends. Two new modes of exploration appeared at this age—what Abravanel calls "pressing ends" and "spanning the bar." In the former, the children literally press the ends toward each other while holding the ends, and in the latter, the children attempt to span the entire bar with the fingers or fingers and palm of one hand.

The seven, eight, and nine year olds performed similarly to each other. In this age range, the primary exploratory mode was holding the ends, and the next most frequent modes were pressing the ends and spanning the bar. In the age range ten to fourteen, the children performed similarly to each other. They used approximately equally often the exploratory modes of holding ends, pressing ends, and spanning the bar. Thus, from age seven on, the primary modes of exploration emphasized the most distant parts of the bar, i.e., the endpoints. Clearly, if the child's task is to determine the length of an object, he will be more likely to extract this information if he actively explores the endpoints, than if he passively holds the object or explores the center regions.

In the third experiment to be discussed, by Vurpillot (1968), the subjects were children between three and ten years of age. They were given a task in which two pictures of two houses were simultaneously presented. Each house had six windows. On three trials, the two houses were identical, and in one trial each the two houses differed by one, three, or five windows (see Figure 36 on p. 220). The children were instructed to look at the pair of houses and tell the experimenter whether the two houses were the same or different. While the children visually explored the houses, their eye movements were recorded.

For purposes of analysis, Vurpillot combined the data into four age groupings, with average ages of approximately four years, five years, six and half

Figure 36
Stimuli used by Vurpillot (1968). The top pair of houses have differences in three corresponding windows. The bottom pair of houses are identical.

years, and nine years. The following were the major results. With the exception of the oldest group, who made essentially no errors, performance was better on trials in which the houses were identical than when the two houses were different. For the "different" pairs, performance was better when five windows differed than when three or one differed. This is intuitively obvious—the greater the number of differences, the greater the likelihood that at least one difference will be noted. Overall, the accuracy of performance (identification) increased with increasing age, with the two youngest age groups performing similarly and the two oldest age groups performing similarly.

Of primary interest is the mode of exploration used by the different age groups. Vurpillot reports two measures: the number of windows fixated, and the number of paired comparisons. Since each house had six windows, the maximum score of the first measure was twelve. For the identical pairs, if peripheral vision gave no information, a minimally acceptable exploration would require a fixation at all windows. For "different" houses, however, the child could stop exploring after the first difference was noted. For the two youngest age groups, the average number of windows fixated was about seven, for both identical and different pairs. For the two oldest age groups, the average number of windows fixated was about seven for the pairs which differed by three and five windows, ten for the pairs which differed by one window, and eleven for the identical pairs. The number of paired comparisons refers to the number of times a child looked in sequence at two windows located in the same place on both houses, e.g., fixated the upper left window on House One and then fixated the upper left window on House Two. Although performance on this measure tends to be grouped by age, as in the first measure, the performance differences between adjacent ages were less marked.

The fourth study, by Lehman (1972), involves three experiments which deal with the selectivity children use in exploring stimuli in order to identify them. In the first and second experiments, the subjects were three groups of children in kindergarten, second, and fourth grades. In both experiments the stimuli consisted of five-sided "random" shapes (the "shape" dimension) with different textured material, e.g., sandpaper, wool, fur, glued in their center (the "texture" dimension). In Experiment I, the children were presented with a "standard" stimulus and two "comparison" stimuli, and on four trials were asked to find the comparison stimulus that had the same shape as the standard, and on four other trials, the same texture as the standard. For the former trials, it is irrelevant to explore the texture dimension for correct identification, and for the latter trials, it is irrelevant to explore shape.

Lehman recorded three measures for each subject:

1. percentage of trials in which only the specified relevant dimension (shape or texture) was explored
2. the order in which relevant and irrelevant dimensions were explored
3. the percentage of trials in which both comparison stimuli were explored.

The major results were: the kindergartners had the lowest percentage of trials in which they explored only the relevant dimensions, and the second and fourth graders performed about the same; the second and fourth graders were more likely than the kindergartners to explore the relevant dimension first; and finally, on trials in which correct identifications were made, the kindergartners were most likely to explore only one comparison object, the second graders next, and the fourth graders least likely to do so. The latter results indicate that as children in this age range get older, they are more likely to "double check" their initial identification in order to assure correct performance.

Experiment II was similar to Experiment I, with the following exceptions: sixteen rather than eight trials were run, and the children were instructed to find the comparison stimulus which was identical to the standard, but they were not told which dimension was relevant. Thus, they had to discover the relevant dimension. For half the children, the stimuli had the same shape on all sixteen trials, and for the other half, the stimuli had the same texture on all sixteen trials. Thus, in Experiment II, children could discover that one dimension never gave them information which would aid their matching the comparison and standard stimuli. The major result of this experiment was that the fourth graders were the only children who systematically changed their mode of exploration from the first half of the trials to the second half. They did this by progressively limiting their search to only the relevant dimension. Also, as in Experiment I, for trials in which a correct identification was made, the older children were more likely than the younger ones to explore more than one object.

In Experiment III, the subjects were four groups of children in kindergarten, second, fourth, and sixth grades. The stimuli were wooden crosses in which the length of the horizontal and vertical bars was equal (either five or twelve inches). On each trial a standard and two comparison stimuli were presented, and the child's task was to find the comparison which was the same size as the standard. Thus, correct solution required only the exploration of one bar (either horizontal or vertical) of each cross. The major results were that there was a progressive increase with age in the frequency with which only one bar was explored; however, only the fourth and sixth graders showed an improvement in "one bar exploration" from the first half of the trials to the second half.

The results of Lehman's study indicate that economical exploration of stimuli, as demonstrated by attending to only the relevant dimension for object identification, shows progressive improvement between the ages of about six and twelve. There appear to be two age-related changes in exploration mode which occur in this age range. In the first, which takes place between the ages of about six and eight, children show a large increment in their ability to ignore (fail to explore) irrelevant information. In the second, which takes place between the ages of about eight and ten, children show a marked improvement in their ability to utilize information gained from previous exploration to govern future exploration. This ability was manifested in the improvement over trials seen for fourth and sixth graders in their exploration of a single relevant dimension, and the absence of this improvement for the kindergarten and second grade children.

When these four studies are considered together, striking parallels can be observed. In the age range from three to about five, children explore limited aspects of objects in ways which make it unlikely that they will identify those objects at some future time. Their exploratory mode can be thought of as uneconomical and incomplete. During the age range from about five to seven, exploratory mode undergoes a rapid change. It becomes more extensive, more economical, more complete, and more task-relevant. These advances are reflected in the more accurate performance of the seven and eight year olds compared to the five and six year olds in difficult tasks. In simple tasks, such as that of Zinchenko et al., the exploratory mode of the five year olds appears to be adequate. From age seven onwards, exploratory mode starts to stabilize, but children from eight to twelve do show progressively more economical exploration with increasing age. In addition, between the ages of eight and ten, children show marked improvement in their ability to benefit from previous explorations. It is noteworthy that the age range seven to twelve is the approximate period during which concrete operations become fully organized.

Selective Attention

This section will summarize research dealing with the question of how well children of different ages are able to select out or segregate certain information from the total information they receive. Three types of research procedures will be discussed:

1. the recognition of visually embedded figures
2. incidental learning of irrelevant information
3. the identification of one auditory message when two are simultaneously given.

Ghent (1956) used children from four to eight years of age as subjects in her experiment. The children performed two tasks. In the first they were asked to recognize from a set of multiple choice items all the geometric figures contained in an array of four or five "overlapping," line-drawn geometric figures. No contours were shared by the overlapping figures, but each figure intersected at least one other figure. In the second task, the children were given four embedded figures trials, in which a complex geometrical figure and a simple geometrical figure were presented. They were asked to trace with their finger the part of the complex figure which looked like the simple figure. Figure 37 on p. 224 depicts all of these trials.

The major results of this study were as follows. For the overlapping figures, of the seventeen possible correct recognitions, the four year olds made an average of one error, the five and six year olds less than one error, and the seven and eight year olds made no errors. On the embedded figures, all of the four year olds and ninety percent of the five year olds made three or four errors (out of four figures), whereas only twenty-five percent of the six year olds and twelve percent of the seven and eight year olds made three or four errors. However, the two older groups did find the task difficult, with only twelve percent of the six year olds and twenty-five percent of the seven and eight year olds making no errors. Since errors were rare for all age groups in the overlapping figures task, it is unlikely that the performance differences in the embedded figures task can be attributed to the young children's not receiving the relevant sensory information. Rather, it would appear that this difficulty lies in their inability to separate parts from wholes, and to select out the relevant from the irrelevant in sensory information. It is interesting that this selection ability starts to emerge at about age six, the age at which economical and strategically appropriate exploratory activity emerges.

We will now consider studies using the incidental learning procedure as a measure of selective attention. In the typical incidental learning situation, a child is shown pictures containing two readily identifiable items belonging to two different categories, e.g., animals and household articles, and asked to remember the items from one of the categories, e.g., animals. The items he is asked to remember are called the "central" items, and the items which he is not specifically asked to remember are called the "incidental" items. The relative extent to which he remembers the incidental as compared to the central items is assumed to be an indication of the extent to which he has attended to irrelevant information; conversely, the relative extent to which central as compared to incidental items are remembered is assumed to be an indication of how well irrelevant information has been excluded. We indicated at the beginning of this section that Gibson (1969) refers to this phenomenon as the exclusivity of attention.

Much of the current research in this area has been carried out by J. W. Hagen and his associates, and is summarized by Hagen (1972) in a recent article. In one of his studies, the subjects were children from the first, third, fifth, and seventh grades. They were presented with eight cards, one at a time, each card containing a drawing of a familiar animal and a familiar household object. After each card was shown, it was placed face down in front of the child. Half the children were initially instructed to remember the locations of the animals, and half the locations of the household objects. After the presentation of the

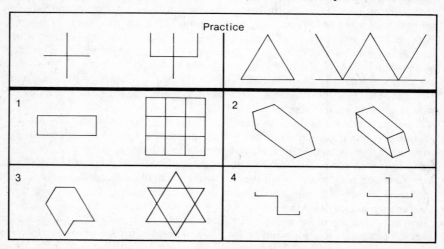

Figure 37

Embedded geometric figures. Each card was approximately 8 x 2 inches. The numbers did not appear on the cards used in testing (From Ghent 1956).

eighth card, half the children were shown separate pictures of the "incidental" stimuli and asked to locate the instructed "central" stimuli, and half were shown separate pictures of the central stimuli and asked to locate them. If the child responded correctly when shown the incidental stimulus, he demonstrated incidental attention and memory for that card. If he responded correctly when shown the central stimulus, he demonstrated central attention and memory for that card.

The major findings were:

1. with increasing age, central memory increases;
2. incidental memory was relatively constant for children in the first, third, and fifth grades, but declined for the oldest group of children (the latter finding is not often seen in other studies);
3. for the youngest children there was a positive correlation between incidental memory performance and central memory performance, i.e., children who had high incidental memory scores tended to have high central memory scores, whereas for the older children there was a negative correlation between these two scores.

In discussing these and other findings, Hagen indicates that with increasing age, children become better able to apportion their attention to the relevant aspects of information at the expense of attending to irrelevant information. This improvement is manifested by the increasing ratio, with increasing age, in amount of central to incidental items remembered. The finding of a drop in incidental learning for the seventh graders is interpreted as reflecting the emergence of a new attentional strategy for dealing with information overload.

An important study by Hale and Piper (1973) calls into question both the generality of the preceding findings and the interpretation of the incidental learning situation as a procedure for assessing selective attention. Hale and Piper point out that selective attention is assumed to be a *central* process, i.e., something individuals do in their heads with information they have received, and not a peripheral process, such as orienting one's view to a particular part of the stimulus array. In the studies carried out by Hagen and others, the central and incidental stimuli were physically separated, and thus it's possible that the performance improvement seen with age comes about in part through improvement in scanning ability, and not only through improvement in selective attention. Some indirect support for this position is found in Wheeler and Dusek's (1973) study, in which it was shown that with increases in the distance between the central and incidental stimuli, amount of incidental learning decreases. Hale and Piper reasoned that if the central and incidental information were part of the same stimulus, then it could be assumed that the subjects had received both types of information, and that any improvements seen in the ratio of central to incidental learning could be attributed to improvements in selective attention.

Hale and Piper used the stimuli shown in Figure 38 on p. 226 with different groups of eight and a half and twelve and a half-year-old children. In the first row, the central and incidental stimuli are animals and household objects. In the second row, the central stimuli are the different geometrical shapes, and the incidental stimuli are the different colors of the different shapes. In the third row, the central stimuli are the different shapes (they were not colored), and the incidental stimuli are the different colored backgrounds of the cards. In the fourth and fifth rows, the central stimuli are the different geometrical shapes and different animals, and the incidental stimuli are the different colored ovals associated with each shape or animal. The crucial stimuli, according to Hale

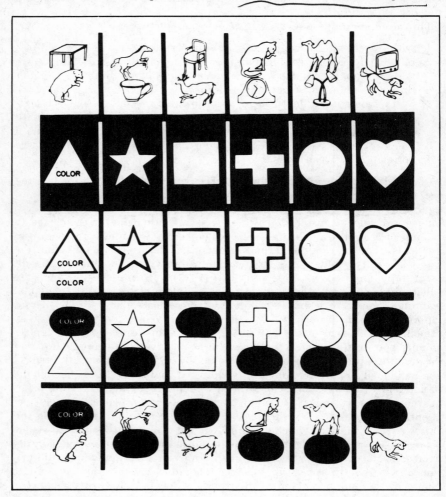

Figure 38

Stimuli of the five tasks in the study. From top to bottom rows, the tasks are: pictures and colored shapes, used in Experiments I and II; colored background, shape-color separated and animal-color separated, used in Experiment II (From Hale and Piper 1973).

and Piper, are those of the second row (the colored shapes), in which the central and incidental stimuli are bound up in the same figure. It seems impossible to identify a yellow triangle as a triangle, for example, without receiving "yellow" information.

The incidental learning procedure Hale and Piper used was similar to that employed by Hagen and others. Two experiments were run. In the first, the stimuli from the first and second rows were used, and in the second, all the stimuli from Figure 38 were used. The major results were:

1. with all stimuli, the central learning of the twelve and a half year olds was greater than that of the eight and a half year olds;
2. for all stimuli but the colored shapes, the incidental learning of the twelve and a half year olds was equal to or less than that of the eight and a half year olds;
3. for the colored shapes, the incidental learning of the twelve and a half year olds was *greater* than that of the eight and a half year olds.

The ratio of central to incidental learning for the eight and a half year olds, for all stimuli, was approximately 2:1; for the twelve and a half year olds, for all stimuli but the colored shapes, it was approximately 4:1. For the colored shapes, however, the ratio for the twelve and a half year olds was approximately 2:1. Hale and Piper interpret these results as follows:

> It is hypothesized that if a stimulus is readily analyzable, then as children grow older they attend increasingly only to those stimulus features that are critical for task performance and ignore other aspects. That is, older children realize the advantage of attending exclusively to task-relevant stimulus features, and this developmental difference in strategy is manifested in performance when the relevant and extraneous stimulus components are easily separable. However, when the components are integrated into a single unit, such as is true of shape and color, children of all developmental levels attend to both of these components in discriminating among stimuli. In this case, even though older children may be potentially more prone to use a focused attentional strategy, children of all ages nevertheless attend to extraneous as well as relevant stimulus features, viewing such features as integral parts of a unitary stimulus. *

The final set of experiments to be discussed in this section were carried out by Eleanor Maccoby and her associates. In these experiments, the typical procedure involved presenting two messages simultaneously through either loudspeakers or earphones, and asking the child to report the content of one of the messages. What is most appealing about this technique, as contrasted with those using the visual modality, is that one can be very confident that the message has been received—that both the relevant and irrelevant sensory information was produced. Unlike vision, where closing your eyes or turning your head will shut out stimulation, there is relatively little that can be done to prevent auditory stimulation.

---

*G. A. Hale and R. A. Piper, "Developmental Trends in Children's Incidental Learning: Some Critical Stimulus Differences," *Developmental Psychology* 8 (1973): 334.

In the first experiment (Maccoby and Konrad 1966), the subjects were children from kindergarten, second, and fourth grades, whose average ages were approximately six, eight, and ten. The children were tested in two conditions, in each of which they heard a list of twenty-three pairs of words. The pairs were presented simultaneously through headphones they were wearing, one word spoken by a woman, and the other by a man. In one condition (the "mixed" condition), both words came through both headphones, and in the other condition (the split condition), the woman's voice came through one headphone and the man's through the other. On one run through the list, the children were asked to report, after each pair was presented, the word the woman said, and in the other run, the word the man said. These instructions were given prior to each run.

The major results were as follows. The kindergarten children performed the least accurately in all conditions, and the fourth graders the most accurately; however, the performance of the second graders was nearly as good as the fourth graders. Performance was better in the split condition than in the mixed condition for all age groups, with the gain in accuracy being approximately the same for each age. Maccoby and Konrad also analyzed the frequency of two types of errors — composite word errors and composite nonsense errors. The former is a word which in some sense combines the two words spoken, e.g., the man says "down" and the woman "wish" and the child reports "dish." The second is a combination which is a nonword, e.g., "squirrel" and "turtle" are reported "squirtle." It was found that the kindergarten children made the fewest composite word errors and the most composite nonsense errors. The reverse was the case for the fourth graders, and the performance of the second graders was close to that of the fourth graders.

In the Maccoby and Konrad (1967) paper, three experiments were reported, two of which will be summarized here. In the first, the subjects were second, fourth, and sixth grade children. The procedure was similar to that of the preceding experiment, except that the man's voice was presented through one loudspeaker, and the woman's through another. The purpose of the experiment was to determine the effects of preparatory instructions on performance. On half of the trials, selected in a random fashion, the children were instructed before the pair of voices was presented to report the man's or woman's word (the "before" condition), and on the other half of the trials, they received the man versus woman instruction after they had heard the words (the "after" condition). The major findings were:

1. overall, the sixth graders performed the best, at about fifty percent correct, followed by the fourth, then second graders;
2. under the before condition, the fourth and sixth graders performed about the same, whereas under the after condition, the performance of the fourth graders was intermediate between that of the second and sixth graders;
3. for both the second and fourth graders, performance was better under the before condition than under the after condition, but for the sixth graders, performance was the same on both.

In the second experiment, the subjects were children from kindergarten, second, fourth, and sixth grades. The procedure was similar to that of the first experiment, with the exception that pairs of two-word phrases were used. Half the phrases consisted of words which have a high probability of following one another in sentences, e.g., "dark night," and half had a low probability, e.g., "dark cheese." As in the first experiment, performance in the before condition was better than in the after condition; however, this relation was observed for all age groups. Performance was better for all age groups with high probability words than with low probability words. Overall, the kindergarten children performed the poorest, the fourth and sixth graders the best and approximately the same, and the second graders intermediate, but more closely resembling the older than the younger children.

The results from the Maccoby and Konrad experiments indicate that the ability to select information from a complex array of auditory information increases from age six to approximately age ten, where it starts to level off. The most marked improvement in this ability occurs between the ages of six and eight, which suggests that during this period new attentional processes start to emerge leading to the ability to exclude irrelevant information. The results are also consistent with the view that between the ages of eight and ten these new processes start to become optimally employed, leading to the more accurate and nearly equal performance of the ten and twelve year olds.

When the selective attention experiments are considered together and compared with the experiments dealing with scanning and exploration, the following inferences can be made. Prior to age five, the ability to explore the environment for task-relevant information and to select relevant from irrelevant incoming information is very impoverished. Between the ages of five and seven, new, more optimal strategies for exploring and selection start to emerge, which is manifested by the superior performance of seven year olds in difficult tasks relative to that of five year olds. Exploratory strategies start to stabilize at about age seven, but children from age eight onward do show progressively more economical exploration. In the selection experiments, it is difficult to determine whether the performance changes observed between seven and ten years are attributable to the emergence of new selection strategies, or to a more optimal use of the old strategies. We have suggested that the latter is the case. As we have already indicated, these interpretations are consistent with the view that a more advanced level of cognitive organization emerges at about age seven, and shows progressive development in subsequent years.

DEVELOPMENT OF MEMORY FROM AGE THREE ONWARD

In the "Overview" of this chapter, we defined a "memory" as an individual's record of an event which consists of a collection of attributes, and a "memory process" as any process which influences either which information stays in the system, how it is organized, or how it is retrieved. Both memories and memory processes change as children mature, and in a very general way we described these changes as reflecting increasing differentiation and hierarchical integration.

Let's explore these ideas a little further. In the experimental literature dealing with memory, processes which influence which information stays in the system are referred to as acquisition processes (e.g., Norman 1969). Acquisition processes are activities that go on "in one's head," no doubt intimately connected with the hippocampus-temporal lobe system which serves to consolidate information. No one knows how many of these acquisition processes there are, but there seems to be a growing consensus that an important psychological aspect of acquiring information is having a "plan" to do so (Flavell 1971, Miller, Galanter, and Pribram 1960, Norman 1969). In the present context, a plan encompasses intentions to remember information, the utilization of strategies to carry out these intentions, and the ability to assess whether the information has been remembered (Flavell, Friedrichs, and Hoyt, 1970, refer to this assessment as "memory monitoring"). We sometimes acquire information without a plan, and sometimes our plans are faulty, but it is quite clear from the psychological literature that having plans has a marked effect in determining which information stays in the system. To anticipate what will presently be dealt with in some detail, it is also quite clear that the planfullness in children's memory undergoes dramatic changes as they mature.

The question of how information is organized in memory is a difficult one to answer, and must be inferred from examining aspects of acquisition and retrieval processes. But neither acquisition nor retrieval processes can be directly observed (no psychological process can be); hence, statements about memory organization are inferences based on other inferences. Organization deals primarily with the way individuals code and order the collection of attributes that constitute a memory. As children mature, they increasingly bring to bear higher symbolic activities to this task. The effect of the utilization of these activities is an increase in memory capacity and easier retrieval of memory information.

Retrieval processes refer to those processes involved with gaining conscious access to information stored in memory. The usual analogy is that of finding a book stored in a library. These processes are particularly complicated to study, primarily because the techniques used rely on an individual's ability to remember previously acquired information. However, failure to remember may be caused by the way the information was acquired, e.g., different items have different strengths, retrieval factors differ, acquired information is lost or decays. The assumption made in studying retrieval processes is that the information is there to be found, and the question asked is how does the individual find it. In our discussion of this topic, an attempt will be made to link the research findings with Tulving's (1974) theoretical viewpoint. The essence of his position is that a failure to retrieve information is a function of a change over time in the individual's "cognitive environment" which characterized his original acquisition of the information. The "cognitive environment" is envisioned as a set of cues linked with the information in storage which give the individual access to that information. Hence, if the cues are not available, or change over time, the individual loses some of his ability to retrieve the stored information.

It may be readily inferred from the preceding discussion that acquisition, organization, and retrieval processes are not, in reality, completely distinct processes. Our separation of them is partly based on pedagogical reasons (the discussion will be easier to follow by separating the three rather than by combining them), and partly on theoretical reasons, i.e., in principle, the three should be separable. Keeping this in mind, we will now move on to a discussion of the research literature.

Development of Intentions, Strategies, and Memory-Monitoring

The logical starting point in planning to remember information is an intention to learn. But obviously humans are not always logical, and this may especially be the case for young humans. Although one cannot be absolutely confident of another's intentions to learn, one may manipulate the degree of this intention by influencing the "set" with which people process information. For example, those individuals asked to remember stimulus information are more likely to have an intent to learn than those who are asked to merely look at or name stimuli. There are three possible outcomes of such an experiment:

1. individuals asked to remember will remember more than those asked to perceive (i.e., look at or name);
2. there will be no memory difference;
3. individuals asked to perceive will remember more than those asked to remember.

The first outcome indicates that intentional memorizing and intentional perceiving are differentiated activities, and suggests that individuals differentially employ them in real life situations. The second outcome is ambiguous, but suggests that individuals do not differentially employ memorizing and perceiving activities in real life situations. The third outcome, though puzzling, indicates that memorizing and perceiving are differentiated activities, and suggests that individuals probably don't employ memorizing activities in real life situations.

There are two recent developmental studies bearing on this question, and, unfortunately, they yield partially conflicting results. In the first one, carried out by Zinchenko (summarized by Smirnov and Zinchenko 1969), the subjects were four groups of children with average ages of approximately three and a half, five and a half, eight and a half, and eleven and a half years, and one group of adults. Different subjects at each age level were tested in two different conditions, called "involuntary" and "voluntary retention with naming." In the first condition, the subjects were presented with fifteen pictures of different familiar objects, e.g., apple, pear, horse, and asked to name them. In the second condition, they were asked to name them and to remember them for subsequent recall. Following a single presentation, the pictures were removed and all the subjects were asked to recall them by naming the objects.

The major results were as follows. Under both the involuntary and voluntary conditions, the number of objects correctly recalled improved with increasing age, stabilizing at eleven and a half years. For the adults and eleven and a half year olds, recall was higher under the voluntary than involuntary condition; for the eight and a half year olds, performance under the two conditions was nearly the same; but for the three and a half and five and a half year olds, performance under the involuntary condition was superior than under the voluntary condition.

The second study was carried out by Appel, Cooper, McCarrell, Sims-Knight, Yussen, and Flavell (1972). Two experiments were conducted using groups of children with average ages of four and a half, seven, and eleven years. In the first experiment, each child was tested under two conditions, called "look" and "memory." In both conditions the child was given between nine and fifteen pictures of common objects for one and a half minutes. In the look condition, he was asked to look at them carefully because it would help him perform more effectively in a subsequent task. In the memory condition, the child was asked to remember the names of the objects. Following the child's examination of the pictures in both conditions, a memory test was run. In the second experiment, the procedure was similar in all ways, except that the pictures were presented with a slide projector one at a time for half a second each, and twelve pictures were used for all subjects.

The major results of both experiments were as follows. Under both conditions, the percentage remembered increased with increasing age. For the four and a half year olds, there was no performance difference between the look and memory conditions; for the seven year olds, in the first experiment look and memory conditions had no differential effect on performance, but in the second experiment, performance was higher under memory than look conditions; and for the eleven year olds, performance was better under the memory than look conditions.

The results of the Zinchenko and Appel et al. studies are in complete agreement for the eleven and eleven and a half year old children, partial agreement for the seven and eight and a half year old children, and disagreement for the three and a half, five and a half, and four year old children. It is not at all clear why the youngest children in Zinchenko's study performed more poorly under instructions to memorize than under instructions to name; however, the results do indicate that these instructions produced different psychological states. Taken as a whole, both studies strongly suggest that the intention to remember, as a *useful* differentiated state of an individual's memory plan, doesn't start to emerge until about age seven, and that by age eleven this state is probably an integrated part of the memory plan. If this conclusion is correct, then it should follow that memory strategies will be nearly absent in children in the age range three to six, will start to emerge at about age seven, and will be highly developed by about eleven years of age. Is this the case?

Before answering this question, the phrase *memory strategy* will have to be defined. Basically, a memory strategy is any activity intentionally used by an individual to improve his memory. From this definition and the preceding discussion, it can be hypothesized that older children will employ memory strategies more frequently than younger ones, and that at a given age level, those who use memory strategies will remember more information than those who don't. The principal strategies which have been studied are: rehearsal, naming, anticipation, and hierarchical grouping during the study period.

The experiments by Flavell, Beach, and Chinsky (1966) and Keeney, Cannizzo, and Flavell (1967) deal with rehearsal as an organizational process. In the Flavell et al. study, the subjects were children from kindergarten (K), second, and fifth grades. In each trial, seven pictures were spread before them. The experimenter slowly pointed to three of the pictures in a given order and then rearranged them. The child's task, after a fifteen-second delay, was to point to (recall) the three pictures in the same order as the experimenter's. During each trial, an experimenter in another room read the lips of the child in order to assess overt rehearsal. The major results were: older children recalled more pictures than younger children, and older children rehearsed more than younger children, i.e., two, twelve, and seventeen children in grades K, 2, and 5 respectively were observed rehearsing.

The Keeney et al. experiment was similar to the one just discussed. In this experiment, three groups of first graders were the subjects. One group consisted of children who rarely or never overtly rehearsed on a pretest (nonrehearsers). The other two groups consisted of children who almost always overtly rehearsed (rehearsers). The nonrehearsers and one group of rehearsers were tested on the following tasks. Ten trials were conducted as in the Flavell et al. study, and the children were instructed to rehearse by whispering audibly the names of the three pictures pointed to. Following this, three trials were run in which the children were given the option of rehearsing or not rehearsing. For the second group of rehearsers, no additional instructions were given, and they received thirteen trials.

The major results were as follows. The organizational rating of the first graders significantly more pictures correctly than the nonrehearsers; during the first ten trials of the experimental procedure, all three groups performed at about the same level of recall; during the final three trials, the majority of nonrehearsers dropped their rehearsal activities and their accuracy of performance also dropped, whereas all of the rehearsers continued to rehearse and to perform at their previous level.

The experiment by Flavell et al. (1970) examines the relationship of the memory strategies of naming, rehearsal, and anticipation. In this experiment, four groups of children in nursery school, kindergarten, second grade, and fourth grade were presented with an array of pictures and asked to study them until they felt they had memorized the location of each picture. The pictures were hidden behind a screen, and by pushing a particular button the child could expose for view a particular picture. Of interest for the present discussion is the type of memory strategy the children used during the study period. The study period was divided into four time quadrants, and an observer out of the child's field of view recorded the presence or absence of the strategies of naming, rehearsal, and anticipation. "Naming" was scored if the child pressed a button and immediately said the name of the exposed picture. "Anticipation" was scored if the child first said a name and then immediately pressed the button corresponding to the name said. "Rehearsal" was scored if the child named an object other than just prior to pushing a button (which would be scored as anticipation) or just after pressing a button (which would be scored as naming).

The major results were as follows. Overall, i.e., averaged across the entire study period, all three strategies were used most often by the fourth graders, next most often by the second graders, and an equal and low amount by the nursery school and kindergarten children. When the use of these strategies is examined over time for the fourth graders and second graders, the frequency of naming decreased over the study period, and the frequency of rehearsal and anticipation increased. For the kindergarten and nursery school children there was essentially no change in the utilization of these strategies. Thus, there appears to be a major break in the use of memory strategies, as we hypothesized, which occurs between the ages of six and eight. Flavell et al. describe their results as follows:

> These interactions taken as a group suggest the developmental emergence, during the early school years, of a fairly complex mnemonic strategy for coping with this sort of memory problem. According to this strategy, S commences each study period by familiarizing himself with the identity and location of each object picture, saying the names of the pictures to himself as he exposes them in an initial effort to get the list into memory storage (Naming). As the list begins to get memorized in this fashion, the temporal and psychological relationships between his perceptual and linguistic responses become more varied, with a more sophisticated Anticipation and Rehearsal activity . . . starting to alternate with and to substitute for this simple Naming behavior. Consequently, by the end of the trial, Rehearsal is just reaching its peak and Anticipation remains high, but Naming has ebbed to quite a low level.*

The final study dealing with memory strategies is that carried out by Niemark, Slotnick, and Ulrich (1971). In their study, children from grades 1, 3, 4, 5, 6, and college students were shown twenty-four pictures which could be grouped into four classes of six pictures each: animals, transportation vehicles, furniture, and articles of clothing. The pictures were presented simultaneously, and the children were told to study them for three minutes, after which they would be asked to recall them. They were also told that during the study period they could move the pictures around if they wished to. During the study period an "organization rating" was determined. This rating assessed the extent to which the subjects systematically rearranged the pictures into categories, i.e., grouped them hierarchically. The minimum possible rating was "0," which reflected no systematic rearrangement of the pictures, and the maximum was "3," which reflected a completely categorized rearrangement of the pictures. Following the study period the subjects were tested for recall.

The major results were as follows. The organizational rating of the first graders (who were about six and a half years old) was about .10, of the third graders, about .30, of the fourth graders, about .70, of the fifth and sixth graders, about 1.0, and of the college students, about 2.2. Thus, there were marked increases in organization with increasing age, with essentially no organization for the six and a half year olds, a "plateau" at about ages ten to twelve, and a progressive

---

* J. H. Flavell, A. G. Friedrichs, and J. D. Hoyt, "Developmental Changes in Memorization Processes," *Cognitive Psychology* 1 (1970): 335.

increase thereafter. For number of pictures correctly recalled, the first graders averaged about eleven, the third graders about sixteen, the fourth, fifth, and sixth graders about nineteen, and the college students about twenty-three. As might be expected, the organization score correlated well with age—about .70, and with amount recalled—about .74. Thus, as we hypothesized, older children make more frequent use of memory strategies than younger ones, and those who use these strategies remember more than those who don't.

The last study to be discussed in this section is that of Flavell et al. (1970). We have already described those aspects of their study concerned with memory strategies, and now we will deal with the aspects concerned with the development of memory-monitoring. Memory-monitoring is the ability to predict one's memory capacity and to evaluate whether to-be-remembered information is in fact remembered. It is obvious that these abilities are important to one's memory plan in that they determine whether you should continue or stop attempts to memorize, and whether you should vary the memory strategies employed.

Flavell et al. used two memory-monitoring tasks. In the first, "predicted object span," the children were presented with series of first two, then three, then four different pictures, and so on, and were asked after each presentation whether they thought they could remember the names and order of the pictures. The experimenter continued increasing the series length by one until either the child said he couldn't remember that many pictures, or until the series length reached ten. When the child said he had reached his limit, the experimenter tested the child's ability to remember his predicted limit. The second task is the one previously described, in which the children were asked to memorize the names and locations of pictures and tell the experimenter when they had done so (this is referred to as the "recall readiness" task). When the child said he had committed this information to memory, the experimenter tested the child's recall. Three trials of this task were run.

For the object span task, the span predicted by nursery school children was about seven pictures, by kindergarten children, about eight, and by second and fourth graders about six. The actual object span for these groups was about three and a half for the nursery school and kindergarten children, four and a half for the second graders, and five and a half for the fourth graders. In the three recall trials of the recall readiness test, only seven percent of the nursery school children and fourteen percent of the kindergarten children performed without error, as contrasted with eighty-two percent of the second graders and eighty-six percent of the fourth graders. Thus, there is a tremendous difference in memory-monitoring between children under age seven, who show very limited and very inaccurate capabilities, and children over seven, who show very substantial capabilities, which tend to improve with age.

The early development of memory planning is usefully summarized by Smirnov and Zinchenko (1969) as comprising the following three stages:

a. A first stage in which children exhibit no purposeful behavior in remembering. The process proceeds, as it were, with no active participation on the child's part, so that it seems less a matter of the children's recalling material than that material presents itself to them for recall.

b. At the second level recall operates as purposeful behavior. The child sets himself the goal of remembering and actively tries to carry out his intention, even though he lacks the appropriate means to do this.

c. It is only at the third level that a child possesses means or methods which will facilitate recall. However, a child's stock of methods is still very slim, and it mostly amounts to repetitions of words which the child names "to himself" (by whispering); only in a few cases does he actually group material in any meaningful way.*

Development of Memory Organization

The two basic techniques for studying memory organization, i.e., the nature of the attributes of information stored in memory, are ① to systematically vary the way information is presented to individuals and note the effects of these variations on what is remembered, and ② to not vary the way information is presented, but note how individuals organize the information when they recall it. For example, if the presence or absence of spatial information during acquisition has no effect on the recall of items for younger children, but does have a positive effect for older children, it may be inferred that younger children do not readily store the spatial attributes of information.

The nature of the attributes individuals use to store information places limits both on the memory strategies employed during acquisition, and on the cognitive environment during recall. In practice, these two factors are difficult to disentangle. In addition, as Flavell (1970) points out, an individual may have a particular memory capacity, but fail to use it. Keeping all these considerations and cautions in mind, let's now examine the results of several experiments.

The first experiment, by Conrad (1971), makes use of the technique of varying information input and examining the nature of recall in order to determine whether there is a developmental trend in the way children store the linguistic aspects of information. Conrad used as subjects children between the ages of three and eleven. They were asked to remember the serial order of pictures of objects. On alternate trials they were presented with a set of eight cards depicting objects whose names either sounded alike (the homophone set), e.g., rat, cat, bat, hat, etc., or whose names did not sound alike (the nonhomophone set), e.g., train, spoon, fist, etc. Previous research with adults has shown that the homophone sets are more difficult to remember than the nonhomophone sets, and this has been interpreted as indicating that adults store the phonological attributes of information. Thus, words that sound alike are more likely to be confused than those that sound different.

The major results of Conrad's study were as follows. For children in the age range three to five, there was no difference in recall between homophone and nonhomophone sets. In the age range five to eleven, nonhomophone sets became progressively easier to recall than homophone sets with increasing age. These results suggest that prior to about age five, children do not use names as

---

*A. A. Smirnov and P. I. Zinchenko, "Problems in the Psychology of Memory," *A Handbook of Contemporary Soviet Psychology*, eds. M. Cole and I. Maltzman (New York: Basic Books, 1969), p. 476.

a memory attribute of visual information, but that after age five, they do use names with progressive frequency.

The experiment by McCarver (1972), which also makes use of the technique of varying information input, was concerned with the utilization of spatial and temporal attributes in the organization of memory. In his study, the subjects were kindergarten, first grade, and fourth grade children and college students. The subjects were tested in one of two conditions. In one condition (no cue condition), they were presented with eight pictures. Each picture was individually shown for two seconds, and then placed face down in front of the subject, forming an evenly spaced horizontal row. Following the last picture, "probe cards" were shown one at a time. The probe cards were identical to the pictures the subject had just seen. As each probe card was presented, the subject was asked to point to the picture which the probe card matched. The other condition (cue condition) differed in three ways: (1) the subjects were instructed to attempt to remember the location of the pictures in sets of two; (2) the pictures were presented for one second each, with three seconds between the second and third, fourth and fifth, and sixth and seventh pictures; and (3) the pictures were not evenly spaced, but placed in horizontal pairs, e.g., the first and second were close together, the second and third far apart, the third and fourth close together, and so on. Hence, temporal and spatial cues were given in this condition.

The major results of this study were as follows. The overall performance of the kindergarten and first grade children was approximately the same, that of the fourth graders was better, and that of the college students was the best. For the kindergarten and first grade children, performance under the cue and no cue conditions was essentially the same, whereas for the older groups, performance was superior under the cue condition. These findings indicate that after about age seven (the average age of the first graders), children start to be able to store the higher order attributes of spatial and temporal pairing in their memory of visual information. By "higher order" we mean a relationship between stimuli which is not inherent in a single stimulus, e.g., the idea of a "pair." This conclusion is consistent with research presented in the next chapter, which indicates that conceptual understanding of spatial relationships starts to emerge at about age six.

The next and final two experiments to be discussed in this section utilize the technique of holding input constant and examining variations in the output. We have already dealt partially with the first experiment, that of Niemark et al. (1971). Recall that in their study children and adults were asked to remember the names of twenty-four pictures following a three-minute study period, and that in general, with increasing age, children remembered more of the to-be-memorized items. What we didn't report are the results of one of the major foci of their study—the method children use in recalling the stored information.

A number of experimenters, using adults as subjects, have found that during the retrieval period, individuals tend to "cluster" their responses. Clustering refers to grouping items during recall on the basis of shared common characteristics, i.e., categories. For example, an individual who clusters tends to recall animals before he shifts to colors, and tends to recall colors before he shifts to types of food, and so on. A measure of clustering reflects the extent to which an individual does this. The clustering measure has a minimum possible score of 0, which indicates no systematic grouping, and a maximum score of 1.0, which indicates complete grouping. It is assumed that the higher the clustering score, the greater is the likelihood that the child has stored the higher order attributes of the visual information. In the Niemark et al. study, these higher order attributes are the semantic categories of the information.

The major findings of their study regarding clustering were: for children in grades 1, 3, 4, 5, 6, and college, the average clustering scores were .40, .46, .50, .62, .70, and .93, respectively. These results indicate that from age six and a half on, children progressively store information about the semantic category of visually presented stimuli. There is no sharp break in the development of this process between the ages of six and a half and twelve. These findings are consistent with those of Conrad, who, using a different technique, found that in the age range five to eleven, children progressively store the name of to-be-remembered visual information.

The final experiment we will discuss was carried out by Lehman and Goodnow (1972). The subjects were groups of children in kindergarten, second, fourth, and sixth grades. Their task was to reproduce, on different trials, three patterns of tapping: (.. ..), (. .. .), and (.. ...). The kindergarten children could do this successfully an average of 1.2 times, second graders 2.6 times, fourth graders 2.9 times, and sixth graders nearly 3.0 (out of 3.0) times. Of interest is the way the children described how they remembered the auditory information. Only about half the kindergartners used numbers to store this information, and all of them who did so merely counted the *number* of taps, e.g., "1, 2, 3, 4, 5." that is, none used numbers to remember the *pattern* of taps. More than eighty-five percent of the older children used numbers, and the extent to which the numbers were used to remember pattern increased with increasing age. Two examples of this are "1,2,1,2,3" and "2,3" for the pattern (.. ...). These results strongly suggest that there is a sharp break between the ages of six and eight in the way children utilize the higher order variable of number to remember auditory information. This conclusion cannot be explained away by noting that kindergartners are not trained to use numbers whereas second graders are, because those kindergartners who have been taught to count use numbers differently than second graders. It is of interest that this break between six and eight is consistent with that found in the McCarver study for the utilization of spatial and temporal cues.

The results in this section may be summarized by quoting from Niemark et al.:

The development of memorization for free recall seems to parallel the pattern of cognitive development from preoperational thought to concrete operations, and from concrete operations to formal operations . . . with respect to component activities and ages of transition. This close correspondence suggests to us that development of memory skills is a part of the more comprehensive process of cognitive development; or possibly that development of procedures for systematic deliberate storage and retrieval of information may be one of the basic processes underlying cognitive development.*

Development of Retrieval Processes

In this, the last section of the chapter, three experiments dealing with the retrieval of stored information in free recall tasks will be briefly discussed. We will attempt to integrate the results of these experiments within the framework of Tulving's (1974) "cue-dependent forgetting" hypothesis. As we have indicated, the essence of his position is that a set of cues is present during the acquisition of memory information which provides access to the stored information. If, for any of a variety of reasons (Tulving doesn't specify them), the cues are no longer available to an individual, then he loses access to these memories. If certain new or old cues are then provided for the individual, such as giving him words that rhyme with those in memory or which are otherwise associated with the stored information, then the cues of the acquisition cognitive environment are assumed to be reinstituted, and the individual retrieves the sought for information. Tulving summarizes a number of experiments of this sort as support for his position. What about children?

Based on what has already been discussed, it may be anticipated that during a recall period, younger children are more likely than older ones to have lost the cues of the acquisition cognitive environment, and hence will have more difficulty retrieving sought-for memory information. If this is so, then an interesting prediction can be made: younger children should benefit more than older children from reinstituting some of the cues from the acquisition cognitive environment. Stated another way, we know that recall performance increases with increasing age, but perhaps the superior ability of older children stems in part from their having more ready access to stored information. If so, then if we give older and younger children the same retrieval cues, the younger children should benefit more than the older ones. The next two experiments test out this hypothesis. Because the acquisition cues used in both experiments are names of categories, which we know young children have difficulty with, the tests of this hypothesis are conservative ones.

In Kobasigawa's (1974) experiment, groups of children in the first, third, and sixth grades were asked to memorize twenty-four names of common objects. The objects were grouped into eight different categories of three objects each. The categories (the cues) in general referred to where the objects belonged, e.g., monkey, bear, and camel belong in a zoo (the category); pear, grapes, and banana belong in a fruit stand (the category). Pictures of the objects were shown to the children with pictures of the appropriate cues, and the experimenter pointed out the relationship between each object and its cue. After this was done, the children were given one of three recall instructions. In the first, the usual free recall condition, they were asked to remember all the objects they could. In the second, the cue recall condition, the experimenter gave the

---

* E. Niemark, N. S. Slotnick, and T. Ulrich, "Development of Memorization Strategies," *Developmental Psychology* 5 (1971): 431.

children the pictures of the cues and suggested that they might want to use them in attempting to recall the names of the objects. In the third, the directive-cue condition, the experimenter presented the cues one at a time to the children and asked them to recall the three objects which went with each cue. Thus, in the third condition, the experimenter not only directed the children's attention to the category cues, but also gave the children an additional cue—the number of objects per category.

The major results were as follows. Under the free recall and cue recall conditions, older children recalled more objects than younger ones. For the first and third graders, there was little performance difference between free and cue recall, but for the sixth graders, cue recall was substantially higher than free recall (twenty versus fifteen objects). Under the directive-cue condition, all age groups performed about the same, recalling between twenty and twenty-one objects, indicating that the younger children benefited the most in this procedure. Additional analysis indicated that the first graders benefited from the directive-cue condition as compared to cue recall in two ways—it allowed them to recall objects from more categories, and it allowed them to recall more objects in each category. The third graders benefited primarily in the latter way, i.e., increased number of objects per category. These results clearly support the view that the poor recall typically found for younger children is largely attributable to their inability either to retain or freely utilize the cues of the acquisition cognitive environment.

The study by Halperin (1974) is very similar to the one just discussed. Children in grades 1, 4, and 7 were asked to memorize thirty-six names of "things" divided into nine categories of uneven size. Two trials were conducted. On each trial, the experimenter called out the name of the category, e.g., "names of zoo animals," and then read the names of the to-be-remembered things. At the end of each trial, the children were tested under one of two recall conditions: free recall, as previously described, or cue recall, in which the child was given the name of the category only. The results were similar to those of the preceding experiment. Older children performed better than younger children under both free and cue recall, but the younger children benefited more than the older ones from the cue condition.

We now turn to the concluding experiment of this chapter, carried out by Piaget and his colleagues. The starting point of their research consists of the following set of assumptions. First, a memory is the outcome of constructive processes, and is not a "copy" of reality. Second, the nature of these constructive processes changes with development; hence the memory of a given event will differ for children who are at different stages of development. Finally, if the nature of the constructive processes changes between the time when the event was first remembered and a time when the individual is asked to recall the event, the memory will undergo changes which correspond to the changes in the constructive processes.

Piaget has shown that preoperational children are unable to understand the concept of an ordered series. For example, if they are given a set of sticks of different lengths and asked to put them in a row from the shortest to the longest, they are unable to do so. Concrete operational children, on the other hand, can do so.

We will summarize one memory experiment which relates to this phenomenon (Piaget and Inhelder, 1973). Children between three and eight years of age were shown an ordered series of ten sticks. They were asked to look at them so that at a later time they could draw them. They were not required to construct the series or manipulate the sticks. One week later they were asked to draw what they had seen, and six months later, without having seen the configuration in the interim, they were again asked to draw what they had seen.

Piaget and Inhelder identified five patterns of responses in the drawings made one week later, which they ordered according to degree of accuracy of recall. The first, which typifies the performance of three and four year olds, consists of a set of sticks lined up, all drawn about the same length, e.g., ||||. The second, which is typical for some four and five year olds, consists of sticks of two lengths. The sticks are drawn lined up, with short and long sticks alternating, e.g., |ı|ı|ı, or in a dichotomous fashion, e.g., |||ııı. The third, which typifies some five and six year olds, consists of a line of sticks of three different lengths drawn in triplets, e.g., |ılı,or ||ııı. The most typical response of five and six year olds was to draw a series of four or five sticks of different lengths, e.g., ,ıl|. The fifth pattern starts to emerge at six years of age. This consists of an accurately drawn series of seven to ten sticks of different lengths. Many of the seven and eight year olds performed in this way.

The drawings made six months later were generally different than the one-week drawings; however, Piaget and Inhelder report that with regard to the preceding five patterns, there was no deterioration of memory. The most striking finding was that seventy-four percent of all the children, and ninety percent of the five to eight year olds, showed progress in the second drawing relative to the first. This improvement was always gradual; for example, a child's drawing moved from the first pattern at one week to the second pattern at six months. Thus, accuracy of memory for an event improved over time.

Piaget and Inhelder interpret these results as follows. The initial memory of the ordered series corresponds to the ways by which the child interprets or constructs his experience. The youngest children, for example, interpret the series as a collection of sticks without order, whereas the oldest children, who understand the concept of order, interpret the ordered series correctly. In the intervening six months, the memory constructions spontaneously change in a more advanced direction, which modifies the memory of the ordered series.

How might we interpret these findings from Tulving's point of view? First, it must be assumed that all the children had in memory some sort of representation of the ordered series of sticks shown to them. This assumption is implicit in Piaget and Inhelder's research. We defined a memory as a collection of attributes. Thus, when a child attempts to recall a memory, he recalls those attributes for which he has the appropriate retrieval cues. If a child lacks a higher order cue, such as the idea of a series, then it is unlikely that he will recall the series attributes of his memory. If a child possesses this cue, it is likely that he will recall the series aspect of the sticks. Thus, in Piaget and

Inhelder's study, as children matured, they tended to develop an understanding of seriation, which gave them greater access to the stored representation of the sticks.

SUMMARY

Life processes are fundamentally involved with the acquisition of knowledge or information. In general, the greater the knowledge an individual has of his environment, the greater is the likelihood that he will act effectively in that environment. Man possesses a superior organ for information acquisition—the brain. As we saw in an earlier chapter, many of the phylogenetically newer regions of the brain underlie the acquisition, identification, storage, and elaboration of information. In general, these are the regions which mature the slowest, and we know that the human brain is still immature at age six. Thus, based on neuroanatomical considerations, it can be hypothesized that the processes which underlie knowledge acquisition will develop slowly.

The two major psychological processes involved with the acquisition of information are attention and memory. These processes operate in tandem, and in reality are never separable. Attentional processes ultimately lead to bringing certain information into sharper focus. Memory processes involve the acquisition, storage, and retrieval of certain information. We saw in this chapter that the development of these processes parallel one another. During the first year of life, the speed with which habituation occurs and the direction of fixating novel stimuli show constant improvement with maturity. Infants progress from being captured by stimuli, to showing intentions. During the second year of life, higher symbolic activities start to play an important role in these processes.

Between the ages of three and twelve, the gains children make in attention and memory can be conceptualized as coming in three stages. Between the ages of three and five, the ability to explore the environment for task-relevant information and select relevant from irrelevant information is very impoverished. The memory plans of children in this age range are essentially nonexistent. Between the ages of five and seven, new, optimal strategies for scanning the environment and selective attending start to emerge. During the latter part of this age range, children start to formulate intentions to memorize, and to utilize simple memory strategies for accomplishing these intentions. Between the ages of nine and eleven, scanning and selective attention stabilize, which may be attributed to the optimal use of old strategies or the emergence of new strategies. Parallel findings exist for memory. Children in this age range effectively use a variety of memory strategies, and have ready access to the information stored in memory. Both attentional and memory processes improve after this age range, but at a slower rate.

Chapter 11

DEVELOPMENT OF AN UNDERSTANDING OF SPATIAL RELATIONSHIPS

OVERVIEW

As we have seen in previous chapters, the evolutionary record indicates that the regions of the brain which underwent the greatest growth during human evolution were the parietal and temporal regions of the neocortex (and possibly the frontal regions also). The neuropsychological data indicate that the parietal regions are intimately involved with spatial understanding and spatial orientation, though not exclusively so. Further, we argued that man's ability to create and utilize cognitive maps—internal representations of the spatial and temporal environments which he utilizes—was crucial to his success as a cooperative hunter of big game. For example, the paleoanthropological record suggests that as long as 500,000 years ago, men either dug deep pits or used natural pits into which they drove elephants for slaughter. This was a very complicated business, involving a profound ability to accurately represent and remember major environmental features and their interrelationships.

From observation of contemporary warm-zone hunter-gatherers, it appears that the choice of a hunting location is largely based on the availability of fruits, nuts, and vegetables suitable for human consumption. These provide the majority of food eaten, and availability varies with the season and the location. We assume that this relationship between hunting location and gathering location also applied to our early ancestors. An omnivorous diet has great survival value, provided that you can remember where the best locations are for gathering and hunting and how these locations vary seasonally. Although choosing the right location at any given time is a somewhat hit-and-miss propcsition, the hunter-gatherer has to be correct most of the time in order to survive beyond a few seasons—the distances travelled are too great and food is

243

frequently too scarce to permit many errors. Seasonal changes play a role in the behavior of human and nonhuman primates, but in a very different way. The nonhuman primates appear to function in the here-and-now much more than humans, either following their game as they change location, or "following" the fruits and vegetables as they ripen.

The evolution of man's motor skills and his ability to create and utilize cognitive maps led to an important evolutionary opportunity—the ability to create external representations which corresponded to the cognitive maps. One of the earliest representations is carved in bone and is believed to be a calendar (Pfeiffer 1972). In this case, the cognitive map was of temporal relationships, and these were represented by spatial relationships. Probably the most important external representations our ancestors created were maps. They allowed man to travel great distances over land and water, and to return safely. A map is usually very different from an aerial perspective, and hence the creation of maps involves much more than perception. In an aerial perspective, nearby objects are larger and distorted differently than distant objects of the same size and shape, and nearby surfaces are larger than distant surfaces of the same size. In a map of a sufficiently small portion of the earth's surface, all of these distortions are eliminated and the distance between two points on a map is proportional to their true distance—a very different situation than in aerial perspectives. Hence, maps represent our conceptions and not our perception. Not only can objects and the distances between them be depicted on maps, but also certain events, either contemporary or historical. For example, in maps made by the Marshall Islanders from the midribs of palm leaves and sea shells (Figure 39 on p. 245), the basic framework represents the sea, the curved lines represent the wave fronts (not currents) approaching the various islands, and the sea shells represent the islands. Bagrow and Skelton (1964) describe these navigation charts as "without parallel" in the history of cartography. They also note that with the introduction of European maps into the region, the islanders stopped making these beautiful maps and eventually forgot how to use them.

The ability to externally represent our conceptions in spatial dimensions underlies much of our symbol-making activity, e.g., writing, music, and dance notation, schematics for machines and roads, plans for building, and ownership deeds. Early maps in the "civilized" world were used for collecting taxes, waging war, and trading. The need for accuracy in these maps affected the development of geometry and astronomy, and may have been the initial impetus for the invention of these disciplines.

Thus far we have indicated that the ability to form cognitive maps was important in man's evolution, and that this ability provided an evolutionary opportunity which was capitalized upon through cultural learning. This opportunity primarily took the form of using external representations to depict in spatial terms what was known. We have implied that man had a great deal of knowledge about his environment prior to the time he started making external representations of it. Thus, the inability to make external representations does not necessarily reflect a lack of knowledge about what can be represented. Further, almost all external representations are somewhat idiosyncratic in that they are tied to a given culture; hence, the inability to use a given representation does not necessarily reflect a lack of knowledge about what is being represented. For example, the Marshall Islanders have forgotten how to use the maps of their ancestors.

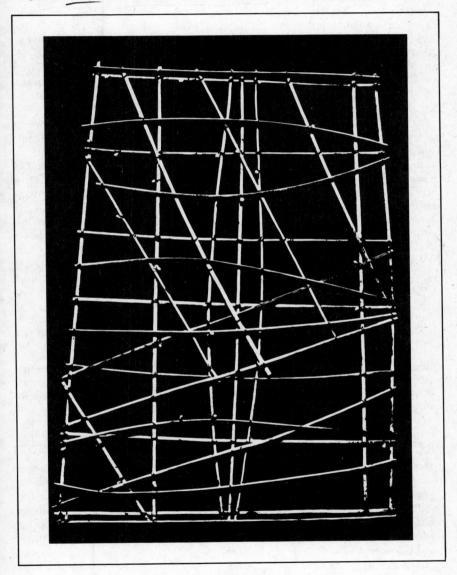

Figure 39
Marshall Islander's Navigation Map (From Bagrow and Skelton 1964).

We will now turn to the child's understanding of spatial relationships. As we have indicated in previous chapters, the development of spatial understanding is a canalized process which proceeds through a number of age-related stages. Superimposed upon this genetically controlled process is cultural learning, which varies from culture to culture. In Western industrial societies, for example, children enter school between the ages of five and seven and start to receive instruction on a variety of subjects which involve spatial understanding, e.g., writing, drawing figures, using maps, measuring with rulers, using music notation. The nature of these experiences may speed up or slow down the child's spatial development, but the extent of these changes in rate is probably very limited.

We believe that the most fundamental aspect of spatial understanding concerns the relationships between objects in the immediate environment. That is, in order for a child to form cognitive maps of distant objects or nonspatial events, he must first have the ability to internally represent what is before him. Given this assumption, the natural starting point for tracking a child's spatial development is the child's perception of the physical environment. An individual's conception of space can be no more accurate than his perceptions. For example, if a child fails to perceive a relationship in the environment, e.g., that a block is in front of a ball, it is doubtful that he has a conception of that relationship. Further, in testing for a child's conception of the environment, the child is usually asked to make a perceptual judgment. For example, on tasks in which the child must select one of a group of drawings to demonstrate his spatial understanding, he can't accurately indicate his understanding if he doesn't accurately perceive the drawings.

Piaget and Inhelder (1956) contrast perception and conception as follows (they sometimes use the terms "conception," "representation," and "imagination" synonymously):

> Perception is the knowledge of objects resulting from direct contact with them. As against this, representation or imagination involves the evocation of objects in their absence, or when it runs parallel to perception, in their presence. It completes perceptual knowledge by reference to objects not actually perceived. Thus, as an example, one may recognize a 'triangle' and liken the given figure to the entire class of comparable shapes not present to perception.*

During the act of perception, one builds up an image of objects which is tied to sensory stimulation. Piaget and Inhelder (1969) refer to this image as a "reproductive" or "copy" image. "Anticipatory" images are linked to the child's conceptions of the environment, and allow the child to anticipate or predict the appearance of objects after they have been transformed in some way, e.g., after objects have been rotated or moved to another viewing position. As children mature, their reproductive images become more complete, and anticipatory imagery emerges, i.e., their perceptual schemes become increas-

---

*J. Piaget and B. Inhelder, *The Child's Conception of Space* (London: Routledge & Kegan Paul, 1956), p. 17.

ingly differentiated and they develop new conceptual schemes. Although in theory the development of copy images and anticipatory images can be separated, in practice it is frequently not possible to do so. As we have noted, the assessment of a child's conceptions usually involves a perceptual task. As we will see later in the chapter, however, periods in development can be identified in which a child's spatial perceptions are very accurate, but his spatial conceptions are very inadequate.

Implicit in the preceding discussion is the idea that children have the capacity to form representations of the permanence of single objects. That is, in order to answer questions about the development of a conceptual or representational understanding of *relationships* between objects, it must be assumed that children understand that a major characteristic of single objects is their durability or permanence, i.e., an object exists independent of the child's actions on the object and independent of the object being perceived. Obviously, if children did not believe objects to have this quality, e.g., out of sight, out of existence, then one could only answer questions about the perceptual relations between objects. Piaget (1954) believes that acquiring the concept of the permanent object is about the most important intellectual acquisition of infancy. Not surprisingly, based upon our previous discussions, the acquisition of this concept occurs over a considerable time period, reaching a relatively mature state between the ages of one and one and a half. We will now turn to a discussion of this topic.

DEVELOPMENT OF THE CONCEPT OF THE PERMANENT OBJECT

In 1954 Piaget described six stages infants go through in their acquisition of the object concept. His findings have been independently tested by a number of investigators, e.g., Bower and Paterson (1972), Evans and Gratch (1972), and, with the exception of some details, his conclusions have been substantiated. In the following discussion we will follow the broad outlines of Piaget's research, with relevant research findings of others interspersed.

From birth to about four to five months of age, the infant is in the first two stages of development. Objects are not readily distinguished, nor are infants able to accurately visually follow (track) moving objects. For example, in one experiment carried out by Bower and his colleagues (Bower 1971), infants of two, three and a half, and four and a half months of age were shown a moving ball that stopped next to a screen. Virtually all the two-month old infants continued to track with their eyes along the path the ball was following, ignoring the stationary ball; most of the three and a half month old infants did this; but essentially all of the four and a half month old infants stopped moving their eyes and gazed at the ball. The type of error the Stage 2 infants made (the two and three and a half month old infants) seemed to reflect their inability to differentiate the property of movement from the concept of the ball.

During Stage 3, which lasts until six or seven months of age, infants are readily able to track moving objects, including assumed complex trajectories the objects follow while hidden from sight. These infants will reach for objects that are partially hidden from sight, but if the object is completely hidden, e.g., covered with a cloth or by an opaque cup, they will not reach for it (Gratch and

Landers 1971). This is a puzzling phenomenon because infants in Stage 3 track with their eyes moving objects which become temporarily hidden, but a static object which is covered becomes both visually and motorically ignored. That infants are capable of removing cups which cover objects, and in fact do so if the cups are transparent, has been demonstrated by Bower and Wishart (1972).

During Stage 4, which typically lasts until a child is nine to eleven months old (Gratch and Landers 1971, Bower and Paterson 1972), a child will reach for and grasp a hidden object. The salient feature of this stage is the following. If an object (almost always a toy) is hidden once or twice in full view of the child at place A, and the child finds it on each occasion, and then, in full view of the child, it is hidden at place B, the child will search for the object at place A. This is almost an unbelievable phenomenon, but it has been replicated a number of times outside of Piaget's laboratory, e.g., Gratch and Landers (1972), Bower and Paterson (1972). In this stage the child appears to have some understanding of object permanence, but this understanding is limited by the child's inability to differentiate between the location of a hidden object and the hidden object itself. It's as if a property of a hidden object is the location at which it was previously found.

During Stage 5, which typically lasts until a child is about one and a half years old, the child accurately searches for an object in the last place it was hidden, irrespective of its previous history of hidden locations. Children in this stage, however, are unable to follow the movements of a hidden object. The typical experiment is to place two cloths on a table, put a toy under one of them in full view of the child, and then, in full view of the child, switch the positions of the two cloths, carrying the toy along. Thus, the toy is initially hidden at A, but moved to B while the child is watching. When given an opportunity to find the toy, the children search at A (Bower and Paterson 1972). In this stage, then, the child has a fairly well developed concept of a permanent object, but his representation of objects is still limited by his inability to move the representation around in his head. That is, success in the preceding type of experiment requires the child to be able to imagine the movement of an unseen object from one place to another. During Stage 6, children can solve this type of problem. Their ability to do so indicates that they have entered the first stage of representational thought (in Piaget's terms, the "preoperational stage"). At this point in development it makes sense to ask questions about children's understanding of the relationships between objects and their conceptions of space.

DEVELOPMENT OF SHAPE PERCEPTION

Piaget and Inhelder (1956) suggest that the natural starting point for an understanding of the child's conception of space is the child's perception of shape. In order to understand how a child *conceives* of the relationships between objects, it is necessary to understand how he perceives these relationships, and in order to understand the latter, it is necessary to understand how he perceives a single object. Piaget and Inhelder argue that the development of shape perception of a single object, perception of a collection of objects, and spatial conception of a group of objects show a striking parallel. That is, the initial correct distinctions made are of a topological nature, and topological distinctions are followed by those of a projective and Euclidian nature. Some of the major topological relationships are proximity (what is next to what), separation (what is distinct from what), order (what precedes what), enclosure (what surrounds or includes what), and continuity or discontinuity. The major projective relationships involve changes in the appearance of an object or group of objects following changes in viewing perspectives, changes produced by rotation, or changes produced by projecting the object or objects on a plane surface as in projecting shadows. The major Euclidian relationships involve exact measurement, such as the size of angles, the distance between two points, proportions, and lengths. In Euclidian space, a stable reference system is used, as in maps. Projective and Euclidian understanding proceed together, both being an outgrowth of topological understanding. These distinctions will become clearer as the relevant research is discussed.

In this section two experiments will be considered. The first, carried out by Piaget and Inhelder, and subsequently replicated by Laurendeau and Pinard (1970), deals with the relationship between topological and Euclidian perception. The second, carried out by Gibson, Gibson, Pick, and Osser (1962), deals with the relationship between topological, Euclidian, and projective perception.

In Piaget and Inhelder's experiment, children between the ages of two and seven were presented with a collection of familiar objects, e.g., key, comb, spoon, and cardboard cutouts of geometrical shapes, some of which are shown in Figure 40 on p. 250. The objects were handed to the child one at a time so that he could tactually explore them, but not look at them. The children were asked to name the familiar objects, and to choose the correct geometrical shape from a set of drawings shown to them. This experimental procedure is very similar to those of Abravanel and Birch and Lefford. If a child understands topological but not Euclidian relationships, he will successfully distinguish between forms that vary in some of the basic topological relationships, but he will make errors or confuse shapes that vary only in Euclidian relationships. For example, he will not confuse the open and closed rings (continuity), the intertwined and superimposed rings (separation), or the surfaces with one or two holes (enclosure), but he will confuse squares and circles, and circles and ellipses, which are alike topologically.

Piaget and Inhelder describe performance in terms of three age-related stages. In the early part of the first stage, from age two and a half to three and a half, the children are able to recognize the familiar objects but none of the geometrical shapes. In the latter part of this stage, from age three and a half to four, the children start to make distinctions between shapes that differ topologically, but they continue to make Euclidian confusions, e.g., circles and squares are not distinguished because they are both closed forms. The tactual exploration of these children was passive, as Abravanel has reported. In the early part of Stage 2, from age four to five, the children make differentiations between rectilinear shapes, e.g., squares, and curvilinear shapes, e.g., circles, and start to make differentiations within rectilinear and curvilinear shapes, e.g., circles

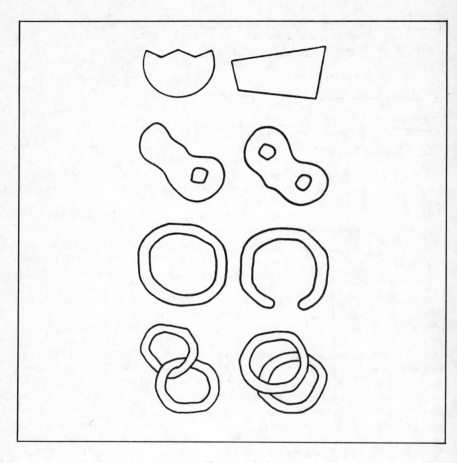

Figure 40

Toothed semi-circle, trapezoid, one and two-holed irregular surfaces, open and closed rings, intertwined and superimposed rings (From Piaget and Inhelder 1956).

and ellipses. In short, they start to perceive Euclidian differences. The tactual exploration of these children was described by Piaget and Inhelder as "global." In the latter part of this stage, from age five to six, the children clearly distinguish between simple rectilinear shapes, e.g., rhombus and trapezium, and simple curvilinear shapes, e.g., circles and ellipses, but they continue to have difficulty with the complex shapes, e.g., stars and crosses. In the third stage, from age six to seven, the children's tactual exploration is quite active and systematic, and they can successfully identify the complex shapes.

In the Gibson et al. (1962) experiment, the subjects were children aged four to eight. They were tested on a matching task in which twelve letterlike forms (the "standards") and twelve transformations of each of these forms were constructed. Some of the standards and several transformations are shown in Figure 41. On each trial the child was presented with one of the standards, all twelve transformations of it, and one or two copies of the standard. He was instructed to pick out all the exact copies of the standard. Three of the transformations changed certain curved portions of the standard into straight lines, or vice versa, e.g., L to C in Figure 41 (Euclidian transformations); five of the transformations either rotated or reversed the standard, e.g., 45° R in Figure 41 (projective transformations); two of the transformations tilted the standard either back or sideways, e.g., Perspective Trs in Figure 41 (perspective transformations); and two of the transformations were topological, either closing lines that were open, or opening lines that were closed, e.g., Close, Break in Figure 41. As you can see in Figure 41, the perspective transformations appear much more similar to the standard than the other transformations, and the children too found this to be the case. Ideally, the various transformations should have been equated for similarity by adult perceivers so that the children's performance could be unambiguously interpreted. However, scaling procedures of this sort are absent in Piaget's research and in almost all other research on children's perception.

An error was defined as the choice of a transformation. The major results were as follows. For the topological transformations, four year olds made about fifteen percent errors, and this percentage declined to about five percent for the eight year olds. For the perspective transformations, four year olds made about eighty percent errors, and eight year olds about sixty percent errors. For the remaining Euclidian and projective transformations, four year olds made about forty percent errors, and this percentage declined to about ten for the eight year

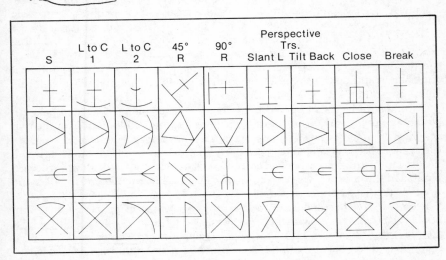

Figure 41

Four standards and Euclidian, projective, and topological transformations of them (From Gibson, Gibson, Pick and Osser 1962).

olds. Hence, these results are highly consistent with those of Piaget and Inhelder. Taken together, the two experiments support the view that topologi- cal relations are accurately perceived prior to Euclidian or projective relations, and that the latter two become accurately perceived at about the same time. These results further suggest that assessing children's conceptions with per- ceptual tasks will be difficult at ages four and five owing to the large percent- age of Euclidian and projective perceptual confusions they make.

SPATIAL RELATIONSHIPS: PERCEPTION AND CONCEPTION OF ORDER

The discussion in this section is based on the research reported by Piaget and Inhelder (1956) in their chapter entitled "Linear and Circular Order." The perception and conception of order implies that the child has notions of proximity, separation, and constant direction of travel. To accurately perceive a linear series of objects, called A, B, C, for example, the child must note that there are three separate objects, that A is next to B and B is next to C, and that they are linked together in the direction of travel A B C or C B A. The series C B A moves in a different direction than A B C, but the two can be put in the same order by reversing the direction of one of them.

The subjects in Piaget and Inhelder's experiment were children between the ages of two and seven and a half. They were given between one and four tasks to perform, depending upon their degree of success. The first task involved the reproduction of a simple linear order. In this task the children were shown a rod strung with seven to nine different colored beads and asked to copy the pattern by placing other beads on a rod located immediately below it. The beads were large so that they could be handled easily, and the children were able to recognize the different colors as demonstrated on a color sorting task. The second task involved transposing a circular order into a simple linear order. In this task the children were presented with a "necklace" containing seven to nine evenly spaced beads and asked to place other beads on a rod located below the necklace so that the order of the beads on the rod and necklace would be the same. The third task involved the reversal of a simple linear order. In this task the children were presented with a rod strung with an odd number of beads and asked to place other beads on a rod located below it so that the order was reversed. If done correctly, the middle beads on the two rods would line up one above the other. The fourth task involved transposing the order of beads arranged on a string twisted in a figure eight. In this task the beads were strung on a necklace, the necklace was twisted to form a figure eight, and the children were asked to place beads on a rod to correspond to the order of the beads on the necklace.

It was discovered that children two to three years of age were generally unable to comprehend even the simplest task. Not only did they fail to copy a simple linear order, but they also failed to select the same color beads as in the model. Children between the ages of three and three and a half started to comprehend the task, in that they matched the colors of the beads to those of the model, but they were unable to line up the beads in the same order as in the model. When the experimenter pointed out to the child that he had made an error, the child was unable to correct it. Hence, children of this age apparently don't perceive proximity relations. Children between the ages of three and a half and four performed somewhat differently than the younger children, in that they arranged some of their beads in pairs, e.g., if the order on the model was A B C D E F G, a child would arrange his beads as B A G F C D E. Thus, children of this age have some perception of proximity, but the proximate pairs are not coordinated, nor is the order between or within pairs perceived. Children between the ages of four and five and a half were generally able to perform the first task correctly when the two rods were lined up one above the other. If their rod was displaced somewhat, or if they were asked to perform the second task, i.e., the necklace to rod task, they made errors. Further, when their errors were pointed out, they were unable to correct them. Thus, children at this stage can perceive the topological relations of proximity, separation, and direction of travel, but only when the rods are lined up. This suggests that they do not have a conception of these relations.

The next stage of development emerges between ages five and six. Children at this stage can solve the necklace problem, but they are unable to reverse order or to transfer the figure eight. When their errors on the reversal task were pointed out, they were unable to correct them. The ability to transpose the circle into a line suggests that anticipatory imagery has emerged, and that direct perception can be transcended. However, this anticipatory imagery is not well developed, in that the children cannot solve the reversal task. The next stage of development emerges between ages five and six and a half. Children at this stage can solve the reversal task by trial and error methods, but they are generally unable to transpose the figure eight. Anticipatory imagery is more fully developed at this stage and reversible operations are starting to emerge. In the final stage, reached between ages six and seven and a half, the children can readily solve the reversal task, and can solve with trial and error methods the figure eight task. At this stage, conceptual thought can augment the child's perception and guide his motor behavior. Children at this stage can solve concrete spatial problems "in their head" and make use of the operations of reversibility.

CONSTRUCTING A STRAIGHT LINE

In the following very simple and very elegant experiment, Piaget and Inhelder demonstrate that a child's conception of a straight line lags several years behind his ability to perceive a straight line. The projective straight line (as contrasted with the topological line, in which straight and curved lines are indistinguishable) is one of the most fundamental aspects of projective and Euclidian space. Hence, the child's conception of it is a natural starting point for the study of more complex spatial relationships.

In this experiment, which has been replicated by Laurendeau and Pinard (1970), the subjects were children from ages two and a half to seven and a half. They were each tested on four experimental tasks. In all tasks the children were given six to ten matchsticks stuck into bases made of modeling clay and asked to pretend that the sticks were telegraph poles. They were then instructed to make a perfectly straight line with the poles which ran along the side of an imaginary road. In the first task, the experimenter placed the first and last poles twenty to forty centimeters apart about three centimeters from one edge of a rectangular table. Correct performance on this task involves placing the poles parallel to the edge of the table, more or less equally spaced between the two end poles. In the second task, the children were given the poles and asked to make a straight line with them on the floor or anywhere on a round table. In the third task, the experimenter placed one end pole near one edge of the rectangular table, and the other end pole near the edge of an adjacent side of the table. Thus, correct performance involves constructing a straight line running at an oblique angle. In the fourth task, the two end poles were placed near the edge of a round table about twenty to forty centimeters apart.

Piaget and Inhelder describe four age-related performance stages on this task, which are summarized in Figure 42 on p. 255. In Stage I, which extends to about age four, children are able to place the poles on the edge of the table and on a line drawn on paper by the experimenter, and they can readily distinguish perceptually between straight and curved lines; but as you can see from Figure 42, they are unable to construct a straight line near the edge of the table connecting the two end points, nor are they able to construct an unguided straight line. In Stage IIA, which extends to about age six, the child can construct a straight line near the edge of a rectangular table, and an unguided line on a round table, but he is unable to construct an oblique line or a line between fixed end points on a round table. When errors are pointed out to children in this stage, they are unable to successfully correct them. For example, when an oblique line is required, the children in attempting to correct their performance merely shift poles from one line to the other, and are unable to join the two lines. In this stage, the child doesn't have the concept of a line, and he is unable to go beyond his perceptions. In Stage IIB, which extends from about age five to six and a half, the children initially make errors, but they can correct them and make oblique lines. In this stage, the children can be induced to use "aiming" as an aid in correcting their errors. Aiming involves viewing the line from a position in which the first pole obscures the perception of the remaining poles if the line is straight. The ability to use aiming, Piaget and Inhelder argue, reflects the understanding that different points of view make the lines appear different, and that one point of view may be most suitable for the task at hand. Hence, in Stage IIB, the child starts to be able to go beyond his immediate perceptions. In Stage III, which emerges between ages six and seven and a half, the children can perform the oblique task without difficulty, and they spontaneously use the technique of aiming. It is at this stage that anticipatory imagery becomes well-developed and the child's conceptions go beyond the perceptual configuration at hand.

It is important to point out that these age-related stages are consistent with the findings of Birch and Lefford. Recall that in their study, children between the ages of five and seven had some difficulty in discriminating the two types of triangles and the two types of diamonds. Also, the five year olds had great difficulty in copying the diamonds (which consist exclusively of oblique lines) freehand, and they had some difficulty in tracing diamonds and connecting dots to form oblique lines.

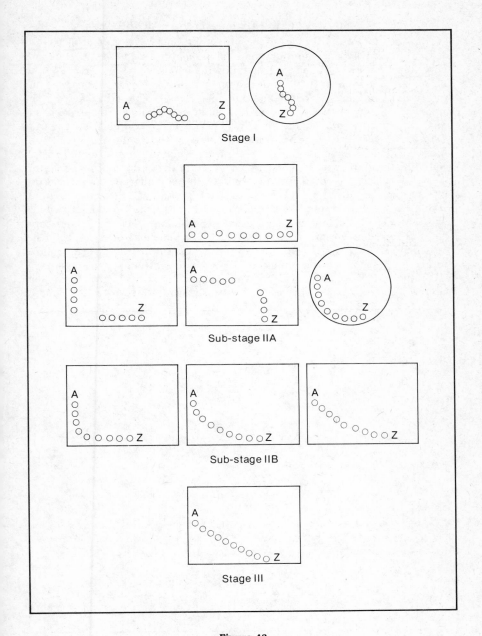

Figure 42

Stages in the ability to construct a straight line (From Piaget and Inhelder 1956).

THE USE OF PHYSICAL REFERENCE SYSTEMS: A MODEL LANDSCAPE

In this section we will discuss the utilization and development of certain topological, projective, and Euclidian relationships in the perception and conception of a group of objects. The following experiment was carried out by Laurendeau and Pinard (1970), and is based on a similar experiment carried out and briefly reported by Piaget and Inhelder (1956). The subjects were six hundred children between the ages of three and twelve. The experiment consisted of two parts. In the first, which can be considered as primarily dealing with perception, the child was presented with two identical miniature landscapes, each thirty-five by forty-seven centimeters, both oriented in the same direction. The experimenter sat across from the child and placed a doll successively at twelve predetermined points on his landscape, and asked the child to place another doll at the corresponding points ("at exactly the same place") on the child's landscape. In the second part of the experiment, which deals with perception and conception, the experimenter rotated his landscape 180° and repeated the procedure. Figure 43 is a schematized version of the landscape showing the twelve points at which the doll was placed (dots A through L), the areas surrounding the dots which correspond to the regions in which the child's doll placements were scored as correct, and the major features of the landscape. The group of three squares located between C and D

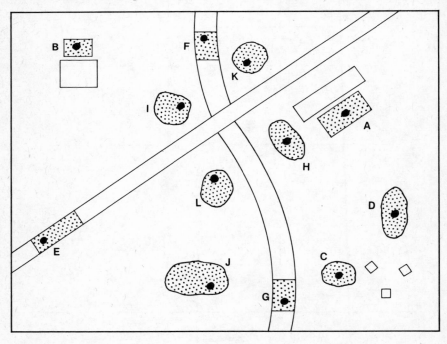

Figure 43

Schematic diagram of landscape (From Laurendeau and Pinard 1970).

were small houses of different colors; the rectangle near A was a red house; the rectangle near B was a yellow house; the parallel lines which enclose E were railroad tracks; and the two lines which enclose F and G were a road. Thus, the landscape was divided by the road and the railroad tracks into four quadrants of different size and shape, two containing no houses, one containing four houses, and one containing one house.

On an *a priori* basis, the twelve points were evaluated in terms of the type and number of topological, projective, and Euclidian relations the child had to deal with in order to perform correctly. Four groups were identified: Group I, which consists of points A-G on Part I; Group II, which consists of points H-L on Part I; Group III, which consists of points A-G on Part II; and Group IV, which consists of points H-L on Part II. Let's examine these. Group I is the easiest, in that these points can be solved by relying primarily on the topological relations of enclosure (E, F, and G) and proximity (A-D). These points only require a minimum coordination, or relating of two topological relations, and they only minimally require the utilization of projective, e.g., left of, right of, and Euclidian relations, e.g., how far from. Group II is next in level of difficulty. For these points, the topological cues are more ambiguous, and the child must utilize projective and Euclidian relations to a greater extent than for Group I. For example, H, I, K, and L are all definable as being located in a field near an intersection. It is important to point out, however, that for all points in Part I, the major topological relation of "proximity to the child" is operating. For example, Point G is near the child and Point F is far from the child, and these placements are rarely missed, i.e., these points are correct more than ninety percent of the time. In Part II, with the rotated landscape, this topological cue interferes with correct performance, and F and G are correct only between forty-five and fifty percent of the time.

Group III is next in level of difficulty, and consists of points A-G on Part II. For these points, the child can make use of topological relations, but in order to be correct he must also make use of at least one projective relation, e.g., left of, in back of, and make at least minimal use of Euclidian measurement. In Part II, in contrast to Part I, the child must apply his *conceptions* of projective and Euclidian relations, and these are in conflict with his *perceptions*. For example, in Part II, the child perceives the experimenter's Point C as being to the left of the road, but relative to both the experimenter's viewing position, and to a fixed physical frame of reference, the doll is to the right of the road. If the child places the doll to the left of the road, responding to his perception, he has responded in a way which Piaget and Inhelder (1956) term "egocentric." When a child is operating in an egocentric fashion, he is failing to coordinate his view with other possible views, and moreover, he is operating as if all views are the same as his. Group IV is the most difficult, consisting of points H-L on Part II. For these points, correct performance requires that the child coordinate two projective relations, i.e., back-front and left-right, and at least minimally make use of Euclidian relations.

In general, the *a priori* grouping of these points corresponds quite well to the children's performance. Overall, the percentage of children who performed correctly on each point in Group I ranged from seventy-six to ninety-two percent; for the points in Group II, the range was sixty-eight to seventy-four percent; for the points in Group III, the range was forty-four to sixty-nine percent; and for the points in Group IV, the range was thirty-seven to fifty-seven percent, with four of the five points below forty-five percent.

Laurendeau and Pinard identified five age-related performance stages in this experiment. In the first stage, which typifies the performance of the three and three and a half year olds and a substantial minority of the four and four and a half year olds, the children apparently understand the task, make some correct placements, but fail to get as many as five of seven correct in Group I or Group III, or four of five correct in Group II or Group IV. An analysis of their errors indicates that these children are unable to utilize projective and Euclidian relations, and they are frequently unable to coordinate two or more of the topological relations, e.g., proximity *and* enclosure. The second stage is defined by Laurendeau and Pinard as solving at least five of seven in Group I, solving not more than three of five in Groups II and IV, and solving at least five of seven in Group III. This stage is typical of children between three and a half and five years of age. An analysis of their errors in Group II indicates that these children are unable to coordinate both left-right and back-front relations. For Groups III and IV, the children's egocentricity interferes with their performance. For example, with points A and B in Group III, eighty-one percent of the errors consisted of placing the doll near the house, but on the side opposite the correct placement (a back-front reversal), and with points E, F, and G in Group III, eighty-nine percent of the errors consisted of placing the doll at the wrong end of the road or railroad tracks (back-front or left-right reversals).

The third stage is defined as solving at least five of seven in Group I and four of five in Group II, and not reaching either of these performance levels on Part II. This stage is characteristic of the six and seven year olds. The primary difference between children at this stage and children at the second stage is that the former are better able to coordinate projective relations on the perceptual task. Their performance on Part II contains a large number of egocentric errors. The fourth stage is defined as success on Part I, correct performance on at least five of seven in Group III, and failure to solve at least four of five in Group IV. This stage is characteristic of seven, eight, and nine year olds. The performance of these children is very interesting. On the relatively simple placements in Part II, the children overcome their egocentric tendencies and correctly coordinate the topological relations and a single projective relation, i.e., either left-right or back-front. On Group IV, however, where the topological cues are more ambiguous and the children must coordinate two projective relations, they make a large number of egocentric errors. In fact, eighty-three percent of their errors were categorized as egocentric. In the fifth and last stage, the children meet criteria on all parts of the test. This stage was reached by seventy percent of the twelve year olds, sixty-four percent of the eleven year olds, and fifty-six percent of the ten year olds. As in the fourth stage, the errors made by these children were primarily egocentric.

In general, the results from this experiment are very consistent with those from experiments dealing with the concept of order and constructing a straight line. Between the ages of three and six, children are rapidly developing the ability to deal with topological relations and simple projective and Euclidian relations on perceptual tasks—their reproductive images have become increasingly differentiated. At about age seven, many children have developed anticipatory imagery which allows them to reverse the order of objects and simple projective relations. At this age, however, they are unable to conceptually (as opposed to perceptually) coordinate two or more projective relations, nor are they able to conceptually deal with a fixed frame of reference. Egocentric intrusions interfere with their conceptual space. During the age range ten to twelve, the children are progressively able to suppress egocentric intrusions and coordinate two or more projective and Euclidian relations.

COORDINATION OF PERSPECTIVES

In this section we will discuss the development and utilization of projective relations in the perception and conception of a group of objects. The starting point is the research of Piaget and Inhelder (1956). In their study, a child was presented with a three-dimensional pasteboard model of three mountains, each painted a different color. The child was tested on three tasks. In the first task, a doll with no facial features was placed in front of the mountains and the child was presented with ten painted pictures representing the mountains as they would be seen from ten different positions. The child was then asked to point to the picture that looked like what the doll would see if the doll took a photograph from his position. In a second task, the child was asked to select one of the ten pictures and then to place the doll in the position it would have to occupy in order to take a snapshot that was similar to the picture that the child had selected. In the third task, the child was given three flat pieces of cardboard shaped and colored like the mountains, and was asked to reconstruct the kind of snapshots the doll would take when it was placed in different positions around the mountains.

Piaget and Inhelder describe three age-related stages in the performance of this task. In the first stage, which occurs between four and seven years of age, the children respond in an egocentric manner. For example, irrespective of where the doll was placed in relation to the mountains, the children either pointed to the picture that looked like what they themselves could see, or they constructed a picture out of the cardboard cutouts which looked like what they could see. Hence, in the egocentric stage, the children act as if they are unaware that there is a viewpoint other than their own. In the second stage, which occurs between seven and eight years of age, the children act as if they are aware that the mountain scene has other perspectives, or as if others seated in a different position would not see the same thing as they do. In this stage, egocentric errors do not predominate; however, the children consistently fail to make correct choices. In the third stage, which occurs at about nine or ten years of age, the mastery of coordination of perspectives is complete. In this stage, the children no longer make egocentric errors, and their performance is generally perfect.

Laurendeau and Pinard (1970) also investigated this problem. The materials they used consisted of three paper cones of different heights and colors placed on a plain cardboard square, and a set of nine sketched scenes, seven of which represented possible perspectives of the cones, and two impossible perspectives. On each trial a small doll was placed near the perimeter of the square and the child was asked to identify, from a set of five of the scenes, the one that the doll could see. Three problems were used with groups of children whose ages ranged from four and a half to twelve years. Consistent with the preceding study, the older children performed better than the younger ones; however, even the twelve year olds made approximately forty percent errors. In their analysis of the types of errors the children made, Laurendeau and Pinard found that the proportion of egocentric errors to total errors for children aged four and a half to six ranged from .21 to .45; for children aged seven to nine, .70 to .73; and for the oldest children, .75 to .81. Hence, the improvement in performance accompanied by egocentric errors is in contradiction to Piaget and Inhelder's findings, but it is consistent with the research reported in the preceding section dealing with the model landscape.

The next experiments to be discussed were carried out by Fishbein, Lewis, and Keiffer (1972), Masangkay, McClusky, McIntyre, Sims-Knight, Vaughn, and Flavell (1974), and Nigl and Fishbein (1974). In the Fishbein et al. paper, it is argued that two relatively independent developmental factors—social and cognitive—are involved in the child's ability to coordinate perspectives.[1] The social factors are conceptualized as three coexisting stages of development, with the later stages being differentiations of the earlier ones. In their most general sense, the social stages refer to the nature of the inferences the child makes about the responses, e.g., perceptions, thoughts, feelings, of other people to external events or objects. They describe these stages as follows:

> Depending upon the situation, these stages may precede, follow, or be coincident with the child's cognitive development. The first stage is that of "egocentrism." In this stage the child believes that others feel, think, or perceive what he does. He is unaware that viewpoints other than his own exist. The second stage which is seen as transitional, is that of "nonegocentricism." In this stage the child is aware that other people may, for example, feel different about an external event than he does but he is not aware that he can ascertain how they feel. The third stage is that of "empathy." In this stage the child is aware of other viewpoints and he has acquired a rule for ascertaining those viewpoints, that is, if he were in the other person's situation, he would respond the way the other person does.*

In the coordination of perspectives task, when the child uses egocentric thought, he attributes his view to the doll. If the doll has a different viewing position, the child's performance will be impaired, but if the child and doll have the same perspective, then his performance will not be impaired by egocentricity. When the child uses nonegocentric thought, he does not make

---

[1] Flavell's (1974) model describing how children develop an inferential understanding of other's visual experiences is similar; however, he considers the social and cognitive factors to be more interconnected.

*H. D. Fishbein, S. Lewis, and K. Keiffer, "Children's Understanding of Spatial Relations," Developmental Psychology 7 (1972): 23.

egocentric errors; however, when he and the doll have different perspectives, the child is correct only by chance. When the child uses empathic thought, he does not invariably perform without error because he still has the problem of figuring out what the doll sees. His ability to do this is a function of his stage of cognitive development. *COGNITIVE*

The stages of cognitive development in this situation refer to the child's ability to deal with projective relations between a set of objects in the perceptual and conceptual aspects of the task. The perceptual task refers to the situation in which the doll and child have the same perspective. Children in the early preoperational stage may have great difficulty with the perceptual task, as in Groups I and II points in the landscape experiment, whereas older preoperational children may experience little difficulty. As children in the operational stage mature, they become increasingly better able to deal with the projective relations in the conceptual task, i.e., when the doll and child have different perspectives. Apart from chance factors, then, success on a given trial on the conceptual aspects of this task requires that a child both utilize empathic thought and coordinate projective relations between objects as seen from a different viewing position.

The Fishbein et al. and Masangkay et al. papers deal with the development and utilization of the social factors, and the Nigl and Fishbein paper deals with the cognitive factors. Fishbein et al. conducted two experiments. In the first, the subjects were children in preschool, first grade, and third grade, with average ages of four, six and a half, and nine respectively. In one condition, the children were presented with a toy on a revolving tray, and four photographs of the toy depicting 0°, 90°, 180°, and 270° rotations of the toy. In a second condition, three toys and four comparable photographs were employed. In a third condition, one toy and eight photographs were used. The additional four photographs depicted 45°, 135°, 225°, and 315° rotations of the toy. In the fourth condition, three toys and eight photographs were used. Thus, all the photographs were of possible perspectives of the array of toys. A schematic diagram is shown in Figure 44 on p. 262.

Each child was tested on two different tasks. In the first, the experimenter took one of the four designated viewing positions and asked the child to point to the photograph which looked like what she could see. In the second task, the experimenter removed the photographs and asked the child to turn the tray so that the experimenter could see a specified view of the toy or toys. The experimenter described the features she wanted to see, using the descriptive labels front, back, and side, e.g., "show me the front of the Santa Claus."

In the second experiment, kindergarten and second grade children were the subjects with average ages of five and a half and seven and a half respectively. This experiment was similar to the first except that only the four photograph conditions were used, and on the turning task the experimenter pointed to a photograph and asked the child to turn the tray so that the experimenter would see the view shown in the photograph.

The major results were as follows. In Experiment I, performance on the turning task was almost perfect for all children, with a range of zero to nine percent errors. On the pointing task, when the experimenter was seated next to the child (front view), the four year olds made approximately twelve percent errors across all conditions, the six and a half year olds approximately six percent errors, and the nine year olds approximately three percent errors. On the nonfrontal positions of the experimenter, i.e., when she had a different viewing perspective than the child, all age groups performed above chance level, with the nine year olds averaging about twenty five percent errors, the six and a half year olds about forty percent errors, and the four year olds about fifty percent errors. For all age groups performance was better on the one toy than three toy conditions, and better on the four photograph than eight photograph conditions. An analysis of the errors indicates that for all age groups the most typical error was an egocentric one, with the older children making relatively more egocentric errors than the youngest children. In Experiment II, the pointing task and turning task were of approximately the same level of difficulty. When the experimenter was at the front view, the five and a half year olds made approximately twenty-five percent errors and the seven and a half year olds approximately ten percent errors. For the nonfrontal views, the five and a half year olds averaged about fifty percent errors and the seven and a half year olds about twenty-five percent errors. Again, performance was better on the one toy than three toy conditions, and as in Experiment I, the predominant

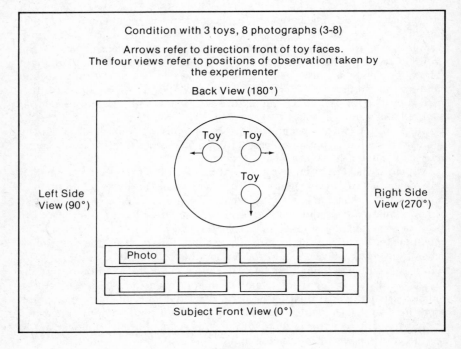

Figure 44

Schematic diagram of the three-toys, eight photographs condition (From Fishbein, Lewis, and Keiffer 1972).

type of error was an egocentric one, with the older children making relatively more than the younger ones.

Fishbein et al. concluded that these results support the position that the stages of social development coexist, and that whether or not the empathic stage is manifested by a child depends upon the difficulty of the task. The results of Experiment I with the turning task indicated that even the youngest children had acquired the empathic mode of thought, and further, that they could use it without error. The authors also suggested the possibility that the children solved these spatial problems by ignoring the internal relationships between the toys, and instead located and used the relevant cues from only one toy. Hence, the experiments made only a limited contribution to the understanding of the cognitive factors in coordination of perspectives.

The study of Masangkay et al. (1974) provides additional information on the early development of social factors. The authors make an important distinction within the empathic mode of responding, referred to as Level 1 and Level 2 understanding. In Level 1, the child understands that another individual can see an object which is invisible to the child, and can specify what the object is. However, the Level 1 child is unable to specify the particular view of the object which the other person sees. In Level 2, the child has this latter ability. The Fishbein et al. experiment only dealt with Level 2 understanding.

In the Masangkay et al. study, three experiments were conducted, two of which will be briefly summarized. In the first, the subjects were two groups of children with average ages of about two and a half and three and a half years. They were tested on a Level 1 task in which the experimenter presented them with an opaque card having either the same or different pictures on the different sides, e.g., a cat on one side and a dog on the other. The experimenter sat across from the child, held up the card, and asked the child what he saw and what the experimenter saw. Approximately sixty percent of the two and a half year olds and ninety-five percent of the three and a half year olds were able to correctly identify the experimenter's view, indicating Level 1 understanding.

In the second experiment, the subjects were five groups of children with average ages of three, three and a half, four, four and a half, and five years. They were tested on the Level 1 task just described, and two Level 2 tasks which bore some similarity to the one toy-four photographs task of Fishbein et al. The major results were that all of the children correctly solved the Level 1 task, but on the Level 2 tasks, the three and three and a half year olds responded at a near chance level, the four and a half and five year olds performed almost without error, and the four year olds performed at an intermediate level. These results are in close agreement with the findings of Fishbein et al., and hence provide strong support of their results.

The Nigl and Fishbein (1974) study was modeled after that of Fishbein et al. Two experiments were conducted, both dealing with the child's ability to perceive and conceive projective relationships. When the experimenter is seated at the front position, the child's task is essentially a perceptual one, and when the experimenter is seated at nonfrontal positions, the child's task is essentially a conceptual one. In the first experiment, the subjects were preschool, first, third, and fifth grade children with average ages of about four, six and a half, eight and a half, and ten and a half, and in the second experiment they were kindergarten, second, fourth, and sixth graders with average ages of about six, eight, ten, and twelve. In both experiments the objects were geometrical shapes constructed in such a fashion that they looked the same following successive 90° rotations, e.g., a cube, a half-sphere. Hence, no single object contained any cue which was unique to a given viewing position. The children were presented with either three, five, or seven of these objects (Experiment I), or four or seven of them (Experiment II). In the first experiment, the objects were all placed on the same rectangular surface, but in the second experiment a two-tiered platform was constructed and at least one object was placed on each surface. In both experiments four photographs were used. They were constructed in such a way as to uncover the confusions the children may have had about left-right, back-front, and up-down projective relationships. In Experiment I, one of the photographs accurately depicted what the experimenter saw, one of them depicted a reversal of the left and right halves of the object array, one of them depicted a reversal of the back and front halves of the array, and one of them reversed both left and right and back and front, which is equivalent to a 180° rotation of the array. The middle two are impossible views of the array because no rotation will produce them. In Experiment II the 180° photograph was replaced by an up-down reversal, i.e., the objects which were on the top tier were shown on the bottom, and vice versa. In order to perform correctly, then, a child had to be able to perceive and conceive left-right relationships, back-front relationships, and up-down relationships. For example, if a child chose a left-right photograph as often as the correct one, it was assumed that he could not utilize that projective relationship.

The major results were as follows. In Experiment I, for the front view, the four year olds performed at about chance level, the six and a half year olds were correct about sixty-five percent of the time, the eight and a half year olds about eighty-five percent, and the ten and a half year olds about ninety-five percent of the time. For the nonfrontal views, the four year olds performed at chance, the six and a half and eight and a half year olds were correct about thirty-five percent of the time, and the ten and a half year olds about sixty percent of the time. Children of all age groups, for frontal and nonfrontal positions, made left-right confusions most frequently, followed by back-front, and then 180° confusions. In Experiment II, for the front view, all age groups performed above a chance level, ranging from fifty percent correct for the six year olds to about ninety percent correct for the twelve year olds. On the nonfrontal views, the six year olds were correct about thirty percent of the time (twenty-five percent is chance responding), eight and ten year olds were correct about thirty-five percent of the time, and the twelve year olds about fifty-five percent of the time. As in Experiment I, left-right confusions were most frequent, followed by back-front, and then up-down confusions, which were rare.

From these results it can be concluded that the accurate perception of projective relationships between objects starts to emerge at about four to five years of age, and becomes highly developed by about age ten. The accurate conception of these projective relations starts to emerge at about age six, but is still very underdeveloped at age twelve. Further, the data suggest that some new conceptual abilities emerge at about age ten, as manifested by the performance jump between the eight and a half and ten and a half year olds in Experiment I, and the ten and twelve year olds in Experiment II.

The final experiment to be discussed in this section is the widely cited study by Davidson (1935). Davidson was interested in the nature of the errors children make in reading the letters of the alphabet. Obviously, if children have difficulty in distinguishing the letters of the alphabet, they will have difficulty in reading words. Davidson was particularly interested in confusions among the letters b, d, p, and q. This is a happy choice from the perspective of the Nigl and Fishbein study. When these letters are compared, three types of errors or confusions can be identified: left-right errors, which involve confusing b and d, or p and q; inversion errors, which bear some similarity to both back-front and up-down errors, and involve confusing b and p, or d and q; and 180° errors, which involve confusing b and q, or d and p, e.g., rotate b 180° and you get q. Fortunately, once again, Davidson reports all these confusions, although he doesn't discuss them in our terms.

Davidson employed two groups of children as subjects—kindergarteners, with an average age of five and three quarters years, and first graders, with an average age of six and three quarters years. They were shown a picture of a single letter, the "standard," and forty "comparison" letters arranged in four lines of ten letters each. They were asked to identify all the comparison letters that looked exactly like the standard. On different trials, the letters b, d, and q were the standards, but the letters d, b, q, and p were always included among the comparison letters along with other letters of the alphabet. This task is very similar to the one used by Gibson et al. (1962), and is primarily a perceptual task.

If the Nigl and Fishbein results are general, one could predict that the older children would perform more accurately than the younger ones, and that both groups would have substantial difficulty with left-right confusions and much less difficulty with either inversions or 180° confusions. This is exactly what was found. The kindergarteners made approximately ninety percent left-right confusions, and approximately forty percent inversion and 180° errors. The first graders made approximately sixty percent left-right errors, and approximately fifteen percent inversion and 180° errors.

When the experiments in this section are considered together, it may be concluded that the social factors in coordination of perspectives develop much earlier than do the cognitive factors for either the perceptual or conceptual aspects of a task. However, depending upon task difficulty, the empathic mode of thought may not be manifested until a much later age. The perceptual abilities to utilize projective relations emerge about a year or two prior to the emergence of the conceptual abilities, and the former are developmentally completed at a much earlier age. Stated in terms of the discussion in the "Overview," children start out dealing with the here-and-now, and later acquire the ability to understand more distant object relationships. The latter ability is still incompletely developed at the onset of adolescence.

SUMMARY

It has been argued that highly developed spatial understanding was a crucial feature in human evolution. Man's ability to form cognitive maps, i.e., representations of his spatial and temporal (seasonal) environment, allowed him to maximize the utilization of food resources in that environment. The starting point in following the child's development of this ability is the child's acquisition of the concept of a permanent object. Piaget and others have shown that children proceed through a number of age-related stages in this acquisition process, which culminate at about age 2 years in the child's ability to represent or imagine the movement of hidden objects from one location to another.

Piaget and Inhelder suggest that the next step in following the child's progress in spatial conceptualization is to examine how he perceives a single object. They show that shape perception of a single object, perception of a collection of objects, and the spatial conception of a collection of objects have parallel developments. Initially, children are confused about topological relationships, and only after they have understood them do they make progress in coping with projective and Euclidian relationships. The research on shape perception indicates that children under five years of age should have difficulty in perceiving or conceiving the relationships between objects owing to Euclidian and projective confusions.

Research was then described which dealt with the perception and conception of order and the construction of a straight line. In brief, the data indicate that children progress through a small number of age-related stages on these tasks, with perceptual understanding preceding conceptual understanding. The latter starts to emerge between the ages of six and seven and a half.

Finally, research bearing on the development of projective and Euclidian understanding of relationships between objects was discussed. Following an earlier suggestion of Piaget and Inhelder, we argued that a child's social development, as well as his perceptual and conceptual development, has an effect on his ability to make accurate projective and Euclidian comparisons. Social development was described as a set of coexisting stages which proceed from egocentric thought, in which the child assumes others have the same perceptions as he, to empathic thought, in which the child assumes that if he were in the other's place, he would see what the other person sees. The research clearly shows that as a child matures, empathic thought increases, but errors frequently stem from egocentric thought. The research also shows that perceptual understanding of Euclidian and projective relations starts to emerge at about age four and becomes highly developed by age nine or ten. Conceptual understanding of these relationships, however, doesn't start to emerge until about age five, and is not highly developed at twelve years of age.

Chapter 12

MORAL DEVELOPMENT

OVERVIEW

We have argued that the key to understanding the form human groups took during the course of evolution is the idea of reciprocal obligations. We described the members of a hunter-gatherer group as involved in a nest of reciprocal obligations, and stated that this nesting had the effect of assuring that nearly everyone was fed, protected, eventually married, and appropriately socialized. It is important to emphasize that reciprocal obligations are *obligations*, that is, they have the status of moral rules. For example, Turnbull (1961) describes an incident in which Cephu, one of the excellent hunters of the Bambuti pygmy group, intentionally and inappropriately placed his net in front of another's net and caught an animal which, had he followed the rules, he would not have caught. Despite the fact that food is shared throughout the group, Cephu was later openly and severely criticized by the group for his "deceitfulness," and he was required to give up his kill.

This example is especially important in two ways. First, it emphasizes that when rules are broken, the group places sanctions on the rule-breaker. This is true for all moral rules. Second, sanctions are frequently imposed on the rule-breaker a considerable time after the discovery that the rule has been broken. This characteristic is apparently absent in the nonhuman primates, where sanctions imposed for "immoral behavior" occur in the here-and-now.

Reciprocal obligations, or moral rules, then, are fundamentally involved with the mutual regulation of members of a social group. Where the moral rules are known and followed, the group will thrive, but in cases where the rules are either not known or not followed, chaos will probably ensue. Thus, two of the chief tasks for any group are to "teach" its members the moral rules, and to insure that its members follow them. As we have consistently maintained, given the nature of man's evolutionary design, these tasks are readily and inevitably accomplished in groups comprised of genetically normal individuals raised in a normal range of environments.

From our perspective, the pertinent question is "why does an individual human act morally?" This is a question which most legal scholars, philosophers, psychologists, sociologists, evolutionists, and theologians have struggled with at one time or another. The variety of answers is marvelous, but some consistencies (which we don't necessarily agree with) emerge. For example, in both the English common law and the teachings of the Catholic church, morality isn't really an issue for a child under the age of seven. This is also about the age, Piaget and other psychologists assert, that children start to consider another's intentions as a basis for making moral judgements. As another example, many theorists consider reciprocal obligations a fundamental concept in morality.

In answering the question "why a human acts morally," a distinction has to be made between one's ability to act morally and one's ability to explain or evaluate moral action. Unfortunately, these two issues are often confused, and as a consequence, some theoreticians, e.g., Kohlberg (1969), Piaget (1932), seem to imply that an individual's ability to give a moral explanation is a prerequisite for his demonstrating moral actions (as contrasted with amoral actions). Moral explanation depends on intellectual and linguistic capabilities, but these capabilities comprise only one determining factor of moral action.

There are at least five broad factors governing moral action. These factors are somewhat interrelated, and the influence they wield on moral action changes throughout an individual's development. They are:

1. authority-acceptance (Waddington 1960b)
2. external reward and punishment
3. internalized standards of right and wrong
4. norm of reciprocity (Gouldner 1960)
5. cognitive-language factors.

"Authority-acceptance" refers to a human predisposition to accept as morality what ethical authorities tell us is moral. Waddington asserts that this human characteristic is an evolved characteristic, hence adaptive, and like other phenotypic characteristics, follows particular developmental pathways. Infancy is the period in which humans develop "authority-bearing systems" (Waddington, 1960b). These systems are initially manifested by obedience, but with further maturation they lead to the acquisition of the moral standards of the group. Authority-acceptance continues to play an important role in moral action throughout one's lifetime, sometimes conflicting with and overriding other factors, e.g., killing innocent people.

The second factor, external reward and punishment, is obviously not restricted to the human species. In general, societies are set up in such a way that moral action frequently leads to rewards, e.g., praise, money, and immoral action frequently leads to punishment, e.g., Cephu's example, prison. The reward or punishment typically fit the magnitude of the moral action, and when they don't, we are either disappointed (in the case of reward), or relieved (in the case of punishment). We certainly perform "good" acts and avoid "bad" acts for their own sake, but without external rewards and punishments, our mutual regulation would be sorely strained.

Intimately related to external reward and punishment is the third factor, internalized standards of right and wrong. Some psychological theorists, e.g., Aronfreed (1969), Gewirtz (1969), imply that individuals acquire these internalized standards through a conditioning process based on rewards and punishments, and that there is little need to investigate other factors in order to understand internalization. In simple terms, one avoids committing bad acts because fear, via external punishment, has been conditioned (internalized) to those acts, and one performs good acts because secondary reward, i.e., good feelings, has been conditioned (internalized) to those acts via external reward. In the psychoanalytic view, e.g., Erikson (1963), Freud (1949), three types of negative internalized standards may be identified: those associated with fear, shame, and guilt. Guilt is a component of superego processes, and is assumed to be the only one (of the three) involved with morality, and related to identification with one's parents. Like external reward and punishment, internalized standards play an important part in governing moral action in infancy and childhood, and continue to do so throughout one's lifetime.

The fourth factor, the norm of reciprocity, refers to obligations or duties one feels toward another in response to the help he has received or the good deeds he has benefited from by the other individual. Gouldner (1960) suggests that this norm imposes at least two demands on people: that we should help those who have helped us, and not injure those who have helped us. It is very likely that this norm imposes two other demands: that we should harm those who have harmed us, and not help those who have harmed us. We think that empathy may underlie, or at least be a crucial component of, the norm of reciprocity. Unless we can predict how another will react to external events, our ability to "reciprocate" is impoverished. What is help to us might be injury to another, and we need to be able to make this assessment. Owing to the complexity of operating in a reciprocal manner, it is very likely that the norm of reciprocity develops at a later age than the three factors just discussed.

The fifth factor, cognitive-language evaluations, i.e., moral judgements, is probably the last of the five factors to emerge in the developing individual and the last to stabilize. As with the norm of reciprocity, the development of empathy is probably crucial to cognitive-language evaluations. The two psychological theorists most influential in the study of moral judgements are Piaget and Kohlberg. In the typical situation studied by them, a child is presented with a dilemma and asked to resolve it by giving an explanation. It is assumed that the explanation given reflects the child's moral understanding and that it is related to his moral actions. One aspect of cognitive-language factors is "ideals," which is typically thought of as a positive attribute of an individual, e.g., "he has high ideals." Ideals frequently have strong motivational consequences in the realm of moral behavior, and unfortunately, not always for the benefit of man. Koestler (1967) points out that more life has been destroyed because of ideals than by "evil" men and women pursuing immoral goals.

In the remainder of this chapter we will discuss research on the development and manifestation of all of these factors except external reward and punishment. Specifically, the following questions will be asked, and tentative answers provided. First, what are the child-rearing antecedents of obedience, and to what extent does obedience change with age? Second, what are the child-rearing antecedents of the acquisition of guilt, identification with one's parents, and imitation? Third, what is the developmental course of the acquisition of empathy? Fourth, what is the developmental course of the acquisition of the norm of reciprocity? And fifth, what is the developmental course of the cognitive-language factor of moral development?

There are at least three major drawbacks in the following discussion. The first is the lack of any firm data on the child-rearing antecedents of individual differences in the acquisition of empathy, the norm of reciprocity, and the cognitive-language factors. Research in these areas has not been carried out. Second, there are apparently no data on the interactions among these factors. And finally, virtually all the research has been carried out with children from Western industrialized societies, whereas the evolutionary processes operated on hunter-gatherer groups. It is doubtful that the processes influencing moral development are the same in both situations. Children in hunter-gatherer groups tend to be raised by the group as a whole, whereas in Western industrialized societies, children tend to be raised by their parents, and especially their mother. There is really no way, based upon the available data, to determine which processes are most affected by these cultural differences.

THE ANTECEDENTS OF OBEDIENCE AND RESISTANCE TO TEMPTATION

With the exception of language development, there is relatively little psychological research dealing with children in their second and third years of life. Although this lack provides an important datum for those interested in the sociology of research, it places uncomfortable strains on researchers who take a developmental perspective. This problem is particularly acute in the area of moral development, where almost all researchers give the impression that moral issues don't exist for children under age three or four. From our perspective, moral issues exist wherever individuals are expected to follow moral rules, i.e., rules which are evaluated from a good-bad point of view and which are involved with the mutual regulation of individuals, e.g., it is bad for a baby to bite his mother's breast. In societies where breast feeding extends much beyond an infant's first year of life, the nursing infant is expected to obey the "no breast biting" rule. In contemporary American society, the rule is rarely an issue because breast feeding either stops when the infant teethes, or the infant is bottle-fed from birth onward. Toilet training is another almost universal moral issue, which takes different forms in different cultures. In hunter-gatherer societies, for example, the child has to learn to obey the rule of defecating at the outskirts of the campsite.

Generally, the principal moral rules for infants revolve around obedience. This makes sense from both an evolutionary perspective and from the view of the infant's psychological capacities. A disobedient, but mobile infant places great risks on his own survival, and in addition may cause harm to others. Obedience is not a moral issue restricted to infancy; rather it continues throughout one's lifetime. One of the typical post-infancy forms it takes is resisting temptation, e.g., don't place your net in front of another's, as Cephu did. Another familiar form revolves around honesty, e.g., don't steal another's weapon or food. Individuals in Western society differ substantially in their tendency to be obedient. Do these differences have something to do with the way they were reared? In other words, what are the child-rearing antecedents of obedience?

Stayton, Hogan, and Ainsworth (1971) studied twenty-five white, middle-class mother-infant dyads during the infant's first year of life. The observations reported in their study deal with behavior in the home during the last quarter of this period, i.e., between nine and twelve months. There were fifteen boys and ten girls, six of whom were first-born. Each mother was rated on three scales concerning the nature of her interactions with her child. The scales are called "sensitivity-insensitivity," "acceptance-rejection," and "cooperation-interference." The sensitive mother is highly attuned to the needs of her infant and responds appropriately to him, whereas the insensitive mother primarily responds to her own needs. The accepting mother is able to accept both her own conflicting feelings towards her infant and the negative and positive actions of her infant, whereas the rejecting mother is frequently resentful of and angry with her infant. The cooperative mother tends to arrange her schedule and activities to accommodate the infant, whereas the interfering mother imposes her schedule on the infant, which frequently interferes with the infant's ongoing activities.

These three variables were correlated with two other aspects of the mother's behavior and two aspects of the infant's behavior. For the mothers, these were "frequency of verbal commands" and "frequency of physical intervention." The former is self-explanatory, and includes commands such as "No, No," "don't touch," "give it to me." The latter refers to the frequency of a variety of physical methods of discipline, such as slapping the infant, dragging him away, and pulling him into a sitting or standing position. The two infant behaviors recorded were the percentage of times the infant obeyed his mother's commands ("compliance to commands"), and the number of times a child started a forbidden activity but self-inhibited carrying it out ("internalized controls").

The major results were as follows. The three scale scores were highly correlated; mothers who scored high on sensitivity also scored high on acceptance and cooperation. In general, there was no relationship between these scale scores and frequency of commands, but there was a moderate negative correlation between these scores and frequency of physical interventions, e.g., highly sensitive mothers tended not to use physical methods of discipline, whereas highly insensitive mothers tended to frequently use physical discipline. Of primary interest were the findings that the scale scores were positively correlated with both internalized controls (about .41) and compliance to demands (about .64), whereas there was essentially no relationship between either mother's frequency of commands or frequency of physical interventions and infant's compliance or self-control. Thus, sensitive, accepting, cooperative mothers tend to have children who obey and use self-control, but mothers who either give a lot of commands or often physically discipline their infants are no more likely to have obedient, self-controlling infants than those who infrequently give commands or use physical discipline. Thus, moderate external punishment apparently has little effect on obedience of infants.

The next study, by Minton, Kagan, and Levine (1971), examined the relationships between several characteristics of mothers' reactions to their infants and the obedience of their first-born, twenty-seven-month-old infants. The mothers were all from the white middle-class, and the observations were made in both the home and the laboratory. Ninety mother-infant dyads were used. For our purposes, the two maternal variables of interest are the frequency with which they gave an explanation to their child when they reprimanded him for violating some standard (explanation reprimands), and the frequency with which they used physical punishment. A reprimand consists of a situation in which the observer noted either a verbal prohibition, a distraction, or a physical punishment by the mother to the child. The two infant variables of interest are the frequency with which they violated maternal standards, as assessed by the presence of a reprimand from their mother, and the frequency with which they disobeyed commands from their mother. The frequency of violation measure is somewhat related to the inverse of the Stayton et al. measure of "internalized controls," and the disobedience to commands measure is somewhat similar to the "compliance" measure of Stayton et al. The measures in the two studies are not the same in that the compliance measure of Stayton et al. includes children's responses to reprimands, e.g., "don't touch."

The major results concerning the relationships between the maternal and child behavior variables were as follows. None of the relationships were strong, but children of mothers who explain their reprimands tend to violate rules less than children of mothers who do not give explanations. On the other hand, children of mothers who frequently use physical punishment tend to violate rules more often than children of mothers who do not frequently use physical punishment. Regarding disobedience, the same relationships hold for the boys, but for the girls there is nearly a zero correlation between the maternal variables and this behavior. There is no obvious explanation for this discrepancy. Thus, for one year olds, moderate physical punishment has essentially no effect on obedience, whereas for two year olds it tends to produce disobedience.

The next study to be discussed, that of Sears, Rau, and Alpert (1965), deals with the relationship between a variety of parental variables and resistance to temptation in white, middle-class boys and girls between the ages of four and five and a half. In their study, the child-rearing practices of the parents were assessed by a very lengthy interview. A large number of child-rearing variables were identified and correlated with measures of the child's resistance to

Resistance -to- temptation

temptation (RTT) in five experimental situations. One of the RTT situations involved leaving the child alone in a room with the task of making sure that a pet hamster did not escape from a cage. In the room were a variety of attractive toys, including a record player and a punching doll, all out of reach from the cage. The child was told that he had to stay near the cage with a rolled-up magazine to prevent the hamster from jumping out. The measure of RTT was how long the child stayed near the cage.

The major results were as follows. First, there was no consistent relationship between age and the various measures of RTT for either boys or girls. Second, in general, the various measures of RTT had a low correlation. These two findings are consistent with other research concerned with age differences and situation specificity in morality (e.g., Grinder 1964, Hartshorne and May 1929–30).

The third set of results deals with the relationship between the parent variables and RTT. For these RTT scores were pooled; thus, each child was given a single score which reflected his ability relative to the rest of the children to resist temptation. Of all the parent variables identified from the interview, for the boys, only ten had correlations with RTT which exceeded chance expectations, and for the girls, only nine had above chance level correlations with RTT. Surprisingly, none of the parent variables which correlated above a chance level for boys did so also for girls, i.e., the nineteen variables were different. For the boys, a high ability to resist temptation, i.e., to be obedient, was positively related to the importance the father attached to teaching right and wrong, the extent to which the father felt hostile to his son, and the extent to which the father was affectionately demonstrative to his son. There was no relation between either mother's or father's permissiveness or punitiveness and RTT. For the girls, a high ability to resist temptation was positively related to the father's dissatisfaction with his daughter, e.g., girls whose RTT was high had fathers who ridiculed them and who were dissatisfied with their development. Also, girls with a high ability to resist temptation had mothers with high achievement standards for them. As with the boys, neither mother's nor father's permissiveness or punitiveness was related to RTT.

The fourth set of results, concerning sex differences, is in great contrast to those of the two previous studies, i.e., parental variables have markedly different effects on boys and girls between the ages of four and five and a half. What stands out in the present study is the tremendous influence of the father on obedience, and surprisingly it is either his ambivalent feelings (with boys) or negative feelings (with girls) which produce obedience. The two consistent trends in the previous studies appear to be the importance of explanation and the ineffectiveness of physical punishment. Recall that mothers who explained their reprimands had more obedient two year olds than those who didn't, and in the present study, fathers who emphasized teaching right from wrong had obedient boys. These comparisons are very tenuous, however, due to the different procedures used in these studies.

The final experiment to be discussed in this section is that of Grinder (1960). Grinder was interested in the relationship between the child-rearing practices parents used on their five and six year old children, and the ability of these same children five years later (at age eleven or twelve) to resist the temptation to cheat. Grinder's subjects were seventy boys and seventy girls from some of the white working and middle-class families studied by Sears, Maccoby, and Levin in their book *Patterns of Child Rearing* (1957). The children participated in the experiment at their school, and did not know that Grinder was following up the earlier research by Sears et al.

The experimental task used was an electronic target shooting game much like those seen in pin ball galleries. Following an initial explanation and demonstration of the game, the children were individually taken to the experimental room. They were told that a score of thirty-five points in twenty shots would earn them a Marksman badge, a score of forty points a Sharpshooter badge, and a score of forty-five points an Expert badge. After showing the children the badges, the experimenter gave them the twenty shot score sheet and told them how to fill it out. Following an indication that the child had understood the whole procedure, the experimenter left the child alone in the room and went down the hall to "do some work." Unknown to the children, the game was rigged so that a child who took twenty shots would score thirty-two points. Thus, any child who reported scoring more than thirty-two points had obviously cheated, i.e., failed to resist the temptation to cheat.

The major results were as follows. Seventeen boys and twenty-five girls turned in scores of 32, and all the rest (ninety-eight) turned in scores of 35 or more, cheating and winning badges. (The experimenter did give the "cheaters" the badges they had "won"). Regarding the relationship between child-rearing practices and game performance, for the boys, ability to resist temptation was positively related to having had a supportive, affectionate mother and parents who had high standards of orderliness and neatness, and who placed little pressure on them to be aggressive. For the girls, the only general aspect of child rearing positively related to resistance to temptation was having had parents who did not follow through on demands for the sake of maintaining their authority. Thus, as in the Sears et al. study (1965), a different pattern of results was found for boys and girls.

The preceding findings can be summarized as follows. First, for white working and middle-class children, relatively high parental punishment has either a negative or a neutral effect on obedience. Second, one and two year olds with sensitive, accepting mothers who explain the rules are more obedient than those with insensitive, rejecting mothers. Third, the child care practices affecting the obedience of boys and girls start to become differentiated at about age two, and by age four these differential effects are marked. Finally, the child care practices producing resistance to temptation between the ages of four and six are different from those producing resistance to temptation at ages eleven to twelve.

What do we make of these findings? As we indicated in a previous chapter, the period of infancy in hunter-gatherer societies is one in which the behaviors of the infant are almost completely accepted, even if not completely approved. Towards the latter part of infancy, at about three years of age, demands are placed on children in some of these societies. No doubt sex-role differentiation starts to be emphasized at about this time also. Thus, the group starts to have different expectations for boys and girls, and starts to emphasize differences in the ways boys and girls are treated. Clearly, punishing an infant is inconsistent with the evolutionary (hunter-gatherer) mode of child rearing, but treating infant boys and girls differentially is consistent with this mode. Due to genetic or cultural reasons, the obedience demands made on boys and girls start to become differentiated in infancy, and as a consequence, the child-rearing techniques required to produce obedience in boys and girls must also become differentiated.

In all cultures something new starts to emerge at about age five—children develop very strong bonds with their friends, and to some extent loosen the bonds with their parents. We ritualize this phenomenon in Western society by sending children away from the home and into school. The child-rearing practices after this age are those of the parents, other adults, and very importantly, other children. Thus, it is not surprising that child care practices producing obedience at four and a half to six years of age are different from those producing obedience at eleven to twelve.

As we implied at the beginning of this chapter, "authority-acceptance," or obedience to authority, is a canalized characteristic necessary for group functioning. Evolutionary processes operate in such a fashion that if a characteristic is important for survival, such as moral behavior, then sufficient mechanisms will be built into the system to ensure the successful manifestation of that characteristic. Authority-acceptance is one of these mechanisms—one which ensures that infants, children, and adults do the "right" thing when told to do so. Authority-acceptance has limited applicability, however, since authorities aren't always around to tell us what to do. One of the evolutionary solutions to this problem was the design of mechanisms for telling ourselves what is right and wrong through the feelings of guilt and self-reward.

SOME ANTECEDENTS OF GUILT, IDENTIFICATION, AND IMITATION

In psychoanalytic theory, e.g., Freud (1949), there are assumed to be three sets of mental processes, called id, ego, and superego. Id processes are present at birth, ego processes start to differentiate out of them shortly thereafter, and superego processes start to emerge at about age four. The main function of superego processes is to guide ego processes so that moral choices are made. This is accomplished through the acquisition of the knowledge of what is wrong and what is right. Psychoanalytic theory emphasizes the obligatory aspects of the superego. One of its processes is the conscience, through which the individual feels warned or punished (by guilt) if he has immoral intentions or acts immorally. The other major superego process involved with moral obligation, the ego-ideal, produces feelings of self-respect or pride when the individual has moral intentions or acts morally. Thus the superego processes take on the rewarding and punishing functions performed by people in the external world.

According to Freud, the obligatory functions of the superego, i.e., the internalization of the conscience and ego-ideal, are developed when the child is required to give up the parent of the opposite sex as a potential love object (the Oedipus complex). The theory is somewhat confusing and contradictory about the events in this process, but basically, in order to allay anxiety about punishment or rejection by the rivaled parent, the child *identifies* with—takes on the characteristics of or attempts to become like—the parent of the same sex (the rivaled parent). In doing so, the child incorporates into himself the standards of that parent. Henceforth, he will have a motive to adhere to the standards even when no one but he would know of a violation. These standards form a major part of superego processes. The child also identifies with the parent of the opposite sex for other reasons, and with other individuals during his lifetime. Thus, superego processes include the moral standards of the society in which the child matures, and the peculiarities of the particular identification models' own standards. Partly because the child incorporates additional ideals and prohibitions when key figures admonish or exhort him, his internalized moral standards continue to be modified throughout his lifetime.

Thus, psychoanalytic theory emphasizes anxiety about loss of parental love and anxiety about a punitive parent(s) as the two most potent child-rearing antecedents of identification and the development of conscience. Others have emphasized yet another factor involved with guilt, identification, and imitation-*power*, e.g., Grusec (1971), Hetherington (1965). According to this view, children seek to model themselves after individuals who control resources that are important to them, independently of loss of love and punishment. Normally parents are involved with all three factors, but it is possible to assess the relative importance of these factors and relate them to children's guilt, identification, and imitation. Before examining some of the experimental literature bearing on these topics, it should be noted that we are sidestepping two issues which have some theoretical importance—the distinction between identification and imitation, and whether the concept of identification is needed (Mussen 1967). Our position is much like Mussen's in that (1) the identification concept is valuable, and (2) imitation involves more limited and more specific behaviors than identification.

As with the other topics which have been discussed in this book, an attempt to give a representative coverage in this section leads to a somewhat dissatisfying state of affairs. This is true for primarily two reasons: treatment of any particular point of view is of necessity minimal, and treatment of several views limits comparisons because of the different techniques and measurements associated with them. We will first discuss two studies dealing with parental antecedents of children's guilt, then one study dealing with parental antecedents of children's identification with and imitation of parents, and finally, one study dealing with the effects of a non-parental model's attributes on children's imitation of that model.

We have already partially dealt with the first study, that of Sears, Rau, and Alpert (1965). Recall that in their study, four to five and a half year old children were presented with a variety of opportunities to resist temptation, and the frequency with which they did so was correlated with a large number of variables assessed during interviews with the children's parents. In the present context, these same variables were correlated with two aspects of the child's behavior called "signs of conscience" and "emotional upset and confession." Signs of conscience is a rating scale, based on interviews with the parents, which assesses the extent to which, at home, the child confesses his misdeeds, acts guilty about his misdeeds, and shows awareness of having done wrong. Emotional upset and confession are measures made of the child's behavior after he has failed to resist temptation in the experimental situation. Presumably the more upset a child becomes for transgressing, and the more readily he confesses, the higher is his guilt. The major findings were as follows. Girls who were rated high by their parents for signs of conscience had mothers who did not use physical punishment, who were democratic, and who were consistent in caretaking. Their fathers praised them a good deal and were empathetic with them. Boys rated high on this measure had mothers who were warm, praiseful, permissive, and who stressed independence, but also stressed neatness and orderliness. The only paternal variable that had any relationship to high conscience was low participation in caretaking during infancy.

Girls rated high on the measures of emotional upset and confession had mothers who placed little pressure on them for conformity, neatness and orderliness, or taking responsibility, but who encouraged their daughter's dependency on them. Their fathers were demonstrably affectionate. Boys rated high on these measures had parents who were nonpermissive of sexuality, and who stressed the importance of teaching right and wrong. In addition, their mothers were typically cold and nonempathetic with them.

Three things stand out from the Sears et al. data. First, the child-rearing antecedents of signs of conscience and the situational manifestations of conscience, i.e., emotional upset and confession, are very different, and to some extent antagonistic, e.g., highly guilty boys had warm mothers for the former, but cold for the latter. This finding may be partially understood by considering the fact that signs of conscience pertain to guilt in the home with respect to the child's parents, but emotional upset and confession pertain to guilt outside the home with respect to non-family adults. Hence, it should not be surprising that the child-rearing antecedents for the two situations are different. Second, and consistent with the obedience literature, the child care antecedents were different for boys and girls. Third, and consistent with the obedience literature, the preceding findings as a whole do not support the view that anxiety over punishment is involved with conscience development, and they give limited importance to the role of anxiety over parent's loss of love in conscience development.

Hoffman and Saltzstein (1967) used white, middle-class seventh grade boys and girls and their parents as subjects in their experiment. They correlated the use of three mother and father punishment practices (treated separately), as assessed by interviews with the children and their parents, with two measures of children's guilt. The three child-rearing punishment practices were called (1) "power assertion," which includes the use of physical punishment, the threat or use of force, and the deprivation of privileges or material goods; (2) "love withdrawal," which includes ignoring the child for wrongdoing, isolating him, and stating dislike for him; and (3) "induction regarding parents," which emphasizes how the parent has been emotionally hurt or disappointed by the child's behavior, thus demonstrating to the child the effect of his actions on others. The two measures of the child's guilt were the mother's rating of his signs of conscience, as in Sears et al. (1965), and his "projective guilt." Projective guilt was assessed by two story-completion projective tests, in which the main characters in the stories commit immoral acts and the child completes the story, indicating what happens to the transgressors.

The major results were as follows. For the boys, the extent of projective guilt was positively correlated with the extent to which the mother used induction, but was not correlated with any of the other practices for either the mother or the father. The extent of signs of conscience was negatively correlated with mother's frequent use of power assertion and father's frequent use of induction, but positively correlated with mother's frequent use of induction and father's frequent use of power assertion. For girls, the extent of projective guilt was negatively correlated with mother's frequent use of power assertion and positively correlated with mother's frequent use of induction, but was not correlated with any other practices for the mother or father. For extent of signs of conscience, there were no reliable correlations with any of the mother or father child care practices.

Thus, as in the Sears et al. study with younger children, anxiety over parental punishment is unrelated to the development of conscience (if anything, it is negatively related). There is also no support for the view that anxiety over direct loss of parental love mediates conscience development. However, there is indirect support for this view if the induction punishment practice is considered. Hoffman and Saltzstein maintain that induction emphasizes the training of empathy and not the withdrawal of love. It is difficult to see how induction can not include the loss of love, e.g., "I'm disappointed in you because you hurt me." It is loss of love plus empathy training. Finally, as in the Sears et al. study, the patterns for boys and girls were different, which is consistent with the view that the different behavioral expectations for boys and girls are reflected in different child-rearing practices.

The experiment by Hetherington (1965) used three groups of children, with average ages of about four and a half, seven, and ten, and their parents as subjects. The major foci of the study were on the relationships between parental dominance and children's identification and imitation. Parental dominance is a measure of which parent "calls the shots." Thus, the dominant parent is assumed to be the more powerful parent, and hence controls resources important for the child. The way Hetherington measured this was by first determining how each parent would solve hypothetical child care problems, and then bringing both parents together to agree on a joint solution. A dominant parent is one who speaks first, speaks last, speaks most, and has his or her solution accepted by the other spouse. The children and parents were selected so that half the boys and girls in each age group came from father-dominant families, and half from mother-dominant families.

Two measures of the children's identification with parents, and one measure of their imitation of parents were taken. The first identification measure was sex-role preference, as determined by the child's performance on the *It Scale For Children*. This is a projective test in which children tell stories about "It," an ambiguous-looking drawing of a figure. It is assumed, for example, that children who identify more strongly with their mother than with their father will project more feminine than masculine roles on "It." The second identification measure was the similarity of personality characteristics between the child and each of his parents. Again, the greater the similarity, the greater the assumed identification. For the imitation task, the child and one parent were seated together and the parent looked through twenty pairs of pictures indicating which one of each pair was the prettiest. This was repeated three times with the same pictures, and then the child was asked to make his selections. One month later the entire procedure was repeated with the other parent. Amount of imitation was determined by the extent of agreement between the child's and each parent's preferences.

If parental power (who controls important resources) is one basis for identification and imitation, then children should tend to identify with and imitate the more dominant parent. The major results were as follows. For sex-role preference, for boys of all ages, there was higher male identification for father-dominant than for mother-dominant families. For girls, there was essentially no difference in female identification as a function of which parent was dominant, although girls identified more with their mother than their father. For parent-child similarity, the results were a bit more complicated, but basically parent dominance had no effect on mother-daughter similarity, but daughters were more similar to fathers in father-dominant than in mother-dominant families. For the seven and ten-year-old boys, mother-son similarity was higher in mother-dominant than in father-dominant families, and for all groups of boys, father-son similarity was higher in father-dominant than in mother-dominant families. For the imitation measure, for all ages and both sexes, children tended to imitate the more dominant parent.

Taken as a whole, these results provide strong support for the importance of parental power in identification and imitation. As Hetherington points out, however, the relationship is a complicated one in that girls are relatively less susceptible to variations in mother-dominance than boys are to variations in father-dominance. Further, boys will generally turn out to be boys (psychologically) and girls, girls (psychologically) despite variations in parental dominance. This is caused partly by the social fabric of a child's environment, and partly by genetic predispositions for sex-role identifications.

The final study to be discussed in this section was carried out by Grusec (1971). Grusec conducted two experiments dealing with the extent to which groups of seven to eleven-year-old children imitated adult models who varied in "power" and "nurturance." In the first experiment, the boys and girls were individually invited to play a game with the experimenter. In the waiting room was a same-sex adult (the model), who purportedly had also been invited to play the game. The child and the model stayed together for ten minutes in the waiting room. When the model was being "highly nurturant," he (or she) played and talked with the child in a warm, friendly manner during the entire waiting time. When the model was being low in nurturance, he (or she) silently worked on some papers during the entire period.

At the end of the waiting period, the child and model were brought into the game room. The experimenter then informed the child that the model was a public relations officer of an airline. In the "high-power" condition the experimenter also said that the model was looking for children to go on a visit to their Toronto terminal, and that after the game the model wanted to talk to the child about his or her possible selection. It was emphasized that the game shortly to be played had absolutely nothing to do with the possibility of the child's being selected for the trip. In the "low-power" condition it was merely mentioned that after the model played the game he would have to return to his office.

Following these "power" instructions, the model played the game while the child watched. The game was a rigged miniature bowling alley in which the player could not directly assess how well he was performing. This information was given by the rigged score lights. Every time the player bowled a high enough score, two marbles were automatically dispensed. The marbles could be traded for prizes—more marbles leading to better prizes. As the experimenter left the room, she mentioned that if either player wanted to, he could donate some of his marbles to the poor children of the city (no specific poor children were identified).

The model bowled twenty trials, winning on five of them. Each time he won, he conspicuously donated one of his two marbles to the poor children, saying "one for the poor children, and one for me." He then knocked on the door to be let out, and was purportedly taken to another room by the experimenter to collect his prize. The child was left alone in the game room and instructed to bowl thirty trials, seven of which were rigged for winning. What did he do with his fourteen marbles?

The basic findings were as follows. Boys and girls responded approximately the same. Children for whom the model was high in power donated more marbles than children who experienced a low-power model. This was true for both the high-nurturant and low-nurturant conditions. Also, children who experienced a high-nurturant model generally donated fewer marbles than those who experienced a low-nurturant model. Thus, children imitated powerful models and low-nurturant models, which is a real puzzler.

In the second experiment, only the power condition was used. The plan of the experiment was essentially the same as the first, but this time the players were asked to reward themselves for their performance on the game. The model bowled twenty trials, receiving scores ranging from forty to eighty. He rewarded himself with one chip for scores of sixty, two chips for scores of seventy or eighty, and no chips for scores of forty or fifty. When he finished bowling, he left the room and the child bowled thirty-six trials, receiving rigged scores ranging from ten to sixty. How many chips did the child give himself?

Again, the performance of boys and girls was about the same. Children who experienced a high-power model used a stringent criterion for self-reward, like the model, and gave themselves fewer chips than those who experienced a low-power model. Thus, in both experiments, children imitated high-power models to a greater extent than they did low-power models.

The peculiar finding linking low nurturance to high imitation is reminiscent of the linkage between cold mothers and the extent of guilt felt by boys, but reminiscence is not the same as explanation. However, Grusec reports contradictory findings from other similar experiments, so perhaps we need not worry about her puzzling finding.

Taken as a whole, the experiments in this section indicate that parental physical punishment is either unrelated or negatively related to the development of conscience. On the other hand, there is a suggestion that anxiety about loss of love from either parent is positively related to conscience development. In addition, if the parent emphasized empathy training in his love-withdrawal discipline, both identification and conscience development were enhanced. Perhaps the most potent parental influence on children's identification and imitation is the perceived power of the parent for giving and withholding valued resources. The fact that power is also a potent influence in imitating strangers with whom the child has had only a brief contact suggests that this characteristic had some evolutionary adaptive advantage. The powerful individuals are the ones who have ready access to and control over resources, and as a consequence, are very likely to survive and reproduce. By modeling oneself after them, rather than after non-powerful persons, one's adaptiveness is probably increased.

DEVELOPMENT OF EMPATHY AND ROLE TAKING

We have suggested in this and previous chapters that the development of empathy is crucial to the development of human moral behavior. We believe that empathy underlies aspects of both the norm of reciprocity and cognitive-language conceptions of morality. During the stage of infancy, the child in hunter-gatherer societies is nearly always in close proximity to his mother, and as we noted, is virtually completely tolerated. Hence, there is essentially no requirement for him to either reciprocate or make moral decisions. As he moves away from the mother, starts to interact with others, and becomes treated with less acceptance and more disapproval, it becomes necessary for him to develop an awareness of the feelings and rights of others. In other words, in order to "get along," he has to move away from his egocentrism.

Following Mead's (1934) usage, "empathy" and "role taking" will be treated as synonymous. In order to take another's role, one has to be empathic with the other person, and the capacity to be empathic is frequently demonstrated by the ability to take the other's role. Although the term "empathy" has been defined in a variety of ways (Stotland, Sherman, and Shaver 1971), we will restrict our discussion to two aspects of what Stotland et al. referred to as "predictive empathy," or what Fishbein et al. (1972) called "empathy." The first aspect of predictive empathy—"simple predictive empathy"—refers to the ability to predict the responses of another. As we saw in the preceding chapter, this ability in the spatial realm is well developed by three years of age.

The second aspect of predictive empathy has no agreed-upon name, but it clearly develops later than simple predictive empathy. We will call it "flexible" predictive empathy, or "flexible empathy." Flexible empathy refers to the ability to predict, keep distinct, and yet simultaneously relate the different viewpoints of others to objectively the same external event(s). This is in contrast, for example, to the coordination of perspectives task, in which the individual predicts, keeps distinct, and simultaneously relates the different perceptions of others from objectively *different* viewing positions. In a situation calling for flexible empathy, the primary reason that everyone doesn't respond the same way to the same event, i.e., have the same viewpoint, is that each has different privileged information. Flexibility refers to the ability to put aside one's own privileged information, and to evaluate the same event from another's view with his privileged information. For example, consider a basketball game which is being won by the home team, the Cougars, by a wide margin. Player A is a Cougar third stringer who rarely plays, and Player B is the Cougar star who needs forty points to set the school record. Player B has thirty-five points already, with ten minutes playing time left. Player A doesn't get into the game, and Player B plays the whole time, but scores only thirty-nine points. Flexible empathy would be reflected by Players A and B accurately predicting each other's feelings, as well as those of their coach and teammates.

Let's now turn to the experimental literature bearing on these issues. The study by Borke (1971) deals with the development of simple predictive empathy in the realm of the feelings of others. Her subjects were two hundred boys and girls between the ages of three and eight years. First the children were shown four drawings of faces which depicted the emotions of "happy," "sad," "afraid," and "angry," and asked to identify them. The experimenter then told the subjects very short stories about other children, e.g., eating a favorite snack, losing a toy, and at the conclusion of each story, presented a picture of a child with a blank face. The subjects were then asked to point to one of the four "emotion" faces and thus indicate how the child in the story probably felt. If the subject pointed to the "correct" face (the face that almost all adults would point to), he demonstrated predictive empathy for that emotion. If the subject lacked predictive empathy, he would be correct in his choices, by chance, twenty-five percent of the time.

The major results were as follows. For the stories calling for a "happy face," about seventy-five percent of the three to three and a half year olds, and more than ninety percent of the older children, made the correct choice. For the "sad face" stories, on average, the three to three and a half year olds responded slightly above chance level, and the remaining children responded correctly between fifty and eighty percent of the time. For the "angry face" stories, children between the ages of three and four and a half responded correctly about forty percent of the time, and the older children about sixty percent of the time. For the "afraid face" stories, the three to three and a half year olds responded correctly about thirty-five percent of the time, children between three and a half and four and a half about sixty percent of the time, and the older children between eighty and one hundred percent of the time. These results strongly indicate that children as young as three years of age are capable of empathetic responses to the feelings of others. The data also suggest that after age four and a half, this capacity starts to stabilize, with little change occurring after that time.

The study by Chandler and Greenspan (1972) deals with the relationship between simple predictive empathy and flexible empathy. The subjects were eighty-six boys and girls from grades 1 through 7. They were tested in a procedure modeled after the studies by Borke (1971) and Flavell, Botkin, Fry, Wright, and Jarvis (1968). In the first part of the procedure, after Borke, the children were presented with three cartoon sequences telling a story about a child, e.g., a boy drops some money down a sewer grating and cannot retrieve it. The stories ended in such a way that the central character would feel one of the three emotions of anger, fear, or sadness, i.e., almost all adults would predict these feelings. At the end of the story, the children were asked to indicate how the central character felt. Virtually every child was correct on every story in predicting the main character's emotion—only three clear-cut errors were noted out of two hundred and fifty-eight stories. Thus, Borke's findings were strongly confirmed.

In the second part of the procedure, after Flavell et al., each story received an addendum. In the addendum, the central character is joined by a second child who is not aware of any of the preceding events, e.g., he does not know that the central character lost money down a sewer. From the time that the central character is joined by the second child, the central character acts in ways consistent with his emotional state, e.g., because he is sad he refuses to accept the second child's invitation to play ball, and the second child is perplexed by this. At this point, the subjects in the experiment were asked to tell the entire story, including the addendum, as they understood it. Then they were asked to tell the story from the perspective of the second child, who did not have the privileged information they possessed, i.e., the subjects knew what had happened prior to the second child's arrival. If a subject told the story from the second child's perspective without intrusions of his own privileged information, then he demonstrated flexible empathy. The results were that flexible empathy systematically increased from only four percent in six year olds to eighty-five percent in thirteen year olds, supporting the view that flexible empathy is a different, more difficult, and later-emerging form of empathy than simple predictive empathy.

There are at least two other experimental procedures which support and amplify the results of the Chandler and Greenspan study. In the first procedure, used by Feffer and his colleagues (Feffer 1970, Feffer and Gourevitch 1960), the children were given a variation of the *Make a Picture Story*. In this procedure, the subjects are given a picture of a background scene and figures of men, women, children, and animals which may be used with the background. The children are first asked to tell a story using at least three of the figures. Then they are asked to retell the story as it would be viewed by each of the three figures, e.g., "now pretend you are the mother in the story you just made up. Tell the story again like you are the mother."

The sequence of three stories, from the three different points of view, is then scored to assess (1) how well the children are able to maintain continuity in the story between all the characters, and (2) how well they are able to keep separate the variety of privileged information each character has. For example, in one story told from the father's view the father comes home from work unhappy because he didn't get the pay raise he had expected. The mother doesn't know this. When told from the mother's view, if she states that his face looks sad, but makes no mention of the pay raise, then the subject has demonstrated flexible empathy. If the mother mentions the pay raise issue, or says that the father looks happy, then flexible empathy has not been demonstrated by the subject.

Feffer (1970) indicates that three age-related response patterns have been observed in studies using this procedure (our terminology is different from Feffer's). For children age six or less, there is typically no evidence of continuity between the various viewpoints, e.g., the father may be sad, but the mother describes him as happy. For seven and eight year olds, there is continuity, but the children do not keep separate the privileged information of the various characters. Finally, at about age nine, the children start to correctly synthesize the various viewpoints, keeping each character's privileged information separate. The frequency of this third pattern increases with increasing age after age nine.

The second procedure for assessing flexible empathy is a variation of Kohlberg's (1969) moral dilemmas, used by Selman and Byrne (1974). Selman and Byrne's subjects were groups of children with average ages of four, six eight, and ten. They were presented with two stories depicting moral dilemmas involving several individuals, and asked to resolve them. Following the child's resolution, the experimenter questioned the child in order to assess (1) the child's awareness of the various viewpoints of the different characters in the story, and (2) how well the child was able to keep separate the privileged information of the various characters. For example, in one story, a girl is asked by her father to promise not to climb trees anymore. The girl promises, but later on in the day her friend's kitten climbs a tree and can't get down. The girl is the only one present with tree-climbing capabilities. Her friends are not aware of the promise she has made, but she is aware of it. What should she do? Selman and Byrne identified four age-related modes of responding, called egocentric role taking, subjective role taking, self-reflective role taking, and mutual role taking. In egocentric role taking, which characterizes the majority of four year olds, the subject is unable to either distinguish the viewpoints of the various characters in the stories, or to relate these viewpoints to one another. In subjective role taking, which characterizes the majority of six year olds, the subject is aware of the different viewpoints of others, but is unable to relate them to one another. At this stage, children have difficulty keeping distinct the privileged information of the various characters. In self-reflective role taking, which typifies the majority of eight and ten year olds, the subjects are able to clearly distinguish the various viewpoints and to readily relate them to one another. In mutual role taking, which typifies the performance of a small number of eight and ten year olds, the subject can, in addition, conceptually take himself out of the situation and view it as an objective outsider.

When the results of these studies are considered together, a fairly consistent picture of the development of empathy is seen. Simple predictive empathy, in the spatial and emotional realm, starts to emerge prior to age three, and to stabilize at about age six. Flexible empathy is virtually nonexistent prior to age six. Six year olds may be aware that different individuals have different privileged information, but they are unable to relate the various viewpoints and to keep privileged information separate. The ability to relate the various views starts to emerge at about age seven, but it is not until age eight or nine (depending upon the procedure used) that children are able to keep separate the various privileged information.

If flexible empathy is a crucial aspect of moral development, then two things should follow. First, children who have relatively low flexible empathy should behave immorally more frequently than those who have relatively high flexible empathy; and second, successful training in flexible empathy should increase moral action. Are these hypotheses valid? The study by Chandler (1973) provides a tentative answer to this question. In his experiment, the subjects were forty-five delinquent boys and forty-five nondelinquent boys between the ages of eleven and thirteen. The category of delinquency was determined on the basis of court records. None of the nondelinquents had a court record, (all the delinquents did), and, in addition, none were judged by their teachers to be involved with serious antisocial activities. All the boys were given the flexible empathy test used by Chandler and Greenspan, which was modeled after the Flavell et al. task.

no longer an affective task.

Following this testing, the delinquents were randomly divided into three groups: a role-taking or empathy-training group, a "placebo" group, and a control group. The empathy-training group met for half a day a week for ten weeks, and made films under the supervision of a psychologist. The films were required to be skits depicting events which typify children of their age, and each of the boys had to play all the parts in each skit. The film making emphasized awareness of other viewpoints and the relationships between these points of view. The boys in the placebo group were treated similarly to those in the empathy-training group, except that they were restricted to making films that involved neither themselves nor children of their own age. The boys in both of these groups received three dollars a session for participating, and they rarely missed a session. The boys in the control group were left alone for the ten weeks.

Following the ten-week period, all the delinquents were given another flexible empathy test. Finally, one and a half years later, the court records of the delinquent boys were examined again. Because the families of twelve of these boys had moved, only thirty-three records were available.

The major results were as follows. On the initial flexible empathy test, the delinquents made on average about 3.3 times as many errors as the nondelinquents, thus confirming the relationship between moral action and flexible empathy. Following the ten-week "training" period, the flexible empathy scores of the empathy-training group improved significantly more than those of the other two delinquent groups. There was no difference between these latter two groups. Finally, the number of arrests in the postexperimental one and a half-year period were compared with those of the one and a half-year period preceding the experiment. Although there was a slight decline in delinquency for the placebo and control groups in the postexperimental period, the frequency of arrests for the empathy-training group was almost cut in half. Thus, empathy training affected both performance on a test of flexible empathy, and frequency of antisocial acts as measured by number of arrests.

confound (delinquents + poor cog. ability).

Chandler is very cautious in interpreting these data. He states that the effects of empathy training may have been specific to his population of subjects, and further, that the improvement seen in the empathy-trained children may have been caused by their having become better able to avoid detection for criminal acts, i.e., that the empathy training was "a school for scoundrels." Nevertheless, his results are very exciting, and promise some socially relevant applications of this highly theoretical research.

THE DEVELOPMENT OF RECIPROCITY

A moment's reflection will indicate how pervasive the norm of reciprocity is in human behavior. All of us have encountered a child who refuses to share some desirable commodity with a peer or sibling because "he didn't share his with me." Or, in seeing two school-age children fighting, we learn that John "hit Bill back." Most of us start to feel squeamish after being invited to a friend's home for dinner for the third or fourth time in a row, knowing that we haven't "reciprocated" in the interim.

The norm of reciprocity has a number of important functions in group life. It leads to the sharing of vital resources; it helps prevent unidirectional coercion, i.e., if someone tries to punish or force others to his will, he will probably receive the same treatment in return; and it provides the framework for a system of justice which employs punishment. Reciprocity underlies cooperation as well as competition, and probably places constraints on the latter. "Winning" implies that someone else is "losing" to the winner. According to the norm of reciprocity, the loser will want to, and perhaps will, attempt to make the winner do some losing. In a close-knit survival unit, like a hunter-gatherer group, this cycle would be disastrous, as Turnbull (1972) has pointed out.

How does one systematically assess the development of the norm of reciprocity? The basic type of technique would involve a realistic situation (from the child's point of view) in which children are given the opportunity to act in a reciprocal manner with one another. The basic measure would be the extent to which children of different ages act in such a manner, i.e., the extent to which their behavior is correlated. For example, in a game situation in which pairs of children have the opportunity to help or hinder one another in achieving some goal, the extent to which they both help or both hinder would provide such a measure. If A always helped B, but B rarely helped A, then they would not be acting reciprocally. If neither A nor B helped the other, or neither A nor B hindered the other, they they would be acting reciprocally.

What do the data show? Based on the empathy research just summarized, it would be expected that the norm of reciprocity would not develop until after the age of six or seven. To a large extent, this is, in fact, what is found, but unfortunately, the published and unpublished data are too sparse to make any firm conclusions. Further, there is a complication in interpreting some of the data owing to the existence of a cultural norm of "taking turns." That is, firm data exist (Kagan and Madsen 1971, 1972) which show that Mexican and American children as young as four years of age will take turns so that first one child will win a prize and then the other will win a prize. On the face of it, these four year olds are manifesting reciprocity, but we feel that "taking turns" is perhaps an early step on the road to acting in a reciprocal manner, and that other experimental procedures would show that the norm of reciprocity is absent in children that young. Indirect support for this belief is found in Taylor's (1975) study, in which six and a half year old girls did not act in a reciprocal manner.

Let's summarize some of the available data bearing on this important issue —the studies by McClintock and Nuttin (1969) and Taylor (1975). McClintock and Nuttin conducted an experiment with second, fourth, and sixth grade children from the United States and Belgium, in which pairs of same-age children played a game called "Maximizing Differences." In this game, the children were instructed to accumulate points. Each child, out of the other's field of view, was asked on every trial (there were one hundred trials in all) to push either the left-hand button on a panel or the right-hand button. They were further instructed that points would be distributed in the following manner. If both children on a given trial pushed the left-hand button, both would win six points. If child A pushed the left-hand button, and child B the right-hand button, A would win zero points, and B would win five points. If A pushed the right-hand button and B the left-hand button, then A would win five points, and B zero points. If A and B both pushed the right-hand button, both would win zero points. At the end of each trial both children were told how many points they had won.

McClintock and Nuttin analyzed the data for each child separately in terms of "competitive" and "cooperative" responses, the former defined as pushing the right-hand button, which precludes the possibility of the partner winning any points, and the latter defined as pushing the left-hand button, which ensures that the partner will win points. Unfortunately for our purposes, no correlations were run on the frequency with which partners acted in a reciprocal manner over all the trials, i.e., we don't know whether children who acted cooperatively had partners who also acted cooperatively. However, sufficient analyses were presented to allow us to make some inferences about the development of reciprocity.

The major results were as follows. Overall, the second graders acted competitively about fifty percent of the time, i.e., pushed the left and right-hand buttons equally often. The fourth graders acted competitively sixty percent of the time, and the sixth graders seventy-three percent of the time. When performance was analyzed over successive blocks of ten trials, the second graders showed essentially no change, the fourth graders showed a moderate increase in competitiveness, and the sixth graders increased competitive responding from about fifty-five percent on the first block of ten trials to about eighty-five percent on the tenth block. The authors report that these changes (or lack thereof for the second graders) were seen for both members of each pair over the course of one hundred trials. Thus, there appears to be a high correlation in reciprocal responding between pairs of children in the fourth and sixth grades. What about the second graders, who seemed to respond randomly, and thus may not have been responding reciprocally? One additional analysis has bearing on this question—the sequence of competitive and cooperative responses. If second graders were responding by chance, and hence independently of their partners' responses, then the sequence of competitive and cooperative responses should have been random) It was not, but rather resembled that of the fourth graders. This result implies that the second graders showed some awareness of the reciprocal nature of the game; however, owing to the absence of correlational data, this study leaves open the question of whether or not second graders are capable of acting reciprocally.

The study of Taylor (1975) provides the clearest answers to the question of the development of reciprocity. In her study, the subjects were pairs of girls of the following age combinations: six and a half years–six and a half years, six and a half–nine and a half, six and a half–eleven and a half, nine and a half–nine and a half, nine and a half–eleven and a half, eleven and a half–eleven and a half. The girls played three variations of a single type of board game. In the first variation, girl A was told by the experimenter that her task was to get her marker from the "start" position to the "home" position in fourteen moves or less. The board has three intersecting circles, each circle comprised of a number of different colored squares. Progress is made in the following way. Girl B selects cards blindly from a stack of cards, and A moves her marker to the color depicted on the card. Half the cards have two colors on them, and for these girl B decides which color A should move to. The only way to move onto the next circle is to land on a square located at the intersection. This game was played twice, once with each girl doing the choosing. In the second variation, both girls played simultaneously, with the game ending when either player reached the home position. As in the first variation, girl B selected cards for A, and girl A selected cards for B. The third variation was like the second, except one girl started on the first circle and the other girl started on the second circle. This game was played twice, once with each girl starting in the advanced position.

The basic measurements Taylor made involved the percentage of times each girl helped the other when given the chance to do so, i.e., on half the trials. "Helping" was defined as choosing the color which moved the other girl closer to the home position. "Hindering" was defined as choosing the color which moved the other girl further from the home position, e.g., given a choice of placing A on the intersection or not on the intersection, if B chose the color not on the intersection, this was scored as a hindering choice.

The major results are shown in Tables 16 and 17. Not shown is the relationship between game variation and percentage of helping. In general, the girls helped one another more frequently in the first variation than in the second and third, in which helping was approximately the same.

In Table 16, the "player" is the girl who does the choosing, and the "partner" is the girl affected by the choice. As you can see, on the average, all groups of players hinder more than they help (fifty percent would be equal helping and hindering), with the six and a half year olds hindering the least, and the nine and a half year olds the most. Also, there is a slight tendency for the eleven and

Table 16

Average Percentage of Helping by Age of Player as a Function of Age of Partner, Pooled Across All Games

		Age of Partner		
		6½	9½	11½
Age of	6½	39	30	40
Player	9½	34	23	25
	11½	41	25	30

Source: A. L. Taylor, *The Development of Children's Social Interaction Behaviors in a Game Situation,* unpublished doctoral dissertation, University of Cincinnati.

a half year olds to be the most flexible in the extent of their hindering. That is, they seem to vary their responses as a function of age of partner more so than the other girls.

Table 17 depicts the extent to which players in the six different age combinations acted in a reciprocal manner. In performing these analyses, Taylor computed the percentage of times for each pair that player A helped player B, and vice versa, and correlated these percentages for each group. It should be noted that it only takes one player of the pair acting in a reciprocal manner to produce a high correlation, e.g., if player B matches player A, but A does not match B, the correlation would be high. What is striking about the data in Table 17 is that when six and a half year olds are playing, there is no significant amount of reciprocity shown; whereas when nine and a half year olds play with each other and with eleven and a half year olds, and when eleven and a half year olds play with each other, a high degree of reciprocity is manifested. When nine and a half year olds and eleven and a half year olds played with six and a half year olds, they apparently sensed that the six and a half year olds didn't reciprocate, and hence they themselves didn't reciprocate.

Based on the results of Taylor's and McClintock and Nuttin's studies, it may tentatively be concluded that by nine and a half years of age, children in

Table 17

Correlations of Helping Behavior Between Players, Pooled Across Games

Age of Players	Correlation Coefficient
6½- 6½	.11
6½- 9½	.46
6½-11½	.10
9½- 9½	.77 *
9½-11½	.68 *
11½-11½	.84 *

*statistically different from chance

Source: A. L. Taylor, *The Development of Children's Social Interaction Behaviors in a Game Situation,* Unpublished doctoral dissertation, University of Cincinnati, 1975.

Western societies have developed the norm of reciprocity. There is very little evidence from Taylor's study that six and a half year olds operate on the basis of this norm, and very scanty evidence from McClintock and Nuttin's study that second graders (who are presumably between seven and eight year old) operate on this norm. As we noted earlier in this section, these results are consistent with the findings concerning the development of flexible empathy, and hence may have validity.

COGNITIVE-LANGUAGE FACTORS IN MORAL DEVELOPMENT

Three of the most important (and related) functions of moral development in regulating the interactions among members of human groups are:

1. to communicate the moral rules to members of the group so that each individual does not have to learn all of them by trial and error;
2. to utilize mechanisms or techniques which aid individuals in extending the norm of reciprocity to generalized "others" in the group;
3. to utilize mechanisms or techniques for teaching or encouraging individuals to, at times, set aside their private interests in favor of public interests.

It is believed that cognitive-language factors, i.e., moral judgements based on verbal communication, are intimately involved with carrying out all of these functions. The extent to which an individual can make use of cognitive-language factors is, at least in part, going to be a function of the extent to which he understands or can conceptualize verbalized moral rules. As might be expected from the research summarized in the preceding sections, a significant change in understanding should occur after six or seven years of age. What do the data show?

The natural starting point is the work of Piaget (1932). Piaget examined children's understanding of rules of games (primarily marbles, which he played with them), and children's answers to moral dilemmas. The two situations provide different and complementary viewpoints from which to study moral development. From a young child's position, there probably is little conceptual difference between rules handed down by parents governing his action at home, and rules handed down by older children or adults concerning how to play a game. Rules are rules.

In the marble-playing situation, Piaget first thoroughly learned the local rules himself, and then strolled up to a small group of children who were playing the game, and joined them. While playing, he would ask them a variety of questions about the rules of the game, exceptions to the rules, who invented the rules, whether the rules could be changed, and so on. In the moral dilemma situation, the children were usually individually interviewed at school. Two of the most widely cited dilemmas are the following (in condensed form): (1) which child is naughtier—one who tells his mother he got a good mark in recitation when in fact he didn't recite that day, or one who told his mother he saw a dog as big as a cow? (2) which child is naughtier—one who, when he opened a door, broke fifteen cups which unknown to him were sitting on a tray behind the door, or one who broke one cup while climbing up to take some jam from the cupboard? In each case, Piaget noted the child's moral judgement and the reasons he gave for that judgement.

Some of the major findings of his research can be summarized as follows. In the game-playing situation, there are three successive stages in children's conscious statements of the rules. In the first stage, between the ages of two and five or six, children know that rules exist, but they are not coercive. The rules are described by Piaget as "motor routines"; that is, the child will perform a certain activity in a repetitive way, and when asked about it he will say "that's the rule." But on another occasion, the child may perform the activity differently. In the second stage, between the ages of five or six and ten, children state that the rules must be followed (they are coercive), and that they can't be changed (they are immutable). They are the rules their fathers used, it is claimed, and they are the rules used everywhere. In the third stage, from age ten on, children see the rules as being coercive, but based on mutual consent. Children of this age acknowledge that rules may differ in different locales, and that if all agree to change them, they may be changed.

For the moral dilemmas, Piaget found two age-related types of judgements. In the first, which is called heteronomy, rules have their force owing to the authority of other more powerful individuals, such as parents and adults. The child follows and understands the rules because these authorities handed them down to him. In other words, children who are heteronomous have a unilateral respect for the superiors who gave them the rules. Heteronomy leads the child to make judgements based on "objective responsibility," e.g., how much damage was done, how big a lie was told, rather than "subjective responsibility," e.g., what were the intentions underlying the act. Thus, the heteronomous individual states that the child who broke fifteen cups was naughtier than the one who broke one cup (more damage was done), and that the child who said the dog was as big as a cow was naughtier than the child who said he had received a good mark in recitation(the former is a bigger lie because dogs are never as big as cows).

Heteronomous thinking is characteristic of six and seven year olds and gradually gives way to autonomy. Autonomous thinking is characteristic of children aged ten and older, and is based on the mutual respect individuals have for one another. This mutual respect leads to an understanding of reciprocity and justice. Rules aren't followed merely because they are the rules, and individuals aren't evaluated only on the objective consequences of their acts. Autonomous children weigh the intentions of others' acts, and thus frequently reach different moral judgements than do heteronomous thinkers.

Hoffman (1970) has recently summarized the experimental literature dealing with tests of the preceding conclusions by Piaget. For experiments carried out with children from Western industrialized countries, the age trends Piaget noted have been confirmed in almost all cases. For children from nonindustrialized cultures, e.g., American Indians, some of the age trends do not occur, e.g., a decrease in the perceived rigidity of rules does not always occur with increasing age.

The aspect of Piaget's theory which has led to the most experimental work is the development of intentionality in making moral judgements. In general, the research carried out since 1970 has confirmed the age trends observed by Piaget, e.g., Hebble (1971), Costanzo, Coie, Grumet, and Farnill (1973). In the Hebble study, it was additionally found that the greatest shift from moral judgements based on amount of damage to moral judgements based on intentions occurred between the ages of nine and ten. In the Costanzo et al. study, the relationship between intentionality and damage was further clarified by the finding that positive intentions are evaluated in making moral judgements at an earlier age than are negative intentions.

Now we turn to the work of Kohlberg and his colleagues and students (summarized in Kohlberg 1969). The basic technique that he and his associates have employed involves individuals resolving dilemmas and giving reasons for resolving them the way they did. The following is one of the dilemmas, taken from Rest (1968):

In Europe, a woman was near death from cancer. One drug might save her, a form of radium that a druggist in the same town had recently discovered. The druggist was charging $2,000, ten times what the drug cost him to make. The sick woman's husband, Heinz, went to everyone he knew to borrow the money, but he could only get together about half of what it cost. He told the druggist that his wife was dying and asked him to sell it cheaper or let him pay later. But the druggist said, "No." The husband got desperate and broke into the man's store to steal the drug for his wife. Should the husband have done that? Why?*

In recent years Kohlberg has used ten such dilemmas, and based on his own thinking, as well as that of Piaget, James Mark Baldwin, and psychoanalytic theorists, he has identified twenty-five aspects of morality by which to score the reasoning used in the resolution of the dilemmas (Kohlberg 1969). Some of these aspects are:

1. how does the individual consider motives in judging moral action;
2. how does the individual consider the consequences of the act in judging moral action;
3. to what extent is punishment involved in moral judgements;
4. how are property rights or possession involved in moral judgements;
5. how are contractual obligations discussed.

Obviously, not every response to a dilemma makes reference to all twenty-five aspects. When the child's reasoning does make reference to a given aspect, the response is classified into a given level and stage of moral development.

Based on his research and thinking about moral knowledge, Kohlberg has identified three age-related levels of moral reasoning, each level divided into two stages. The levels are called "preconventional," which typifies the reasoning of four to ten year olds, "conventional," which typifies the reasoning of

---

*J. Rest, *Developmental Hierarchy in Preference and Comprehension of Moral Judgment*, Unpublished doctoral dissertation, University of Chicago, 1968.

most adolescents and adults, and "postconventional," which typifies the reasoning of an unknown percentage of adults.

Preconventional moral thinking (Stages 1 and 2) interprets moral acts in terms of the physical consequences of the act, e.g., punishment, reward, or exchange of favors, or in terms of deference to the superior physical power of the individual or individuals who make up the rules. Conventional moral thinking (Stages 3 and 4) is described as conformist since it attempts to maintain and support the social order as it is. The rules are seen as valuable in and of themselves. On the individual level, the conventional moral thinker sees moral behavior as pleasing others and doing what is expected of him. The postconventional moral thinker (Stages 5 and 6) views morality in terms of principles or rules which are applicable to a whole range of societies and individuals. These principles are autonomous, in that they do not depend upon the particular individuals or groups who hold them (Kohlberg 1968, 1969). Table 18 presents some concrete examples of the various stages of moral thinking as applied to the dying-wife dilemma.

As you can see from Table 18 and the preceding discussion, as one moves up the scale of moral reasoning, one's conceptions move from the particular act and concrete outcome to the general or abstract principle. Each higher stage, according to Kohlberg, contains all the elements of the lower stage, but the lower elements have been transformed in accordance with the principle of increasing differentiation and hierarchical integration. That is, the individuals

Table 18

Six Stages of Orientation to Intentions and Consequences (Aspects 1 and 2) in Response to a Moral Dilemma

Stage 1.   Motives and need-consequences of act are ignored in judging badness because of focus upon irrelevant physical form of the act (e.g., size of the lie), or of the consequences of the act (e.g., amount of physical damage).

Pro—He should steal the drug. It isn't really bad to take it. It isn't like he didn't ask to pay for it first. The drug he'd take is only worth $200, he's not really taking a $2,000 drug.

Con—He shouldn't steal the drug, it's a big crime. He didn't get permission, he used force and broke and entered. He did a lot of damage, stealing a very expensive drug and breaking up the store, too.

Stage 2.   Judgement ignores label or physical consequences of the act because of the instrumental value of the act in serving a need or because the act doesn't do harm in terms of the need of another. (Differentiates the human need-value of the act from its physical form or consequences.)

Pro—It's all right to steal the drug because she needs it and he wants her to live. It isn't that he wants to steal, but it's the way he has to use to get the drug to save her.

Con—He shouldn't steal it. The druggist isn't wrong or bad, he just wants to make a profit. That's what you're in business for, to make money.

Stage 3.   Action evaluated according to the type of motive or person likely to perform the act. An act is not bad if it is an expression of a "nice" or altruistic motive or person, and it is not good if it is the expression of a "mean" or selfish motive or person. Circumstances may excuse or justify deviant action. (Differentiates good motives to which an act is instrumental from human but selfish need to which it is instrumental.)

Pro—He should steal the drug. He was only doing something that was natural for a good husband to do. You can't blame him for doing something out of love for his wife, you'd blame him if he didn't love his wife enough to save her.

Con—He shouldn't steal. If his wife dies, he can't be blamed. It isn't because he's heartless or that he doesn't love her enough to do everything that he legally can. The druggist is the selfish or heartless one.

Stage 4.   An act is always or categorically wrong, regardless of motives or circumstances, if it violates a rule and does forseeable harm to others. (Differentiates action out of a sense of obligation to rule from action for generally "nice" or natural motives.)

Pro—You should steal it. If you did nothing you'd be letting your wife die, it's your responsibility if she dies. You have to take it with the idea of paying the druggist.

Con—It is a natural thing for Heinz to want to save his wife but it's still always wrong to steal. He still knows he's stealing and taking a valuable drug from the man who made it.

Stage 5.   A formal statement that though circumstances or motive modify disapproval, as a general rule the means do not justify the ends. While circumstances justify deviant acts to some extent they do not make it right or lead to suspension of moral categories. (Differentiates moral blame because of the intent behind breaking the rule from the legal or principled necessity not to make exceptions to rules.)

Pro—The law wasn't set up for these circumstances. Taking the drug in this situation isn't really right, but it's justified to do it.

Con—You can't completely blame someone for stealing but extreme circumstances don't really justify taking the law in your own hands. You can't have everyone stealing whenever they get desperate. The end may be good, but the ends don't justify the means.

Stage 6.   Good motives don't make an act right (or not wrong); but if an act follows from a decision to follow general self-chosen principles, it can't be wrong. It may be actually right to deviate from the rules and concrete violation of a moral principle. (Differentiates good motives of following a moral principle from natural motives as following a rule. Recognizes that moral principles don't allow exceptions any more than do legal rules.)

Pro—This is a situation which forces him to choose between stealing and letting his wife die. In a situation where the choice must be made, it is morally right to steal. He has to act in terms of the principle of preserving and respecting life.

Con—Heinz is faced with the decision of whether to consider the other people who need the drug just as badly as his wife. Heinz ought to act not according to his particular feelings toward his wife, but considering the value of all the lives involved.

Source: J. Rest, *Developmental Hierarchy in Preference and Comprehension of Moral Judgment.* Unpublished doctoral dissertation, University of Chicago, 1968.

at the higher levels of moral thinking can make finer moral distinctions than those at the lower levels, and the decisions they make have wider applicability than those made at the lower levels. When an individual is identified as being in a given stage of moral thinking, it means that the typical moral reasoning he uses is at that stage. For instance, an individual at Stage 3 will typically solve about one-half the dilemmas at Stage 3 thinking, about one-fourth below Stage 3, and about one-fourth above Stage 3.

At least three types of empirical research confirm the validity of these stages (summarized by Kohlberg 1969). First, a group of individuals with initial ages of ten to sixteen were intermittently tested over a twelve-year period on the moral dilemmas. It was found that their level of moral reasoning increased progressively over the twelve-year period. Important for the view that moral knowledge develops in an epigenetic sequence is the fact that as the individuals' moral knowledge increased, they did not skip any intervening stages.

Second, in cross-cultural studies of urban youths aged ten to sixteen in the United States, Taiwan, and Mexico, and rural youths in Turkey and Yucatan, great similarity in the age-related progression of moral thinking was found. In all these cultures, the most prevalent thinking at age ten were Stages 1 and 2; at age thirteen, Stages 3 and 4 thinking showed an increase at the "expense of" the lower level of moral thought, and for the urban youths at age sixteen, the frequency of Stages 5 and 6 moral thought increased and Stages 1 and 2 thinking decreased further. The rural youths showed no evidence of Stages 5 or 6 thinking at age sixteen, but Stages 1 and 2 thinking did decrease at that age.

The third type of evidence is as follows. When individuals from the United States were asked to paraphrase other individuals' moral statements, they could successfully do so for statements at or below their own level of moral thinking; they could paraphrase some statements one stage above their own level of moral thinking; but they could only infrequently paraphrase statements two or more stages above their own. This finding implies that the stage of moral thinking typically employed in solving moral dilemmas is approximately at the upper limit of an individual's cognitive-verbal level of moral understanding.

Although Kohlberg has provided us with a profound analysis of the development of moral thinking, his research has serious, but not insurmountable, deficiencies from an experimental view. The basic problem, as Kurtines and Grief (1974) point out, lies with his "clinical" method of measuring moral thought. It seems that the only individuals who can use and score Kohlberg's moral dilemmas reliably are those who have been trained by Kohlberg or his students. Further, the reliability of their scoring is far from perfect. However, others are developing more objective and reliable tests, and their research is starting to appear in the published literature.

SUMMARY

We started this chapter with the statement of an idea and a question. The idea was that moral development goes to the core of the mutual regulation of members of subsistence groups. The question was, Why does an individual act morally? Based on the writing of a variety of scholars, it was asserted that there are at least five factors which determine moral action: authority-acceptance, or obedience; external rewards and punishments; internal rewards and punishments or ego-ideal and conscience; the norms of reciprocity; and cognitive-language factors. Following up an idea expressed earlier in the book, it was asserted that the development of empathy probably underlies the development of the norms of reciprocity and the development of cognitive-language factors.

In the ensuing discussion of research and theory, some of the major conclusions reached were as follows. First, regarding the development of obedience and resistance to temptation, children whose parents physically punish them for being disobedient tend to be less obedient than children who are not physically punished; young children with sensitive, "accepting" mothers tend to be more obedient that those with insensitive, "rejecting" mothers; and from about age 4 onwards, when sex-role differentiation is heavily emphasized, the child-rearing antecedents producing obedience in boys and girls become differentiated.

Second, regarding the development of identification and conscience, children whose parents frequently used physical punishment tended to identify less with their parents and show less guilt than those children whose parents infrequently physically punished them; however, there were strong indications that children whose parents used explanation as a vehicle for producing moral action, and whose parents were seen as controlling important resources showed greater conscience development and greater identification than children whose parents lacked these characteristics.

Third, regarding the development of empathy, a distinction was made between "simple" predictive empathy, and "flexible" predictive empathy. The former deals with the ability to predict the responses of another from the other's point of view. The latter deals with the ability to predict another's responses from the same point of view. Simple predictive empathy in the spatial and emotional realms starts to emerge prior to age 3 and to stabilize at about age 6. Flexible predictive empathy starts to emerge at about age 7, but it is not until children are about 9 years old that they can integrate the different responses of others.

Fourth, regarding the development of the norm of reciprocity, it was noted that few studies exist which bear on this important topic. The limited data indicate, consistent with the "empathy" data, that it is not until after the age of 7 or 8 that children are capable of regularly operating in a reciprocal fashion. It is clear that younger children are capable of taking turns and "hitting back," but these capabilities are seen as being early steps on the road to reciprocity.

Fifth, regarding the development of the cognitive-language factors, some of the research of Piaget and Kohlberg and their followers was summarized. Consistent with the empathy data, a shift in the understanding of moral rules occurs at about age 7. At this age children start to consider intention as a major component in making moral decisions, and start to verbally express the idea of reciprocity. As individuals mature from age 8 to adulthood, their conceptualizations of morality shift from concerns with the physical consequences of acts, e.g., rewards and punishments, to concerns with maintaining social conventions, e.g., conforming, to concerns with universal principles or rules.

The above summary concludes the final chapter of the book. As was stated on page 1, you might want to reread Chapter One to help you sort out and synthesize the myriad ideas and facts presented here. The act of writing this book has been an exciting, intellectual experience, some of which, hopefully, has been transmitted to you. This book should be seen, however, primarily as a beginning towards an integration of how, what, and why children learn. As more facts, clearer questions, and better intellectual guides come forth, we should be able to make more headway in our understanding of this important topic.

REFERENCES

Abravanel, E. 1968. The development of intersensory patterning with regard to selected spatial dimensions. *Monographs of the Society for Research in Child Development* 33, no. 118.

Alland, A., Jr. 1967. *Evolution and human behavior.* Garden City, New York: Natural History Press.

Anderson, S., and Messick, S. 1974. Social competency in young children. *Developmental Psychology* 10: 282–93.

Appel, L. F., Cooper, R. G., McCarrell, N., Sims-Knight, J., Yussen, S. R., and Flavell, J. H. 1972. The development of the distinction between perceiving and memorizing. *Child Development* 43: 1365–81.

Aronfreed, Justin. 1969. The concept of internalization. In *Handbook of socialization theory and research,* ed. D. A. Goslin. Chicago: Rand Mc-Nally.

Bagrow, L., and Skelton, R. A. 1964. *History of Cartography.* London: C. A. Watts.

Baldwin, J. M. 1895. *Mental development in the child and the race.* New York: Macmillan.

———. 1902. *Development and evolution.* New York: Macmillan.

Bartlett, F. C. 1932. *Remembering.* Cambridge: Cambridge University Press.

———. 1958. *Thinking: an experimental and social study.* New York: Basic Books.

Bernstein, I. S., and Gordon, T. P. 1974. The function of aggression in primate societies. *American Scientist* 62: 304–11.

Bicchieri, M. G., ed. 1972. *Hunters and gatherers today.* New York: Holt, Rinehart & Winston.

Birch, H. G., and Lefford, A. 1963. Intersensory development in children. *Monographs of the Society for Research in Child Development* 28, no. 5.

————. 1967. Visual integration, intersensory integration, and voluntary motor control. *Monographs of the Society for Research in Child Development* 32, no. 11.

Blinkov, S., and Glezer, I. I. 1958. *The human brain in figures and tables: a quantitative handbook.* New York: Basic Books.

Borke, H. 1971. Interpersonal perception of young children. *Developmental Psychology* 5: 263–69.

Bower, T. G. R. 1971. The object in the world of the infant. *Scientific American*: 225: 30–38.

Bower, T. G. R., and Paterson, J. G. 1972. Stages in the development of the object concept. *Cognition* 1: 47–56.

Bower, T. G. R., and Wishart, J. G. 1972. The effects of motor skill on object permanence. *Cognition* 1: 165–72.

Bowlby, J. 1969. *Attachment and loss,* vol. 1. New York: Basic Books.

Braidwood, R. J. 1967. *Prehistoric man.* 7th ed. Glenview: Scott, Foresman.

Braine, M. D. S. 1963. The ontogeny of English phrase structure. The first phase. *Language* 39: 1–14.

Broverman, D. M., Klaiber, E. L., Kobayashi, Y., and Vogel, W. 1968. Roles of activation and inhibition in sex differences in cognitive abilities. *Psychological Review* 75: 23–50.

Brown, R. 1965. *Social psychology.* New York: The Free Press.

————. 1973. Development of the first language in the human species. *American Psychologist* 28: 97–106.

Brown, R., and Bellugi, U. 1964. Three processes in the child's acquisition of syntax. *Harvard Educational Review* 34: 133–51.

Brown, R., Cazden, C., and Bellugi, U. 1969. The child's grammar from one to three. In *Minnesota symposia on child psychology,* ed. J. P. Hill, volume 2. Minneapolis: University of Minnesota Press.

Bruml, H. 1972. Age changes in preference and skill measures of handedness. *Perceptual and Motor Skills* 34: 3–14.

Bruner, J. S. 1970. The growth and structures of skill. In *Mechanisms of motor skill development,* ed. K. Connolly. New York: Academic Press.

————. 1972. Nature and uses of immaturity. *American Psychologist* 27: 687–708.

————. 1973. Organization of early skilled action. *Child Development* 44: 1–11.

Campbell, B. G. 1966. *Human evolution.* Chicago: Aldine.

————. 1972. Man for all seasons. In *Sexual selection and the descent of man,* ed. B. Campbell. Chicago: Aldine.

Caron, A. J., Caron, R. F., Caldwell, R. C., and Weiss, S. J. 1973. Infant perception of the structural properties of the face. *Developmental Psychology* 9: 385–99.

Chandler, M. J. 1973. Egocentricism and anti-social behavior: the assessment and training of social perspective-taking skills. *Developmental Psychology* 9: 326–32.

Chandler, M. J., and Greenspan, S. 1972. Ersatz egocentricism: a reply to H. Borke. *Developmental Psychology* 7: 104–6.

Chomsky, C. 1969. *The acquisition of syntax in children from 5 to 10.* Cambridge: M. I. T. Press.

Clark, W. E. Le Gros. 1959. *The antecedents of man.* Edinburgh: Edinburgh University Press.

Cohen, Y. A., ed. 1968a. *Man in adaptation: the cultural present.* Chicago: Aldine.

———. ed. 1968b. *Man in adaptation: The biosocial background.* Chicago: Aldine.

Conel, J. L. 1939–67. *The postnatal development of the human cerebral cortex.* Vols. 1–8. Cambridge: Harvard University Press.

Connolly, K. 1970. Response speed, temporal sequencing, and information processing in children. In *Mechanisms of motor skill development,* ed. K. Connolly. New York: Academic Press.

Conrad, R. 1971. The chronology of the development of covert speech in children. *Developmental Psychology* 5: 398–405.

Costanzo, P. R., Coie, J. D., Grument, J. F., and Farnill, D. 1973. Reexamination of the effects of intent and consequence on children's moral judgments. *Child Development* 44: 154–61.

Cragg, B. G. 1967. The density of synapses and neurones in the motor and visual areas of the cerebral cortex. *Journal of Anatomy* 101: 639–54.

Critchley, M. 1953. *The parietal lobes.* Baltimore: Williams & Wilkins.

Darlington, C. D. 1969. *The evolution of man and society.* New York: Simon & Schuster.

Davidson, H. P. 1935. A study of the confusing letters b, d, p, and q. *Journal of Genetic Psychology* 47: 458–68.

Dekaban, A. 1970. *Neurology of early childhood.* Baltimore: Williams & Wilkins.

DeValois, R. L., and Jacobs, G. H. 1971. Vision. In *Behavior of nonhuman primates,* eds., A. M. Schrier and F. Stollnitz, vol. 3. New York: Academic Press.

DeVore, I., ed. 1965. *Primate behavior: field studies of monkeys and apes.* New York: Holt, Rinehart and Winston.

Diamond, I. T., and Hall, W. C. 1969. Evolution of the neocortex. *Science* 164: 251–62.

Dobzansky, T. 1962. *Mankind evolving.* New Haven: Yale University Press.

Dolhinow, P. J., and Bishop, N. 1970. The development of motor skills and social relationships among primates through play. In *Minnesota symposia on child psychology,* ed. J. P. Hill. Minneapolis: University of Minnesota Press.

Douglas, R. J. 1968. The hippocampus and behavior. *Psychological Bulletin* 70: 416–42.

Dunn, L. C. 1965. A short history of genetics. New York: McGraw-Hill.

Eichorn, D. 1970. Physiological development. In *Carmichael's manual of child psychology*, ed. P. Mussen, New York: Wiley.

Eiseley, L. 1958. *Darwin's century*. Garden City: Doubleday.

Erikson, E. H. 1963. *Childhood and society*. 2nd ed. New York: W. W. Norton.

Evans, W. F., and Gratch, G. 1972. The Stage IV error in Piaget's theory of object concept development: difficulties in object conceptualization or spatial localization? *Child Development* 43: 682–88.

Fantz, R. L. 1961. The origin of form perception. *Scientific American* 204: 66–72.

———. 1964. Visual experience in infants: decreased attention to familiar patterns relative to novel ones. *Science* 146: 668–70.

Fantz, R. L., and Nevis, S. 1967. Pattern preferences in perceptual-cognitive development in early infancy. *Merrill-Palmer Quarterly* 13: 88–108.

Feffer, M. 1970. Developmental analysis of interpersonal behavior. *Psychological Review* 77: 197–214.

Feffer, M., and Gourevitch, V. 1960. Cognitive aspects of role-taking in children. *Journal of Personality* 28: 383–96.

Finley, G. E., Kagan, J., and Layne, O., Jr. 1972. Development of young children's attention to normal and distorted stimuli: a cross-cultural study. *Developmental Psychology* 6: 288–92.

Fishbein, H. D., Lewis, S., and Keiffer, K. 1972. Children's understanding of spatial relations. *Developmental Psychology* 7: 21–33.

Fitts, P. M., and Posner, M. I. 1967. *Human performance*. Belmont, Ca.: Brooks/Cole.

Flavell, J. H. 1970. Developmental studies of mediated memory. In *Advances in child development and behavior*, eds. H. W. Reese and L. P. Lipsett. New York: Academic Press.

———. 1971. First discussant's comments: what is memory development the development of? *Human Development* 14: 272–86.

———. 1974. The development of inferences about others. In *Understanding other persons*, ed. T. Mischel. Oxford: Blackwell, Basil, & Mott.

Flavell, J. H., Beach, D. R., and Chinsky, J. M. 1966. Spontaneous verbal rehearsal in a memory task as a function of age. *Child Development* 37: 283–99.

Flavell, J. H., Botkin, P. T., Fry, C. L., Wright, J. W., and Jarvis, P. E. 1968. *The development of role-taking and communication skills in children*. New York: Wiley.

Flavell, J. H., Friedrichs, A. G., and Hoyt, J. D. 1970. Developmental changes in memorization processes. *Cognitive Psychology* 1: 324–40.

Fraser, A. S. 1961. The inconstant constant, evolution of living constancy. *Australian Scientist* 1: 35–42.

Freud, S. 1949. *An outline of psychoanalysis*. New York: W. W. Norton.

Gallup, G. G., Jr. 1968. Mirror image stimulation. *Psychological Bulletin* 70: 782–93.

————. 1970. Chimpanzees: Self-recognition. *Science* 167: 86–87.

Garcia, J., and Koelling, R. A. 1966. Relation of cue to consequence in avoidance learning. *Psychonomic Science* 4: 123–24.

Gardner, H. 1971. Children's duplication of rhythmic patterns. *Journal of Research in Music Education* 19, 355–60.

Gardner, R. A., and Gardner, B. T. 1969. Teaching sign language to a chimpanzee. *Science* 165: 664–72.

Geschwind, N. 1972. Language and the brain. *Scientific American* 226. 76–83.

Gesell, A. 1930. *A history of psychology in autobiography*, ed. E. G. Boring, vol. 4. Worcester, Mass.: Clark University Press.

Gesell, A., and Ames, L. B. 1947. The development of handedness. *Journal of Genetic Psychology* 70: 155–75.

Gewirtz, J. L. 1969. Mechanisms of social learning: some roles of stimulation and behavior in early human development. In *Handbook of socialization theory and research*, ed. D. A. Goslin. Chicago: Rand McNally.

Ghent, L. 1956. Perception of overlapping and embedded figures by children of different ages. *American Journal of Psychology* 69: 575–87.

Ghiselin, M. T. 1973. Darwin and evolutionary psychology. *Science* 179: 964–68.

Gibson, E. J. 1969. *Principles of perceptual learning and development*. New York: Appleton-Century-Crofts.

Gibson, E. J., Gibson, J. J., Pick, A. D., and Osser, H. 1962. A developmental study of the discrimination of letter-like forms. *Journal of Comparative and Physiological Psychology* 55: 897–906.

Gibson, J. J. 1966. *The senses considered as perceptual systems*. Boston: Houghton Mifflin.

Gouldner, A. W. 1960. The norm of reciprocity: a preliminary statement. *American Sociological Review* 25: 160–78.

Gratch, G., and Landers, W. R. 1971. Stage IV of Piaget's theory of infant's object concepts: a longitudinal study. *Child Development* 42: 359–72.

Grinder, R. E. 1960. *Behavior in a temptation situation and its relation to certain aspects of socialization*. Unpublished doctoral dissertation, Harvard University.

————. 1964. Relations between behavioral and cognitive dimensions of conscience in middle childhood. *Child Development* 35: 881–93.

Grusec, J. E. 1971. Power and the internalization of self-denial. *Child Development* 42: 92–105.

Hagen, J. W. 1972. Strategies for remembering. In *Information processing in children*, ed. S. Farnham-Diggory, New York: Academic Press.

Hale, G. A., and Piper, R. A. 1973. Developmental trends in children's incidental learning: some critical stimulus differences. *Developmental Psychology* 8: 327–35.

Hall, K. R. L. 1968. Social learning in monkeys. In *Primates: studies in adaptation and variability*, ed. P. C. Jay. New York: Holt, Rinehart and Winston.

Hallowell, A. I. 1961. The Protocultural foundations of human adaptation. In *Social life of early man*, ed. S. L. Washburn. Chicago: Aldine.

————. 1963. Personality, culture, and society in behavioral evolution. In *Psychology: A study of a science*, ed. S. Koch, vol. 6. New York: McGraw-Hill.

Halperin, M. S. 1974. Developmental changes in the recall and recognition of categorized word lists. *Child Development* 45: 144–51.

Harlow, H. F. 1971. *Learning to love*. San Francisco: Albion.

Harlow, H. F., Gluck, J. P., and Suomi, S. J. 1972. Generalization of behavior data between nonhuman and human animals. *American Psychologist* 27: 709–16.

Harlow, H. F., and Harlow, M. K. 1962. Social deprivation in monkeys. *Scientific American* 207: 136–46.

Harlow, H., Harlow, M., Dodsworth, R., and Arling, G. 1966. Maternal behavior of Rhesus monkeys deprived of mothering and peer associations in infancy. *Proceedings of the American Philosophical Society* 110: 58–66.

Harrison, R. I., and Montagna, W. 1969. *Man*. New York: Appleton-Century-Crofts.

Hartshorne, H., and May, M. A. 1928–30. *Studies in the nature of character*, vol. 1; *Studies in deceit*, vol. 2; *Studies in service and self-control*, vol. 3; *Studies in organization of character*. New York: Macmillan.

Hays, J. D., and Berggren, W. A. 1971. Quateruary boundaries and correlations. In *The micropaleontology of oceans*, eds. B. M. Funnell and W. R. Riedel. Cambridge: Cambridge University Press.

Hebble, P. W. 1971. The development of elementary school children's judgment of intent. *Child Development* 42: 1203–15.

Hein, A., and Held, R. 1967. Dissociation of the visual placing response into elicited and guided components. *Science* 158: 390–92.

Held, R., and Bauer, J. A., Jr. 1971. Visually guided reaching in infant monkeys after restricted rearing. *Science* 155: 718–20.

Held, R., and Hein, A. 1963. Movement-produced stimulation in the development of visually guided behavior. *Journal of Comparative and Physiological Psychology* 56: 872–76.

Herrick, C. J. 1956. *The evolution of human nature*. Austin: University of Texas Press.

Hetherington, E. M. 1965. A developmental study of the effects of sex of the dominant parent on sex-role preference, identification, and imitation in children. *Journal of Personality and Social Psychology* 2: 188–94.

Hilgard, E. R., and Bower, G. H. 1966. *Theories of learning*. 3rd ed. New York: Appleton-Century-Crofts.

Hinde, R. A. 1966. *Animal behavior*. New York: McGraw-Hill.

————. 1971. Development of social behavior. In *Behavior of nonhuman primates*, eds. A. M. Schrier and F. Stollnitz, vol. 3. New York: Academic Press.

Hockett, C. F. 1960. The origin of speech. *Scientific American* 203: 88 *ff.*

Hockett, C. F., and Ascher, R. 1964. The human revolution. *Current Anthropology* 5: 135–47.

Hoffman, M. L. 1970. Moral development. In *Carmichael's manual of child psychology,* ed. P. H. Mussen. New York: Wiley.

Hoffman, M. L., and Saltzstein, H. D. 1967. Parent discipline and the child's moral development. *Journal of Personality and Social Psychology* 5: 45–57.

Holloway, R. L., 1968. The evolution of the primate brain: some aspects of quantitative relations. *Brain Research* 7: 121–72.

———. 1972. Australopithecine endocasts, brain evolution in the hominoidia, and a model of hominid evolution. In *The functional and evolutionary biology of primates,* ed. R. Tuttle. Chicago: Aldine-Atherton.

Howell, F. C. 1972. Recent advances in human evolutionary studies. In *Perspectives on human evolution,* eds. S. L. Washburn and P. Dolhinow, vol. 2. New York: Holt, Rinehart and Winston.

Howells, W. 1973. *The evolution of the genus Homo.* Reading, Mass.: Addison-Wesley.

Hulse, F. S. 1963. *The human species.* New York: Random House.

Itani, J. 1972. A preliminary essay on the relationship between social organization and incest avoidance in nonhuman primates. *Primate socialization,* ed. F. E. Poirier. New York: Random House.

Jarvis, P. E. 1968. Verbal control of sensory-motor performance: a test of Luria's hypothesis. *Human Development* 11: 172–83.

Jay, P. ed. 1968. *Primates: studies in adaptation and variability.* New York: Holt, Rinehart and Winston.

Jerison, H. J. 1963. Interpreting the evolution of the brain. *Human Biology* 35.: 263–91.

———.1973. *Evolution of the brain and intelligence.* New York: Academic Press.

Jolly, A. 1972. *The evolution of primate behavior.* New York: Macmillan.

Jones, N. B., ed. 1972. *Ethological studies of child behavior.* Cambridge: Cambridge University Press.

Kagan, J. 1970. The determinants of attention in the infant. *American Scientist* 58: 298–306.

———. 1972. Do infants think? *Scientific American* 226: 74–82.

Kagan, S. and Madsen, M. C. 1971. Cooperation and competition of Mexican-American, and Anglo-American children of two ages under four instructional sets. *Developmental Psychology* 5: 32–39.

Kagan, S. and Madsen, M. C. 1972. Rivalry in Anglo-American and Mexican-American children of two ages. *Journal of Personality and Social Psychology* 2: 214–20.

Kaplan, S. 1973. Cognitive maps in perception and thought. In *Cognitive mapping: images of spatial environments,* eds. R. M. Downs and D. Stea. Chicago: Aldine.

Kawai, M. 1965. Newly acquired precultural behavior of the natural troop of Japanese monkeys on Koshima islet. *Primates* 6: 1–30.

Keeney, J. T., Cannizzo, S. R., and Flavell, J. H. 1967. Spontaneous and induced verbal rehearsal in a recall task. *Child Development* 38: 953–66.

Kimble, D. P. 1968. Hippocampus and internal inhibition. *Psychological Bulletin* 70: 285–95.

Kobasigawa, A. 1974. Utilization of retrieval cues by children in recall. *Child Development* 45: 127–34.

Koestler, A. 1967. *The ghost in the machine*. New York: Macmillan.

Koestler, A., and Smythies, J. R., eds. 1968. *Beyond reductionism*. New York: Macmillan.

Kohlberg, L. 1968. The child as a moral philosopher. *Psychology Today* 2: 24–30.

————.1969. Stage and sequence: the cognitive developmental approach to socialization. In *Handbook of socialization theory and research*, ed. D. Goslin. Chicago: Rand McNally.

Konner, M. J. 1972. Aspects of the developmental ethology of a foraging people. In *Ethological studies of child behavior*, ed. N. B. Jones. Cambridge: Cambridge University Press.

Kramer, P. E., Koff, E., and Luria, Z. 1972. The development of competence in an exceptional language structure in older children and young adults. *Child Development* 43: 121–30.

Kummer, H. 1971. *Primate societies*. New York: Aldine-Atherton.

Kurtines, W., and Greif, E. B. 1974. The development of moral thought: review and evaluation of Kohlberg's approach. *Psychological Bulletin* 81: 453–70.

Laughlin, W. S. 1968. Hunting: An integrating biobehavior system and its evolutionary importance. *Man the Hunter*, eds. R. B. Lee and I. DeVore. Chicago: Aldine.

Laurendeau, M., and Pinard, A. 1970. *The development of the concept of space in the child*. New York: International Universities Press.

Leakey, L. S. B. 1960. *Adam's ancestors*. New York: Harper & Row.

Lee, R. B., and DeVore, I., eds. 1968. *Man the hunter*. Chicago: Aldine.

Lehman, E. B. 1972. Selective strategies in children's attention to task-relevant information. *Child development* 43: 197–209.

Lehman, E. B., and Goodnow, J. 1972. Memory for rhythmic series: age changes in accuracy and number coding. *Developmental Psychology* 6: 363.

Lenneberg, E. H. 1966. The natural history of language. In *The genesis of language*, eds. F. Smith and G. A. Miller. Cambridge: M.I.T. Press.

————. 1967. *Biological foundations of language*. New York: Wiley.

Lewis, M. 1969. Infants responses to facial stimuli during the first year of life. *Developmental Psychology* 2: 75–86.

Lewis, M., Goldberg, S., and Campbell, H. 1969. A developmental study of information processing within the first three years of life. Response decrement to a redundant signal. *Monographs of the Society for Research in Child Development* 34, no. 9.

Lieberman, P. 1973. On the evolution of language: a unified view. *Cognition* 2: 59–94.

Longwell, C. H., and Flint, R. F. 1955. *Introduction to physical geology.* New York: Wiley.

Lorenz, K. Z. 1966. *On aggression.* New York: Harcourt, Brace and World.

————.1969. Innate bases of learning. In *On the biology of learning,* ed. K. Pribram. New York: Harcourt, Brace, and World.

————.1972. The enmity between generations and its probable ethological causes. In *Play and development,* ed. M. W. Piers. New York: W. W. Norton.

Luria, A. R. 1960. Verbal regulation of behavior. In *The central nervous system and behavior: transactions of the third conference,* ed. M. A. B. Brazier. New York: Josiah Macy, Jr., Foundation.

————.1969. Speech development and the formation of mental processes. In *A handbook of contemporary Soviet psychology,* eds. M. Cole and I. Maltzman. New York: Basic Books.

————.1970. The functional organization of the brain. *Scientific American* 222: 66–78.

Maccoby, E. E., and Konrad, K. W. 1966. Age trends in selective listening. *Journal of Experimental Child Psychology* 3: 113–22.

————.1967. The effect of preparatory set on selective listening: developmental trends. *Monographs of the Society for Research in Child Development* 32: no. 4 (Series no. 112).

MacLean, P. D. 1954. Studies on limbic system ("visceral brain") and their bearing on psychosomatic problems. In R. Cleghorn and E. Wittkower (eds.) *Recent Developments in Psychosomatic Medicine.* London: Pittman.

————. 1962. New findings relevant to the evolution of psychosexual functions of the brain. *Journal of Mental Disease* 135: 289–301.

————. 1967. The brain in relation to empathy and medical education. *Journal of Nervous and Mental Disorders* 144: 374–82.

————.1970. The triune brain, emotion, and scientific bias. In *The neurosciences: second study program,* ed. F. O. Schmitt. New York: Rockefeller University Press.

————.1973. Clarence M. Hincks Memorial Lectures, 1969. In *A triune concept of the brain and behavior,* eds. T. J. Boag and D. Campbell. Toronto: University of Toronto Press.

Magoun, H. W. 1969. Advances in brain research with implications for learning. In *On the biology of learning,* ed. K. Pribram. New York: Harcourt, Brace and World.

Marler, P. M., and Hamilton, W. J., III. 1966. *Mechanisms of animal behavior.* New York: Wiley.

Masangkay, Z. S., McCluskey, K. A., McIntyre, C. W., Sims-Knight, J., Vaughn, B. E., and Flavell, J. H. 1974. The early development of inferences about the visual percepts of others. *Child Development* 45: 357–66.

Mayr, E. 1963. *Animal species and evolution.* Cambridge: Harvard University Press.

McCarver, R. B. 1972. A developmental study of the effect of organizational cues on short-term memory. *Child Development* 43: 1317–28.

McClintock, C. G. and Nuttin, J. M. 1969. Development of competitive game behavior in children across two cultures. *Journal of Experimental Social Psychology* 5: 203–18.

McGraw, M. B. 1935. *Growth: a study of Johnny and Jimmy.* New York: Appleton-Century-Crofts.

Mead, G. H. 1934. *Mind, self, and society.* Chicago: University of Chicago Press.

Miller, G. A., Galanter, E., and Pribram, K. 1960. *Plans and the structure of behavior.* New York: Holt, Rinehart and Winston.

Miller, S. A., Shelton, J., and Flavell, J. H. 1970. A test of Luria's hypothesis concerning the development of self-regulation. *Child Development* 41: 651–66.

Milner, B. 1968. Visual recognition and recall after right temporal lobe excision in man. *Neuropsychologia* 6: 191–209.

————.1971. Interhemispheric differences in the localization of psychological processes in man. *British Medical Bulletin* 27: 272–77.

Milner, P. M. 1970. *Physiological psychology.* New York: Holt, Rinehart and Winston.

Minton, C., Kagan, J., and Levine, J. A. 1971. Maternal control and obedience in the two year old. *Child Development* 42: 1873–94.

Moore, K. L. 1973. *The developing human.* Philadelphia: W. B. Saunders.

Mussen, P. 1967. Early socialization: learning and identification. In *New directions in psychology III,* eds. N. Kogan, G. Mandler, P. Mussen, and M. A. Waltach. New York: Holt, Rinehart and Winston.

Niemark, E., Slotnick, N. S., and Ulrich, T. 1971. Development of memorization strategies. *Developmental Psychology* 5: 427–32.

Neisser, U. 1967. *Cognitive psychology.* New York: Appleton-Century-Crofts.

Nelson, K. 1973. Structure and strategy in learning to talk. *Monographs of the Society for Research in Child Development* 38: nos. 1-2.

————.1974. Concept, word, and sentence: interrelations in acquisition and development. *Psychological Review* 81: 267–85.

Newell, N. D. 1963. Crises in the history of life. *Scientific American* 209: 76.

Nigl, A. J., and Fishbein, H. D. 1974. Perception and conception in coordination of perspectives. *Developmental Psychology* 10: 858–66.

Norman, D. A. 1969. *Memory and attention.* New York: Wiley.

Oakley, K. P. 1972. Skill as a human possession. In *Perspectives on human evolution*, vol. 2, eds. S. L. Washburn and P. Dolhinow. New York: Holt, Rinehart and Winston.

Palermo, D. S., and Molfese, D. L. 1972. Language acquisition from age five onward. *Psychological Bulletin* 78: 409–28.

Pavlov, I. P. 1927. *Conditioned reflexes*. Translated and edited by G. V. Anrep. Oxford: Oxford University Press.

Penfield, W. 1969. Consciousness, memory, and man's conditioned reflexes. In *On the biology of learning*, ed. K. Pribram. New York: Harcourt, Brace, and World.

Penfield, W., and Roberts, L. 1959. *Speech and brain-mechanisms*. Princeton: Princeton University Press.

Peters, R. 1973. Cognitive maps in wolves and men. In *Environmental Design Research*, vol. 2, ed. W. F. E. Preiser. Stroudsburg, Pa.: Dowden, Hutchinson & Ross.

Pfeiffer, J. E. 1972. *The emergence of man*. 2nd ed. New York: Harper & Row.

Piaget, J. 1948. *The moral judgment of the child*. Glencoe, Ill.: Free Press (originally published in 1932).

———.1950. *Psychology of intelligence*. London: Routledge & Kegan Paul.

———.1954. *The construction of reality in the child*. New York: Basic Books.

———.1970. Piaget's theory. In *Carmichael's manual of child psychology*, ed. P. H. Mussen. 3rd ed. New York: Wiley.

———.1971. *Biology and knowledge*. Chicago: University of Chicago Press.

Piaget, J., and Inhelder, B. 1956. *The child's conception of space*. London: Routledge & Kegan Paul.

———.1969. *The psychology of the child*. New York: Basic Books.

———.1973. *Memory and Intelligence*. New York: Basic Books.

Pilbeam, D. 1972. *The ascent of man*. New York: Macmillan.

Poirier, F. E. 1973. Socialization and learning among nonhuman primates. In *Learning and culture*, eds. S. T. Kimball and J. H. Burnett. Seattle: University of Washington Press.

Poirier, F. E., and Smith, E. O. 1973. Socializing functions of nonhuman primate play behavior. Paper presented at the meetings of the American Association for the Advancement of Science, Houston.

Premack, A. J., and Premack, D. 1972. Teaching language to an ape. *Scientific American* 227: 92–99.

Pribram, K. 1969. The four R's of remembering. In *On the biology of learning*, ed. K. Pribram. New York: Harcourt, Brace, and World.

Rand, C. W. 1973. Copying in drawing: the importance of adequate visual analysis versus the ability to utilize drawing rules. *Child Development* 44: 47–53.

Rensch, B. 1959. *Evolution above the species level*. New York: Columbia University Press.

Rest, J. 1968. *Developmental hierarchy in preference and comprehension of moral judgment.* Unpublished doctoral dissertation, University of Chicago.

Riesen, A. H. 1958. Plasticity of behavior: psychological aspects. *Biological and biochemical bases of behavior,* eds. H. F. Harlow and C. N. Woolsey. Madison: University of Wisconsin Press.

Robinson, B. W. 1972. Anatomical and physiological contrasts between human and other primate vocalizations. In *Perspectives on human evolution,* vol. 2, eds. S. L. Washburn and P. Dolhinow. New York: Holt, Rinehart and Winston.

Romer, A. S. 1966. *Vertebrate paleontology.* 3rd ed. Chicago: University of Chicago Press.

Rothstein, A. L. 1972. Effect of age, feedback, and practice on ability to respond within a fixed time interval. *Journal of Motor Behavior* 4:113–19.

Rozin, R., and Kalat, J. W. 1971. Specific hungers and poison avoidance as adaptive specializations of learning. *Psychological Review* 78: 459–86.

Rumbaugh, D. M. 1970. Learning skills in anthropoids. In *Primate behavior,* vol. 1, ed. L. A. Rosenblum. New York: Academic Press.

Salapatek, P. 1973. The visual investigation of geometric pattern by the one- and two-month-old infant. In *The competent infant,* eds. L. J. Stone, H. T. Smith, and L. B. Murphy. New York: Basic Books.

Saxen, L., and Rapola, J. 1969. *Congenital defects.* New York: Holt, Rinehart and Winston.

Schaffer, H. R., Greenwood, A., and Parry, M. H. 1972. The onset of wariness. *Child Development* 43: 165–76.

Schiller, P. H. 1952. Innate constituents of complex responses in primates. *Psychological Review* 59: 177–91.

Schlesinger, I. M. 1971. Production of utterances and language acquisition. In *The ontogenesis of grammar,* ed. D. I. Slobin. New York: Academic Press.

Schmidt, R. A. 1968. Anticipation and timing in human motor performance. *Psychol. Bulletin* 70: 631–46.

———.1971. Proprioception and the timing of motor responses. *Psychol. Bulletin* 76: 383–93.

Schultz, T. R., and Pilon, R. 1973. Development of the ability to detect linguistic ambiguity. *Child Development* 44: 728–33.

Scott, J. P. 1968. *Early experience and the organization of behavior.* Belmont, Ca.: Brooks/Cole.

Sears, R. R., Maccoby, E. E., and Levine, H. 1957. *Patterns of child rearing.* Evanston, Ill.: Row, Peterson.

Sears, R. R., Rau, L., and Alpert, R. 1965. *Identification and child rearing.* Stanford: Stanford University Press.

Seligman, M. E. P. 1970. On the generality of the laws of learning. *Psychological Review* 77: 406–18.

Selman, R. L., and Byrne, D. F. 1974. A structural-developmental analysis of levels of role taking in middle childhood. *Child Development* 45: 803–06.

Semmes, J., Weinstein, S., Ghent, L., and Teuber, H. L. 1955. Spatial orientation in man after cerebral injury: I, analyses by locus of lesion. *The Journal of Psychology* 39: 227–44.

Simons, E. L. 1964. The early relatives of man. *Scientific American* 211: 51–63.

Simpson, G. G. 1949. *The meaning of evolution.* New Haven: Yale University Press.

Slobin, D. I. 1966. Grammatical transformations and sentence comprehension in childhood and adulthood. *Journal of Verbal Learning and Verbal Behavior* 5: 219–27.

———. 1971. *Psycholinguistics.* New York: Scott, Foresman.

———. 1972. Seven questions about language development. In *New horizons in psychology 2*, ed. P. C. Dodwell. Harmondworth, England: Penguin.

Smirnov, A. A., and Zinchenko, P. I. 1969. Problems in the psychology of memory. In *A handbook of contemporary Soviet psychology*, eds. M. Cole and I. Maltzman. New York: Basic Books.

Smith, K. U., and Sussman, H. 1969. Cybernetic theory and analysis of motor learning and memory. In *Principles of skill acquisition*, ed. E. A. Bilodeau. New York: Academic Press.

Snow, C. E. 1972. Mother's speech to children learning language. *Child Development* 43: 549–65.

Sokolov, E. N. 1960. Neuronal models and the orienting reflex. In *The central nervous system and behavior*, ed. M. A. B. Brazier. New York: Josiah Macy Foundation.

Spencer, H. 1870-72. *The principles of psychology.* 2nd ed., 2 vols. London: Williams and Norgate.

Sperry, R. W. 1952. Neurology and the mind-brain problem. *American Scientist* 40: 291–312.

———. 1972. Mental unity following surgical disconnections of the cerebral hemispheres. In *Perspectives on human evolution*, vol. 2, ed. S. L. Washburn and P. Dolhinow. New York: Holt, Rinehart and Winston.

Stayton, D. J., Hogan, R., and Ainsworth, M. D. S. 1971. Infant obedience and maternal behavior: the origins of socialization reconsidered. *Child Development* 42: 1057–70.

Stebbins, G. L. 1971. *Processes of organic evolution.* 2nd ed. Englewood Cliffs, N.J.: Prentice-Hall.

Stephan, H. 1972. Evolution of primate brains: a comparative anatomical investigation. In *The functional and evolutionary biology of primates*, ed. R. Tuttle. Chicago: Aldine-Atherton.

Stephan, H., and Andy, O. J. 1970. The allocortex in primates. In *The primate brain*, eds. C. R. Noback and W. Montagna. New York: Appleton-Century-Crofts.

Stephan, H., Bauchot, R., and Andy, O. J. 1970. Data on size of the brain and of various brain parts in insectivores and primates. In *The primate brain*, eds. C. R. Noback and W. Montagna. New York: Appleton-Century-Crofts.

Stotland, E., Sherman, S., and Shaver, K. G. 1971. *Empathy and birth order.* Lincoln: University of Nebraska Press.

Strommen, E. A. 1973. Verbal self-regulation in a children's game: impulsive errors on "Simon says." *Child Development* 44: 849–53.

Surwillo, W. W. 1971. Human reaction time and period of the EEG in relation to development. *Psychophysiology* 8: 468–82.

Tanner, J. M. 1962. *Growth at adolescence.* Oxford: Blackwell.

———. 1970. Physical growth. In *Carmichael's manual of child psychology*, ed. P. H. Mussen, 3rd ed. New York: Wiley.

Taylor, A. L. 1975. *The development of children's social interaction behaviors in a game situation.* Unpublished doctoral dissertation, University of Cincinnati.

Teleki, G. 1973. The omnivorous chimpanzee. *Scientific American* 228: 32–42.

Tinbergen, N. 1965. Behavior and natural selection. In *Ideas in evolution and behavior*, ed. J. A. Moore, Garden City, N.Y.: Natural History Press.

Tizard, B., Cooperman, O., and Tizard, J. 1972. Environmental effects on language development: a study of young children in long-stay residential nurseries. *Child Development* 43: 337–38.

Tobias, P. V. 1970. *The brain in hominid evolution.* New York: Columbia University Press.

Torrey, T. W. 1971. *Morphogenesis of the vertebrates.* 3rd ed. New York: Wiley.

Travers, W., and Van Lawick, H. 1973. *The baboons of Gombe.* Film, Los Angeles: Metromedia Producers Corporation.

Tulving, E. 1974. Cue-dependent forgetting. *American Scientist* 62: 74–82.

Turnbull, C. M. 1961. *The forest people.* New York: Simon & Schuster.

———.1972. *The mountain people.* New York: Simon & Schuster.

Turner, E. A., and Rommetveit, R. 1967. The acquisition of sentence voice and reversibility. *Child Development* 38: 649–60.

Underwood, B. J. 1969. Attributes of memory. *Psychological Review* 76: 559–73.

Van Lawick-Goodall, J. 1968. The behavior of free living chimpanzees in the Gombe Stream Reserve. *Animal Behavior Monographs* 1: 165–301.

———.1973. In *The baboons of Gombe* (A Film). Bill Travers and Hugo Van Lawick, producers. Los Angeles: Metromedia Producers Corporation.

Van Valen, L. 1974. Brain size and intelligence in man. *American Journal of Physical Anthropology* 40: 417–24.

Vurpillot, E. 1968. The development of scanning strategies and their relation to visual differentiation. *Journal of Experimental Child Psychology* 6: 622–50.

Waddington, C. H. 1957. *The strategy of genes.* London: Allen and Unwin.

————. 1960a, Genetic assimilation. In Advances in Genetics, eds. E. W. Caspari and J. W. Thoday. New York: Academic Press.

————. 1960b. The ethical animal. London: George Allen & Unwin.

————.1962. New patterns in genetics and development. New York: Columbia University Press.

————. 1968. The theory of evolution today. In Beyond reductionism, eds. A. Koestler and J. R. Smythies. New York: Macmillan.

Washburn, S. L. 1960. Tools and human evolution. Scientific American 203: 62.

————. 1970. Comment on: "A possible evolutionary basis for aesthetic appreciation in man and apes." Evolution 24: 824–25.

Washburn, S. L., and Hamburg, D. A. 1965. The study of primate behavior. In Primate behavior: field studies of monkeys and apes, ed. I. De Vore. New York: Holt, Rinehart and Winston.

————.1968. Aggressive behavior in Old World monkeys and apes. In Primates. Studies in adaptation and variability. New York: Holt, Rinehart and Winston.

Washburn, S. L., and Lancaster, C. S. 1968. The evolution of hunting. In Man the hunter, eds. R. B. Lee and I. De Vore. Chicago: Aldine.

Washburn, S. L., and Moore, R. 1974. Ape into man. Boston: Little, Brown and Co.

Went, F. W. 1968. The size of man. American Scientist 56: 400–13.

Werner, H. 1961. Comparative psychology of mental development. New York: Science Editions (originally published in 1948).

————. 1957. The concept of development from a comparative and organismic view. In The concept of development, ed. D. B. Harris. Minneapolis: University of Minnesota Press.

Wetherford, M. J., and Cohen, L. B. 1973. Developmental changes in infant visual preferences for novelty and familiarity. Child Development 44: 416–24.

Wheeler, R. J., and Dusek, J. B. 1973. The effects of attentional and cognitive factors on children's incidental learning. Child Development 44: 253–58.

White, B., Castle, P., and Held, R. 1964. Observations on the development of visually-directed reaching. Child Development 35: 349–64.

White, B. L., and Held, R. 1966. Plasticity and sensorimotor development in the human infant. In The causes of behavior: readings in child development and educational psychology, 2nd ed., eds J. F. Rosenblith and W. Allin-Smith. Boston: Allyn & Bacon.

White, L. A. 1959. The evolution of culture. New York: McGraw-Hill.

White, R. W. 1960. Competence and the psychosexual stage of development. In Nebraska symposium on motivation, ed. M. R. Jones. Lincoln: University of Nebraska Press.

————.1969. Motivation reconsidered: the concept of competence. Psychological Review 66: 297–333.

White, S. H. 1965. Evidence for a hierarchical arrangement of learning processes. In *Advances in child behavior and development*, vol. 2, eds. L. P. Lipsitt and C. C. Spiker. New York: Academic Press.

―――. 1969. Some general outlines of the matrix of developmental changes between five and seven years. Paper given at the symposium "Cognitive development: The years five to eight" at the International Congress of Psychology, London.

White, S. H., and Fishbein, H. D. 1971. Children's learning. In *Behavioral science in pediatric medicine*, eds. N. B. Talbot, J. Kagan, and L. Eisenburg. Philadelphia: W. B. Saunders.

Whiting, J. 1968. Are the hunter-gatherers a cultural type? In *Man the hunter*, eds. R. B. Lee and I. DeVore. Chicago: Aldine.

Wickler, W. 1972. *The sexual code*. Garden City, N.J.: Doubleday.

Woolsey, C. N. 1958. Organization of somatic sensory and motor areas of the cerebral cortex. In *Biological and biochemical bases of behavior*, eds. H. F. Harlow and C. N. Woolsey. Madison: University of Wisconsin Press.

Wright, R. V. S. 1972. Imitative learning of a flaked stone technology—the case of an orangutan. *Mankind* 8: 296–306.

Young, J. Z. 1971. *An introduction to the study of man*. New York: Oxford University Press.

Zinchenko, V. P., Chzhi-tsin, V., and Tarakanov, V. V. 1962. The formation and development of perceptual activity. *Soviet Psychology and Psychiatry* 2: 3–12.

AUTHOR INDEX

315

SUBJECT INDEX